Room for Development

Room for Development

Housing Markets in Latin America and the Caribbean

César Patricio Bouillon, Editor

Inter-American Development Bank

palgrave macmillan

ROOM FOR DEVELOPMENT

First published in 2012 by
PALGRAVE MACMILLAN®
in the United States—a division of St. Martin's Press LLC,
175 Fifth Avenue, New York, NY 10010.

Where this book is distributed in the UK, Europe and the rest of the world, this is by Palgrave Macmillan, a division of Macmillan Publishers Limited, registered in England, company number 785998, of Houndmills, Basingstoke, Hampshire RG21 6XS.

Palgrave Macmillan is the global academic imprint of the above companies and has companies and representatives throughout the world.

Palgrave® and Macmillan® are registered trademarks in the United States, the United Kingdom, Europe and other countries.

ISBN: 978–1–137–00564–9 (hardback)
ISBN: 978–1–137–00563–2 (paperback)

Library of Congress Cataloging-in-Publication Data

Room for development : housing markets in Latin America and the Caribbean / César Patricio Bouillon, Editor ; Inter-American Development Bank.
pages cm
ISBN 978–1–137–00564–9—
ISBN 978–1–137–00563–2
1. Housing—Latin America. 2. Housing—Caribbean Area. I. Bouillon, César Patricio. II. Inter-American Development Bank.

HD7305.5.A3R66 2012
333.33′8098—dc23 2011049337

A catalogue record of the book is available from the British Library.

Design by Newgen Imaging Systems (P) Ltd., Chennai, India.

First edition: April 2012

10 9 8 7 6 5 4 3 2 1

Printed in the United States of America.

SUSTAINABLE FORESTRY INITIATIVE Certified Sourcing www.sfiprogram.org SFI-00453

Contents

List of Boxes vii

List of Figures ix

List of Tables xv

Acknowledgments xix

About the Contributors xxiii

Preface xxv

Introduction 1

1 Dirt Floors and Unpaved Streets: Why Housing Markets Matter 5

2 Portrait of a Problem: The Housing Sector 23

3 Two Bedrooms, Two Bathrooms, and a Big Yard? Housing Demand in Latin America and the Caribbean 51

4 To Buy or Not to Buy: Expanding the Rental Housing Market 87

5 Digging up the Truth about Land Markets 109

6 A Construction Industry in Need of Remodeling 149

7 Too Small to Thrive: The Housing Finance Market 187

8 Doing It Yourself 211

9 Hammering Out a Housing Policy That Works 239

Notes 281

References 289

Index 311

Boxes

1.1	Consequences of Land Titling Programs: An Experiment in Argentina	10
4.1	The Potential for Rental Housing: Habitat for Humanity in Buenos Aires	105
5.1	A Virtuous Circle: Financing Basic Infrastructure with Land-Based Revenue	142
5.2	Colombia's Macroproyectos: A Successful Case of Low-Income Housing in a Mixed-Use Setting	146
6.1	Energy Efficiency in Barbados	178
7.1	Securitization and Mortgage Financing in Latin America and the Caribbean	194
8.1	Patrimonio Hoy	224
8.2	Market-Based Slum Upgrading: Terra Nova in Brazil	227
8.3	A Joint Venture to Foster Low-Income Housing in Paraguay	229
8.4	A Public-Private Partnership for Low-Cost Housing in El Salvador	235

Figures

1.1	Projections of Urban Land Cover for Latin America and the Caribbean, 2000–2050	18
2.1a	Housing Conditions by Income Quintile in Latin America and the Caribbean, Mid-1990s and Late 2000s: Quantitative Deprivations	30
2.1b	Housing Conditions by Income Quintile in Latin America and the Caribbean, Mid-1990s and Late 2000s: Dwellings of Disposable Materials or Overcrowded	30
2.1c	Housing Conditions by Income Quintile in Latin America and the Caribbean, Mid-1990s and Late 2000s: Inadequate Infrastructure	30
2.1d	Housing Conditions by Income Quintile in Latin America and the Caribbean, Mid-1990s and Late 2000s: Lack of Secure Tenure	31
2.2a	Housing Shortages by Country in Latin America, 2009: Quantitative	33
2.2b	Housing Shortages by Country in Latin America, 2009: Qualitative	33
2.3a	Housing Shortages by City, 2009: Quantitative	34
2.3b	Housing Shortages by City, 2009: Qualitative	34
2.4	Slum Population and Income Per Capita, Select Countries Worldwide, 2005	37
2.5	Slum Population and Income Per Capita by Population, 2005	38
2.6	Change in Population Density in Select Cities Worldwide, 1990–2000	42
2.7	Urbanized Area Population Density in Select Cities Worldwide, 1800–2000	43
2.8	Total Housing Deficit for Select Cities in Latin America and the Caribbean, 2009	48

3.1 Change in Urban Growth Rate and Total Population, 2010–2025 53
3.2 Affordability Gap Due to Low Household Income in Select Latin American Cities 58
3.3 Interest Rate Affordability Gap in Select Latin American Cities (Sorted by Income Effect) 61
3.4a Affordability Gap in Select Latin American Cities: Inability to Document Income (Sorted by Income Effect) Due to Self-Employment 63
3.4b Affordability Gap in Select Latin American Cities: Inability to Document Income (Sorted by Income Effect) Due to Lack of Affiliation to Social Security 64
3.5 Effect of House Prices on Affordability in Select Latin American Cities 67
3.6a Housing Supply in Bogota, 2008: Housing Supply and Capacity to Pay 68
3.6b Housing Supply in Bogota, 2008: Housing Supply by Income Deciles 68
3.7 Total Affordability Gap in Latin American and Caribbean Cities 70
3.8 Tenure Choices by Gender of Household Head, Argentina, 2009 76
3.9a Distribution of Monthly Household Income Per Capita by Tenure Choice in Brazil: Formal Workers 78
3.9b Distribution of Monthly Household Income Per Capita by Tenure Choice in Brazil: Informal Workers 78
4.1 Rental Tenure: Latin America and the Caribbean vs. Select European Union Countries 91
4.2 Rental Tenure by City Size: Largest Cities in Latin America and the Caribbean, 2010 92
4.3 Rental Tenure Evolution in Urban Latin America, 1995–2007 93
5.1 Land Prices and Income for 18 Latin American Cities 114
5.2a Effect of Land Prices on Housing Affordability by Plot Size, Select Latin American and Caribbean Cities: 60-Square-Meter Plot Size 115
5.2b Effect of Land Prices on Housing Affordability by Plot Size, Select Latin American and Caribbean Cities: 100-Square-Meter Plot Size 116

5.3a Housing Supply and Population Distribution Arranged by Land Cost and Family Capacity to Pay in Select Cities in Latin America: Buenos Aires 118
5.3b Housing Supply and Population Distribution Arranged by Land Cost and Family Capacity to Pay in Select Cities in Latin America: Cordoba 118
5.3c Housing Supply and Population Distribution Arranged by Land Cost and Family Capacity to Pay in Select Cities in Latin America: Rosario 118
5.3d Housing Supply and Population Distribution Arranged by Land Cost and Family Capacity to Pay in Select Cities in Latin America: Rio de Janeiro 118
5.3e Housing Supply and Population Distribution Arranged by Land Cost and Family Capacity to Pay in Select Cities in Latin America: Santiago 118
5.4a Housing Supply by Income Deciles in Select Cities in Latin America: Buenos Aires 119
5.4b Housing Supply by Income Deciles in Select Cities in Latin America: Cordoba 119
5.4c Housing Supply by Income Deciles in Select Cities in Latin America: Rosario 119
5.4d Housing Supply by Income Deciles in Select Cities in Latin America: Rio de Janeiro 119
5.4e Housing Supply by Income Deciles in Select Cities in Latin America: Santiago 119
5.5 Plot Size Effect on Affordability, Cities with Minimum Plot Size Regulations 132
5.6 Time to Register Property in Latin American and Caribbean Countries, 2010 134
5.7 Cost to Register Property in Latin American and Caribbean Countries, 2010 135
5.8 Cost of Registering Property (Percent of Property Value) and Income Per Capita around the World, 2009 135
6.1 Construction Costs as a Share of the Total Price of the Cheapest Housing Solution, Select Cities, 2010 152
6.2a Construction Costs in Select Latin American and Caribbean Cities and Countries (Base Year 2000 = 100): Overall Costs 154

6.2b Construction Costs in Select Latin American and Caribbean Cities and Countries (Base Year 2000 = 100): Material Costs 155
6.2c Construction Costs in Select Latin American and Caribbean Cities and Countries (Base Year 2000 = 100): Labor Costs 156
6.3 Cost of Construction Permits and Income Per Capita, 2009 163
6.4 Construction Technologies 164
6.5 Type of Construction for New Social Housing in Select Latin American Countries 172
B6.1 Viability of Renewable Distributed Generation (DG) in Barbados 179
B6.2 Average Power Consumption by the Hotel Sector in Barbados 181
B6.3 Cost Effectiveness of Energy-Efficient Appliances in Barbados 182
7.1a An International Comparison of House Price Levels (Constant Prices): Advanced Economies and Emerging Economies, 1990–2010 188
7.1b An International Comparison of House Price Levels (Constant Prices): Select Developing Countries and Regions, 2000–2010 188
7.2a Mortgage Debt as a Percent of GDP, 2009: Western Europe and North America 191
7.2b Mortgage Debt as a Percent of GDP, 2009: Asia and the Pacific 191
7.2c Mortgage Debt as a Percent of GDP, 2009: Eastern Europe 192
7.2d Mortgage Debt as a Percent of GDP, 2009: Latin America and the Caribbean 192
7.2e Mortgage Debt as a Percent of GDP, 2009: Africa and Middle East 192
B7.1 Securitized Mortgages as a Percent of Total Mortgage Portfolio 195
7.3 Brazil: Net Requirements and Total Housing Loans by Private Lenders 203
7.4a Mexico: Evolution of Loan Origination by Main Participants: Percent of Mortgage Loans 205
7.4b Mexico: Evolution of Loan Origination by Main Participants: Number of Mortgage Loans 205

7.5 Colombia: Mortgage Disbursements for Social and Nonsocial Housing 208
8.1 Critical Market Failures along the Low-Income Housing Value Chain 213
8.2 Basic Starting Options for a Core House, Guyana Incremental Housing Program 217
8.3 Expansion Possibilities for a Core House, Guyana Incremental Housing Program 218
9.1 Housing Policy in Argentina: Approaches and Trends 249
9.2 Housing Policy in Chile: Approaches and Trends 251
9.3 Housing Policy in Colombia: Approaches and Trends 254
9.4a Housing Sector Results, Household Formation, and Formal Housing: Argentina 256
9.4b Housing Sector Results, Household Formation, and Formal Housing: Chile 256
9.4c Housing Sector Results, Household Formation, and Formal Housing: Colombia 257
9.5 Percent Distribution of Beneficiaries of Select Public Housing Programs by Income 265
9.6 Argentina: Changes in Housing Conditions for Beneficiary Families Due to Housing Programs 270
9.7 Colombia: Changes in Housing Conditions for Beneficiary Families Due to Housing Programs 271
9.8 Colombia: Changes in Distance to Amenities for Beneficiary Families Due to Housing Programs 272
9.9 Argentina: Level of Satisfaction with Housing Programs 273

Tables

1.1	Negative Health Impacts Resulting from Poor Conditions in Housing and Surrounding Neighborhoods	8
1.2	Ranking of Select Megacities Based on Ambient Air Quality and Road Travel Speed	16
2.1	Basic Housing Market Outcomes	25
2.2	Regional Housing Shortages in Latin America and the Caribbean, 2009	26
2.3	Total Housing Deficits in Latin America and the Caribbean by Country, 2009	28
2.4	Urban Housing Deficits in Latin America and the Caribbean by Country, 2009	29
2.5	Housing Report Card for Latin American and Caribbean Countries	32
2.6	Perception of Dwelling Surroundings in Latin America and the Caribbean, 2007	40
2.7	Segregation Measures Based on Educational Attainment of Adults in Select Cities in Latin America and the United States	46
3.1	Composition of Cities' GDP Growth in Latin America and the Caribbean, 2007–2025	54
3.2	Housing Demand in Select Latin American and Caribbean Cities, 2007–2025	55
3.3	Mortgage Interest Rates in Latin American and Caribbean Countries, 2010	60
3.4	Price of the Cheapest Private-Sector Housing Solution Offered and Number of Months Needed to Buy It in Select Latin American and Caribbean Cities, 2010	65
3.5	Affordability Scorecard of Latin American and Caribbean Cities	71
4.1	Rental Tenure in Select Cities Worldwide	92
4.2	Qualitative Shortage in Urban Areas, 2006	95

5.1	Housing Cost Components in Latin American and Caribbean Cities, 2010	112
5.2	Chile: Evolution of Housing Cost Components in Social Housing Programs, 1994–2004	113
5.3	Land Affordability in Select Cities in Latin America	121
5.4	Categories and Instruments for Land Use Regulation	125
5.5	Urban Planning Systems in Latin America, Select Countries	128
5.6	Land Regulations in 15 Latin American and Caribbean Cities	131
5.7	Developed and Urban Land Premiums, Select Cities in Latin America and the Caribbean	133
5.8	Factors That Reduce Private Investment in Land Development Targeted at Low-Income People in Argentina	138
5.9	City-Level Subdivision Regulations in Three Cities in Argentina	140
5.10	Costs of Providing Housing Infrastructure in Regular Land Development and Slum Upgrading Programs	144
6.1	Construction Costs by Type of Finishes in Select Cities	151
6.2	Construction Costs and Household Income, Select Cities, 2010	153
6.3	Special Characteristics of the Construction Industry	157
6.4	Concentration and Dispersion of the Construction Industry in Select Cities in Latin America and the Caribbean, 2010	159
6.5	Legal Costs and Time Needed to Obtain Construction Permits, Select Latin American and Caribbean Cities, 2010	161
6.6	Effort, Time, and Money Required to Obtain Construction Permits in Latin American and Caribbean Countries, 2009	162
6.7	Advantages and Disadvantages of Industrialized Construction	166
6.8	Differences between Traditional and Modern Construction Technologies	168
6.9	Savings of Industrialized Construction	171
7.1	Market Share of Government-Sponsored Credit Institutions in Real Estate Lending in Select Latin American Countries	189
7.2	Factors Favoring the Provision of Housing Finance	198
8.1	Residents' Own Investments in Housing Improvements in Chile's Progressive Housing Programs	221

8.2	Household Housing Investments by Type of Initial Housing Solution, El Salvador	222
8.3	Comparative Investment Patterns of Households That Do and Do Not Receive Remittances	232
9.1	Constitutional Provisions Concerning Housing in Select Latin American Countries	240
9.2	Dos and Don'ts of the Enabling Markets Approach to Housing	243
9.3	Housing Programs in Latin America and the Caribbean	244
9.4	Annual Housing Production in Each Submarket in Argentina, Chile, and Colombia	257
9.5	Housing Programs in Argentina, Chile, and Colombia	258
9.6	Features of the Most Important Housing Programs in Argentina, Chile, and Colombia	262
9.7	Coverage of Housing Programs	268

Acknowledgments

Development in the Americas (DIA) is the flagship publication of the Inter-American Development Bank. This issue was produced under the direction of César Patricio Bouillon, lead research economist of the Research Department. The general editor of the volume was Rita Funaro, publications coordinator of the Research Department, who was assisted by Nancy Morrison. The technical editor was Carlos Andrés Gómez-Peña, economics associate. Eduardo Lora, the chief economist (a.i.) and general manager of the Research Department, provided extremely valuable guidance and advice throughout the life of this project. Vicente Fretes, chief of the Fiscal and Municipal Management Division of the Institutional Capacity and Finance Sector and Eduardo Rojas, former principal specialist in Urban Development and Housing at the Inter-American Development Bank, provided useful inputs to the entire project. Santiago Levy, the vice president for Sectors, provided overall support for the project.

The principal authors of each individual chapter are as follows:

Introduction: César Patricio Bouillon
Chapter 1: César Patricio Bouillon, Viviane Azevedo, and Katia Herrera
Chapter 2: César Patricio Bouillon, Nadin Medellín, and Cynthia Boruchowicz
Chapter 3: César Patricio Bouillon, Viviane Azevedo, Nadin Medellín, and Cynthia Boruchowicz
Chapter 4: Andrés Blanco, César Patricio Bouillon, Vicente Fretes, and Andrés Muñoz Miranda
Chapter 5: César Patricio Bouillon, Cynthia Boruchowicz, David Dowall, and Nadin Medellín
Chapter 6: Cynthia Boruchowicz, César Patricio Bouillon, and Sebastian Miller
Chapter 7: Alessandro Rebucci, Arturo Galindo, Frank Warnock, and Veronica Warnock

Chapter 8: Viviane Azevedo, César Patricio Bouillon, and Ophélie Chevalier

Chapter 9: Fernando Cuenin, Carolina Piedrafita, Eduardo Rojas, and Nadin Medellín

Several individuals collaborated with valuable inputs for specific chapters: Viviane Azevedo (chapter 2), Cynthia Boruchowicz (chapter 1), Fernando Cafferata (chapter 6), Marc Godbout (chapter 4), Ophélie Chevalier (chapter 5), Edgardo Demaestri (chapter 7), Bruce Ferguson (chapter 8), and Christiaan Gischler (chapter 6).

Many researchers were involved in the preparation of the background papers employed as the basis for this report: Raúl Abreu-Lastra, Shlomo Angel, María Angélica Arbeláez, Etna Mabel Artiga de Soundy, Sebastián Auguste, Fernando Balderrama, Nelson Baltrusis, Ricardo Bebczuk, Alejandro Becerra, Guillermo Bermúdez, Manuel Bonilla, María Isabel Bonilla, Carolina Camacho, Rosario Casanova, Juan Casazza, Roberto Chávez, Marcela Cristini, Mario Cuevas, Johanna Fajardo, Bruce Ferguson, Yolanda Gaete, Sebastián Galiani, Natalia Garabato, George Gattoni, Christiaan Gischler, Reinhard Goethert, Margarita Greene, Marc Hofstetter, Sigfrido Lée, Julie Litchfield, Marco A. López-Silva, Eduardo Lundberg, James Magowan, Bruno Martins, Rosa Massena, Pauline McHardy, Helena Menna Barreto, Alejandro Micco, Felipe Morris, Paavo Monkkonen, Ramiro Moya, Miguel Palomino Bonilla, Eric Parrado, Agustín Paulín-Hutmacher, Manuel Perló Cohen, Bernardita Piedrabuena, Caio Piza, Alberto Saracho-Martínez, Magdalena Ramada-Sarasola, Ernesto Schargrodsky, Eduardo Reese, Lucas Ronconi, Alejandro Sparacino, Maria Teresa Souza, Roberto Steiner, Eugenia Suárez, Tony Takeda, Jorge Tovar, Pablo Trivelli, Jorge Enrique Torres Ramírez, Miguel Urrutia, Irene Vance, David Vetter, Marcia Vetter, Daniel Wills, and Rudy Wong Barrantes.

The following research assistants contributed to the preparation of the project: Johanna Fajardo, Luis Felipe Sáenz, and Ana Virginia Mujica.

Several individuals provided useful input to specific studies and earlier drafts of this volume. In particular, Samuel Berlinski, José Brakarz, Matías Busso, Ana Corbacho, Julián Cristia, Pablo Federico, Eduardo Fernández-Arias, Kurt Focke, Kirsten Funes Deras, Jane Katz, Fernanda Magalhães, Shagun Mehrotra, Andrew Powell, Ana María Rodríguez, Inder Ruprah, Héctor Salazar, Ernesto Stein, and María Luisa Zanelli.

This book could not have been produced without the immense effort and dedication of the administrative team of the Research Department and, in particular, Patricia Arauz, Carla Carpio, Cathleen Conkling-Shaker, Myriam Escobar-Genes, Raquel Gómez, Elton Mancilla, Luis Daniel Martínez, Mariela Semidey, and Federico Volpino.

The comments and opinions expressed in this publication are those of the coordinator of the project and authors of the corresponding chapters and do not reflect the views of the Inter-American Development Bank or its executive directors in any form.

Contributors

Viviane Azevedo, a Brazilian citizen, received a PhD in Economics from the University of Illinois at Urbana-Champaign and is a specialist in the Opportunities for the Majority Sector of the Inter-American Development Bank.

Andrés Blanco, a citizen of Colombia, is an assistant professor in the Department of Urban and Regional Planning at the University of Florida. He holds a PhD (c) in City and Regional Planning from Cornell University.

Cynthia Boruchowicz, a national of Argentina, received a master of Public Policy from the University of Chicago and is a research fellow in the Research Department of the Inter-American Development Bank.

César Patricio Bouillon, a citizen of Peru, received a PhD in Economics from Georgetown University and is a lead research economist in the Research Department of the Inter-American Development Bank.

Ophélie Chevalier, a national of France, received a master of International Affairs at Columbia University and is a housing and urban development specialist in the Fiscal and Municipal Management Division of the Institutional Capacity and Finance Sector of the Inter-American Development Bank.

Fernando Cuenin, a citizen of Argentina, received an MA in Economics from Universidad Nacional de La Plata and is an operations specialist in the Andean Country Group Department of the Inter-American Development Bank.

David Dowall, a citizen of the United States, is a professor of city and regional planning at the University of California at Berkeley and holds a master's degree in Urban and Regional Planning and a PhD in Economics from the University of Colorado.

Vicente Fretes, an Argentine citizen, received an MBA and a PhD in Economics from the University of Pennsylvania and North Carolina State University, respectively. He is the chief of the Fiscal and Municipal Management Division of the Institutional Capacity and Finance Sector of the Inter-American Development Bank.

Arturo Galindo, a national of Colombia, is the regional economic advisor for the Andean Country Group Department of the Inter-American Development Bank. He holds a PhD in Economics from the University of Illinois at Urbana-Champaign.

Katia Herrera, a Mexican citizen, is completing her PhD studies in Economics and Education at Columbia University.

Nadin Medellín, a national of Mexico, received an MA in Economics and Public Policy from Tecnológico de Monterrey.

Sebastian Miller, a citizen of the United States and Chile, received a PhD in Economics from the University of Maryland at College Park. He is a research economist in the Research Department of the Inter-American Development Bank.

Andrés Muñoz Miranda, a Colombian citizen, received a PhD (c) in Public Administration from New York University and is a senior associate in the Fiscal and Municipal Management Division of the Institutional Capacity and Finance Sector of the Inter-American Development Bank.

Carolina Piedrafita, a citizen of Argentina, received a master's degree in Public Policy and Management from Columbia University and is a housing and urban development specialist in the Fiscal and Municipal Management Division of the Institutional Capacity and Finance Sector of the Inter-American Development Bank.

Alessandro Rebucci, a national of Italy, received a PhD in Economics from the University of London and is a lead research economist in the Research Department of the Inter-American Development Bank.

Eduardo Rojas, a Chilean citizen, holds an MBA from Johns Hopkins University. He is a former principal specialist in Urban Development and Housing at the Inter-American Development Bank.

Frank Warnock, a citizen of the United States, is an associate professor of Business Administration at the University of Virginia. He received a PhD in Economics from the University of North Carolina at Chapel Hill.

Veronica Warnock, a national of the Philippines, is a senior lecturer at the School of Business of the University of Virginia. She holds a PhD in Economics from Fordham University.

Preface

Cities are truly engines of growth and innovation, attracting jobs, investment, and people. But along with the promise come a number of challenges, including how to accommodate ever-larger populations with services, employment, and shelter. The stark differences in housing conditions between rich and poor families are a reminder of how difficult this task is and of the socioeconomic differences that persist throughout Latin America and the Caribbean.

The urban housing ills of the region date back decades. Many surfaced in the 1950s with the waves of rural to urban migration and were fed by poor urban planning and deficient investment in infrastructure. Since then, many cities and countries have made great strides to meet diverse needs—witness the impressive progress in access to power and potable water. The region needs to accelerate this progress, build upon its experience, and learn from better managed cities outside the region where living conditions and quality of life are much higher.

This year's edition of *Development in the Americas* is about that quest. It takes a closer look at the causes and consequences of poor housing outcomes and seeks to learn from both successes and failures around the region in order to improve the homes and neighborhoods of Latin American and Caribbean families. The book challenges conventional wisdom on many housing issues, and at the same time it makes clear that fixing the housing problems of the urban poor is a multifaceted venture that demands action in seemingly disparate policy areas ranging from finance, taxation, and regulation to infrastructure, land development, and innovation.

Governments must play a large role in building a better housing sector, but families and the private sector should be—under the right regulatory and policy framework—the main actors in improving housing conditions. The investment opportunity for the private sector is enormous, as is the opportunity for millions of families to substantially improve their quality of life. Focusing more attention on low-income housing is a win-win situation for our cities. On the one hand, it generates employment and economic growth. On the other, it helps to reduce social inequality and improve the prospects for all children.

The Inter-American Development Bank (IDB) has a long history of supporting government housing and urban development programs, as well as policy changes in willing countries and cities in the region. The Bank finances projects to improve urban transportation, supply housing to low-income households, and open up green spaces and parks. All of the Bank's urban development programs aim to expand the fiscal, financial, and planning capacity of the local governments with whom it partners. Through its new initiative to support emerging sustainable cities, the IDB provides loans and technical assistance to strengthen urban planning and regulation, rebuild and preserve downtown areas and historical centers, and upgrade infrastructure and urban services to create better homes and neighborhoods. Recently it has also turned its attention to promoting innovation and scaling up private sector investments aimed at serving the needs of the lower-income residents in the region's cities through its Opportunities for the Majority (OMJ) program.

Despite its many achievements, the Bank is committed to deepening its efforts in this sector, especially those directed toward low-income families. The IDB is ready to meet this challenge and to support governments, entrepreneurs, and families in their efforts to improve their housing and living conditions in the coming years.

It is with great pleasure that I present this book to policymakers, entrepreneurs, academics, and all of those interested in the development of the region. I hope that the tools and the blueprints for housing progress that this volume presents will help make *Room for Development* in our cities.

Luis Alberto Moreno
President
Inter-American Development Bank

Introduction

Latin American and Caribbean countries are the most urban in the developing world, enjoy very high home ownership rates, and boast high average family incomes by developing world standards. Despite significant progress over the past two decades, many of the region's city inhabitants are still poorly housed. Of the 130 million urban families in the region, 5 million rely on another family for shelter, 3 million live in houses that are beyond repair, and another 34 million live in houses that lack either title, water, sewerage, adequate flooring, or sufficient space. Most of these dwellings and many more otherwise satisfactory homes are located in neighborhoods that lack basic urban amenities, such as public transportation, parks, and hospitals. Paradoxically, most families living in inadequate housing are not poor; rather they come from the lower middle-income sector.

Room for Development: Housing Markets in Latin America and the Caribbean looks at both the determinants and consequences of poor housing in Latin American and Caribbean cities. Even though some housing outcomes such as access to potable water, sanitary disposal of household waste, and poor-quality building materials are worse in rural areas, this book focuses only on urban areas. Urban and rural housing problems are quite different. In rural areas, precisely because the population is scattered and in some cases isolated, provision of basic infrastructure and access to social services is costly and sometimes not even feasible. Moreover, certain factors that are key to the functioning and outcomes of housing markets in urban areas are simply not relevant to rural areas. These include access to certain amenities such as open spaces and green areas or avoiding congestion. They also include so-called economies of agglomeration that come from the concentration of populations, such as links between public transportation and job opportunities, and the lower cost involved in providing basic services to a large number of people.

Housing and neighborhood conditions strongly influence the health, nutrition, and education of the population, the environment in which they live, and therefore their access to economic opportunities and vulnerability to social ills.

This book taps new data sources and applies rigorous analytical methods as it examines the three interrelated factors most often blamed for the region's poor housing outcomes: high housing prices relative to family income, lack of access to mortgage credit, and key factors influencing housing costs such as high land and construction prices. The book looks at the roles that the private sector and the construction industry play in serving—or underserving—low-income housing markets. It also explores the role of government policies and regulations, along with public housing programs, at both the local and federal level, in shaping housing outcomes in the region.

The book is based on the premise that a house is more than four walls and a roof. It focuses on individual home characteristics, including traditional housing inadequacies ("deficits") such as lack of access to piped water and sanitation. But it then expands that focus to examine the importance of neighborhood location, access to urban amenities, urban form, density, and segregation. These factors are a result of how well housing markets function—or fail to function—from how land is developed and serviced to the way homes are built. This approach departs from the traditional analysis of housing issues that focuses mostly on the attributes of the house and leads to a more complete understanding of how housing influences the quality of life in an urban setting.

To sharpen the understanding of urban housing in Latin America and the Caribbean, the book uses a variety of data sources, including the most recent household surveys, and new information on housing, land prices, and regulation for a sample of cities in the region. With these data, the analysis in the book goes beyond national indicators and focuses on housing indicators disaggregated for 41 cities in the region. The use of household surveys allows for the analysis of housing gaps by family income level and affordability.

Closing the region's current housing gap will require an investment of at least US$310 billion, or 7.8 percent of the region's GDP. The investments needed to meet future housing demand require at least US$70 billion each year. Families, businesses, and governments together must meet this challenge. The private sector must move down market and expand mortgage and microfinancing for housing. Households need to mobilize savings, seek technical and public assistance, and inform themselves about the potential of new construction technologies. Municipalities must step up efforts to ensure the supply of neighborhood amenities; together with central governments and utility companies they are major stakeholders in enacting key regulation and providing basic infrastructure.

Policy change is necessary to enable families and the private sector to interact effectively in a healthy housing market and to help poor households meet minimum housing standards. This book revisits the old and traditional housing policies and programs enacted in recent decades to address quantitative and qualitative shortcomings in urban housing. These policies have clearly not been sufficient to close the housing gaps in the region, and a broader scope is needed.

The findings in this book point to some of the blueprints for policy change in housing programs and regulations in our cities. One of the key findings is that housing policies and regulations should respect and enable household choice in the housing market. The bias in the region for home ownership and for new homes needs to be replaced by a broader vision that values the contribution of, and provides incentives for renting. Barriers to residential mobility need to be overcome to allow families to move rather than remain in substandard housing. Since millions of families in the region build their own homes slowly over time (in so-called incremental housing), improving this process is also important. However, it is important to recognize that families that build their homes themselves can build inefficiencies into their homes and end up in substandard dwellings. Even with government assistance, some of the savings, environmental efficiency, and innovation that come with industrialized construction by the private sector cannot be realized under the practice of "do it yourself" housing.

Providing more and better housing choices to low- and middle-income families necessarily implies increasing the incentives and easing the constraints to expanding the reach of the formal housing sector, especially those that limit land development, affordable home construction, and long-term financing.

Expanding choice in housing markets requires policies and regulation to address the causes rather than treat the symptoms of poor functioning housing markets. This implies focusing on improving land and mortgage markets, ensuring an adequate regulatory framework for these markets to function properly, and providing infrastructure and subsidies to service land for poor households. These policies and regulations should also be retailored to encourage sustainable "green housing" by promoting land preservation, greater density of city populations, and green construction.

Finally, this DIA confirms that many housing programs and expenditures do not benefit the poorest households. This bias toward serving middle-class and wealthier households should be redressed by rerouting direct housing provision and housing demand subsidies toward low-income households. The oversight and advisory role of housing ministries should be strengthened in order to control local regulations that discriminate against low-income housing development and mixed land uses. Tax incentives and subsidies should be put in place when appropriate and public-private partnerships should be promoted to encourage land development and innovative construction technologies for low-income housing. With steps like these, the millions of people residing in cities across Latin America and the Caribbean—and their children—should be able to look forward to better homes, better neighborhoods, and better futures.

1

Dirt Floors and Unpaved Streets: Why Housing Markets Matter

Latin America and the Caribbean is the most urbanized developing region in the world. More than four out of five people in the region live in cities. This is a good thing, as urbanization has many benefits, not the least of which is that it helps reduce poverty. Cities attract poor people, which—as economist Edward Glaeser argues in his recent book, *Triumph of the City: How Our Greatest Invention Makes Us Richer, Smarter, Greener, Healthier, and Happier* (2011)—is a sign of urban strength, not weakness.

Unfortunately, urbanization's effect on poverty is not uniform. As the rural poor move to urban areas, rural poverty declines. Unhappily, urban poverty tends to fall more slowly; while some poor rural migrants to cities overcome poverty, the ones that remain poor drag down the process of reducing urban poverty (Ferre, Ferreira, and Lanjouw 2010).

The poor flock to cities in pursuit of more employment opportunities, better access to basic services, and an array of amenities. Cities let people and firms enjoy the benefits that come from locating near one another—a process that economists call "agglomerating." The benefits of agglomeration arise from economies of scale and network effects, which reduce the cost of providing services such as transportation, lower production costs, increase worker productivity (through competition, specialization, and division of labor), foster innovation, and decrease the per capita cost of providing amenities.

Even though cities provide many economic opportunities and access to better services and amenities, they may also be tough on their citizens. Glaeser identifies the three great scourges of urban life: crime, disease, and congestion. Inadequate housing conditions and bad neighborhoods are key factors in explaining these scourges. Bad housing and neighborhoods worsen the quality of life of city dwellers, may negatively impact children's development, and in turn may limit the potential that cities offer the poor to overcome poverty.

For example, in Argentina in recent years, households have been moving to urban areas where jobs are being created quickly. Since housing supply has not kept pace with the population influx, housing has become dangerously overcrowded[1] (Cristini, Moya, and Bermúdez 2011).

But overcrowding is only one aspect of bad housing. A good house is more than a well-built dwelling with enough rooms, running water, and a solid floor. Building a good house starts much earlier—well before a floor, walls, and roof are erected. It starts when a legal plot within city boundaries with access to trunk infrastructure (including water, sanitation, drainage, main roads, and other forms of public transportation) is subdivided into individual plots, each with its own connections to infrastructure. If the original plot is large enough, urban amenities such as parks, community centers, schools, and in some cases health centers must be planned, land for them should be reserved, and public-private arrangements should be made to guarantee funding for their operations.

Neighborhood population density that is neither too low nor too high, the amenities associated with its location, and proximity to city centers are also important components of a good house, as they enable families and society to enjoy the benefits and efficiencies of urban agglomeration. These benefits include access to jobs and other economic opportunities, cheap transportation costs, the environmental benefits that come with dense urban land use (such as lower energy consumption), network externalities (such as more suppliers for inputs and amenities), beneficial peer effects (the positive influence of neighbors or classmates on an individual's behavior), access to cultural amenities and sports, and political participation.

Given the pervasiveness of poor housing, the stereotypical, modern Latin American and Caribbean city is a conglomerate that combines a vast array of informal settlements, or slums, surrounding pockets of formal residential neighborhoods and business districts. But the problem is not merely cosmetic. The need to fix these problems—by improving the functioning of housing markets, enacting smart regulation, and increasing the effectiveness of public housing policies—is immediate and essential. Fundamentally, living in a good house influences people's quality of life, the health and education of their children, their carbon footprint, and their vulnerability to crime and natural disasters.

Health Begins at Home

Living in a bad house is not good for your health, especially if you are a young child. Poor health is one of the most detrimental effects of poor housing. A bad house can become a breeding ground for disease and desolation instead of being a nest of security and comfort.

In cities throughout Latin America and the Caribbean, millions of households still live in overcrowded houses with dirt floors and without sanitation, water, and garbage collection. Overcrowding increases the possibility that contagious diseases will spread within the household when one member falls ill. Dirt floors compound the problem as they help transmit parasitic diseases. Lack of water, electricity, and sanitation make it costly and difficult to obtain clean drinkable water, to prepare and store food safely, and to maintain good personal hygiene, compromising the health of residents and fostering the spread of communicable and food-borne diseases. Other housing problems such as poor regulation of temperature and humidity can lead to respiratory disease. The main consequences of poor housing on certain diseases are summarized in table 1.1.

The characteristics of neighborhoods also affect health in important ways, especially from the broad perspective of public health. Many neighborhoods in Latin America and the Caribbean spring up as informal settlements located on floodplains or hillsides on the periphery of big cities. Often, such neighborhoods are located near sources of heavy traffic and pollution, industrial activity, solid waste dumps, or vector breeding sites.[2] Living in a neighborhood without parks and places for outdoor recreation and leisure activities also negatively impacts mental and physical health, and may contribute to obesity.

A child's health is highly influenced by the house in which he or she lives. Consequently, the risk of illness and malnutrition during early childhood is high for low-income children, who tend to live in substandard housing. The effects of infirmity are hard to undo and likely to affect school enrollment and performance, even into adulthood. Many childhood diseases can be traced back to the lack of access to clean water and adequate sanitation, the prevalence of dirt floors, and the overall unhealthy homes in which these children were raised.

Disentangling and measuring the impact of housing conditions on health is not an easy task, but very important insights can be extracted from rigorous impact evaluations of programs that aim to solve some specific housing problems. For example, a recent study evaluates the impact

Table 1.1 Negative Health Impacts Resulting from Poor Conditions in Housing and Surrounding Neighborhoods

Risk factors	Associated contagious diseases	Accidents and noncontagious diseases	Associated mental diseases
Poor construction, overcrowding, inadequate air flow, dampness, and dirt floors	• Diseases due to insect infestation, parasites, rodents, and animal bites (malaria, chagas) • Acute respiratory infections • Tuberculosis	• Heart disease • Lung and respiratory chronic diseases (including asthma) • Lung cancer • Wounds • Burns • Prenatal diseases	• Poor cognitive and psychomotor development in young children • Learning disabilities and behavior disorders from exposure to toxic materials (lead) • Neurosis • Domestic violence • Alcoholism and drug addiction
Inadequate water and sanitation	• Fecal, oral, and parasitic diseases (typhoid, cholera, hepatitis, polio, among others)	• Heart disease • Stomach cancer • Diseases associated with microbiological toxins • Diseases associated with insect infestation	
Areas surrounding dwelling (inadequate garbage collection and storage, pollution, proximity to industrial zones or to congested roads, poor recreation facilities and parks)	• Diseases due to insect infestation, parasites, rodents, animal bites • Intoxication • Acute respiratory infections	• Heart disease • Lung and respiratory chronic diseases • Obesity • Cancer • Traffic accidents and other accidents	• Neurosis • Psychiatric disorders associated with chemicals and other contaminants

Source: Authors' compilation.

of the Mexican program Piso Firme (Firm Ground) on young children's health and cognitive development, as well as on the mental health and happiness of their mothers. The program replaced dirt floors with cement floors, a one-time intervention that cost about $150 per household. Results of the evaluation indicate that Piso Firme significantly decreased the incidence of parasitic infestations, diarrhea, and anemia, and improved the cognitive development of children who benefited from the program (as measured through the Peabody Picture Vocabulary Test[3]). Furthermore, adults reported being happier and scored significantly lower on assessment tools that measure depression and perceived stress. The results are summed up by Cattaneo et al. (2009): "Piso Firme has a comparable absolute impact on child cognitive development when compared to Mexico's anti-poverty conditional cash transfer program, Oportunidades, formerly called PROGRESA...Our results also indicate that replacing dirt floors with cement floors appears to be at least as effective as nutritional supplementation and early childhood cognitive stimulation" (p. 77).

Access to safe water also has important consequences for health. Waterborne diseases such as intestinal diarrhea, cholera, typhoid fever, and dysentery, caused by contaminated water supplies, are linked to deficient or nonexistent sanitation and sewage disposal facilities. Safe water is especially important for child health. A number of studies point to access to safe water as a key to better child health (for example, Merrick 1985; Esrey et al. 1991; Lee, Rosenzweig, and Pitt 1997; Jalan and Ravallion 2003). Deficient child health, in turn, has a significant impact on how well a child fares in school.

The importance of access to water and sanitation can be illustrated by the effects on child health of steps in Argentina to privatize water service and improve water provision (including increasing coverage; improving water and sanitation supply, sewage treatment, water cleanliness, and water pressure; lessening water leaks; and speeding repairs). Galiani, Gertler, and Schargrodsky (2005) found that the improvements in water provision helped reduce child mortality by 8 percent, mainly thanks to fewer deaths from infectious and parasitic diseases. The effect is even higher (26 percent) in the poorest areas, which probably had lower quality and coverage of water and sanitation before the services were privatized. Land titling has also been found to affect child health, as results from a natural experiment in Argentina illustrate (see box 1.1).

The damage from childhood diseases and malnutrition can be irreversible. Not only do children often miss school due to illness, they can permanently lose cognitive capacity from parasitic infections.

Box 1.1 Consequences of Land Titling Programs: An Experiment in Argentina

Many countries in Latin America and the Caribbean have promoted large-scale titling programs, including Peru, El Salvador, and Brazil. Even though opinions vary about the efficiency of such programs, research has shown that: (1) formalization programs have not increased access to formal credit (Deininger and Feder 2009); (2) people do not need titles to invest in their informal houses (Payne and Fernandes 2001); (3) formalization policies are associated with improvements in children's nutrition, fewer days missed at school, lower teenage pregnancy rates (Galiani and Schargrodsky 2004), and increased labor force participation (Field 2007).

While the correlation of land titling and improvements in social indicators has been established, causation is more difficult to determine (Fernandes 2011). In general, beneficiaries of title allocation are not selected randomly but on the basis of preferential criteria such as political favoritism or family connections. That in turn creates a selection bias that prevents the proper evaluation of the causal linkage between land titling and social outcomes.

To overcome the selection bias problem, an experiment could randomly give land titling to a group of squatters (treatment) and not give it to others (control) who share the same initial characteristics. This is, however, hard to implement in real life. Nevertheless, Galiani and Schargrodsky (2004) take advantage of a natural experiment in land rights in San Francisco Solano, County of Quilmes, Province of Buenos Aires, Argentina. In 1981, nearly 1,800 families occupied a large plot of wasteland that turned out to be comprised of thirteen plots of land belonging to different private owners. In 1984, the Congress of the Province of Buenos Aires passed a law expropriating these lands and transferring them to the squatters. Nine of the land owners accepted the compensation given by the local government, but four did not (lawsuits are still pending). As a consequence, some of the initial squatters now have formal property rights, while others do not. However, they share similar characteristics and arrived at the same time; the fact that some "got lucky" and some did not was completely random.

Based on this experiment, an evaluation of urban land titling on child health shows that children in titled parcels enjoyed better nutritional levels, but only in the short run (weight-for-height scores but not height-for-age).Teenage girls in formal plots had lower pregnancy rates than those in untitled parcels, which is consistent with the idea that access to land titles encourages households to invest in human capital.

Sources: Deininger and Feder (2009), Fernandes (2011), Field (2007), Galiani and Schardgrodsky (2004), and Payne and Fernandes (2001).

Housing and Education: A Two-Way Street

Housing affects educational outcomes, and as in the case of health, measuring the direct effect is challenging given the interconnected variables that affect housing and educational outcomes. For instance, families with higher incomes can afford both better housing and better education for themselves and their children. They can pay for higher-quality schooling or out-of-school resources such as textbooks, supplementary materials, or tutoring. In addition, their children enjoy better diets, which translate into lower rates of illness and better performance in school. Elite social networks such as those found in better neighborhoods, also place a higher premium on education and thus influence families to invest in more and better education. In other words, people who live in better homes tend to enjoy better education but how much of that is due to their incomes and what that can buy them?

Despite these complex interactions, housing does affect educational outcomes through several causal pathways—both direct and indirect. For example, lack of piped water supply and electricity effectively reduce the number of hours a child can study by forcing him to fetch water or limiting his work to daylight hours. Overcrowding creates distractions and thus limits the academic performance of students, as do low levels of sanitation (Goux and Maurin 2005).

Interestingly, the sword cuts both ways when it comes to housing and education. While housing conditions affect educational outcomes, school quality may affect the prices of homes in a neighborhood. Evidence from the United States and Europe shows that real estate (housing) prices are higher in neighborhoods with good public schools. Clearly, this pricing reflects demand for good schools (Black 1999; Figlio and Lucas 2004; Fack and Grenet 2010).

Poorly functioning housing markets and land markets may also lead to residential segregation. This in turn affects outcomes such as education through peer and neighborhood effects. Peer effects in the context of education are the influence that classmates have on an individual student's performance and choices. Students who live in segregated low-income areas are likely to have peers who also live in inadequate overcrowded housing, and have few resources to invest in education. Having low-achieving peers decreases the academic performance of individual students and the cohort (Altermatt and Pomerantz 2005). Furthermore, schools in segregated areas lack resources to provide an adequate environment for learning, perpetuating the poverty cycle.

In addition, studies for developed countries show that moving to neighborhoods with a higher proportion of home ownership increases educational stability, with lower dropout and repetition rates. Not surprisingly, constantly changing houses or schools negatively affects student performance (Brennan 2011). Although more research is required in the context of Latin America to understand the relationship between housing, neighborhood effects, and education, research on public housing programs finds a positive effect due to home ownership, less crowding, and housing quality. However, no significant effects were found on educational performance as measured by school attendance. A possible explanation is that often public housing programs are built on the periphery of cities, leading to segregation of low-income families (Ruprah 2011).

Clearly, living conditions and educational attainment are both critical ingredients of poverty reduction and economic growth in cities. Thus, policymakers and planners need to consider the positive spillover effects of housing improvements on education—and vice versa—and shape housing programs to jointly optimize their impact.

Segregation, Neighborhood Quality, and Social Ills

House surroundings and neighborhoods have an effect on the overall quality of life of families, for better or worse. Residential spillover effects are also important, with residents benefiting from or being disadvantaged by neighborhood effects[4] (Sampson and Raudenbush 1999).

Poorly planned, deteriorated, and unsafe residential areas negatively affect a range of social outcomes. Such areas usually lack adequate public services, parks, or playgrounds, and have been associated with an increase in obesity rates, poor cognitive development among children, and other social ills such as difficulties socializing.

Families living in "bad neighborhoods"—that is, neighborhoods that are run down, segregated, isolated, and typically characterized by violence or other social ills—are more likely to feel marginalized by society. People living in segregated, run-down neighborhoods are more likely to harbor feelings of insecurity and mistrust. Children growing up in distressed neighborhoods may lack access to good-quality education and employment, and may be exposed to social risks such as drug addiction, idleness, and gang activities, among others.

Neighborhood characteristics, both physical and socioeconomic, play a key role in defining the opportunities available to individuals and their families. Certain amenities may directly affect education outcomes as well as health outcomes, such as obesity. Indirectly, the degree of social cohesion influences crime and psychological well-being.

During the last 50 years, the region has experienced a rapid process of urbanization, resulting in cities and megacities (those with 10 million inhabitants or more) that are characterized by high levels of income inequality and poor housing conditions. Economic growth has also fed an obviously segregated pattern of housing, with gated communities for middle-income and high-income families proliferating in the suburbs. Although gated communities promote the concentration of the poor in periphery neighborhoods that lack proper infrastructure and promote the formation of slums, some researchers argue that this phenomenon does not represent a major change in the current pattern of segregation in the region (Roberts and Wilson 2009).

Rigorously measuring the impact of segregation and neighborhood quality is difficult because people sort themselves into different neighborhoods. An unbiased way of assessing the impact of neighborhoods on educational outcomes is through randomized control trials (RCTs). Such RCTs for housing programs are expensive and rare in developing countries. In the United States, programs in which families that won a lottery were allocated vouchers to occupy houses in better locations have been evaluated. The winners of vouchers (treatment group) were compared to the families that did not win the lottery (control group). Adequate, safe, and stable housing was found to have several beneficial outcomes. Moving to better neighborhoods offers youth a better, safer environment as rates of criminal victimization are lower, and household members are less likely to engage in criminal activities. The treatment group has positive mental health outcomes and lower levels of obesity (Katz, Kling, and Liebman 2001; and Kling, Liebman, and Katz 2007).

Finally, urbanization and population growth in Latin America has frequently outpaced the capacity of governments to provide public services that are crucial to development. Consider, for example, the range of negative spillover effects that a lack of quality public schools can perpetuate. Poorer households have no alternative but to send children to neighborhood public schools while more affluent families usually pay for private schools, even in faraway neighborhoods—what economists would call a substitute good. The children from poorer families not only suffer the consequences of a bad education, but the dangers of an unsafe, unhealthy neighborhood. The lack of adequate housing, together with low-quality, or in some cases no public services in the neighborhood, perpetuates inequalities and hinders economic and social development.

Better Housing Markets, Greener Cities?

Housing and land markets matter for the environment in numerous ways. For example, the fuel residents use for cooking depends on whether a house is connected to the electrical grid or to a natural gas pipeline. The layout and insulation of the dwelling impacts energy use for heating and cooling. The density and location of neighborhoods and their access to roads and public transportation networks affects energy consumption for transportation.

Cities account for 40 percent to 70 percent of global greenhouse gas (GHG) emissions (UN-HABITAT 2011a). With rapidly growing cities, declining urban densities, and rising incomes, the contribution of cities to emissions is projected to balloon. For the first time, more than half of the world's population lives in cities—a threshold crossed in 2008 (UNFPA 2007). By 2050, it is estimated that the urban population will have doubled; most of the population and economic growth is projected to take place in cities in what are today classified as developing countries, which would concentrate the new sources of emissions.

Latin America and the Caribbean is no exception to these trends; both the share and the absolute number of urban residents will increase dramatically during the next 40 years. Latin America is the only developing country region with high urbanization rates; as noted, more than 80 percent of the Latin American population lives in cities (UNFPA 2010). The urban population in the region totals around 470 million people and is expected to exceed 680 million by 2050 (Angel 2011, p. 46).

Residences and transportation constitute two of the most important sources of emissions in cities; as such, they represent important determinants of the carbon footprint of cities. Greenhouse gas emissions—particularly those coming from the combustion of fossil fuels for energy to light, heat, and cool residences and to power automobiles and other modes of transportation—are major culprits in rising global temperatures (UN-HABITAT 2011a). According to the International Energy Agency, Latin American residences account for 7 percent of total greenhouse gas emissions in the region while transportation accounts for 35 percent (World Resources Institute 2005). Urban transport is a source of air pollutants, such as suspended particles (a contributor to smog), sulfur dioxide, and nitrogen dioxide, that have adverse health impacts (see table 1.2). Thus, the idea of internalizing the cost of pollution through price mechanisms should be further explored (Parry and Timilsina, 2010).

As cities grow and households become wealthier, their energy consumption increases. Higher salaries allow people to buy cars, use less public transport, purchase larger homes, and consume more products. Furthermore, poor households need better quality housing. Thus, as cities in developing countries grow, so will their emissions (Wilbanks et al. 2007; UN-HABITAT 2011a). Greenhouse gas emissions in Latin America and the Caribbean are growing rapidly. The region's carbon dioxide (CO_2) emissions per person increased from 4.6 percent to 5.9 percent from 1990 to 2007. The increase in CO_2 emissions per capita in Latin America was higher than the world's average (World Resources Institute 2011). High emission levels negatively impact the environment and demand difficult trade-offs. Both governments and citizens should make an effort to reduce emissions. Even though Latin American cities are not big greenhouse gas emitters when compared to more industrialized countries,[5] the region will likely have to share the global burden to curtail emissions in the future, and may benefit from global incentives to do so.

Intermediate cities are growing faster than megacities, and density in cities is declining (Lora, Powell, and Sanguinetti 2008; Angel 2011). This is problematic because lower-density cities have higher per capita energy consumption than higher-density cities. How the housing market works, and, in particular, how land is developed and how houses are built are key factors that influence city emissions.

Urban Form, Carbon Use, and Housing Markets

The shape of a city, the population density in its built areas, and its compactness[6] represent key determinants of the energy consumption—and hence greenhouse gas emissions—of its inhabitants, particularly for transportation (Angel 2011). Urban sprawl boosts dependence on cars as households must commute longer distances for work and services.[7]

High-density cities have significantly lower greenhouse gas emissions than sprawling suburbia (Glaeser and Kahn 2010). The closer households are to their work areas and the more efficient the public transport system, the less the emissions per person. Dependence on cars has other adverse effects on human health. For instance, it increases air pollution that affects the respiratory system, and increases automobile crashes, pedestrian injuries, and fatalities. Low-density cities promote a more sedentary lifestyle,

Table 1.2 Ranking of Selected Megacities Based on Ambient Air Quality and Road Travel Speed

Megacities in 2000	Road Speed Average		Multi-pollutant index (MPI)		Total suspended particles (TSP)		Sulfur dioxide (SO_2)		Nitrogen dioxide (NO_2)	
	mph	Rank	μg m^{-3}	Rank	μg m^{-3}	Rank	μg m^{-3}	Rank	μg m^{-3}	Rank
Beijing	11.1	1	2.01	2	377	5	90	2	122	2
Buenos Aires	18.6	10	−0.01	13	185	11	20	8	20	18
Cairo	12.4	3	1.93	3	593	2	37	5	59	9
Delhi	14.4	7	0.92	7	405	4	18	10	36	16
Dhaka	n.d.	n.d.	2.4	1	516	3	120	1	83	4
Jakarta	11.6	2	1.24	5	271	7	35	6	120	3
Karachi	n.d.	n.d.	1.81	4	668	1	13	12	30	17
Kolkata (Calcutta)	n.d.	n.d.	0.59	9	312	6	19	9	37	15
Los Angeles, Long Beach, Santa Ana	29.5	15	−0.25	15	39	16	9	13	66	6

Mexico City	14	6	0.52	10	201	10	47	4	56	10
Moscow	18.6	10	1.07	6	150	12	15	11	170	1
Mumbai (Bombay)	13.8	5	0.39	11	243	9	19	9	43	14
New York—Newark	23.9	14	−0.23	14	27	18	22	7	63	7
Osaka—Kobe	20.5	13	−0.37	18	34	17	19	9	45	13
Rio de Janeiro	18.6	10	0.11	12	139	13	15	11	60	8
Sao Paulo	15	8	−0.29	17	53	14	18	10	47	12
Shanghai	12.4	4	0.87	8	246	8	53	3	73	5
Tokyo	16.2	9	−0.27	16	40	15	19	9	55	11

Source: Parry and Timilsina (2010, p. 196).

Notes: Megacities are as of 2000. Pollution data are for 2000. Road speed is for 2005. MPI is a multipollutant index combing all three pollutants.

Argentina (Buenos Aires), Bangladesh (Dhaka), Brazil (Rio de Janeiro, Sao Paulo), China (Beijing, Shanghai), Egypt (Cairo), India (Delhi, Kolkata, Mumbai), Indonesia (Jakarta), Japan (Osaka—Kobe, Tokyo), Mexico (Mexico City), Pakistan (Karachi), Russia (Moscow), United States (Long Beach, Los Angeles, New York—Newark, Santa Ana).

n.d. = no data

$\mu g/m^3$ = micrograms per cubic meter

mph = miles per hour

while higher-density cities allow for a lifestyle that generates fewer emissions per capita (Frumkin 2002).

Many factors affect city growth, its density, and the urban land cover—the total built-up area occupied by cities. Factors include population growth, income, inequality, land market regulations, infrastructure, fuel prices, and geographical characteristics. For instance, population growth is associated with higher-density cities, but rising incomes are associated with lower-density cities. Land market regulation, when enforced, is a major determinant of the intensity of land use.

Urban land cover in the region has increased since the beginning of the century and is projected to increase substantially in the coming years, particularly as density declines (Angel 2011). Urban land cover in Latin America was 91,300 square kilometers in 2000, and is projected to rise 74 percent by 2050, assuming density remains constant. However, assuming a 1 percent decline in density, urban land cover would increase 187 percent by 2050 (see figure 1.1). City growth tends to be carbon-intensive; as density declines, growth will be more carbon-intensive. Countering the carbon-intensive growth of cities requires providing the right incentives to encourage dense urban settlements.

Figure 1.1 Projections of Urban Land Cover for Latin America and the Caribbean, 2000–2050

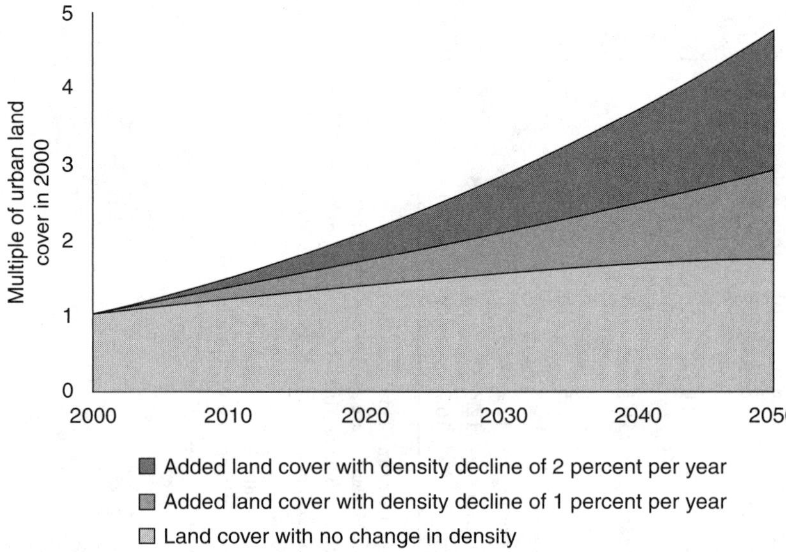

Source: Angel (2011).

Dense urban settlements provide efficient and effective responses to climate change by reducing per capita greenhouse gas emissions, and improving standards of living. First, urban density reduces transaction costs as households and service providers are closer to each other. Thus, cities have the potential to coordinate transport and land use, thereby reducing the distance traveled per person. Mass transportation can use energy-efficient fuels, decreasing emissions, pollution, and congestion. An example is the bus rapid transport (BRT) system implemented in Curitiba, Brazil, during the 1970s, and now running in several cities in Latin America, including Bogota, Lima and Mexico City, reducing auto use.

Second, there are benefits due to economies of scale in service delivery. High urban densities allow multiple households to be provided with networked services such as water, transport, and electricity at a minimal incremental cost. Serviced urban land boosts real estate value. For example, in Curitiba, property values rose for real estate with access to the BRT system (FTA 2009).

Third, higher-density cities can achieve economies of scope, reaping efficiency gains through joint production of some services, such as water and sanitation. Fourth, cities encourage innovation, thanks to additional benefits derived from knowledge spillovers. Fifth, agglomeration economies reduce production costs for firms because of the benefits of collocation of firms (O'Flaherty 2005; Glaeser 2011).

Housing Markets: In the Eye of the Climate-Change Storm

Climate change is already affecting the lives of almost everybody on earth. To assess the risks to urban areas posed by climate change, Mehrotra et al. (2011) developed a comprehensive framework. This framework articulates risk as a combination of the extent of climate hazards, vulnerability of households and firms, and the ability and willingness of city leaders to take action (agency). *Climate hazards* refer to the change in mean and extreme temperature, sea level, and precipitation. These climate variables impact the city through changes in the magnitude and frequency of heat waves, droughts, and floods. Sea-level rise (SLR) primarily affects coastal cities—for Latin America and the Caribbean, particularly those in El Salvador, Guyana, and coastal Buenos Aires (Magrin et al. 2007), as well as Caribbean countries. The temperature in Latin America is expected to rise from 1 to 4°C by 2050.

Vulnerability refers to the conditions of the people, their dwellings, and their assets that make them vulnerable to hazards. These vulnerabilities vary by the socioeconomic characteristics of the population. Cities in Latin America are segregated by income, and often poor people live in neighborhoods developed irregularly and located in zones prone to hazards, such as steep slopes, fault lines, and coastal areas. Extreme events, such as flooding, affect poor people more than the rest of the city because they live in lower-quality housing. Climate change adversely affects labor productivity and has economic costs, particularly for the poor. Warmer temperatures stress the health of the elderly and children; and the probability of vector-borne diseases such as malaria and dengue increases in cities with poor drainage systems (Barata et al. 2011). Historically, cities have been situated close to water and in low-lying areas, where flooding and the rise in sea level pose a threat. Flooding disrupts public transportation, electricity (traffic lights), telephone lines, and drainage systems, and harms dwellings and their contents. In extreme situations, people living in low-lying neighborhoods must be evacuated. Extreme climate events such as coastal flooding and decline in food production can expedite migration from rural areas to medium and large cities, as well as migration from cities in poor countries to those in wealthier ones (UNEP 2010).

Risk mitigation depends on well-functioning land markets and regulation that prevents residential land development in vulnerable locations and promotes investment in mitigating infrastructure, such as dikes, and earthquake-resistant buildings. *Adaptive capacity* is a function of city leadership's ability and willingness to prepare for climate change. The more city leaders adopt policies to mitigate and adapt to climate change, the lesser the risk. In Latin America, the focus on adaptation is as important as mitigation. The more prepared cities and households are, the lower their costs will be.

Housing and the Quality of Life

Enjoying good health, having children succeed in school, not having to face very long commutes, living free from exposure to pollutants, and being able to relax at home and not worry about crime all contribute to a good quality of life. Thus, it is logical to conclude that housing quality has a strong impact on how satisfied people are with their lives.

Life satisfaction can be broadly defined as a person's level of happiness with all aspects of life (Campbell 1976). It is natural that the houses in which people live and their neighborhood are major factors influencing their life satisfaction.

Surveys and studies reveal that in Latin America and the Caribbean people's satisfaction with their homes and the cities in which they live weigh heavily in their overall life satisfaction. Dwelling and neighborhood characteristics and urban amenities such as parks and cultural facilities have both direct and indirect effects on life satisfaction through health channels, for example (Lora et al. 2010). The influence of these factors on life satisfaction can be measured through an objective approach (by measuring their effect on home prices, gauging what housing amenities convey the highest prices) or by an indirect approach (measuring what housing amenities influence more self-reported life satisfaction). Through the life satisfaction approach, where individuals are asked to evaluate their own perception of a neighborhood amenity, multiple studies have shown that surroundings and access to neighborhood amenities are important determinants of the quality of urban life (Lora, Powell, and Sanguinetti 2008).

Another question concerning life satisfaction and housing outcomes relates to the importance of home ownership. Are homeowners happier than nonhomeowners? From an individual perspective, the social impacts of homeownership are not clear. On the one hand, investments in one's home and neighborhood might boost life satisfaction by improving the social, psychological, emotional, and financial health of individuals. On the other hand, homeownership might lead to distress and lower levels of life satisfaction, negatively impacting psychological or physical health, as, for example, when homeowners live in distressed neighborhoods, face financial losses, or simply cannot pay their mortgage.

Results of studies on the empirical evidence between homeownership and life satisfaction should be considered in light of the difficulties ascertaining whether the relationship is causal: that is, are homeowners happier or do happier individuals tend to buy homes? The available evidence is limited; there are many confounding variables that are difficult to control and can lead the results.

Using data for 17 countries in the region from the opinion survey Latinobarometer,[8] Ruprah (2010a) argues that homeowners are happier than nonhomeowners in Latin America. The results are confirmed through statistical analysis and impact measurements and are robust to a set of control variables such as the level of education and employment status.

Finding the Keys to Better Homes in the Region

Unfortunately, while living in a good house built in a good neighborhood is very important for an array of development outcomes, for both individuals and society, a high percentage of families in many Latin American cities do not live in good houses or neighborhoods. Of the 130 million families living in the region's cities, 5 million depend on another family for shelter; 3 million live in houses that are beyond repair; and 34 million live in houses that lack title or need some major improvement, such as providing proper water and sewerage facilities, replacing a dirt floor, or adding some extra rooms to avoid overcrowding. Most of these dwellings and an even higher number with no apparent problems are located in neighborhoods that lack many basic urban amenities.

Why do so many Latin Americans live in relatively bad homes? In some cases, families cannot afford even a simple basic house. In other cases, even if they earn sufficient income to afford better housing, they cannot get a mortgage, cannot document their income, credit markets are too shallow, or mortgage credit is too expensive. In still other cases, no home is available for them to buy. Why don't private sector builders and developers offer good basic homes for these families? Such units are not as profitable as building homes for wealthier households, or they may not be sufficiently profitable if land or construction costs are too high, or regulations make them too expensive to produce in some markets. Finally, some families would not want a good home built by the private sector even if they could afford it if they think that they can get it more cheaply by obtaining the land from an illegal developer or by taking over (invading) and building the house themselves.

Gauging which of these factors is more relevant in explaining the region's housing gaps and identifying the policies and regulation changes that may ease them is pivotal for ensuring that Latin American children are well-educated and healthy, that they and their parents enjoy not only good shelter but also a good quality of life, that families are not vulnerable to natural disasters or pollution, that cities have cleaner air and less congestion, and that ultimately all city inhabitants can enjoy the economic and social benefits that urban life has to offer.

2

Portrait of a Problem: The Housing Sector

Anyone who lives in or visits a Latin American or Caribbean city comes face to face with the housing problems that ail most neighborhoods in the region. There is nothing subtle or hidden about the ramshackle dwellings that crowd most of the regions' capitals. Upon arrival, visitors to Caracas are greeted by the spectacle of tens of thousands of dilapidated houses jam-packed precariously along the hillsides that line the main road between the airport and the city. Overcrowded *conventillos* (tenement houses) still abound in the historical downtown areas and neighborhoods of old capital cities such as Bogota and Buenos Aires. In a region notorious for its high levels of income inequality, the contrast between the haves and the have-nots is nowhere more striking than in the housing sector. Poor inhabitants of *favela*s (Brazilian slums) in Rio de Janeiro share the same view of Ipanema Beach with very wealthy households living lavishly in some of the most expensive real estate on the planet. In Lima, households living in jerry-built shacks devoid of running water or toilets watch luxury cars speed by to modern mansions in the exclusive sector of La Molina or to beach houses south of the Peruvian capital.

Informal housing in the region usually has a common origin: irregular land development. Houses spring up in lots without access to basic services. Over time, owners add to their dwellings themselves, ignoring poorly enforced building codes or municipal regulation. Even in the success stories—such as the former Villa El Salvador Pueblo Joven in Lima, or *favela*s in Brazilian cities that benefited from the public upgrading program Favela-Bairro—streets may still be too narrow, access to key urban amenities such as parks may be low, and access to public transport may be difficult.

Housing problems currently affect more than one-third of Latin American and Caribbean families living in cities, and have major consequences for their well-being and quality of life, their vulnerability to natural disasters and social ills, the likelihood that their children will succeed later in life, their capacity to adapt to changes in their life circumstances, and their access to economic opportunities. Good housing reflects well-functioning housing markets, in which households can access good-quality housing and improve their housing conditions as their incomes increase. The right incentives for preserving land as protected areas and encouraging intensive land use of unprotected areas are also key to promoting stable growth and greener cities. A well-functioning housing system also affects economic cycles, both for individual households and the larger economy. Residential construction is an important factor for business cycles. For most households, investment in housing makes up the lion's share of their investment portfolios and savings.

Economic growth will likely help narrow the region's housing gaps, but not enough. By 2015, economic growth will have helped only 36 percent of the families currently living in substandard houses (Ruprah 2009).[1] Existing public housing programs in the region will likely help only another 5 percent of families. With these projections, by 2015 about 36 percent of families—nearly 59 million people—in both urban and rural areas will still be living in inadequate houses, compared to 37 percent of households in 2009.

Housing Gaps in Latin America and the Caribbean

Measuring the magnitude and the characteristics of the housing problem in the region will help policymakers at the local, regional, and national levels pinpoint the most acute housing needs, analyze the investment requirements for households, the private sector, and local and city governments, and understand the nature of the inadequate and dysfunctional regulation that contributes to those gaps.

Measuring housing outcomes thoroughly and consistently allows for clear-cut comparisons among countries and cities and facilitates setting reasonable targets for improving housing conditions over time.[2] One shortcoming of the traditional definition of "housing outcomes" in the literature is that it focuses on only a subset of outcomes: those related to the dwelling (see table 2.1). These measures ignore the plethora of factors that contribute to the quality of life in urban areas beyond the physical characteristics of housing. Housing comprises far more than just a roof

Table 2.1 Basic Housing Market Outcomes

Dwelling	Surroundings, neighborhood, and city level
Structure and materials	*Urban form*
• Floor	• Prevalence of slums
• Walls	• Congestion
• Roof	• Density
• Flow, design	• Suburbanization
• Resistance to earthquakes	• Fragmentation (scattered development) and dispersion (fragmentation + lack of access or connectivity)
Basic services	*Services*
• Water	• Street lighting
• Sanitation	• Garbage collection
• Electricity	• Drainage
• Telephone, cable, Internet	• Roads and access to public transport
	• Parks and recreation
	• Police and security services
Living space	
• Households per dwelling	
• Persons per dwelling	
• Persons per bedroom	
• Rooms per dwelling	
Tenure	
• Ownership	
• Title	

Source: Authors' compilation.

and four walls; it refers to the services the dwelling enjoys, its location, the safety of the neighborhood, and a myriad of other factors that contribute to a person's quality of life.

Measures of *housing gaps*, often called *housing deficits*, are widely employed to assess housing problems and access to basic urban services. Although relatively easy to define, measure, and compare across countries and regions, the measure has many drawbacks. First and foremost, it depends upon establishing a subjective standard for adequacy. Such "needs" are famously unlimited. However, the measure of "housing gaps" does not determine market demand. The measure also omits important aspects of community services: access to jobs and commuting distance to major employment centers, quality of education and health services, safety of the surrounding areas, income segregation/integration, and cultural and market amenities (high-quality, competitively priced food and consumer goods, libraries, museums, and the like). Neighbors and community also contribute to life prospects and outcomes as much as physical housing conditions and basic urban services.

Housing gaps are usually divided into "quantitative" and "qualitative" shortages based on achieving minimum standards for housing outcomes. *Quantitative shortages* measure households in dwellings unsuitable for living that cannot be repaired plus households that share units. *Qualitative shortages* include households in dwellings with insecure tenure, walls made from discarded materials (such as palm fronds or throwaway materials such as cardboard), dirt floors, no access to piped water, inadequate sanitation, or overcrowding (three or more people per room). Table 2.2 presents estimates for these deficits using recent household surveys.

Table 2.2 Regional Housing Shortages in Latin America and the Caribbean, 2009 (Percent of Households)

				Urban quintiles by per capita household income				
Housing gaps	**National**	**Urban**	**Rural**	**I**	**II**	**III**	**IV**	**V**
Total shortages	*37*	*32*	*60*	*52*	*39*	*32*	*24*	*16*
Quantitative shortages	*6*	*6*	*5*	*9*	*8*	*6*	*5*	*3*
Additional households	4	4	3	6	5	4	3	2
Improvised dwellings	2	2	3	3	3	2	2	1
Qualitative shortages	*31*	*26*	*55*	*43*	*31*	*26*	*19*	*12*
Materials	12	7	32	16	10	6	4	2
Dirt floor	6	2	22	5	3	2	1	0
Poor roof	3	2	6	3	2	2	1	1
Poor walls	2	1	6	2	1	1	0	0
Overcrowding	6	4	13	10	6	3	2	0
Infrastructure	21	16	43	30	20	16	10	6
Lack electricity	4	1	17	2	1	1	0	0
Lack sanitation	15	13	27	25	16	12	7	4
Lack piped water	9	6	20	11	7	6	4	3
Lack of secure tenure	11	11	15	16	12	10	9	6

Source: Authors' calculations based on Rojas and Medellín (2011).

Table 2.2 updates the existing studies that review housing outcomes for the region (see Angel 2000; Arriagada 2000; Fay 2005, Ruprah 2009; Szalachman and Collinao 2010). The latest available information for a large number of countries (MacDonald and Simioni 1999) utilizes data from the population and housing censuses taken a decade ago; data from a new set of censuses will not be available for analysis until around 2013–2014.

Lack of infrastructure (especially water and sanitation) constitutes one of the main housing deficits in urban areas of the region. Around 21 million households live in dwellings lacking at least one basic service. Inadequate sanitation is the main infrastructure problem, affecting 13 percent of households (almost 17 million). Around 8 million households (6 percent) lack piped water. By contrast, coverage of electricity is almost universal (table 2.2).

Housing shortages vary across income quintiles, and consistently worsen as household income declines. This pattern is especially evident for gaps in access to infrastructure, use of inadequate building materials, or overcrowded dwellings. In 2009, the percentage of poor households (using ECLAC's food poverty line definition) lacking infrastructure was six times higher than that of high-income households. Overcrowding and poor-quality building materials are almost nonexistent in high-income households but affect 16 percent of poor households. Even though the poor suffer the highest incidence of housing shortages, most households experiencing housing deficits are not poor (32.3 million households compared to 9.8 million that are poor).

Table 2.2 presents averages for the region, but there are significant differences among countries in the structure of their housing shortages. Some must solve significant quantitative shortages while reducing qualitative shortages; others face problems mostly concerning housing quality, commonly related to lack of access to infrastructure. Table 2.3 presents total housing deficits by country and income quintile. Table 2.4 breaks down urban quantitative and qualitative shortages by country.

The variation suggests that different countries need different solutions for their housing problems. As Rojas and Medellín (2011) stress, there is no "one-size-fits-all" solution to the urban housing problems of the region; countries should base their housing policies and programs on detailed and well-documented diagnoses of their housing situations, thereby avoiding the temptation to imitate policies and programs that have worked in other countries but that may not work as well in their own.

Moreover, the government's use of housing gaps, by itself, to set production goals often creates substantial problems. Housing programs should

Table 2.3 Total Housing Deficits in Latin America and the Caribbean by Country, 2009 (Percent of Households)

				Urban quintiles (per capita household income)				
Country	**National**	**Urban**	**Rural**	**I**	**II**	**III**	**IV**	**V**
Argentina	32	32	n.d.	55	38	28	20	16
Bolivia	75	64	93	83	77	61	60	39
Brazil	33	32	44	52	38	31	23	14
Chile	23	19	53	29	22	18	15	10
Colombia	37	27	71	47	32	26	19	12
Costa Rica	18	12	26	24	15	9	9	5
Dominican Republic	41	35	56	54	39	34	28	18
Ecuador	50	41	66	63	52	43	31	18
Guatemala	67	56	79	77	70	59	46	30
Honduras	57	42	72	65	55	44	30	18
Mexico	34	28	58	46	33	27	19	14
Nicaragua	78	70	88	87	83	72	68	41
Panama	39	37	58	62	46	31	26	14
Peru	72	60	98	71	74	64	53	37
Paraguay	43	39	50	62	46	33	30	22
El Salvador	58	50	74	78	61	51	38	20
Uruguay	26	26	n.d.	51	31	20	15	11
Venezuela	29	29	n.d.	44	35	27	22	15

n.d. = no data.
Source: Authors' calculations based on Rojas and Medellin (2011).

pay as much or more attention to the location and quality of projects, target the poor and leave the lower middle-class to the private sector, set subsidies for poor households at a level high enough for them to really afford them, give as much choice to households as possible in the use of subsidies, and improve communities and local services. These steps may be even more important than meeting production goals for physical units intended to reduce housing gaps.

A Housing Report Card for the Region

The percentage of urban households facing quantitative and qualitative shortages decreased between 1995 and 2009, except for households lacking security of tenure. However, because the population has grown, the number of households facing shortages has increased in the period. Housing

Table 2.4 Urban Housing Deficits in Latin America and the Caribbean by Country, 2009 (Percent of Households)

		Qualitative shortages				
Country	**Quantitative shortages**	**Total**	**Materials**	**Overcrowding**	**Infrastructure**	**Lack of secure tenure**
Argentina	*5*	*27*	9	6	13	16
Bolivia	*30*	*34*	27	23	32	11
Brazil	*6*	*25*	2	0	22	7
Chile	*3*	*16*	1	1	2	14
Colombia	*9*	*19*	7	4	9	10
Costa Rica	*2*	*10*	5	1	1	6
Dominican Republic	*3*	*32*	5	3	25	9
Ecuador	*10*	*31*	14	8	19	13
Guatemala	*11*	*46*	32	27	32	10
Honduras	*2*	*41*	18	14	26	12
Mexico	*2*	*26*	9	5	8	15
Nicaragua	*12*	*58*	33	28	52	10
Panama	*8*	*29*	7	6	22	13
Peru	*14*	*46*	34	11	29	21
Paraguay	*3*	*36*	13	9	25	10
El Salvador	*8*	*41*	21	16	30	17
Uruguay	*0*	*25*	4	3	4	22
Venezuela	*8*	*20*	13	6	5	6

Source: Authors' calculations based on Rojas and Medellín (2011).

conditions have improved for all income groups, particularly for the lowest income quintiles (see figure 2.1).

Some of the 18 countries studied are doing better than others in improving housing conditions in general and for the poor in particular. Table 2.5 presents a housing report card for all countries in the region for which recent household survey data are available. Countries are graded in the four main measures of deficiency (quantitative deficits, problems with materials and overcrowding, infrastructure, and tenure) according to four criteria: countries with the lowest gap; countries with the worst progress; countries that didn't improve the gap between the richest and poorest households; and countries in which the gap among the poorest households didn't improve.

Most countries have made significant progress in reducing quantitative housing shortages in urban areas (table 2.4). All countries have gaps

Figure 2.1 Housing Conditions by Income Quintile in Latin America and the Caribbean, Mid-1990s and Late 2000s

Quantitative Measures

a. Quantitative Deprivations

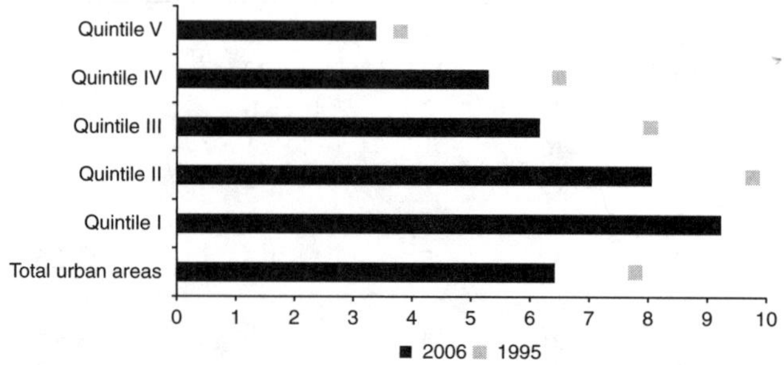

Qualitative Measures

b. Dwellings of Disposable Materials or Overcrowded

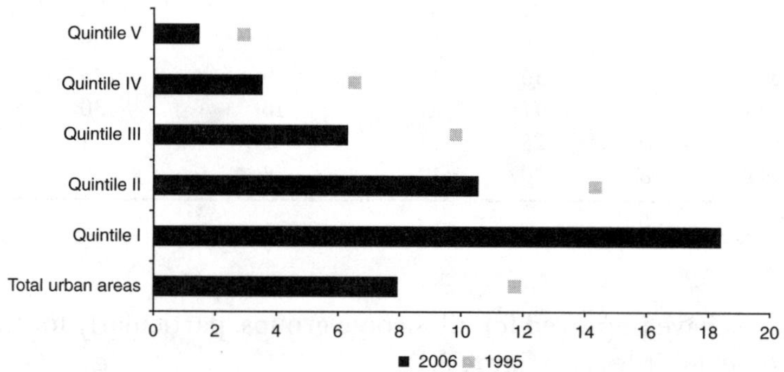

c. Inadequate Infrastructure

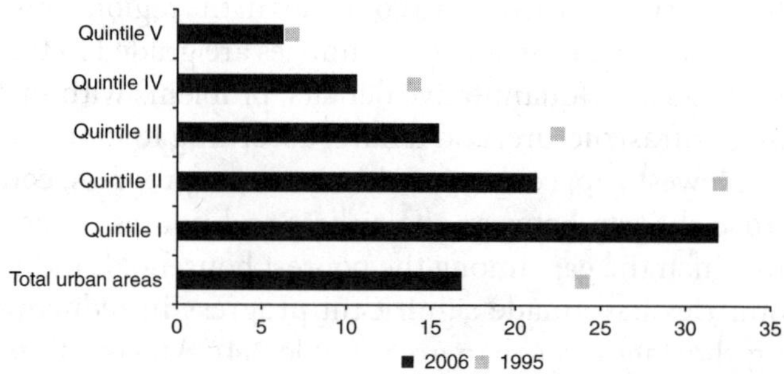

d. Lack of Secure Tenure

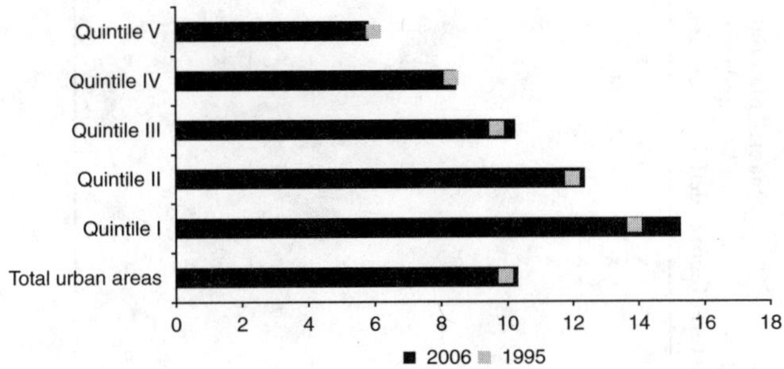

Source: Calculations based on Rojas and Medellín (2011).

below 12 percent, with the exception of Bolivia (30 percent) and Peru (14 percent). Nicaragua, Peru, and Guatemala have the highest aggregated qualitative gap (over 45 percent). Materials gaps for households in the lowest-income quintile surpass 50 percent in Bolivia, Guatemala, Nicaragua, and Peru. Nicaragua has the highest infrastructure gap (51 percent); however, in the lowest quintiles of Bolivia, the Dominican Republic, Guatemala, and El Salvador, the rate exceeds 50 percent. Only in 5 of the 18 countries is the infrastructure gap for the lowest quintile below 20 percent.

With respect to security of tenure, at 21 percent, the highest shortages are among the bottom quintile in Argentina, Panama, and Uruguay (around 30 percent).

Housing Deficits, Income, and City Size

Both at the country and city levels, income is one of the principal determinants of housing deficits (see figure 2.2). As average income increases, the percentage of families living in bad homes should decrease, since more families can afford to buy good homes. But this pattern is distorted by the ability of families to obtain credit, and the ability of the private sector to develop land and build houses for households of all income levels. Nicaragua, Bolivia, and Argentina have the highest deficits when compared with what would be expected by the level of income of the country. On the other hand, Costa Rica shows very low shortages, given its level of income. Costa Rica was one of the pioneers in the region in implementing ABC-type (Ahorro, Bono y Credito [Saving, Bonus, and Credit]) housing

Table 2.5 Housing Report Card for Latin American and Caribbean Countries

	Countries with the lowest gap[a]				Countries with the worst progress[b]				Countries that didn't improve the gap between the richest and poorest households				Countries in which the gap among the poorest households didn't improve			
Country	Quantitative deficits	Materials and overcrowding	Basic infrastructure	Tenure	Quantitative deficits	Materials and overcrowding	Basic infrastructure	Tenure	Quantitative deficits	Materials and overcrowding	Basic infrastructure	Tenure	Quantitative deficits	Materials and overcrowding	Basic infrastructure	Tenure
Argentina	✓	–	–	–	–	x	–	x	–	x	x	x	–	x	–	x
Bolivia	–	–	–	–	–	x	–	x	–	–	–	x	–	–	–	x
Brazil	–	✓	–	–	–	–	–	–	–	–	–	x	–	–	–	–
Chile	–	✓	✓	–	–	–	–	–	–	–	–	x	–	–	–	–
Colombia	–	–	–	–	–	–	x	x	–	–	–	x	–	–	x	x
Costa Rica	✓	✓	✓	–	–	–	–	–	–	–	–	x	–	–	–	x
Dominican Republic	–	–	–	–	–	–	–	–	–	–	–	–	–	–	–	–
Ecuador	–	–	–	–	x	–	–	x	–	–	x	–	–	–	–	–
Guatemala	–	–	–	–	–	–	–	–	–	x	–	–	–	x	–	–
Honduras	–	–	–	–	–	–	–	–	–	–	x	x	–	–	–	x
Mexico	✓	–	–	–	–	x	–	x	–	–	–	–	–	–	–	x
Nicaragua	–	–	–	–	x	–	–	x	x	x	x	–	x	x	–	–
Panama	–	–	–	–	–	–	x	x	–	–	–	–	–	–	–	x
Peru	–	–	–	–	–	–	–	–	–	x	–	–	–	x	–	–
Paraguay	✓	–	–	–	–	–	–	–	–	–	–	x	–	–	–	x
El Salvador	–	–	–	–	–	–	–	x	–	x	x	–	–	x	–	–
Uruguay	✓	✓	✓	–	–	–	–	x	–	–	–	x	–	–	–	x
Venezuela	–	–	✓	–	x	x	–	x	x	–	–	–	x	–	–	x

A "✓" = positive result.
A "x" = negative result.
A "–" = neither positive nor negative result.
[a] Less than 5 percent of households with deficit.
[b] Less than 10 percent make progress in closing the gap.
Source: Authors' compilation based on methodology developed by Rojas and Medellín (2011).

Figure 2.2 Housing Shortages by Country in Latin America, 2009

a. Quantitative

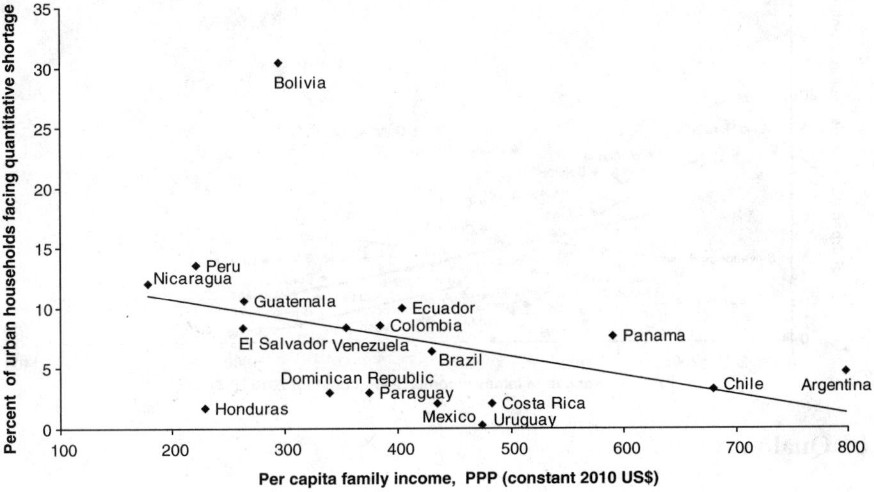

b. Qualitative

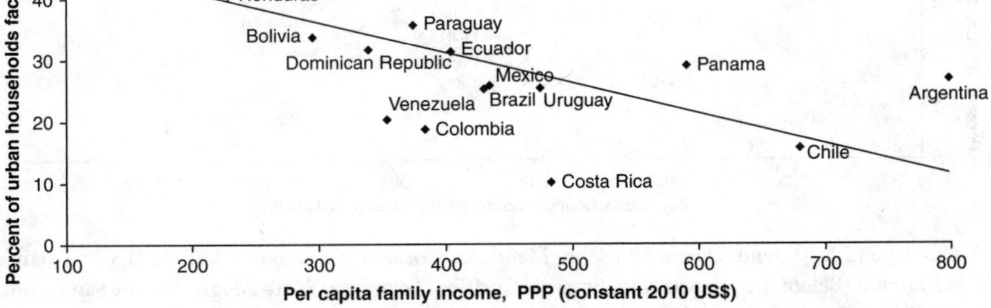

Source: Authors' calculations based on Rojas and Medellín (2010).

Figure 2.3 Housing Shortages by City, 2009

a. Quantitative

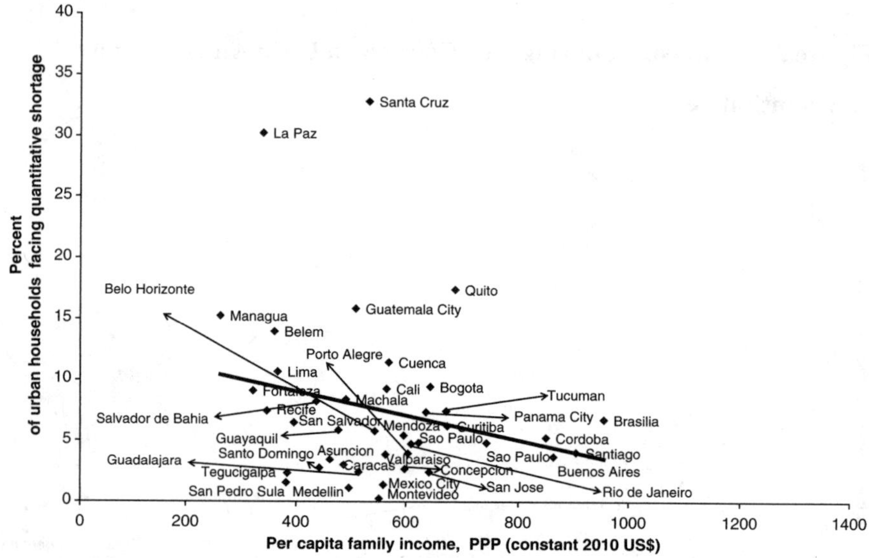

b. Qualitative

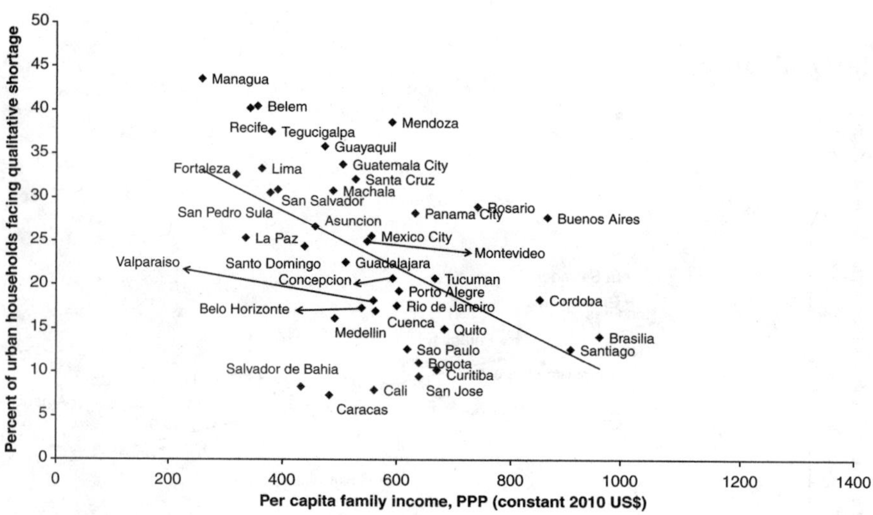

Note: Argentina (Buenos Aires, Cordoba, Mendoza, Rosario, Tucuman), Bolivia (La Paz, Santa Cruz), Brazil (Belem, Belo Horizonte, Brasilia, Curitiba, Fortaleza, Porto Alegre, Recife, Sao Paulo), Chile (Concepcion, Santiago, Valparaiso), Colombia (Bogota, Cali, Medellin), Costa Rica (San Jose), Dominican Republic (Santo Domingo), Ecuador (Cuenca, Guayaquil, Machala, Quito), El Salvador (San Salvador), Guatemala (Guatemala City), Honduras (San Pedro Sula, Tegucigalpa), Mexico (Guadalajara, Mexico City), Nicaragua (Managua), Panama (Panama City), Paraguay (Asuncion), Peru (Lima), Uruguay (Montevideo), Venezuela (Caracas).

Source: Authors' calculations based on Rojas and Medellín (2010).

programs; between the early 1990s and late 2000s, the program benefited 23 percent of families in the country with 270,000 housing solutions.

At the city level, the most severe quantitative shortages are evident in cities in Bolivia (Sucre, Santa Cruz, Cochabamba, Oruro, and Tarija). Bogota enjoys one of the lowest qualitative deficits when compared to its income level thanks in large part to the efforts of its government to create partnerships and implement incentives and policies to promote land development and housing construction for most income levels in the city (see figure 2.3).

Location, Location, Location

Analyzing individual housing deficits is only one of the angles from which housing market performance can be measured. Another angle, which may be as important, is how housing markets—especially land development for residential use—shape the characteristics of the areas immediately around dwellings and surrounding neighborhoods: the shape and structure of cities, and urban segregation.

One of the most important channels through which land and housing markets impact neighborhood characteristics, city size, and urban segregation is through the formation of slums, a process that overlaps strongly with housing informality.

Informality in housing markets is a complex phenomenon with many complementary features (Dowall 2007; Fernandes 2011). Housing informality encompasses overlapping layers of illegality that make quantification a serious challenge. Informal housing takes a variety of forms; known by such names as *favelas, barriadas, barrios, pueblos jóvenes, villas-miseria, villas-emergencia, chabolas*, or *tugurios*, all of these are essentially national variations of shantytowns. Informal housing usually entails the occupation of public, communal, or private land. Dwellings have no access to basic infrastructure or basic urban amenities. Informality may also arise with the unlicensed subdivision of private, communal, or public land (urban or rural land in the urban fringe), followed by the sale of individual plots and construction by residents, resulting in *barrios ilegales*, *loteos piratas*, *loteamentos irregulares*, or *loteamentos clandestinos* (different names in different countries for the same sort of informal neighborhood built on illegally acquired land). In some cases, informality evolves from poorly designed public housing projects (*conjuntos habitacionales*) that have gradually become extralegal. In most cases, irregular land development is followed by irregular, self-built housing with no compliance to construction codes.

Since housing informality is a complex issue with multiple consequences, its precise measurement remains a challenge. Data on informality at all levels, from global to local, tend to be fragmented, imprecise, and often questionable (Fernandes 2011). UN-HABITAT, the World Bank, Cities Alliance, and other international bodies have attempted to provide reliable statistics. Based on an assessment of 15 Latin American countries, MacDonald (2004) argues that at least 25 percent of the urban population of the region lives in informal settlements. In Brazil, 20 to 25 percent of dwellings in main cities originated from illegal land occupation (Fernandes 2011). The population living in *villas-emergencia* in Buenos Aires has grown by 25 percent over the past few years, housing 7 percent of the city's total population, around 200,000 people (Clichevsky 2006). Informality in the region has been growing since the mid-1950s. In Rio de Janeiro, for example, from 1961 to 2009, dwellers in *favelas* and other informal settlements rose from 10 percent of the population to more than 20 percent (from 300,000 to 1.25 million); the rates of informal growth have been higher than the growth rates of both the urban population and poverty incidence (Fernandes 2011). In São Paulo, informal dwellings rose from 6.9 percent to 11.4 percent of the total from1991 to 2001 (Dowall 2007).

Housing informality can lead to the formation of slums, which can be described as a "heavily populated urban area characterized by substandard housing and squalor" (UN-HABITAT, 2007, p. 1). According to UN-HABITAT, nowadays slums have come to include the vast majority of informal settlements, which are quickly becoming the most visible manifestation of urban poverty in developing world cities. The limits in the definitions of informal housing and slums are not clear, and the two concepts tend to overlap in the literature.

To quantify the prevalence of slums using existing data (household surveys and censuses), UN-HABITAT developed a household-level definition to identify individual slum dwellers among the urban population. A slum dweller is defined as any household lacking one of the following: access to improved water (sufficient amount at an affordable price obtained without extreme effort); access to improved sanitation (disposal of human waste); security of tenure (proven documentation or perceived protection from eviction); durability of housing (a permanent and adequate structure in a nonhazardous location); and sufficient living area (not more than two people sharing the same room). This definition implies an upper bound for the measurement of slum dwellings. It does not take into account the local context of the household, or if it shares the same characteristics as other neighboring dwellings.

Using the previous definition, UN-HABITAT estimates that in 2001, almost 32 percent of the world's urban population was living in slums. By region, 60 percent of those slum dwellers were in Asia, 20 percent in Africa, 14 percent in Latin America and the Caribbean, and 6 percent in the developed regions (Fernandes 2011).

Figure 2.4 shows slum population as a percentage of the total urban population plotted against GDP per capita for 87 countries in the developing world as of 2005. It reveals that, among those countries with a higher incidence of slums than expected given their level of GDP per capita (above the trend line), around 37 percent are from Latin America and the Caribbean. These countries include Brazil and Argentina, two of the most influential actors of the region given their size and income level.

Figure 2.5 zeroes in on Latin America, focusing on the correlation between the prevalence of slum population (as a percentage of total urban population) and GDP per capita, but taking into account each country's

Figure 2.4 Slum Population and Income Per Capita, Select Countries Worldwide, 2005

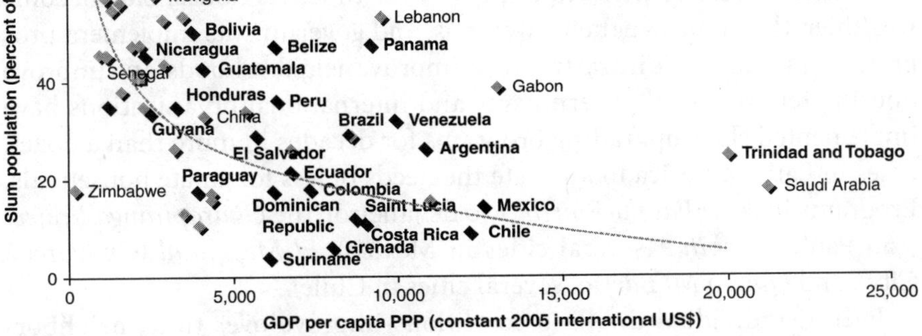

Note: Slum population measured as a percentage of urban population.
Sources: Data for slums, UN-HABITAT (2010); GDP per capita, World Bank (2011c).

Figure 2.5 Slum Population and Income Per Capita by Population, 2005

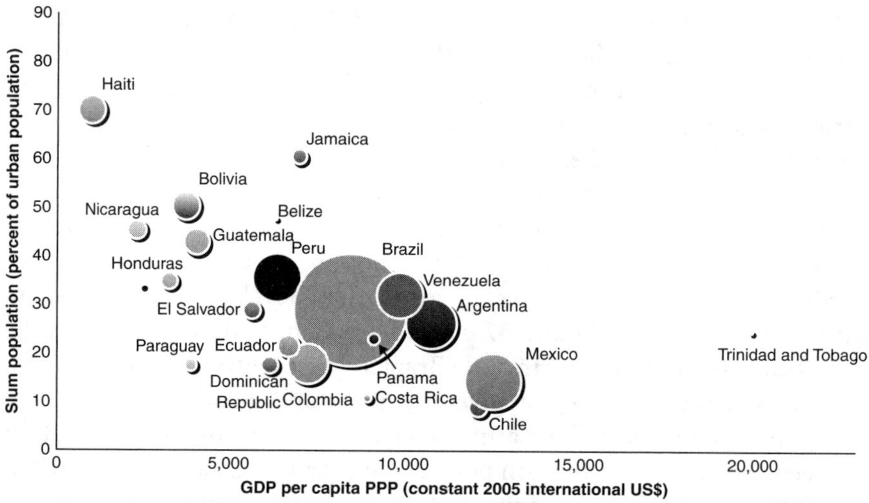

Note: Slum population measured as a percentage of urban population. The size of the circles respresents cities' populations by thousands of people.
Sources: Data for slums, UN-HABITAT (2010); GDP per capita, World Bank (2011c).

total population. Thus, countries can have a high incidence of slums that affect only a limited number of people, and vice versa. On the one hand, in Haiti, slum incidence is high; more than 70 percent of the urban population lives in slums, but that amounts to 2.7 million people. On the other hand, Brazil has a relatively low incidence of slums (29 percent of its urban population lives in slums), but that totals around 45.6 million people.

Informal housing tends to improve over time. As households become wealthier, they improve their dwellings, and governments implement programs to provide basic infrastructure, improve neighborhoods, and improve housing tenure. Local governments and international organizations have implemented slum upgrading programs for decades in more than a dozen cities in Latin America to alleviate the needs of less fortunate households. Programs include *Favela-Bairro* (Rio de Janeiro), the *Guarapiranga Project* (São Paulo), *Habitat* (several cities in Mexico), *El Mezquital* (Guatemala City), and *Quiero Mi Barrio* (several cities in Chile).

Even if individual dwelling conditions improve over time, neighborhood amenities may not improve at the same pace. In some slums, poor surroundings and lack of amenities endure, as fixing these problems requires costly public investments and expropriations of land to make room for amenities and access roads. In other cases, these deficits persist due to lack of planning and funding from local governments, which face increased demand for these services from irregular land developments that did not include funding for them.

Few comprehensive data sources on the situation of neighborhood and housing amenities in the region exist, but some insights can be gained from surveys that collect data on citizen satisfaction with these services. One of them is the Gallup poll, which surveys urban dwellers to learn about their overall satisfaction with their city, as well as such aspects as basic urban infrastructure, for example, roads, sidewalks, and pedestrian ways; basic services such as public transportation; amenities such as sports facilities, parks, and green spaces; the cleanliness of air and water; and problems such as traffic congestion. Table 2.6 reports these results.

Overall, more than two-thirds of Latin Americans are satisfied with the city they live in and with the quality of their water and air, but only half are satisfied with basic services such as roads and sidewalks, and with public spaces such as sports facilities, parks, and green spaces. At the national level, citizens of poorer countries tend to report worse neighborhood conditions. Peruvians report low satisfaction for many aspects of city life, possibly because of the prevalence of slums and housing informality in the country. Argentines are among the most dissatisfied with their sidewalks—perhaps because even some federal public housing lack paved roads and sidewalks, which are supposed to be the responsibility of municipalities.

Housing Markets and the Shape of Cities

Among the most important outcomes of housing markets and land markets are the shape, size, and urban structure of cities; together, these elements make up a dwelling's surroundings. Poorly functioning housing markets and land markets frequently create and feed endless cities, with low urban densities, fuzzy boundaries between the city and the countryside, single-use (commercial, industrial, recreational, or residential) rather than mixed-use neighborhoods, scattered and poorly connected urban developments, and fragmented open spaces (Angel 2011).

Housing informality goes hand in hand with chaotic urban sprawl, since irregular land development and construction usually result in the widespread occupation of public spaces such as streets, pavements, and viaducts, or the occupation of protected forest or coastal land, riverbanks, water reservoirs, mountain sides, and other environmentally protected or disaster-prone areas.

Table 2.6 Perception of Dwelling Surroundings in Latin America and the Caribbean, 2007 (Percent of People Satisfied with Each Category)

Country	Overall satisfaction		Public infrastructure: percentage of people satisfied with...		Public services: percentage of people satisfied with...		Public space: percentage of people satisfied with...			
	Satisfied with the city or area where they live	Would recommend the city or area where they live as a place to live	Roads and highways	Sidewalks or pedestrian ways	Public transportation systems	Flow of traffic	Availability of public sports facilities	Availability of public parks and green areas	Quality of air	Quality of water
Argentina	84.8	84.4	45.9	38.6	51.1	52.1	56.1	n.d.	72.3	69.0
Belize	69.6	69.4	35.3	46.2	41.4	53.9	44.4	49.0	75.1	67.8
Bolivia	83.0	76.3	60.0	46.3	71.5	56.9	58.1	53.1	70.8	81.1
Brazil	81.9	81.0	60.3	53.3	64.9	60.5	49.3	52.3	71.5	80.4
Chile	77.6	74.0	73.8	53.9	58.8	65.7	41.4	53.7	60.5	82.9
Colombia	84.5	83.9	53.6	59.1	76.0	65.5	54.9	55.0	69.2	78.4
Costa Rica	87.3	84.0	51.1	47.0	78.4	62.9	53.5	52.5	85.3	88.9
Dominican Republic	76.8	72.6	49.7	50.8	58.3	67.1	46.5	41.3	72.2	57.2

Ecuador	83.7	82.4	61.3	51.2	70.9	63.9	56.0	54.7	68.8	70.1
El Salvador	85.3	77.7	65.0	59.0	73.5	65.6	48.6	47.0	76.7	71.0
Guatemala	91.6	84.8	57.5	55.4	69.7	54.3	54.8	52.3	74.2	68.6
Guyana	77.1	75.4	73.2	50.9	72.4	65.8	48.4	40.0	81.1	54.6
Honduras	82.9	71.5	48.5	34.7	70.8	53.1	50.3	46.0	74.1	71.7
Haiti	52.1	57.9	35.8	n.d.	35.5	n.d.	n.d.	n.d.	48.8	46.2
Jamaica	66.6	69.7	45.6	n.d.	74.4	n.d.	n.d.	n.d.	86.3	90.0
Mexico	82.3	77.5	60.0	54.0	66.9	59.9	53.4	55.6	72.9	71.2
Nicaragua	85.7	79.9	54.9	45.1	64.2	66.3	44.0	42.6	81.7	65.2
Panama	86.2	75.4	46.4	46.1	45.4	55.1	55.0	52.0	84.4	83.6
Peru	72.3	73.2	49.2	43.7	60.2	48.6	42.0	48.2	60.5	64.7
Puerto Rico	87.3	85.7	42.3	n.d.	45.3	n.d.	n.d.	n.d.	64.4	61.0
Paraguay	85.9	83.9	47.7	49.6	53.8	69.0	66.5	61.4	86.7	87.2
Trinidad and Tobago	75.1	79.0	47.2	n.d.	57.6	n.d.	n.d.	n.d.	75.6	72.0
Uruguay	81.7	79.1	70.9	57.9	72.3	72.1	60.7	70.1	88.4	92.4
Venezuela	86.8	88.0	54.4	n.d.	65.8	n.d.	n.d.	n.d.	79.1	82.2
Region's average	*80.3*	*77.8*	*53.7*	*49.6*	*62.5*	*61.0*	*51.8*	*51.5*	*74.2*	*73.2*

n.d. = no data.
Source: Gallup (2007).

The average urban population density, measured as the ratio of the total population to the total built-up area of a city, constitutes one of the housing outcomes used in the literature to determine how land development shapes a city and its carbon footprint. Illegal subdivision of land and construction of houses may result in higher population densities than formal land subdivisions when individual plot size regulations and floor-to-area ratios (FARs) are stringent. But they may have the opposite effect when land use regulations, incentives, and city characteristics favor multiunit vertical developments (high rises). This has important implications for the greening of cities.

Contrary to popular belief, cities in the developing world are not suffering from overcrowding, constant compactness, and less expansion at the periphery than developed cities (Angel et al. 2010). The average urban population density has declined in most cities in the developing world, and cities in Latin America and the Caribbean are no exception. For the Latin American cities with data available, 75 percent had a lower density in 2000 than in 1990 (see figure 2.6). The main reason for this phenomenon is that the land area of cities has expanded at a faster rate than their

Figure 2.6 Change in Population Density in Select Cities Worldwide, 1990–2000

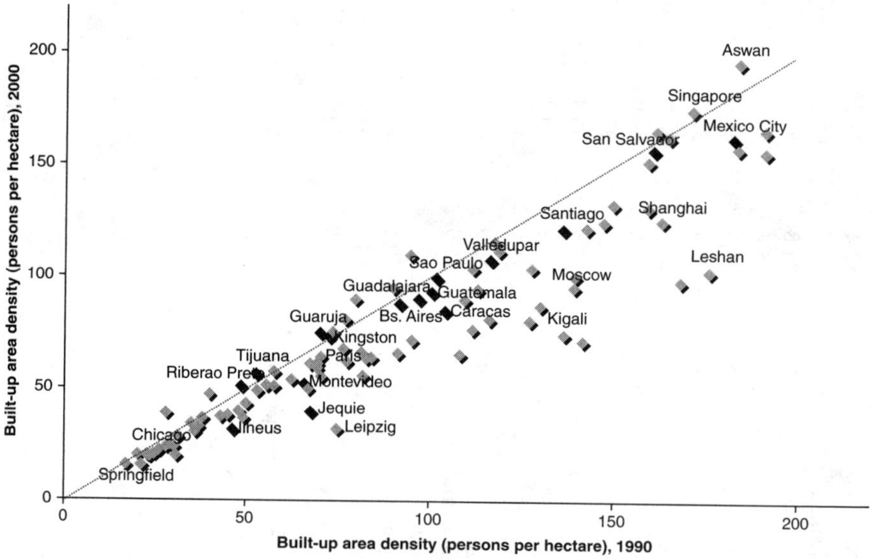

Source: Angel et al. (2010).

Figure 2.7 Urbanized Area Population Density in Select Cities Worldwide, 1800–2000

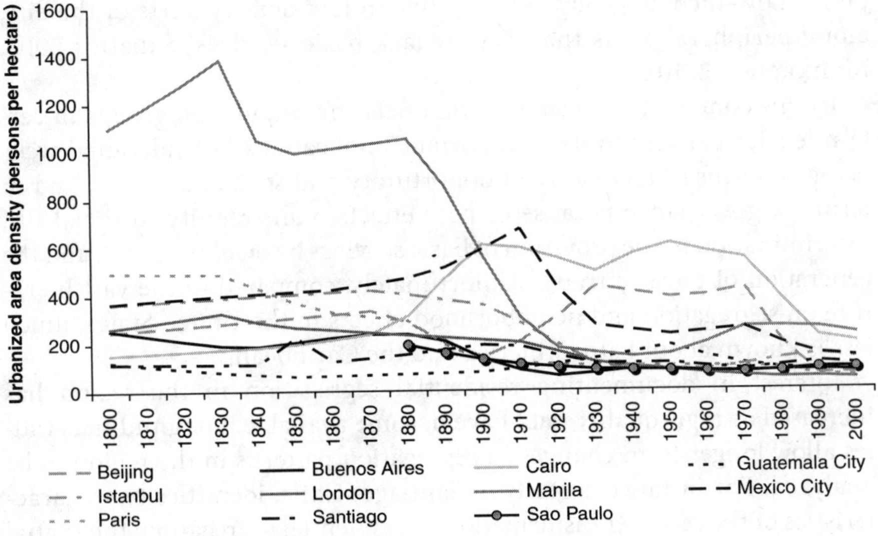

Source: Angel et al. (2010).

population growth. In less-developed regions, this might in part reflect the lack of urban planning and the expansion of informal housing.

Historically, urban densities peaked around 1890, and were then followed by periods of declining densities. In the twentieth century, the territory of cities grew 27 percent faster than their population. Especially in the last two decades of the twentieth century, cities became less dense both in the developed and developing world. Figure 2.7 documents this trend for selected cities around the world between 1800 and 2000.

Segregation

An important outcome of housing and land markets is urban segregation: the grouping together in close proximity ("spatial agglomeration") of families with similar social conditions, including socioeconomic status, ethnicity, migratory origin, and age.

Latin America has high levels of income inequality, pronounced socioeconomic differences based on race and ethnicity, and very large metropolitan areas. Certain patterns tend to predominate in Latin

American cities. High-income groups tend to cluster in one area of the city. Income heterogeneity is higher in high-income areas than in low-income ones (that is, poorer neighborhoods are more uniformly poor). Low-income groups tend to live in low-density parts of the city, along peripheral areas that usually lack basic services (Sabatini 2003; Monkkonen 2010).

In this context, the concentration of certain population groups in certain locales is likely to have important implications for individual well-being in terms of inequality of opportunity and social outcomes, and in terms of governance because of peer effects, vulnerability to social ills, discrimination in the provision of basic services by neighborhood, and the generation of poverty traps.[3] Unfortunately, compared to the vast literature on segregation and neighborhood effects in the United States, much less is known about Latin America and the Caribbean.

Interest in documenting residential segregation in the region has increased as high-quality data have become available. Longitudinal studies allow longer-term changes in segregation patterns in the region to be analyzed. For instance, a study of Santiago, Chile, identifies two characteristics of the recent transformation in residential segregation: the spatial dispersion of the elites; and the physical proximity of the poor to both the residential areas of the elites and to subcenters or dynamic areas within the city to gain access to jobs and opportunities to generate income (Sabatini et al. 2009). This pattern is also present in Brazil: small urban slums have been increasing in São Paulo's metropolitan areas (Marques and Torres 2005), while they have been established in Rio de Janeiro's affluent neighborhoods for longer periods.

Using data for over 100 Mexican cities, Monkkonen (2010) analyzes segregation patterns at the national level and finds that most low-income urban households live in low-density areas of cities. This pattern contrasts with the dense urban slums in other developing countries, especially in Asia. Additionally, larger cities in Mexico tend to be more segregated, and the regional differences in segregation are significant. The study pays special attention to segregation of informally employed workers, indigenous people, and low-income households. It finds that indigenous people occupy less space per household and tend to live more in the periphery relative to either low-income households or those that include informal workers. Variations in levels of income segregation across cities of different sizes and regions are significant, as expected. This can be explained by the greater differentiation of neighborhood characteristics in larger cities, which leads to more segregation. However, this result does not hold for informal workers and indigenous people, meaning other reasons besides income must explain the residential location of both groups.

In Mexico, levels of segregation of low-income households and ethnic minorities pale when compared to the United States or Europe and likely reflect a mix of factors such as the structure of local governments, the conditions of the land and housing markets, and prevailing land use regulations (Monkkonen 2010).

Other countries besides Mexico present quantitative results, although, as Monkkonen (2010) points out, analysis of more robust measures of segregation is needed. Racial segregation in 35 cities in Brazil is moderate by US standards (Telles 1992). Furthermore, segregation in Brazil increases the development of housing markets; socioeconomic status is a strong predictor of overall residential segregation. "Segregation is significantly higher in urban areas with high occupational inequality, low mean income, high levels of housing turnover, and high homeownership," Telles concludes (p. 186).

For Peru, Peters and Skop (2007) analyze segregation in Lima using level of education, type of employment, tenancy of dwelling, and socioeconomic status. This study indicates that segregation is stronger by socioeconomic status and tenancy than by either education or employment. Additionally, the findings indicate that segregation across Lima's Metropolitan Region is not widespread; instead, there are segregated "pockets" in some areas.

Roberts and Wilson (2009) study the patterns of socioeconomic segregation in seven Latin America cities and in one city in the United States, Austin, Texas, allowing for interregional comparison. Table 2.7 depicts the results of three segregation measures based on educational attainment of adults for two points in time. The dissimilarity index measures the proportion of the poor population that needs to be moved from one spatial unit (say, a neighborhood) to another in order to make the distribution of the population homogeneous. The dissimilarity index ranges from 0 to 1, and a higher value implies more segregation. The isolation index measures the probability that a poor individual shares his or her neighborhood with other poor individuals. Finally, the Moran's I index measures the degree to which the characteristics of a particular locale resemble adjacent locations ("spatial autocorrelation") .

The evolution of spatial segregation in recent years in Latin American cities has been smooth, without abrupt changes in segregation levels. Two cities deserve special attention: Santiago and Montevideo. In the case of Santiago, the reduction in overall poverty has led to lower

Table 2.7 Segregation Measures Based on Educational Attainment of Adults in Select Cities in Latin America and the United States

	Dissimilarity Index (0 to 1 Scale)		Isolation Index (probability)		Global Moran's I (−1 to 1 Scale)	
City	**Year 1**	**Year 2**	**Year 1**	**Year 2**	**Year 1**	**Year 2**
Austin	0.383	0.416	0.204	0.213	0.520	0.610
Buenos Aires	0.268	0.270	0.658	0.499	0.851	0.775
Campinas	0.300	0.256	n.d.	n.d.	0.593	0.581
Lima	0.330	n.d.	0.700	n.d.	0.556	n.d.
Mexico City	0.170	0.148	0.272	0.249	0.590	0.670
Montevideo	0.305	0.373	0.420	0.380	0.780	0.790
Santiago	0.467	0.411	0.267	0.410	0.728	0.686
Sao Paulo	0.276	0.276	0.681	0.577	n.d.	0.740

Note: For explanations of the measures, see text.
n.d. = no data.
Source: Roberts and Wilson (2009).

socioeconomic segregation as elites have dispersed through metropolitan areas. Meanwhile, public housing has been built on a large scale, spatially concentrating the poor—and thereby counteracting the dispersion of the poor in the metropolitan area. In Montevideo, segregation by educational level has increased. New patterns of residential segregation have emerged, such as greater contrast between the center and periphery, an increase in the number of irregular settlements on the periphery, loss of population in the city center, and a greater number of elderly residents (Roberts and Wilson 2009). In São Paulo, educational segregation of adults has decreased as segregation by income has increased. Importantly, in all the cities in the region, overall educational levels have increased, thereby shrinking the educational gap; thus, segregation by education is likely to decline.

Millions or Billions? The Price Tag for Closing the Region's Housing Gaps

How much do households need to invest to close their housing gaps? This section simulates these costs using the housing shortage data presented earlier and the market costs for standardized housing units and basic dwelling upgrades needed to close each gap. The estimates provide a lower boundary, as they focus only on fixing deficiencies in individual dwellings; they do not cover costs associated with improving neighborhoods, basic infrastructure such as sidewalks and roads, and urban amenities.

Closing the gap for poor households in the region[4] suffering from quantitative deficits in housing would require a minimum investment of at least US$25.5 billion. This estimate assumes that poor households live in a basic standard dwelling with 40 square meters of built area and in a 60-square-meter plot valued at US$15,000.[5] For households that are not poor, closing the quantitative gap would require an investment of at least US$148 billion. This estimate assumes that these households live in a $23,000 home, which is the current average price of the cheapest dwelling offered by the private sector in the region from data compiled by the Inter-American Development Bank (IDB). Closing the qualitative infrastructure gap would require an investment of at least $107 billion, assuming an investment of $5,000 per household. Finally, closing the qualitative materials gap would imply an investment of at least $30 billion, assuming an investment of $3,000 per household.

These combined investments for poor and nonpoor households total around $310 billion, or 7.8 percent of the region's GDP. Closing the gap in the quantitative deficit and in the infrastructure deficit for all the poor households in the region would amount to around $53 billion, or 1.4 percent of the region's GDP.

For the cities for which representative data are available, taking into account that the market cost of a standardized dwelling varies widely, the investment needs range from more than US$10 billion in some of the biggest cities to less than US$0.5 billion in the smaller ones (figure 2.8).

Currently, Latin American countries devote 1 percent of their GDP, on average, to public programs for housing and urban development issues. For the countries spending the most on the housing sector, expenditures reach 2 percent of GDP (ECLAC, 2010). In terms of public social expenditures, housing accounts for 11 percent of the budget, on average (ECLAC, 2010). However, these figures must be viewed with caution; public accounts are not strictly comparable among countries and some housing expenditures are included in other expenditure classifications, depending on national criteria. For instance, Chile classifies some vouchers as social security expenses.

One study (Ruprah 2009) estimates that if the public sector alone were to eliminate individual housing shortages by 2015, the budget of the region's ABC (Ahorro, Bono y Credito) housing programs would have to

Figure 2.8 Total Housing Deficit for Select Cities in Latin America and the Caribbean, 2009 (US$ billion)

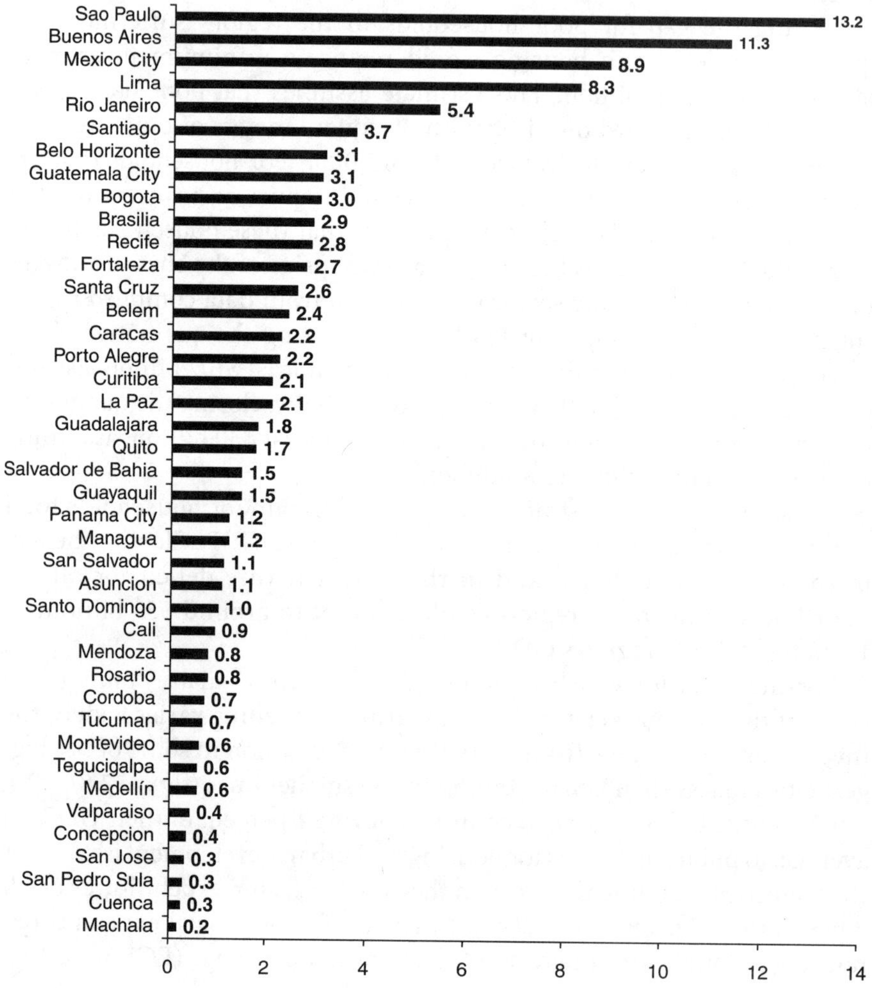

Note: Argentina (Buenos Aires, Cordoba, Mendoza, Rosario, and Tucumán), Bolivia (La Paz, Santa Cruz), Brazil (Belem, Belo Horizonte, Brasilia, Curitiba, Fortaleza, Porto Alegre, Recife, and Sao Paulo), Chile (Concepcion, Santiago, and Valparaiso), Colombia (Bogota, Cali, and Medellin), Costa Rica (San Jose), Dominican Republic (Santo Domingo), Ecuador (Cuenca, Guayaquil, Machala, and Quito), El Salvador (San Salvador), Guatemala (Guatemala City), Honduras (San Pedro Sula and Tegucigalpa), Mexico (Guadalajara and Mexico City), Nicaragua (Managua), Panama (Panama City), Paraguay (Asuncion), Peru (Lima), Uruguay (Montevideo), and Venezuela (Caracas).
Source: Authors' calculations based on Bouillon and Medellín (2011).

be scaled up an average of 14 times—a level the author considers infeasible, both fiscally and politically. The pace at which the region's housing shortage will shrink—1.1 percent over five years—seems agonizingly slow for a region undergoing sustained economic growth and reductions in poverty. Economic growth and housing programs alone will likely do little to reduce the share of Latin American and Caribbean households suffering from housing shortages.[6]

This chapter has painted a picture of the present and future housing sector that is far from rosy. This panorama implies that policymakers in the region must understand and address two of the main dysfunctions in the housing market: why families that can afford a good home end up in a bad one, and what factors reduce the incentives of the private sector to develop land and produce good, affordable homes for most urban families in the region. With these issues in focus, the broad brushstrokes of a brighter housing landscape will have to include a combination of regulatory reform, improvements in credit and labor markets, and enhanced coordination between local, regional, and federal governments to provide incentives and key infrastructure for land development for mixed income uses.

3

Two Bedrooms, Two Bathrooms, and a Big Yard? Housing Demand in Latin America and the Caribbean

Demand is usually defined as the "willingness and ability to purchase a commodity or service at a specific price and time" (Merriam-Webster.com). The concept of demand encompasses the desire to own a good, and the ability and willingness to pay for it at a given point in time. Demand for housing is no different. This chapter focuses on the forces driving housing demand in the Latin American and Caribbean region. Where will housing demand be the strongest in the future? Should policymakers keep worrying about the continued strong growth of mega and capital cities? What factors influence households' preferences for certain types of housing, and what factors constrain these households in making their housing choices?

The notion of meeting future demand and filling the existing shortages of housing in the region with good-quality dwellings located in well-designed neighborhoods with access to basic services and urban amenities is based on a powerful assumption: that to purchase or rent a home, all households in the region's cities must have access to well-functioning formal land and housing markets. Many households in Latin American and Caribbean cities do not participate in the market for formal privately produced housing, or in the formal housing rental market; thus they do not "demand" housing from these formal markets. Many of these households end up living in substandard dwellings that they build themselves on irregularly developed land. Are these households opting out of the formal market by choice? Or are they being "priced out" of the market because of a series of factors including low income, lack of access to credit, or dysfunctional formal land and housing markets that translate into formal housing that is too expensive?

Living in the City

Latin America is the second most urbanized region globally after North America and the most urbanized region in the developing world. Some 80 percent of the population now lives in cities; thus, most housing demand in the region comes from city dwellers. The 198 cities in the region with populations of 200,000 or more currently host 260 million people and have a combined gross domestic product (GDP) of US$3.6 trillion. By 2025, those cities are expected to house 315 million inhabitants and to generate 65 percent of the GDP of the region, amounting to US$7.4 trillion (MGI 2011a). Even though Latin America has already ridden the wave of urbanization that most of the other developing regions are expected to ride in the next 15 years, it will still experience important changes in underlying patterns of income, population, and household formation in the next few decades that will modify the composition of overall housing demand.

Until now the region's urbanization growth has been concentrated in its leading cities (MGI 2011a). Even though the biggest cities remain the largest contributors to GDP, their relative weight in the economy is declining. Growth in both population and GDP is expected to dip below average in the top ten largest urban areas in Latin America between 2007 and 2025, based on their GDP in 2007. On the other hand, the rest of the cities with populations of 200,000 or more will not only expand their populations at above-average rates but also generate almost 1.5 times the growth in GDP of the top ten cities (MGI 2011a).

Population and income growth, along with changes in household size and composition, are among the macrodrivers of housing demand. The anticipated growth of Latin America suggests that housing demand will spike in the near future. However, demographic and economic trends suggest that medium-sized cities, rather than the largest ones, will drive most of the quantitative growth.

Small and medium-sized cities will lead population growth between 2010 and 2015 (figure 3.1). In all countries, the highest rates of urban growth will be concentrated in cities of fewer than 1 million inhabitants. For example, in Venezuela, cities between 500,000 to 1 million people will grow around 60 percent between 2010 and 2015, whereas the largest cities (between 1 and 5 million people) will grow only around 18 percent. In Argentina, cities of fewer than 500,000 people will grow a little more than 20 percent, on average, whereas the megacities of more than 10 million people will grow around 3 percent. Smaller cities will also dominate the new demand for houses in absolute terms (number of dwellings).

Figure 3.1 Change in Urban Growth Rate and Total Population, 2010–2025

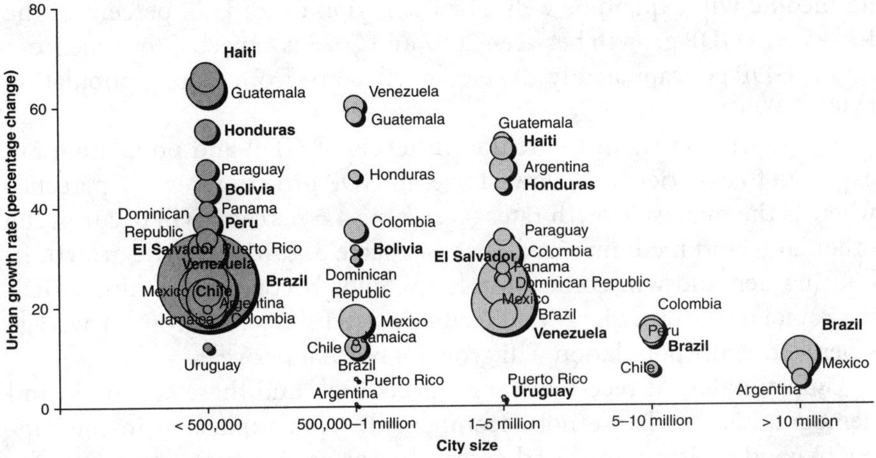

Note: The size of the circles represents cities' population change in thousands of people between 2010 and 2025.
Source: UN (2007).

Even if the number of people in a city remains stable, demand for housing can increase as a result of changes in the make-up of families. By 2025, urban Latin America will have more but smaller families. The size of the average household is expected to drop 18 percent, from 3.8 people per household in 2007 to 3.1 by 2025 (MGI 2011b). Therefore, housing demand in Latin America will expand not just because the number of people living in cities will increase, but also because the average number of people sharing the same household will decline. Increases in the number of households with a single parent, young adults who used to live with their parents but are moving out earlier than they used to, and seniors living without their adult children will add to the number of households, even if population growth remains the same. For cities in the region with more than 200,000 inhabitants, population growth from 2011 to 2025 implies an increase in household demand of about 15 million dwellings. However, factoring in the smaller household size, the increase in housing demand more than doubles to around 33 million dwellings.

The other macroeconomic driver of housing demand is the growth in per capita income. As people grow wealthier, they demand larger houses in better locations. Demand for second homes is also likely to swell. With income expected to grow 1.5 times more in medium-sized cities than in megacities, medium-sizes cities will significantly boost housing demand not only because their populations will increase, but because per capita income will expand as well. For the region overall, 77 percent of the increase in GDP growth between 2007 and 2025 is expected to come from higher GDP per capita; only 23 percent will come from a larger population (MGI 2011a).

The top ten cities in the region in terms of GDP and population are expected to experience the lowest overall GDP growth rates (3.7 percent), whereas the highest growth rates (averaging 4.5 percent) will occur in the other large and medium-sized ones (see table 3.1). Most of the growth in housing demand will come from households becoming wealthier. GDP per capita in the other large and medium-sized cities will grow on average 3 percent, while population will grow 1.4 percent per year.

Unfortunately, if recent history repeats itself and these economic and demographic trends are not accompanied by an expansion in the supply of good housing units and access to mortgage finance, especially for middle-low- and low-income households, many families may remain, or end up, in substandard housing. Even in the biggest, most mature cities, demand will likely expand substantially from the need to close existing gaps, accommodate new households, and meet the demand for second homes (table 3.2). For example, housing demand in Bogota is expected to surge 95 percent between 2007 and 2025 compared to a projected population increase of around 15 percent between 2010 and 2025.

Table 3.1 Composition of Cities' GDP Growth in Latin America and the Caribbean, 2007–2025

City type	GDP per capita (percent)	Population growth (percent)	GDP growth (percent)[a]
Top 10	2.9	0.8	3.7
Biggest 11–50	3.2	1.3	4.5
Other large and medium-sized cities	3.0	1.4	4.4
Small cities and rural areas	3.0	0.7	3.8

[a] GDP growth has two components: GDP per capita growth and population growth.

Note: Top 50 cities are the largest cities according to their GDP in 2007 (not population). Large cities are those with populations of 200,000 or more; they include megacities (10 million or more) and medium-sized cities (200,000 to 10 million). Small cities have populations of 200,000 inhabitants or less.

Source: MGI (2011a).

Table 3.2 Housing Demand in Select Latin American and Caribbean Cities, 2007–2025 (In Thousands)

City	Stock of dwellings in 2007	Current gap	New households (2007–2025)	Demand for second homes	Total dwelling demand in 2025	Percent increase in housing demand
Bogota	1,931	370	1,304	155	3,760	95
Mexico City	5,636	570	2,124	172	8,501	51
Monterrey	1,017	156	401	33	1,607	58
Rio de Janeiro	3,892	323	1,724	132	6,072	56
Sao Paulo	6,632	550	2,864	289	10,336	56

Source: MGI (2011a).

Affordability in Latin America

Why do people end up living in substandard housing? Is it because their incomes are too low? Is it because there is no credit, interest rates are too high, or they cannot qualify for credit because they cannot document income? Is it because builders do not care about serving low-income markets? Is it because construction costs for private builders are too high? Is it because formal serviced land is too expensive? Or is it because people are willing to sacrifice housing quality and basic features to live in cheaper dwellings?

These questions are very relevant for policymakers. Latin American governments deploy an array of public policies and programs to promote access to a minimum standard of housing for all citizens and to reduce the number of households in need of shelter. Despite these interventions, millions of vulnerable households still have little option but to share a dwelling with other household(s) or live as squatters in houses they built themselves on plots in irregular land subdivisions. The key to resolving this dilemma lies in affordability.

To measure the restrictions that may limit families' housing choices, this chapter looks at the determinants of private formal housing affordability in the region. *Formal housing affordability* can be defined as the capacity of a household to buy outright or qualify for a private mortgage loan for a house built using legal building codes on legally subdivided and serviced land. Affordability is measured with data from the most recent household surveys in 18 countries in the region (accounting for around 95 percent of the Latin American urban population in 2009), combined with interest rate, housing, and land market indicators.[1]

The most obvious reason households cannot afford a dwelling is that they do not earn enough income. However, other factors constrain affordability in Latin American cities, and they may rival insufficient income in importance.

Access to financial markets plays an important role in determining the capacity of households to buy a formal finished dwelling. A better developed mortgage market can offer reasonably priced mortgage credit. Status in the labor market also affects the ability to obtain mortgage credit. Informal workers have difficulty providing reliable information about their income, and thus may be denied credit.

The third factor that influences housing affordability is the price and available supply of privately produced formal housing units. Housing supply may remain limited if the private sector lacks incentives to go down-market, either because it is less profitable than serving wealthier markets and capital and access to credit are scarce, or because there is unfair competition from informal land developers and from people who build their own homes. In addition, there may be constraints on technology or inputs, such as land availability; or regulation costs and taxes may affect the ability to produce housing units below a certain cost threshold.

The affordability gap for each city is calculated as the percentage of households in the city that would spend more than 30 percent of their reported household income to service a 20-year mortgage with a 10 percent down payment to purchase a house at a given price and at a given interest rate. The percentage of households that can or cannot afford a dwelling is thus a function of the distribution of household income, the interest rate, and the price of the dwelling. Changing the last two factors permits their marginal contributions to affordability to be measured. To focus on housing affordability for low-income households, the simulations are calibrated for the purchase of a standardized basic dwelling with 40 square meters of habitable (built) area, either in a multiunit housing complex or in a single 60-square-meter plot with all basic services and formal title, in a legal subdivision.

Affordability Begins at Home

Not surprisingly, a household's first hurdle in being able to afford a home is its income. The *affordability gap* due to insufficient household income is the percentage of households that will spend more than 30 percent of their income to service a mortgage loan with a real interest rate of

6 percent to purchase a basic standardized dwelling that costs US$15,000 (assuming US$11,000 in construction costs and US$4,000 in serviced subdivided land costs—values reflecting the average construction costs of a low-income dwelling and land average costs for the region; Bouillon and Medellín 2011). This estimate represents the base scenario (benchmark) to measure the effects of higher interest rates, lack of access to credit due to labor informality, and higher dwelling prices due to housing supply factors. Figure 3.2 shows the simulation results.

On average, 19 percent of households have difficulty affording a dwelling solely because of insufficient income. However, a much higher percentage of households are precluded from home ownership because of their low incomes in some cities such as La Paz (55 percent), Managua (43 percent), and Santa Cruz (36 percent). Cities with moderate average household income and high inequality (monthly household income of around $US1,000; a Gini Index greater than 0.50) will likely suffer worse problems with affordability.

Various policy interventions aim at addressing the low-income constraint on affordability. First, policies can focus on promoting widespread income growth. Second, in cities with high inequality, redistributive policies can boost the income of the poorest households. Third, targeted housing programs can subsidize home ownership for the poorest. Fourth, policies can promote the development of low-income rental markets and direct subsidies to the poorest to access those markets.

Even if a household allocates less than 30 percent of its income to service a mortgage, this expenditure can push it below the extreme poverty line, implying that the household will not be able to cover food expenses. These households fall into what the literature usually calls *shelter-induced poverty* (Kutty 2005; Ruprah 2010b). To measure shelter-induced poverty, this chapter uses national official extreme poverty lines based on the income needed to cover a basic food basket that provides an intake of 2,300 calories per day per capita.

Taking into account shelter-induced poverty widens the affordability gap to an average of 22 percent. In addition, the number of cities where more than 30 percent of households face affordability problems jumps from 3 to 11 cities (see figure 3.2). Shelter-induced poverty is more pronounced in cities where a relatively greater number of households have incomes that slightly exceed the extreme poverty line. Remarkable cases include Caracas, Mexico City, and Guadalajara, which have income effects below the region's average, but very large shelter-induced poverty effects.

Figure 3.2 Affordability Gap Due to Low Household Income in Select Latin American Cities

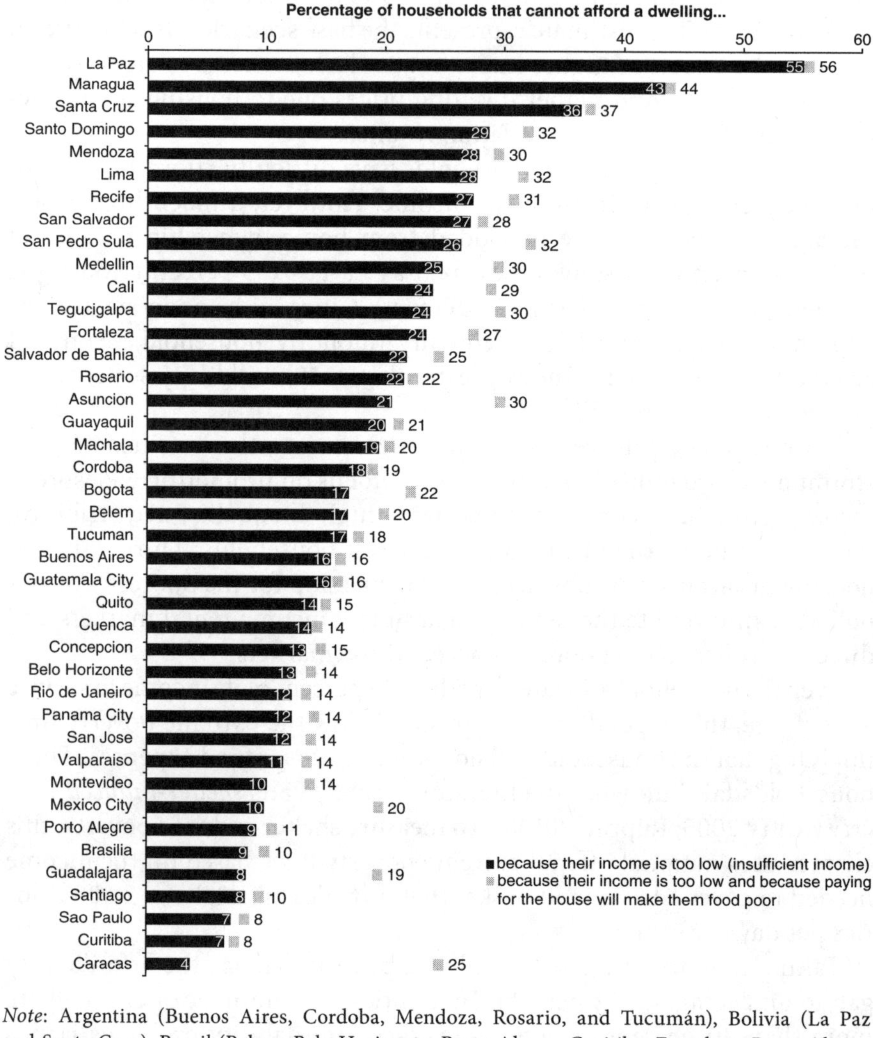

Note: Argentina (Buenos Aires, Cordoba, Mendoza, Rosario, and Tucumán), Bolivia (La Paz and Santa Cruz), Brazil (Belem, Belo Horizonte, Porto Alegre, Curitiba, Fortaleza, Porto Alegre, Recife, Rio de Janeiro, Sao Paulo, and Salvador de Bahia), Chile (Concepcion, Santiago, and Valparaiso), Colombia (Bogota, Cali, and Medellin), Costa Rica (San Jose), Dominican Republic (Santo Domingo), Ecuador (Cuenca, Guayaquil, Machala, and Quito), El Salvador (San Salvador), Guatemala (Guatemala City), Honduras (Tegucigalpa and San Pedro Sula), Mexico (Guadalajara and Mexico City), Nicaragua (Managua), Panama (Panama City), Peru (Lima), Paraguay (Asuncion), Uruguay (Montevideo), and Venezuela (Caracas).

Source: Authors' calculations based on Bouillon and Medellín (2011).

Financial Markets and Affordability

Access to mortgage credit depends on various factors: macroeconomic stability, financial market regulations, the cost of credit (interest rate), and household characteristics that influence credit risk. This section focuses on two factors that may hamper households' access to residential mortgages. First, the high real interest mortgage rates that prevail in the region make it too difficult for low-income households to service housing debt. Second, the status of the breadwinner's employment in the labor market may prevent a household from qualifying for a mortgage; informal workers cannot document their household income.

To estimate the affordability gap effects of current interest rates in the region, a simulation recalculates the mortgage servicing needed to purchase a standard US$15,000 dwelling using each country's current real mortgage interest rates (shown in table 3.3) instead of the "fair" real rate of 6 percent. With this information, the simulation calculates the percentage of households above the original benchmark that will allocate more that 30 percent of their monthly income to service their mortgage.[2]

Real interest rates in Latin American countries average 8.1 percent—higher than the rates charged in OECD countries. However, exceptions where the private sector rate is very competitive include Panama (2.7 percent) and Chile (4.6 percent). In contrast, some countries such as Brazil, Honduras, Nicaragua, and Venezuela are still charging double-digit real interest rates (see table 3.3).

Figure 3.3 illustrates the interest rate effect on affordability. On average, considering both high interest rates and low income, the affordability problem climbs to 24 percent. In some cities, the problem escalates even more. For instance, in San Pedro Sula, Honduras, the gap doubles and about half of the households cannot afford a standard dwelling because the interest rate is too high. In Brazilian and Colombian cities, the affordability problem also increases considerably: by around 10 percentage points.

Labor Informality: Closing the Door to Credit

Being able to document income is a prerequisite to accessing the mortgage market. If a household can't prove its income, it can't get a mortgage; it's as simple as that. This chapter considers two alternative definitions to gauge whether a household can document income: i) if the household has a wage earner or a qualified self-employed professional (including an entrepreneur); and ii) if the household has a wage earner or self-employed earner who contributes to the social security system.

Table 3.3 Mortgage Interest Rates in Latin American and Caribbean Countries, 2010 (Percentage)

Country	Nominal mortgage interest rate	Real interest rate	Estimated inflation 2010	Indexed
OECD	4.3	3.2	1.1	n.a.
Latin America and the Caribbean (average)	11.4	8.1	6.4	n.a.
Argentina	12.8	5.1	7.7	n.a.
Bolivia	9.9	6.4	3.5	n.a.
Brazil	10.9	10.9	5.2	Indexed to reference rate
Chile	4.6	4.6	3.7	Indexed to inflation (UF)
Colombia	13.0	9.8	3.2	n.a.
Costa Rica	15.3	9.8	5.5	n.a.
Dominican Republic	12.9	6.6	6.3	n.a.
Ecuador	10.7	7.0	3.7	n.a.
Guatemala	11.7	6.2	5.5	n.a.
Honduras	18.9	13.2	5.7	n.a.
Nicaragua	10.2	10.2	7.0	US dollar
Mexico	14.3	9.8	4.5	n.a.
Panama	6.8	2.7	4.1	n.a.
Peru	11.7	8.8	2.8	n.a.
Paraguay	11.6	6.1	5.5	n.a.
El Salvador	8.5	8.5	1.5	US dollar
Uruguay	6.3	6.3	7.0	Indexed to inflation
Venezuela	14.4	14.4	33.3	Indexed and regulated rate

Note: Average data for Latin America and the Caribbean is based on the simple average of the countries' data. Since one-third of the countries have indexed interest rates, the remainder after deducting the average inflation rate to the nominal interest rate are not equal to the real interest rate.

For Brazil, Chile, El Salvador, Nicaragua, Uruguay, and Venezuela the remainder after deducting the inflation rate to the nominal interest rate is not equal to the real interest rate since they have indexed interest rates. That is why the nominal mortgage interest rate is equal to the real interest rate for those countries.

n.a. = not applicable.

UF = unidad de fomento (unit of account indexed to consumer price inflation).

Source: Authors' compilation.

Figure 3.3 Interest Rate Affordability Gap in Select Latin American Cities (Sorted by Income Effect)

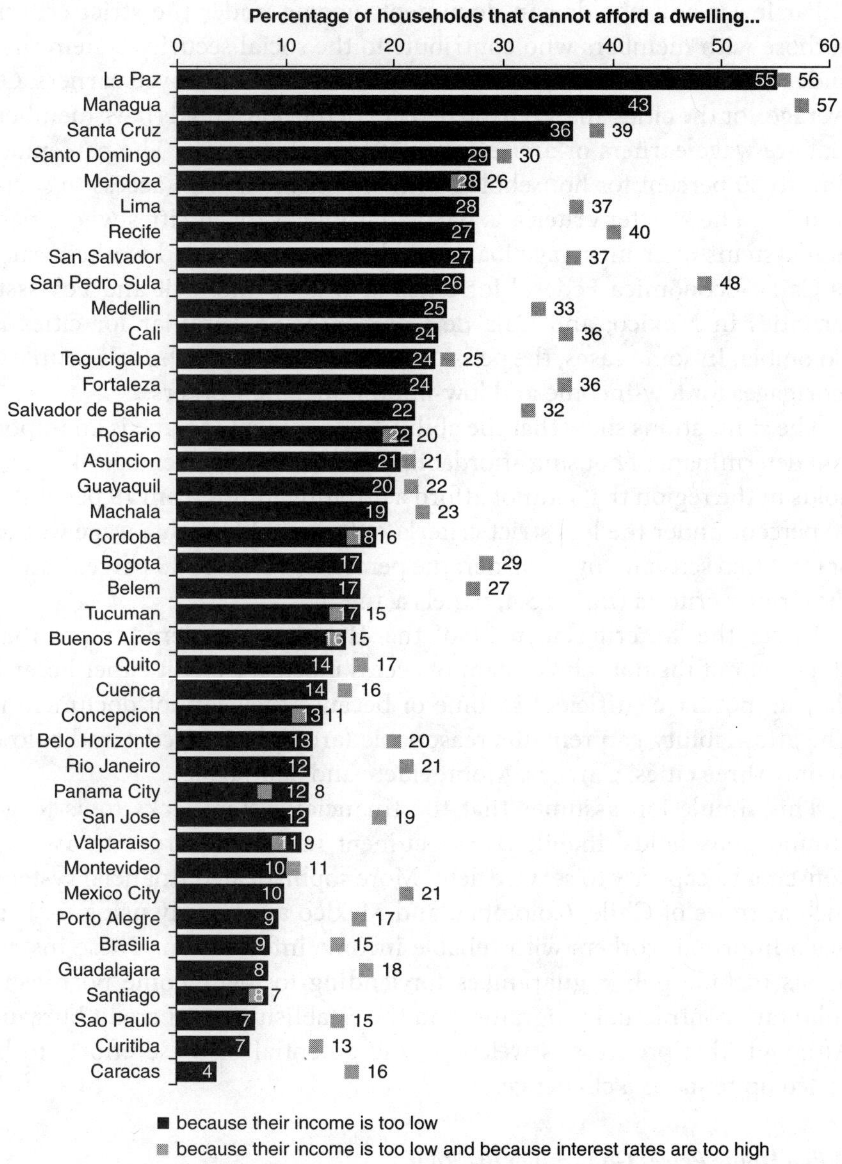

Note: Argentina (Buenos Aires, Cordoba, Mendoza, Rosario, and Tucumán), Bolivia (La Paz and Santa Cruz), Brazil (Belem, Belo Horizonte, Porto Alegre, Curitiba, Fortaleza, Porto Alegre, Recife, Rio de Janeiro, Sao Paulo, and Salvador de Bahia), Chile (Concepcion, Santiago, and Valparaiso), Colombia (Bogota, Cali, and Medellin), Costa Rica (San Jose), Dominican Republic (Santo Domingo), Ecuador (Cuenca, Guayaquil, Machala, and Quito), El Salvador (San Salvador), Honduras (Tegucigalpa and San Pedro Sula), Mexico (Guadalajara and Mexico City), Nicaragua (Managua), Panama (Panama City), Peru (Lima), Paraguay (Asuncion), Uruguay (Montevideo), and Venezuela (Caracas).
Source: Authors' calculations based on Bouillon and Medellín (2011).

Far fewer households can document income under the strict criteria of those with members who contribute to the social security system than under the criteria of wage earners and qualified self-employed earners. On average, for the cities analyzed, 80 percent of the households have members that are wage earners or are self-employed professionals. The percentage slips to 60 percent for households with any member with access to social security. The stricter criteria is particularly relevant in cities where pension systems offer mortgage loans as a benefit to affiliated workers, such as Caixa Econômica Federal for cities in Brazil; Infonavit and Fovissste for cities in Mexico; and Caja de Compensación Familiar for cities in Colombia. In some cases, the pension system constitutes the sole source of mortgages for low-income and low-middle-income workers.

The simulations show that the ability to document income is an important determinant of housing affordability. The average percentage of households in the region that cannot afford a dwelling jumps from 19 percent to 30 percent under the less strict criteria of households with a wage worker or qualified self-employed earner; the percentage rises to 45 percent under the stricter criteria (figure 3.4, panels a and b).

Under the lax criteria, in 21 of the 41 cities considered, more than 30 percent of the households cannot access mortgage credit either because they do not have sufficient income or because they cannot document it. The affordability gap remains reasonable (around 15 percent and below) in only three cities: Caracas, Montevideo, and Santiago.

This simulation assumes that the financial system lacks tools to get around households' inability to document income in order to assess a household's capacity to service debt. More sophisticated financial systems such as those of Chile, Colombia, and Mexico are already using tools to reach informal workers with reliable income information. These instruments include public guarantees for lending to low-income borrowers, voluntary contractual programs, and the establishment of credit bureaus. Although this progress is welcome, the potential of these efforts to be scaled up remains a challenge.

When Home Prices Go through the Roof

The assumption has been that the private sector can supply a basic housing unit at a low price of US$15,000. However, the private sector may not live up to this expectation for several reasons: lack of interest in servicing low-income families due to concerns about profitability, credit constraints, high cost of land or of servicing land for residential use, excessive regulations, and high property registration costs. The effect of market prices on affordability (relative to the standardized house price of US$15,000) is measured as the increase in the percentage of households that cannot service a mortgage at a 6 percent real interest rate to purchase a home at the minimum price that the private sector currently offers in the urban fringe.

The cheapest dwelling offered by the private sector without construction subsidies averaged around US$24,000 in 2010, and families need

Figure 3.4 Affordability Gap in Select Latin American Cities: Inability to Document Income (Sorted by Income Effect)

a. Due to Self-Employment

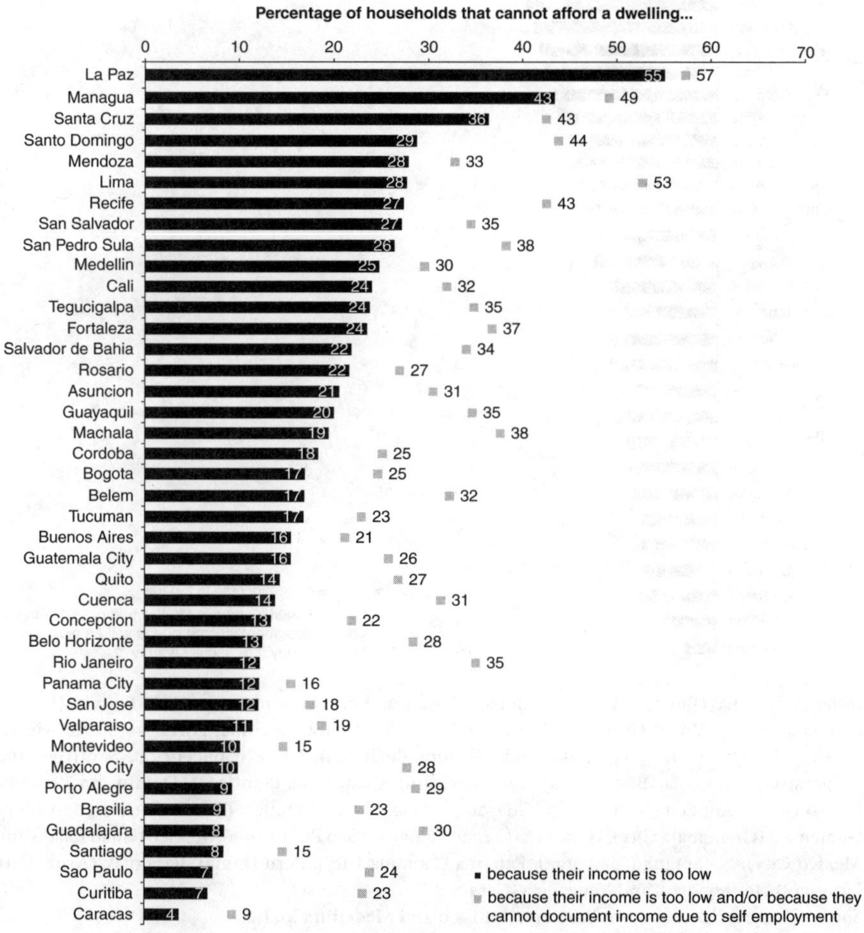

Figure 3.4 Continued

b. Due to Lack of Affiliation to Social Security

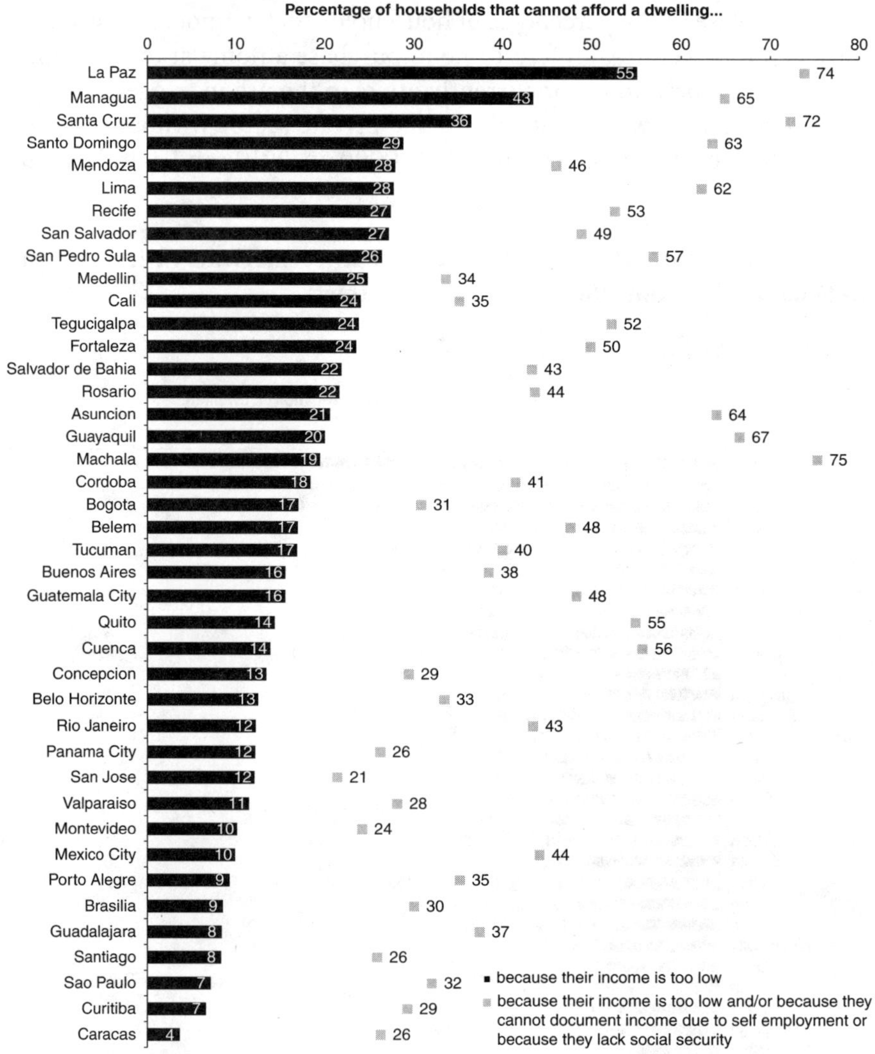

Note: Argentina (Buenos Aires, Cordoba, Mendoza, Rosario, and Tucumán), Bolivia (La Paz and Santa Cruz), Brazil (Belem, Belo Horizonte, Porto Alegre, Curitiba, Fortaleza, Porto Alegre, Recife, Rio de Janeiro, Sao Paulo, and Salvador de Bahia), Chile (Concepcion, Santiago, and Valparaiso), Colombia (Bogota, Cali, and Medellin), Costa Rica (San Jose), Dominican Republic (Santo Domingo), Ecuador (Cuenca, Guayaquil, Machala, and Quito), El Salvador (San Salvador), Guatemala (Guatemala City), Honduras (Tegucigalpa and San Pedro Sula), Mexico (Guadalajara and Mexico City), Nicaragua (Managua), Panama (Panama City), Peru (Lima), Paraguay (Asuncion), Uruguay (Montevideo), and Venezuela (Caracas).
Source: Authors' calculations based on Bouillon and Medellin (2011).

21 months (1.8 years) of full income to afford it (see table 3.4). The private sector in La Paz offers the cheapest house in the region (about US$11,000), but families in that city need 22 times their monthly income to buy it. The specter is a little better in Bogota, where the cheapest market solution costs around US$12,300 and households must devote only 10 months of their income to afford it. Caracas not only has the most expensive solution (around US$54,000), but families need to save 31 months (2.6 years) of their income to buy a dwelling. Buenos Aires has the second most expensive solution (around $US44,000) and the monthly period for which families must save to afford it is the highest of the sample (45 months, or 3.8 years).

Public housing policies could play an important role in encouraging the private sector to go down-market. It is no coincidence that some of the lowest prices and price-to-income ratios, such as the ones in Bogota and

Table 3.4 Price of the Cheapest Private-Sector Housing Solution Offered and Number of Months Needed to Buy It in Select Latin American Cities, 2010

City	Price of the cheapest private-sector housing solution (US$)	Number of months of full income needed to buy the cheapest private-sector dwelling
Caracas	54,054	31
Buenos Aires	44,228	45
Santiago	42,420	21
Sao Paulo	38,936	23
Montevideo	36,474	30
Panama City	31,795	25
Santo Domingo	21,105	24
Quito	20,000	18
Mexico City	19,697	16
Lima	18,120	24
Guatemala City	17,766	16
San Jose	17,053	12
Guadalajara	15,095	12
Tegucigalpa	15,073	16
San Salvador	15,000	20
Bogota	12,290	10
Guayaquil	12,000	13
Managua	12,000	20
La Paz	10,983	22

Source: Authors' calculations based on Bouillon and Medellín (2011).

Guadalajara, result from strong public programs such as Macroproyectos in Colombia, and the Vivienda Económica campaign in Mexico. Both programs have encouraged the private sector to expand its participation in the affordable-market sector by increasing the supply of affordable land and strengthening low-income households' access to mortgages, respectively. In contrast, in Argentina and Venezuela, the high prices and ratios can be blamed in part on an active public sector giving away housing solutions to low-income households (if properly targeted), thereby crowding out private sector penetration for that market segment.

On average, high prices explain why another 9 percent of households cannot afford a dwelling in the region, in addition to those that cannot because of low income. In Buenos Aires, 62 percent of households cannot afford to buy the cheapest dwelling offered by the private sector, even if they could find a fair market mortgage. Similarly, in Caracas, 49 percent of households cannot afford a private solution. In contrast, in some other cities, the private sector has been relatively successful and offers dwellings at reasonable prices. In La Paz and Managua, the private sector offers dwellings below the standardized dwelling price, which actually cuts the affordability gap by 15 percent and 7 percent, respectively. Other cities that reduce the affordability gap with down-market penetrations are Recife, Guayaquil, and Bogota (figure 3.5). Interestingly, in cities with over 5 million inhabitants, with the exception of Bogota and Guadalajara, low down-market penetration contributes to the affordability problem.

The lowest-priced housing solution offered by the private sector provides an indication of how deeply downstream the private sector can penetrate in a city. But a comprehensive analysis should also consider whether the supply of low-priced dwellings matches the demand for them. This is more difficult to assess in the region, as databases about private sector supply are scarce.

In the case of Bogota, almost 14 percent of the population cannot afford even the lowest-priced house in the city (the distributions of both the supply and the maximum unit values that families can purchase are shown in figure 3.6, panel a). However, even though a significant proportion of the population cannot afford even the cheapest home, around 16 percent can afford a dwelling that costs between US$19,000 and US$29,000. Housing supply is densest in the moderately priced range, with the largest number of units priced around US$23,000. Still, nearly 40 percent of available new housing units cost less than US$23,000 and almost 19 percent cost no more than the benchmark US$15,000.

Another way to evaluate housing supply relative to income level is to examine the distribution of supply per income deciles. The first 10 percent

Figure 3.5 Effect of House Prices on Affordability in Select Latin American Cities

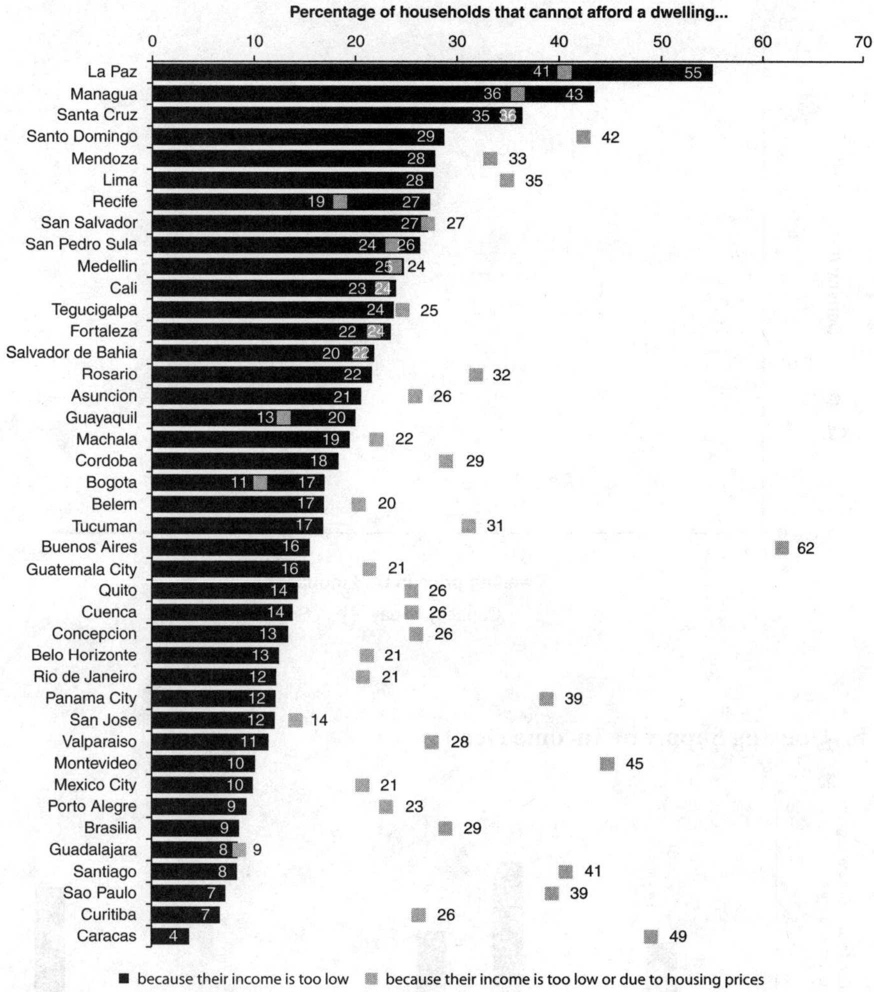

Note: Argentina (Buenos Aires, Cordoba, Mendoza, Rosario, and Tucumán), Bolivia (La Paz and Santa Cruz), Brazil (Belem, Belo Horizonte, Porto Alegre, Curitiba, Fortaleza, Porto Alegre, Recife, Rio de Janeiro, Sao Paulo, and Salvador de Bahia), Chile (Concepcion, Santiago, and Valparaiso), Colombia (Bogota, Cali, and Medellin), Costa Rica (San Jose), Dominican Republic (Santo Domingo), Ecuador (Cuenca, Guayaquil, Machala, and Quito), El Salvador (San Salvador), Guatemala (Guatemala City), Honduras (Tegucigalpa and San Pedro Sula), Mexico (Guadalajara and Mexico City), Nicaragua (Managua), Panama (Panama City), Peru (Lima), Paraguay (Asuncion), Uruguay (Montevideo), and Venezuela (Caracas).

Source: Authors' calculations based on Bouillon and Medellin (2011).

Figure 3.6 Housing Supply in Bogota, 2008

a. Housing Supply and Capacity to Pay

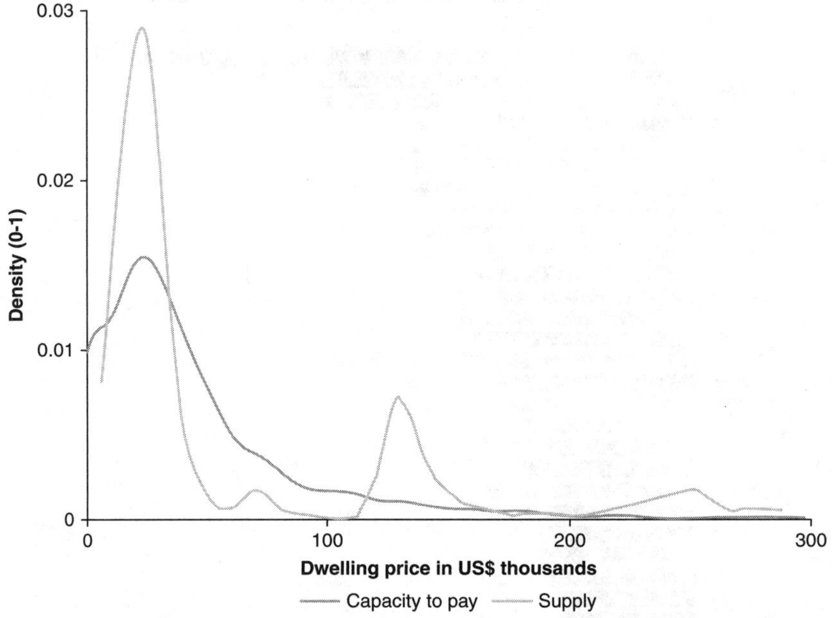

b. Housing Supply by Income Deciles

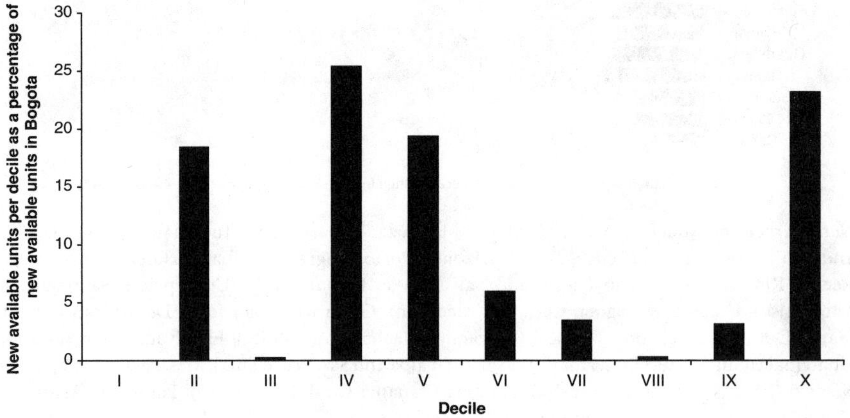

Source: Authors' calculations based on DANE (2008a, b).

of the population cannot afford any house on the market, while about 20 percent of the supply serves the second and third deciles of the income distribution (figure 3.6, panel b). Even though only 0.3 percent of the supply is on the market at the highest price families in the third decile of the income distribution can afford, those families can also buy dwellings aimed at families in the second and first deciles. Few houses are directed specifically at households in the seventh, eighth, and ninth deciles of the income distribution, but they can still afford homes built for families with lower incomes.

These figures for Bogota contrast dramatically with those for Lima, where between 2010 and 2011, 90 percent of housing supply was built for the richest top quintile of families, and only 1.6 percent of formal housing was built for the bottom 40 percent. What explains the divergence between these two cities? Bogota has actively developed land for low-income housing and engaged the private sector in generating housing supply for low-income households. In contrast, in Lima, land policies are practically nonexistent and most public housing interventions are geared to middle-income housing. Low-income households in Lima are targeted through microcredit for building housing in stages (incremental housing). And, as will be discussed, the lack of houses built for low-income households may also reflect other affordability problems, such as the ability to document income.

Adding Up the Affordability Gap

All things considered, more than four out of ten households (43 percent) in 41 Latin American cities cannot afford a proper dwelling in the formal sector using their own means (see figure 3.7). Some exceptions include cities in Bolivia, Ecuador, Guatemala, and Nicaragua, whose social security systems cover fewer low-income households. Total affordability gaps vary in the region's cities, from 26 percent in San Jose to 79 percent in Caracas. Results are evenly distributed; around half the cities in the sample performed below the average.

Insufficient income represents the most important factor hampering housing affordability across cities. In some cities, however, the inability to document income and the prices of private sector dwellings are more important factors. In contrast, the interest rate effect is not the most important factor in any city studied.

Table 3.5 presents an affordability scorecard that summarizes the results. Cities facing major affordability challenges in each dimension and overall are marked with an "x" while those that are relatively successful

Figure 3.7 Total Affordability Gap in Latin American and Caribbean Cities

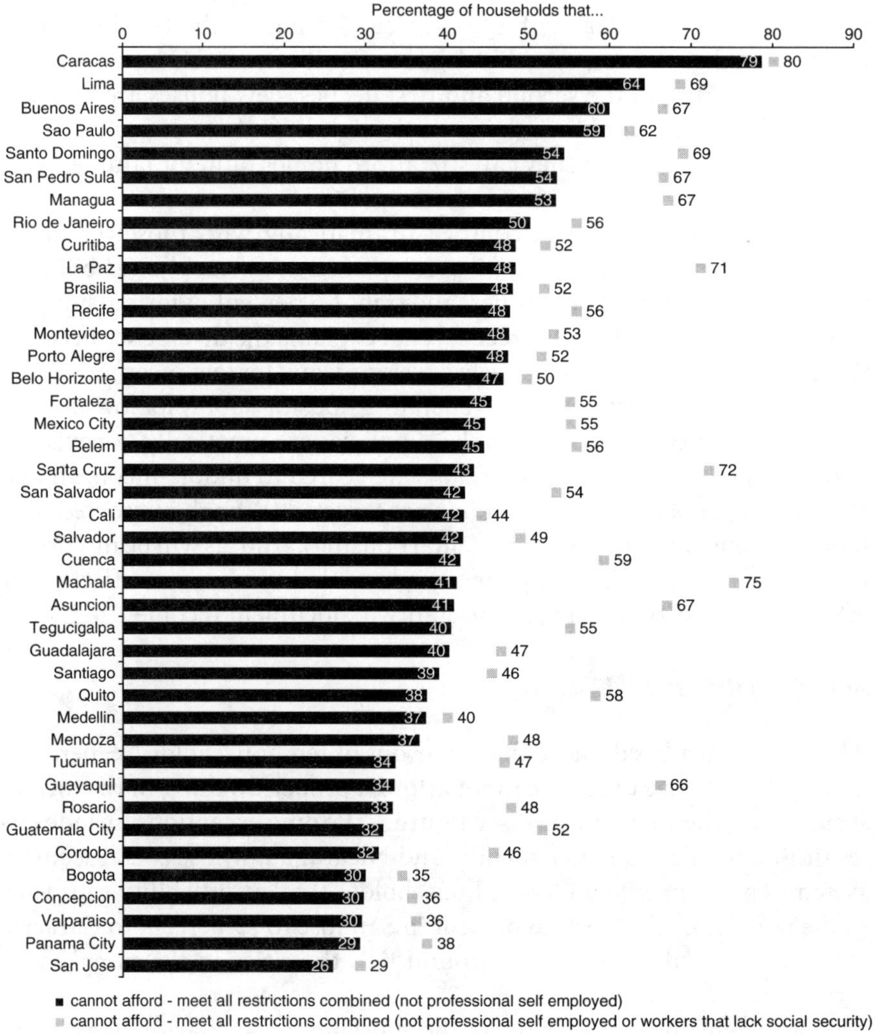

Note: Argentina (Buenos Aires, Cordoba, Mendoza, Rosario, and Tucumán), Bolivia (La Paz and Santa Cruz), Brazil (Belem, Belo Horizonte, Porto Alegre, Curitiba, Fortaleza, Porto Alegre, Recife, Rio de Janeiro, Sao Paulo, and Salvador de Bahia), Chile (Concepcion, Santiago, and Valparaiso), Colombia (Bogota, Cali, and Medellin), Costa Rica (San Jose), Dominican Republic (Santo Domingo), Ecuador (Cuenca, Guayaquil, Machala, and Quito), El Salvador (San Salvador), Guatemala (Guatemala City), Honduras (Tegucigalpa and San Pedro Sula), Mexico (Guadalajara and Mexico City), Nicaragua (Managua), Panama (Panama City), Peru (Lima), Paraguay (Asuncion), Uruguay (Montevideo), and Venezuela (Caracas).
Source: Authors' calculations based on Bouillon and Medellin (2011).

Table 3.5 Affordability Scorecard of Latin American and Caribbean Cities

		Affordability gap due to:					
Country	City	Overall affordability gap	Low income	Poverty effect	Interest rate	Documenting income[a]	Housing price
Argentina	Buenos Aires	x			✓	✓	x
	Cordoba				✓		
	Rosario				✓		
	Tucuman				✓		
	Mendoza				✓		
Bolivia	La Paz		x				✓
	Santa Cruz		x			x	
Brazil	Belem						
	Fortaleza				x		
	Recife				x		✓
	Salvador				x		
	Belo Horizonte						
	Rio Janeiro					x	
	Sao Paulo	x	✓	✓			x
	Curitiba		✓	✓			
	Porto Alegre		✓	✓			
	Brasilia		✓	✓			
Chile	Santiago		✓	✓	✓	✓	x
	Concepcion	✓			✓	✓	
	Valparaiso	✓			✓	✓	
Colombia	Bogota	✓			x		✓
	Medellin						
	Cali				x		

Continued

Table 3.5 Continued

Country	City	Affordability gap due to:					
		Overall affordability gap	Low income	Poverty effect	Interest rate	Documenting income[a]	Housing price
Costa Rica	San Jose	✓				✓	
Dominican Republic	Santo Domingo					x	
Ecuador	Quito					x	
	Guayaquil					x	✓
	Cuenca					x	
	Machala					x	
El Salvador	San Salvador						
Guatemala	Guatemala City					x	
Honduras	Tegucigalpa						
	San Pedro Sula				x		
Mexico	Mexico City		✓	x	x		
	Guadalajara		✓	x		x	
Nicaragua	Managua		x		x		✓
Panama	Panama City	✓			✓	✓	
Paraguay	Asuncion					x	
Peru	Lima	x				x	
Uruguay	Montevideo		✓			✓	x
Venezuela	Caracas	x	✓	x	x	✓	x

[a] Labor market attachment proxy.

Source: Authors' compilations.

receive a "✓." The first column presents the overall affordability gap. In Bogota, Concepcion, Panama City, San Jose, and Valparaiso, only three out of ten households face at least one affordability constraint. In contrast, in Caracas, Buenos Aires, Lima, and Sao Paulo, six out of ten households face affordability constraints.

San Jose's performance is exemplary; all factors except for interest rates remain well below the average for the region. The main problem preventing affordability, insufficient income, affects only 12 percent of households. The case of Panama City also deserves kudos; levels are similar to San Jose, but low market penetration presents the principal barrier, affecting 27 percent of households.

Not surprisingly, affordability problems loom large for the cities with the most expensive housing supply in the region: Caracas, Buenos Aires, and Sao Paulo. In all these cases, low down-market penetration is the biggest culprit. In contrast, in Lima, low income and the inability to document income in a labor market dominated by informal employment boost the number of households for whom houses are out of reach.

In some countries, affordability may represent less of an issue in smaller cities. For example, a household in Buenos Aires City needs 60 percent more months of savings than one in Tucumán to acquire a similar dwelling. In general, the smaller the city, the more affordable it is. In cities with fewer than 800,000 inhabitants, household's savings time to buy one square meter is some 30 to 40 percent lower than in the big cities of the country (Cristini, Moya, and Bermúdez 2011).

Buyers, Renters, or Builders: Household Choices in Housing Markets

Even when households can access mortgage credit relatively easily, they may opt out of the formal housing market and build their homes themselves—most likely on irregularly developed land. The decision to buy, build, or rent a house depends on the state of the housing market, the availability of specific public housing policies and regulations, and the household's own characteristics and preferences. Many countries in the region promote homeownership through a range of programs; however, rental programs are not as widespread as those promoting home ownership. How do housing programs and policies affect formal housing choices and rental markets?

In developing countries, there is a wider range of tenure choices than in developed countries. For developed countries, households usually choose between buying or renting a dwelling in the formal market. In developing countries, the informal market offers another important choice. Within this "informal market," options include owning or renting a house built illegally by the resident on irregularly developed land, occupying land or buildings without the owner's permission (squatting), illegally renting subdivisions of a home or land, or illegally sharing or subleasing a dwelling unit (De Wandeler and Khanaiklang 1992; Coccato 1996).

For policymakers, it is important to understand what drives households' decisions to select among housing alternatives: that is, what drives housing demand in the region. For example, do richer, better-educated households prefer to own their homes rather than rent them? Do younger couples with fewer and younger children prefer to rent a home initially while saving to buy one when their family grows? Do poor households with no access to public programs for subsidized rental housing or ownership opt to live precariously while they improve their home gradually (even if living in substandard housing jeopardizes the health and safety of their children)? Do significant transaction costs for buying and selling homes limit residential mobility, and push families that want to significantly expand their living space to opt against buying a bigger home and instead build a home gradually, adding rooms and expanding as the family grows?

Do access and proximity to transportation matter for tenure choice? Proximity to labor market opportunities, schools, or the need to reduce commuting time for child caregivers (working mothers, for example) can force families to live in worse, but better-located houses; opting for one or two rooms in a downtown overcrowded *conventillo* (tenement houses), rather than in a low- or low-middle-income housing development in the periphery of the city. Informal workers may also want to build a home gradually without committing to a stream of rent or mortgage payments if they feel that their income is too volatile.

Measuring What Drives Housing Choices

Statistical tenure choice models use household surveys to better understand what drives household choices. These models estimate the probability that a family will select one type of housing tenure over another based on household characteristics such as age, level of education, type of employment and gender of the household head, family size, and migration conditions. In the standard approach, the choice is generally restricted to owning versus renting; however, recent studies also include other characteristics such as formality and the quality of the dwelling.

Life cycle models of tenure choice predict that both ownership and home quality will increase with the age of the head of the household (Ortalo-Magné and Rady 1998). Evidence from the region supports this result. In Colombia, older heads of the household are more likely to buy than rent, and to buy homes built by the formal sector (Arbeláez, Camacho, and Fajardo 2011). In Brazil, the older the head of the household, the higher the probability of being a homeowner (Piza, Litchfield, and Balderrama 2011). In Uruguay, age also increases the probability of owning a formal home. Interestingly, age decreases the probability of being a formal renter more than the probability of informally owning a unit (Garabato and Ramada-Sarasola 2011).

Gender also matters. Male heads of household tend to rent and purchase informal dwellings more frequently than females. Women value quality much more than men. Female heads of household are more likely to rent or own a good-quality home than males. In the Uruguayan formal market, the predicted probability of renting increases by 0.024 if a man heads the household (Garabato and Ramada-Sarasola 2011). In Brazil, a male head of household reduces the probability of owning a formal dwelling by 1.7 percentage points (Piza, Litchfield, and Balderrama 2011). Figure 3.8 displays the probabilities of different tenure choices by gender in Argentina.

How does family size affect tenure choice? Although causality cannot be confirmed, bigger families tend to own their dwelling. In Argentina, households with more children are more likely to own a house than to rent one of similar quality. Households with more children tend to own a low-quality house rather than rent a good-quality unit. Among households that rent, the preference is for a low-quality unit (Cristini, Moya, and Bermúdez 2011). In Brazil, large families tend to own a dwelling, as do childless couples. For individuals who live (or used to live) as a couple, the probability of renting is higher than buying in Colombia (Arbeláez, Camacho, and Fajardo 2011).

In Argentina, Cristini, Moya, and Bermúdez (2011) find that household income and educational level are not good predictors of choices between owning and renting a home of the same quality, but they do influence the quality of the home. For example, a 1 percent increase in income

Figure 3.8 Tenure Choices by Gender of Household Head, Argentina, 2009

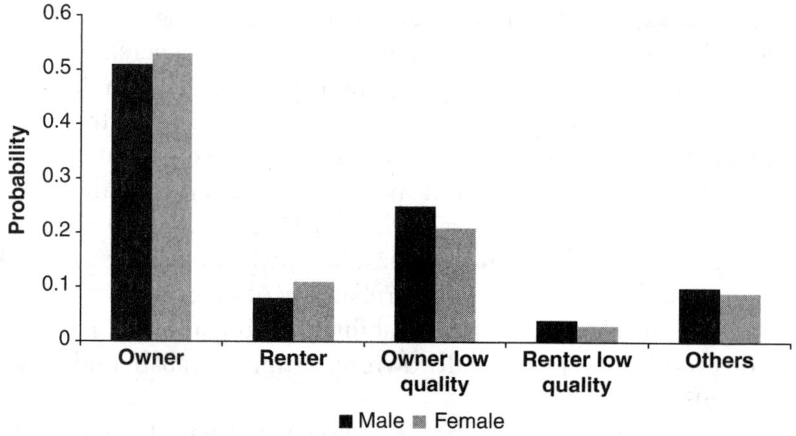

Source: Cristini, Moya, and Bermúdez (2011).

level substantially increases (by about 42.6 percent) the probability that a household will rent a good-quality unit rather than own a low-quality one. Findings for Colombia indicate that more educated individuals tend to rent. When they opt to own a dwelling, they prefer formal units. Colombians with more income opt to own rather than rent a formal unit (Arbeláez, Camacho, and Fajardo 2011).

In Brazil, as incomes rise, households are less likely to own homes. A 10 percent hike in a households' monthly income reduces the likelihood of formal ownership by 2 percent and the likelihood of informal ownership by 3.7 percent, while boosting the likelihood of formal renting by 1.2 percent. However, if instead of income a wealth index is used—that is, the possession of durable goods—better-off households are more likely to own a formal dwelling. In terms of education, renters tend to be better educated, and poorer households are more likely to own than to rent a dwelling, perhaps because of the programs that help poor households buy a dwelling (Piza, Litchfield, and Balderrama 2011).

Labor market formality also affects households' choices. Colombians working in the informal sector are more likely to own an informal dwelling than those who work for the formal sector; this probability is statistically higher than the likelihood of buying or renting formal dwellings. Conversely, inactive household heads, who are most likely retired, are more frequently owners (formal or informal) than formal workers. Being unemployed in Colombia does not seem to impact tenure decisions, as there are no significant differences in tenure choice between employed and unemployed individuals (Arbeláez, Camacho, and Fajardo 2011). The same holds for Argentina, where unemployment is not a determinant of any particular type of tenure or even housing quality (Cristini, Moya, and Bermúdez 2011).

Evidence from Brazil points in the same direction: informal workers are less likely to own or rent a formal dwelling, probably due to credit constraints resulting from labor market informality. Figure 3.9 displays the distribution of rented and owned household units along the deciles of the income distribution in Brazil. Among formal workers, the preferences for owning or renting units are similar for all deciles, with the proportion of rented dwellings increasing slightly starting at the sixth decile (roughly, the 40 percent best off). For informal workers, the proportion of rented units is higher across the income distribution and for all income deciles.

Interestingly, domestic workers are more likely to be in the formal housing market. In Argentina, domestic workers have a higher probability of living in a substandard unit relative to buying a higher-quality house (Cristini, Moya, and Bermúdez, 2011). This comes as little surprise given the meager wage level of domestic workers; furthermore, Goytia, de Mendoza, and Pasquini (2010) emphasize that working in the domestic service sector is a significant determinant of land tenure in Argentina. In Brazil, a formal domestic worker is less likely to be an owner, but more likely to be a renter of a formal dwelling, which generally are of higher quality than their informal counterparts (Piza, Litchfield, and Balderrama 2011).

Migrants are more likely to rent a dwelling than own one, as evidenced in Argentina and Colombia. In Argentina, foreign migrants (from neighboring countries) tend to rent low-quality houses, while migrants from other provinces tend to rent better-quality units (Cristini, Moya, and Bermúdez 2011). In Colombia, no significant differences exist between migrants and non-migrants in terms of owning formal or informal dwellings (Arbeláez, Camacho, and Fajardo 2011).

Eligibility for housing subsidies likely affects the household's decision to own or rent. In Colombia, households eligible for subsidies and income-poor are more likely to buy a house—either formal or informal—compared to the total population (Arbeláez, Camacho, and Fajardo 2011).

Figure 3.9 Distribution of Monthly Household Income Per Capita by Tenure Choice in Brazil

a. Formal Workers

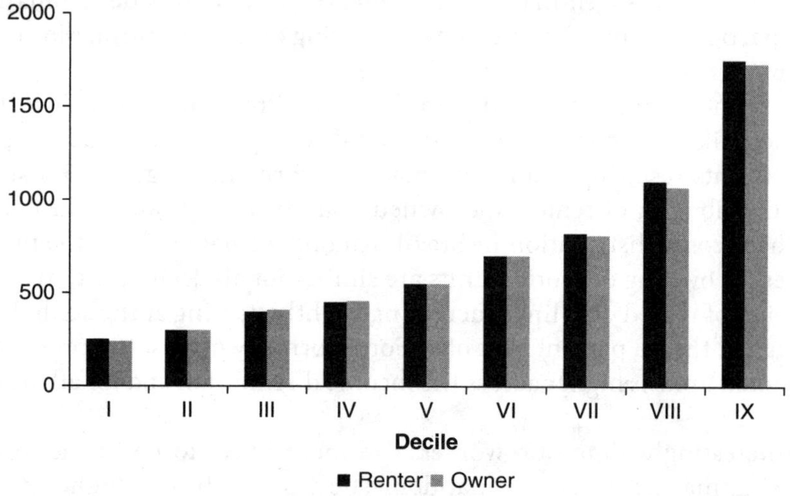

b. Informal Workers

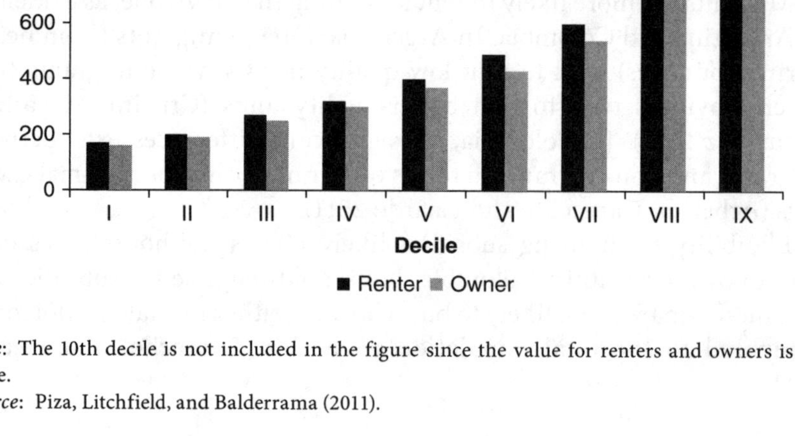

Note: The 10th decile is not included in the figure since the value for renters and owners is the same.
Source: Piza, Litchfield, and Balderrama (2011).

In Search of a Dream Home

Families tend to value housing attributes differently according to their circumstances, needs, and preferences. For example, do households value proximity to parks and recreation facilities? How much does distance to employment opportunities or amenities matter compared to having a larger or smaller home or having a lawn or a patio?

Policymakers or urban planners may ignore some of these attributes, especially for markets that are currently underserved by the private sector. Yet what families need and want in a house matters greatly for the design of public housing programs and for regulation. Public housing programs have placed much emphasis on increasing access to affordable housing in the outskirts of cities, where land is less costly. But if some families value proximity highly, alternative programs should be considered, such as rental vouchers, location subsidies, or costlier investments to improve the supply of mixed housing developments in central areas. Similarly, land and building regulations may intentionally or unintentionally increase the price of attributes that households may value, such as increasing density or mixed land use.

Valuing Housing Attributes

Trying to gauge what families want and are willing to pay for in a dwelling is not a simple task, as houses comprise a wide array of attributes. The number of bedrooms and bathrooms, the square footage of the house, the size of the yard, its location, access to urban amenities, and type of neighbors all figure into the mix, and what is a dream home for one family, may not be for another. When shopping for a home, individuals and families weigh a number of housing and neighborhood characteristics. However, preferences affect prices. A good-quality house situated in a neighborhood with premium amenities likely costs more than a similar unit in a less endowed neighborhood.

A class of statistical models called hedonic regressions use housing prices and rents, together with housing characteristics, to assess the price of housing and other neighborhood characteristics; these models are commonly used to obtain an index of relative housing prices. The hedonic method places monetary values on amenities such as number of bedrooms and quality of the floor, as well as on public goods such as the presence of green areas in a neighborhood.What variables are most likely to determine housing prices? The characteristics of the unit carry enormous weight in determining prices. Location and individuals' perceptions of neighborhoods also matter. In Brazil's formal housing market, adding a bathroom to the median of one bathroom per unit increases the price of the dwelling by around 18 percent. Doubling the number of bedrooms from two to four raises the price by about 24 percent. Expanding the median number of other rooms (excluding bedrooms) by 20 percent (from five to six rooms), raises the price of a dwelling by 14 percent (Piza, Litchfield, and Balderrama 2011) in the formal rental market. In Uruguay, the biggest impact on housing value stems from the unit's type of construction, which combines the type of materials in the floor, walls, and roof. Increasing the number of rooms and bathrooms also boosts the value of the housing unit. Similarly, neighborhoods with more services or better socioeconomic conditions command higher prices. Curiously, Uruguayans pay a premium of 11.7 percent on average for houses over apartments as a dwelling unit (Garabato and Ramada-Sarasola 2011). In Mexico, considering only new housing units, size matters most: a 1 percent increase in the area built raises prices by 0.63 percent (Fontenla, González, and Navarro 2009).

Location and access to services also affect prices. For example, access to running water, electricity, and sanitation services within Montevideo has no discernible impact on the value of housing in higher-income neighborhoods, as the entire neighborhood likely enjoys access to basic services. In these premium locations, housing values respond more to additional rooms and bathrooms. In contrast, in very poor Montevideo neighborhoods, access to running water, electricity, and sanitation services affects housing prices significantly, by around 18 percent. Small construction problems significantly impact the value of housing in more affluent neighborhoods relative to poorer ones. While the existence of moderate construction problems impacts housing prices by up to 30 percent in the better-endowed neighborhoods of Montevideo, in the rest of the country it reaches a maximum of only 17 percent. In Mexico, the federal government categorizes municipalities according to three minimum wage zones related to the cost of living. Housing units in the two top zones are 23 percent and 8 percent more expensive, respectively, than housing units located in the least-endowed zone (Fontenla, González, and Navarro 2009).

Proximity to urban amenities matters for households. A recent study that uses a combination of hedonic prices and life satisfaction models for the city of Manizales, Colombia, reveals that housing prices do not properly capture the provision of public goods. The availability of a green or sports area, proximity to places of cultural value, and neighborhood security are valued by households in Manizales and are not properly captured by housing markets (Velásquez 2011). In Chile, in recent years, informal settlements have sprung up as poor households made strategic decisions about location. Celhay and Sanhueza (2011) find that slum dwellers tend to have the same demographic characteristics as beneficiaries of public housing programs, but show better socioeconomic outcomes and stronger preferences for a better location in the city. In addition, "living in slums is correlated to better labor outcomes for men: higher rates of labor participation and employment rates, and lower rates of inactivity (employment or schooling attendance), even after controlling for geographic location" (p. 15).

Family Matters

Demographic characteristics also influence the size and quality of the houses that families prefer. In general, males demand less housing (smaller and lower-quality houses) than females, while married couples and more educated heads of household demand more housing. In Argentina, older heads of household demand more and better housing. Apparently, access and progressive completion of the house improves with the age of the head of household and might be related to a higher probability of getting a loan or accumulating savings (Cristini, Moya, and Bermúdez 2011).

Surprisingly, in the Uruguayan informal market and in Mexico, families with more children demand less housing (Fontenla and González 2009; Garabato and Ramada-Sarasola 2011). The same holds for married couples in Argentina (Cristini, Moya, and Bermúdez 2011). The availability of less income for housing given the costs of rearing children may explain this finding and seems reasonable since no significant effect is found in the formal market.

Age boosts housing demand at the national level and in the formal market. However, demand for housing initially increases with age and then starts declining once the household begins to shrink as children leave to form their own households; that is, age displays an inverse U-shaped relationship with housing demand in the overall sample. Intriguingly, in the informal market in Uruguay, age impacts housing demand negatively; this may indicate that older households in the informal housing market are generally in the poorest-income strata.

On average, more educated households demand more housing. However, the relationship is not as clear for informal housing markets (an example is Uruguay; see Garabato and Ramada-Sarasola 2011).

Residential Mobility

Residential mobility is important. Family circumstances or income may change or labor market opportunities may require households to move to different cities or neighborhoods. If the housing market works well, households should be able to change the place where they live easily. Elasticity (the percentage change in the price that a household is willing to pay for a house when its income increases by 1 percent) measures how fluid the market is. A high elasticity implies that the market is fluid and that people can move relatively freely. A low elasticity implies that the residential mobility of households is low, either because they are constrained in the housing decision or because they prefer to stay in the houses they live in even when their circumstances change. Usually these elasticities are estimated using changes in permanent income, as households make decisions about major purchases based on long-term income expectations rather than short-term income.

Likewise, price elasticity measures households' changes in the size, location, quality, and amenities of the houses they demand when the prices of those characteristics change. Specifically, price elasticity gives the percentage change in the amount that a household is willing to pay for a house when the price of that house changes by 1 percent.

Some studies analyze housing demand elasticities by pooling owners and renters together, while others estimate elasticities separately for each group. Separating the groups is likely more appropriate since in some countries owners have lower elasticities—reflecting, as mentioned, lower residential mobility, which can reflect high transaction costs in the owners' housing market. Rental markets in general have higher elasticities and are more dynamic. Households tend to be more mobile when renting relative to owning. (Malpezzi and Mayo 1987).

Elasticities also vary between formal and informal houses. The market for informal housing in most countries is less regulated and transaction costs tend to be much lower than those for formal houses.

Recent estimates of income and price housing demand elasticities for Latin America vary significantly across countries in the region. The new estimates confirm previous results and show that owners' elasticities are lower than those of renters. In addition, income elasticities for owners are lower than those for developed countries in other parts of the world, with the exception of Mexico. Low income elasticities indicate low residential mobility.

Price elasticities for owners are low in Uruguay and Mexico compared to developed countries or relative to Peru and Brazil. A low price elasticity can indicate lower supply than demand for housing units, which limits households' ability to adjust their housing demand to prices, and also reveals limited mobility in the housing market. Price elasticity goes up significantly in absolute value when considering only the informal market in Brazil, Peru, and Uruguay, for example.

A caveat regarding elasticities is that price and income elasticity of demand vary depending on the model of the home, the level of aggregation, income, housing price, and the estimating technique used (Zabel 2004). In Argentina, estimates of permanent income and price elasticities refer to renters and owners as well as the overall market. In Peru, the elasticities used are for the share of renters, owners, and for the informal housing market. In Uruguay, the elasticities are calculated according to formality status (formality defined as legal tenure), as well as for the entire market.

Price elasticities in Argentina indicate that owners are more inelastic relative to renters: that is, they respond less to changes in prices than renters. This result is somewhat expected and reflects a less efficient mortgage market. Cristini, Moya, and Bermúdez (2011) pinpoint an inefficient mortgage market and the existence of transaction costs for real estate operations as potential culprits. Once the household owns a house, it tends to remain in the unit and modify it when necessary to avoid moving. In Mexico, for instance, the lack of good substitutes to owning a housing unit reduces the price elasticity of demand. Many households become owners by building a house themselves and adding to it or improving it over time (Fontenla and González 2009).

In Brazil, the relatively high income elasticity for renters and the positive impact of schooling on renters' elasticity suggest that better-educated household heads might prefer to rent an expensive dwelling than to own a simple house. Also, better-educated renters might be postponing homeownership because they are relatively young and their households are smaller (Piza, Litchfield, and Balderrama 2011).

In Uruguay, the income elasticity for housing demand in the formal market is much lower than in the informal market. As Garabato and Ramada-Sarasola (2011) note,

> This result seems to be consistent with the findings on the type of qualitative deficits faced by households in Uruguay and the lack of use of housing policies by the eligible population. In this sense, Uruguayan households seem to display [a]certain

> inertia with respect to improving their housing conditions and this may be also reflected in the low elasticity found with respect to income. (P. 37)

In Mexico, problems with data limit the estimates to owners. Permanent income elasticity for this group is in line with developed countries and much higher than owners' permanent income elasticity in other countries of the region. The estimate for the price elasticity of housing demand in Mexico is around -0.3, lower than the value observed in developed countries. Fontenla and González (2009) note the lack of good substitutes to owning in Mexico, resulting in a lower price elasticity of demand, and inducing households to own a dwelling by building it themselves and adding to it or improving it over time.

Easing Housing Demand Constraints

Residential mobility is low in Latin America and the Caribbean. Many families start in bad homes and improve them over time as income rises. This has many costs, especially for young children who begin life exposed to developmental risks that compromise their capacity to live full lives in the future. Many families do not make this choice willingly. They end up in bad houses because their income is too low and there are no other alternatives (public subsidies or rental options), because they have no access to credit (due to their labor market status, the high cost of credit, or simply because the mortgage markets in their city are very shallow), or because the private sector has not built good homes in the city where they live.

Why are some families underserved by the private sector in the housing market? Lack of affordable land is one possible explanation, but only a partial one. High construction costs may make housing unaffordable for poor households. Such costs have been rising in some cities, but the dynamism of that sector of the population that builds its own homes suggests that these costs are not a binding constraint in most of them. Regulations, red tape, and taxes are other contributing factors. In many cities, regulations favor land development and construction for high-income households. Red tape may eliminate the profitability of housing projects with low margins, such as those for low-income housing. The chapters that follow explore these restrictions in more detail, particularly those affecting land markets and the construction sector.

Housing policies have had little success addressing most of these restrictions. With notable exceptions, such as the case of Bogota, housing policies have ignored regulatory reforms, investments in key infrastructure, and active government action needed to improve the provision of affordable land for low-middle-income and low-income households. Access to credit represents an important constraint for many households. A series of building blocks are needed to establish and maintain a deep and healthy mortgage market, and many are not in place in the region. The labor market, by preventing informal workers from documenting income, also influences access to mortgages. Even though credit technologies exist to circumvent this problem, scaling them up is a challenge. Above all, housing policies must offer households more and better choices: to rent or own; to move or stay; to borrow or not; to buy or build. A larger menu of options would go a long way toward easing the constraints that bind housing demand today.

4

To Buy or Not to Buy: Expanding the Rental Housing Market

Home ownership may be a good choice for many people, but it is not necessarily the best for all (Apgar 2004). Renting may offer a better option for some families for whom home ownership may not be the right fit given their needs, lifestyle, or life cycle (Retsinas and Belsky 2002; UN-HABITAT 2003b). For this reason, a well-functioning rental housing market is a critical part of a sustainable, integral, and healthy housing system. Expanding the rental housing market in Latin America and the Caribbean could broaden the choice of housing options for households, injecting flexibility into housing markets to respond to the full spectrum of citizens' housing needs and preferences. In addition, rental housing could provide policy alternatives for policymakers to tackle the quantitative and qualitative shortages affecting most countries in the region. An efficient rental housing market could also have a beneficial impact on the economies of the region, helping to alleviate the housing shortage, improve labor mobility and earnings potential, and reduce the macroeconomic risks borne by low-income families.

Unfortunately, the availability and affordability of good-quality rental housing in Latin America and the Caribbean is low. Traditionally, most poor households in the region have been excluded from owning or renting good houses produced by the private sector. The affordability problem for owning a good house stems from a series of factors, including insufficient income, lack of financial resources, or limited access to mortgage markets (see chapter 3). Consequently, a considerable proportion of low-income households live in bad homes, which they build themselves on informal land settlements located in peripheral areas; typically, they lack titles, planning permits, and access to basic infrastructure services. Indeed, as much as 70 percent of the population in some cities in the region lives in informal housing (see chapter 2).

The beneficial choice offered by rental housing is evident for middle-income households in countries such as Argentina, Brazil, and Colombia, where renters tend to be younger people with fewer or no children and with higher education levels. These individuals prefer to rent a higher-quality dwelling rather than own a low-quality one (Arbeláez et al. 2011; Cristini, Moya, and Bermúdez 2011; Piza, Litchfield, and Balderrama 2011). Yet broader choice also benefits low-income households. In central areas of Mexico City, for instance, low-income families headed by young women working in the informal sector prefer renting a room rather than living in informal housing on the periphery so they can save on commuting time and avoid the costs associated with building their homes themselves (Miraftab 1997).

Renting as a Solution

The housing shortage is one of the greatest challenges to social and economic development in Latin America and the Caribbean. As of 2009, nearly one out of three households in the region (32 percent) suffered from inadequate housing, and the housing deficit is growing (see chapter 2). Rental housing could help address the shortage by increasing urban density and improving housing conditions.

One of the most important factors underlying the housing shortage in Latin America and the Caribbean is the scarcity of serviced urban land for low-income housing (see chapter 5; and Smolka 2002; Abramo 2006; Buckley and Kalarickal 2006). This scarcity of land has contributed to irregular land development in most cities, resulting in substandard housing in neighborhoods devoid of green areas and public spaces, and contributing to fragmented city spaces, urban segregation, and chaotic urban sprawl, all of which generate a series of negative externalities, including increasing the urban carbon footprint of the region (see chapter 1).

Rental housing can accommodate dense populations in multistory structures and thus offers the potential for higher-density urban areas. By utilizing urban serviced land more efficiently, rental housing could help remedy the quantitative and qualitative deficit of low-income housing. Public interventions that support rental housing may also provide access to housing for lower-income households in more cost-effective ways than other types of interventions. Moreover, such housing could be centrally located in consolidated areas that have better employment and income opportunities. Unlike the case of informal urbanization, this increase in density would not stem from overcrowding but from "verticalization" and capital-intensive buildings that provide adequate open spaces and social infrastructure.

Rental Housing and Mobility

One key advantage of the rental housing market is greater mobility for individuals and families seeking jobs (UN-HABITAT 2003b; 2011b). Rental housing removes barriers to mobility by avoiding the transaction costs associated with buying and selling a property.[1] Oswald (1996) argues that homeowners buy not only an asset, but immobility as well, and are thus substantially more exposed to shocks in local labor markets than renters. In a cross-country analysis of developed countries between 1960 and 1990, he finds that unemployment increased because of the rise in home ownership and the decline in private renting. Oswald concludes that by increasing the owner-occupied rate, developed country governments have undermined the efficiency of labor markets and may inadvertently have created unemployment. Improved labor mobility facilitates a quicker adjustment of the labor market when labor demands changes across jurisdictions (Green and Hendershott 2001; Belsky and Drew 2007), thereby helping to lower unemployment, improve productivity, and foster economic growth.

Similarly, rental housing expands access to social opportunity, particularly for poorer residents, bringing them closer to areas with better access to urban services and amenities. For this group, greater mobility could not only mean access to jobs, but also access to better schools and safer neighborhoods (Belsky and Drew 2007).

Shelter from Financial Exposure

For most homeowners, especially the poor, their housing unit is an undiversified investment. By putting all their wealth into one asset, families are exposed to the risks of a market downturn and thus to losing their lifetime savings (Goodman 1997; Belsky, Retsinas, and Duda 2005). The recent housing crisis in the United States highlights this point with its extraordinary levels of foreclosure, which underscore the serious risks of homeownership. As of August 2010, families in the United States had US$6 trillion less in housing wealth than they did three years before (Kiviat 2010); by the end of that year, 23.1 percent of mortgaged homes (11.1 million) were underwater (Associated Press 2011). While providing the same housing services as home ownership, rental housing minimizes this risk and allows households to invest in assets other than housing.

Wanted: Homes to Rent

In 2007, 24 million households—approximately 17 percent of total households in Latin America and the Caribbean—rented their dwellings. The significance of rental tenure, however, varies considerably by country. Renting is extensive in Colombia (31 percent of households) and the Dominican Republic (27 percent), but less common in Venezuela (10 percent), Peru (7 percent), and Nicaragua (3 percent). In most Latin American and Caribbean countries, the level of rental tenure ranges from 11 to 18 percent (see figure 4.1).

The rental market in Latin America and the Caribbean seems underdeveloped in comparison to the euro area (see table 4.1). The proportion of tenant households in Latin America and the Caribbean is slightly above half that of the 28 percent average of the euro area in 2009. The level of rental tenure in the euro area ranges from 43 percent in Austria and 37 percent in France to 24 percent in Greece and 17 percent in Spain.

Moreover, rental tenure in the largest Latin American and Caribbean cities remains well below the levels found in major cities in developed and developing countries, even though the region's cities are densely populated (see table 4.1). For example, the proportion of urban households that paid rent for their dwellings in Mexico City (20 percent), Sao Paulo (20 percent), Rio de Janeiro (19 percent), and Buenos Aires (15 percent) is much lower than that of Berlin (89 percent), Cairo (63 percent), New York (55 percent), Montreal (54 percent), Lagos (49 percent), and Bangkok (41 percent).

In addition, the significance of rental tenure in Latin America and the Caribbean varies little with city size. The levels of rental tenure in the 40 largest cities in Latin America and the Caribbean with over 1 million inhabitants are fairly similar (see figure 4.2). The average levels of rental tenure in the major capitals with over 8 million inhabitants—20 percent—is similar to that of smaller cities with average population size of 1.5 million inhabitants: for example, Quito (36 percent), Tegucigalpa (26 percent), San Jose (21 percent), La Paz (20 percent), and Montevideo (19 percent).

In addition to being relatively small, the rental sector in Latin America and the Caribbean remains stagnant. The average level of rental tenure for urban areas in 17 countries in the region grew from 18 percent in 1995 to

Figure 4.1 Rental Tenure: Latin America and the Caribbean vs. Select European Union Countries (Percent of Population)

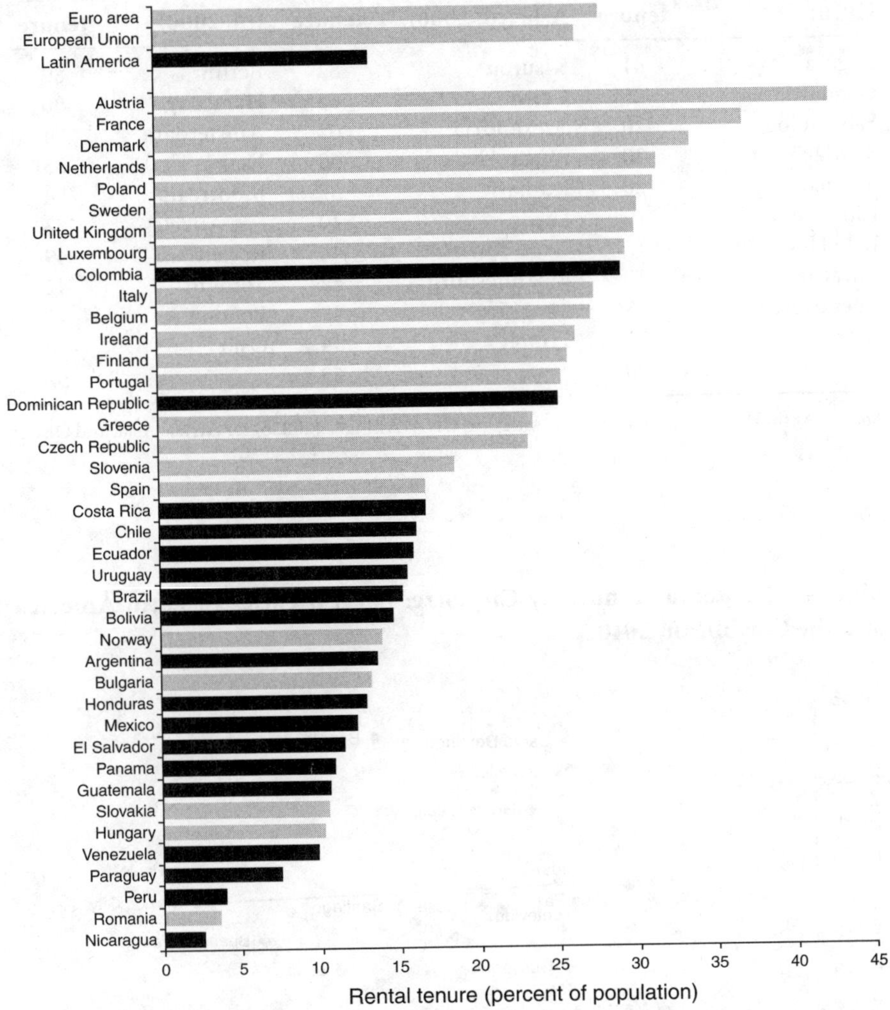

Note: Values for European Union, Euro Area, and Latin America are simple averages. Latin America includes Argentina, Bolivia, Brazil, Chile, Colombia, Costa Rica, Dominican Republic, El Salvador, Guatemala, Honduras, Mexico, Nicaragua, Panama, Paraguay, Peru, Venezuela, and Uruguay; European Union includes Austria, Belgium, Bulgaria, Czech Republic, Denmark, Finland, France, Greece, Hungary, Ireland, Italy, Luxembourg, Netherlands, Norway, Poland, Portugal, Romania, Slovakia, Slovenia, Spain, Sweden, and the United Kingdom; Euro Area includes Austria, Belgium, Finland, France, Greece, Ireland, Italy, Luxembourg, Netherlands, Portugal, Slovakia, Slovenia, and Spain.

Sources: Authors' calculations based on Rojas and Medellin (2011) and Eurostat (2011).

Table 4.1 Rental Tenure in Select Cities Worldwide (Percent of Urban Households That Rent Their Dwelling)

Latin America (2010)	Rental tenure	Africa and Asia (*ca.* 2000)	Rental tenure	OECD (*ca.* 2000)	Rental tenure
Bogota	41	Kisumu	82	Berlin	89
Guadalajara	25	Cairo	63	Hamburg	80
Sao Paulo	20	Alexandria	62	Amsterdam	74
Santiago	20	Addis Ababa	60	New York	55
Mexico City	20	Kumasi	57	Montreal	54
Rio Janeiro	19	Lagos	49	Los Angeles	53
Belo Horizonte	17	Cape Town	44	Rotterdam	49
Caracas	15	Johannesburg	42	Toronto	42
Buenos Aires	15	Bangkok	41	London	41
Lima	11	Tripoli	34	Oslo	30
Average	*20*		*53*		*57*

Source: Authors' calculations for Latin America. UN-HABITAT (2003b) for Africa, Asia, and OECD cities.

Figure 4.2 Rental Tenure by City Size: Largest Cities in Latin America and the Caribbean, 2010

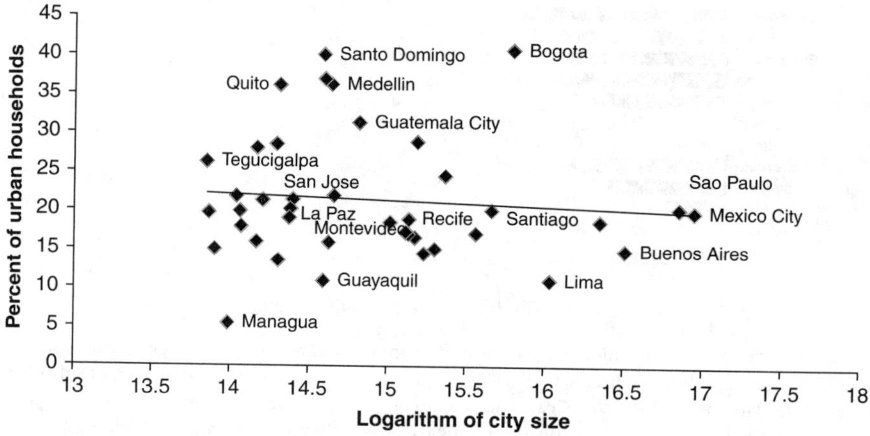

Note: Argentina (Buenos Aires), Bolivia (La Paz), Brazil (Recife, Sao Paulo), Chile (Santiago), Colombia (Bogota, Medellin), Costa Rica (San Jose), Dominican Republic (Santo Domingo), Ecuador (Guayaquil, Quito), Guatemala (Guatemala City), Honduras (Tegucigalpa), Mexico (Mexico City), Nicaragua (Managua), Peru (Lima), and Uruguay (Montevideo).
Source: Authors' calculations based on Rojas and Medellín (2011).

19 percent in 2007: a meager increase of 1 percentage point in one decade (see figure 4.3). Again, the extent of renting over time varies by country. During this period, the proportion of urban households renting in Honduras and Costa Rica grew significantly while renting plummeted in Nicaragua, Peru, and Paraguay. In most other countries, the growth in the share of urban renters was very modest at best.

Rental tenure in Latin America and the Caribbean seems to be disassociated with wealth. Rojas and Medellín (2011) show that for 18 Latin American and Caribbean countries in 2006, the proportion of tenant households in both the highest- and lowest-income quintiles were on average fairly equal. The rental sector in the region thus displays a unique

Figure 4.3 Rental Tenure Evolution in Urban Latin America, 1995–2007

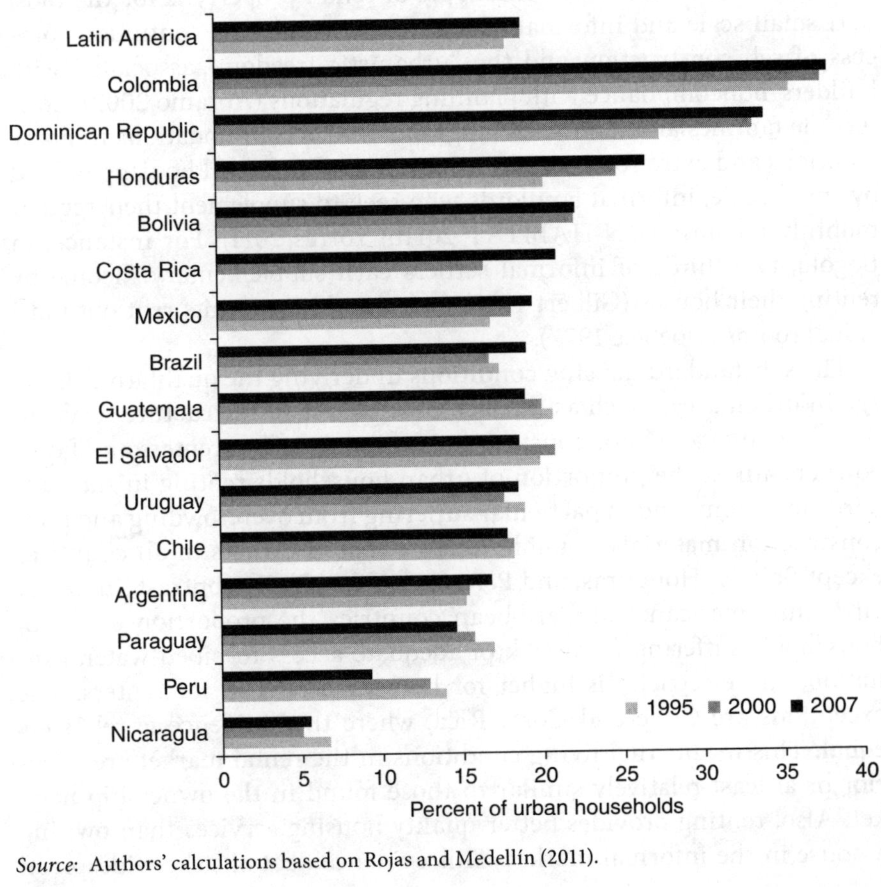

Source: Authors' calculations based on Rojas and Medellín (2011).

profile, especially when compared to that of member countries of the Organisation for Economic Co-operation and Development (OECD), where the incidence of renting tends to be very high in the lowest-income quintiles and very low in high-income quintiles (Pomeroy and Godbout 2011). Nonetheless, the average figures mask considerable differences across the region. In eight countries (Brazil, Colombia, Costa Rica, Ecuador, El Salvador, Honduras, Nicaragua, and Peru), rental tenure across income quintiles was either similar or more prevalent in middle-income households. In six countries (Bolivia, the Dominican Republic, Mexico, Panama, Paraguay, and Uruguay), renting was more prevalent among the lowest quintiles. In four countries (Argentina, Chile, Guatemala, and Venezuela), renting was more extensive among high-income households (Rojas and Medellín 2011).

In most cities in the region, commercial investors offer a limited supply of large-scale rental units. The supply of rental property is for the most part small scale and informal in nature: the result of a continuous process of self-construction and the "urbanistic freedom" associated with builders' noncompliance with planning regulations (Abramo 2007). Low-income families and many new migrants find accommodations in home additions and extra rooms built in substandard informal housing offered by small-scale, informal landlords who seek to supplement their regular monthly incomes (UN-HABITAT 2011b; Torres 2011). For instance, in Bogota, two-thirds of informal settlers earn supplementary income by renting their houses (Gilbert 1999) and one-third of units rent out individual rooms (Doebele 1977).

The substandard housing conditions underlying the qualitative shortage in urban areas, such as the lack of adequate infrastructure services, overcrowding, and poor construction materials, affect renters and homeowners alike. The proportion of urban households renting in substandard conditions, and in particular suffering from overcrowding and poor construction materials, roughly mirrors that of owners in all countries except Bolivia, Honduras, and Peru (see table 4.2). By contrast, in nearly all Latin American and Caribbean countries the proportion of urban households suffering from lack of adequate access to piped water, sanitation, and electricity is higher for homeowners than for renters. The exceptions are Chile and Costa Rica, where the incidence is relatively equal. This means that living conditions in the rental market are superior or at least relatively similar to those found in the ownership market. Also, renting provides better-quality housing services than owning a house in the informal market. This evidence debunks the widespread

Table 4.2 Qualitative Shortage in Urban Areas, 2006 (Percent of Households)

	Renters			Owners					
				Formal			Informal		
Country	Poor construction materials	Overcrowding	Infrastructure[a]	Poor construction materials	Overcrowding	Infrastructure[a]	Poor construction materials	Overcrowding	Infrastructure[a]
Argentina	8	6	5	8	5	13	19	15	22
Bolivia	35	30	32	24	19	31	33	28	34
Brazil	1	0	9	1	0	14	3	1	19
Chile	2	1	2	1	1	2	3	2	6
Colombia	5	4	5	5	3	7	12	6	18
Costa Rica	6	1	1	4	0	0	18	3	7
Dominican Republic	5	4	23	5	2	25	9	4	32
Ecuador	7	5	3	15	8	16	14	9	12
Guatemala	24	21	14	20	17	22	35	32	28
Honduras	29	28	9	8	6	14	27	23	39
Mexico	10	8	4	7	4	9	13	9	11
Nicaragua	20	22	25	34	27	31	7	18	23
Panama	10	9	14	5	4	22	21	20	43
Peru	18	14	9	12	5	15	33	19	35
Paraguay	7	5	3	11	8	15	30	28	26
El Salvador	11	10	10	18	14	15	19	14	21
Uruguay	2	2	1	3	2	3	8	7	8
Venezuela	6	6	0	5	4	1	8	5	2
Average	*11*	*10*	9	*10*	7	*14*	*17*	*13*	*21*

[a] Infrastructure includes: access to piped water, sanitation, and electricity.
Source: Authors' calculations based on Rojas and Medellín (2011).

belief that associates renting with poor-quality housing services (Gilbert 1998; UN-HABITAT 2003b).

Thus, the evidence indicates that the rental market in Latin America and the Caribbean is shallow and underdeveloped, despite its potential. As explained further in this chapter, the shallowness of the rental housing market could be the result of market distortions or a strong bias toward home ownership.

Constraints to the Development of the Rental Housing Market

The four main constraints to the development and expansion of the formal rental housing market in Latin America and the Caribbean are the excessive focus of public policies on promoting home ownership, an overly protective regulatory framework that favors tenants over landlords, the limited availability of urban land with services, and underdeveloped credit markets, which limit access to long-term financing for landlords.

The Policy Bias toward Home Ownership

One of the foremost problems with housing policy in most Latin American and Caribbean countries is the strong emphasis on encouraging home ownership rather than the general provision of safe, salubrious, and inclusive housing. Typical approaches reduce the up front investment costs that a homeowner would bear through direct housing subsidies, favorable tax treatment of capital gains and the imputed income earned, and lower financing costs. These policies lower ownership costs and tilt households' tenure decision toward owning, thus making housing services provided through ownership cheaper than through renting. The excessive focus on home ownership in Latin America and the Caribbean has made rental units much more expensive or not available, reducing welfare significantly for many.

The policy bias is based on the belief that home ownership in itself leads to better financial and social outcomes (Retsinas and Belsky 2002). Several studies suggest that home ownership, compared to other types of housing tenure, primarily renting, leads to higher life satisfaction (Rohe, Quercia, and Van Zandt 2007; Ruprah 2010a for Latin America and the Caribbean), better physical health (Rossi and Weber 1996; Page-Adams and Vosler 1997), greater community and political engagement (DiPasquale and Glaeser 1999), higher neighborhood stability (Herbert and Belsky

2008), accumulation of more real estate assets and wealth (Boehm and Schlottmann 2002; Case and Marynchenko 2002), higher property values in surrounding areas (Ellen et al. 2001), and better education for children as well as higher future earnings as they enter the labor market (Haurin, Parcel, and Haurin 2001).

The empirical evidence is not as conclusive as it is often presented in policy circles. First, the benefits of homeownership may occur only under certain circumstances (Retsinas and Belsky 2002) or may not accrue to all homeowners, particularly low-income homeowners (UN-HABITAT 2003b). For instance, owners' ability to make mortgage payments influences health outcomes such as stress levels or self-esteem. Second, the effects of home ownership must be disentangled from factors such as income, education, and location (Retsinas and Belsky 2002). For example, the beneficial neighborhood effects of home ownership actually derive from families having lived in one place for a long time rather than from being owners. Third, previous studies have omitted the risks associated with home ownership and the social costs imposed on low-income households (Rohe, Van Zandt, and McCarthy 2002; Kiviat 2010). For instance, mortgage default and the loss of mobility certainly impact adversely on employment and self-esteem. In addition, while homeowners may save more, they also hold most of their wealth in a single asset, whose price volatility can wipe out a lifetime of savings.

Despite the weaknesses in the empirical findings, governments in Latin America and the Caribbean continue to pursue universal home ownership. The region's housing markets demonstrate very high home ownership rates (Rojas and Medellín 2011). Countries such as Venezuela (80 percent), Brazil (74 percent), Paraguay (75 percent), and Costa Rica (72 percent) have the highest home ownership rates in the region and some of the highest rates in the world.

Home ownership rates in most Latin American and Caribbean countries are even higher than in most OECD countries. This discrepancy is remarkable given the lower income levels that prevail in Latin America and the Caribbean. Tax policies help explain such a discrepancy. For instance, the three OECD countries with the lowest home ownership rates—Switzerland, Germany, and Denmark—all until recently taxed the imputed rental income on housing, making after-tax ownership more expensive than renting. So too did France, the Netherlands, and Finland, the next three countries with lower homeownership rates after Austria. By contrast, in general, Latin American and Caribbean countries do not levy taxes on imputed rental income and property taxes are low, favoring ownership. Thus, these patterns suggest that tax policy matters considerably in the choice of home ownership versus renting.

The home ownership bias is also evident in the main policies used to promote low-income housing in the region: public housing, upgrading and titling, and demand subsidies. First, in contrast to most OECD countries, in general, public housing in Latin American and Caribbean countries has been produced for sale and not for rent. Despite the allocation of considerable resources, public units have been insufficient to meet the need and in many cases have been "poached" by middle- and even high-income groups (see chapter 9; and Gilbert 1998).

In addition, even though neighborhood upgrading and titling policies are needed to improve the current stock of deficient houses, both policies, combined with lax enforcement of land regulations, reinforce the home ownership bias because they aim to consolidate informal housing and legalize its tenure.

An Overly Protective Regulatory Framework

The regulatory framework mediating tenant-landlord relationships is one of the main factors hampering the supply of rental housing in Latin America and the Caribbean. Legislation and the judiciary system tend to favor tenants' rights over landlords' rights, thus making it extremely difficult and costly for landlords to evict tenants and repossess their properties. This situation increases investment risk and deters owners and investors from investing in the private rental market. As Casas-Arce and Saiz (2006) argue, when legal enforcement of contracts is costly, there will be a shift from arrangements that rely on such enforcement toward other forms that do not. In this case, the shift will be from investments in rental housing to other types of ventures.

In Colombia, Law 56 of 1985 effectively empowered tenants to extend rental agreements for as long as they wanted to live in the dwelling by abolishing the expiration of a rental agreement as a means to evict a tenant and repossess the property (Jaramillo and Ibáñez 2002). While Law 820 of 2003 eliminated some of these legal barriers and shortened the time required to evict a tenant from five years to approximately one year, repossession continues to be a lengthy, cumbersome, and costly process (Torres 2011). In Uruguay, Law 14219 of 1974 grants tenants a grace period of six months to vacate properties if the landlord is notified after the rental agreement has expired, or one year if the agreement has not expired yet. The situation is fairly similar in Argentina, where an eviction lawsuit may take from six months to one year. The outcome depends on a judge's decision, which often considers the tenant's situation, such as whether children occupy the property. The accelerated repossession regulations enacted and used in recent years in a few Argentine provinces allow landlords to recover the property in two to four months. Nevertheless, the process continues to be uncertain and landlords must deposit a refundable amount just to begin the judicial process, which is often a deterrent. Legal costs for both procedures in Argentina are relatively low: about 1 percent of the total contract amount. However, this does not take into account the economic cost incurred during the time of litigation when the property cannot be rented (Moya 2011). Additionally, if damages to the property are discovered after eviction, another judicial procedure ensues, further increasing the costs associated with a rental dispute.

Rent control regimes have also severely constrained the development of the private rental market in Latin America and the Caribbean.[2] Rent control sets the rate and frequency of rent increases, often linked to some measure such as the consumer price index. In some places, rent increases are allowed only while a tenant continues to rent a unit. Once a unit is vacated, the restriction is lifted and rents may be adjusted to the market level. However, the rent is capped again once a new tenant occupies the dwelling. Tight rent control laws impinge upon the ability of landlords to generate a sufficient rate of return to remain invested in the development of this sector and reduce their incentive to invest in more rental units (Pomeroy and Godbout 2011). Le Blanc (2009) states that "countries that have imposed hard types of rent control have witnessed a dwindling of the rental sector. Unsatisfied rental demand, as well as investors' money, has carried over to the informal housing sector, with price outcomes depending on the countries" (p. 373). This issue has been critical in Colombia, where government authorities tightly regulate rental prices and rent increases. The rent control system that froze rent prices from 1956 to 1983, when it was abandoned, stunted the development of the rental sector. The problem continues, as existing rental legislation mandates that monthly rent cannot exceed 1 percent of the commercial value of a property and that the annual rent increase must be tied to the inflation rate foreseen for the upcoming year.

The Urban Paradox: Vacant Land but No Services

As mentioned, one of the most important factors underlying the housing shortage in Latin America and the Caribbean is the scarcity of land with urban services. The causes for this scarcity relate to the region's accelerated process of urbanization in a context of low incomes, high inequality, and inadequate mechanisms to finance infrastructure. In effect, the high rate of rural-to-urban migration in the second half of the twentieth century increased the demand for serviced land faster than the ability of public officials to provide infrastructure (Gilbert 1998).

Not only did most of the new demand come from low-income families that were unable to pay for the capital cost of expanding services, but local governments failed to implement mechanisms to fund infrastructure by capturing part of the land revalorization that it produces. For instance, property taxes have been traditionally weak in Latin America and the Caribbean, representing only 0.37 percent of the region's GDP, compared to 2.12 percent in OECD countries (Uribe and Bejarano 2009). Other mechanisms to capture the value of land, such as impact fees and improvement taxes, have started to be implemented in the region only in the last decade. This pattern is reinforced by elitist planning regulations that mandate low densities in areas with good services, and by the strong tendency of landlords to speculate with vacant land holdings. As a result, Latin American and Caribbean cities experience a paradoxical dynamic in which serviced land is undersupplied in the market but vacant land is abundant (see chapter 5).

The scarcity of serviced land has constrained the supply of housing in Latin American and Caribbean cities, making finished homes unaffordable and pushing the poor to informal housing arrangements. As noted, rental housing, because it encourages high density and multifamily units, could use the scarce land more efficiently, helping to solve the housing deficit in the region. For instance, the Planning Department in Bogota has calculated that about 100,920 low-income multifamily housing units could be built on the "fattening lots," slicing the housing deficit by at least 20 percent (SDP 2009).

Money Matters

In a well-functioning rental housing market, an owner-investor should be able to contract a long-term mortgage loan to finance the construction, acquisition, or rehabilitation of a rental housing project. Longer-term loans increase the amortization period, which could lower the monthly mortgage payment considerably, reducing monthly operational expenses and increasing the profitability of a rental housing project.

In most OECD countries, access to long-term mortgage financing for rental construction is easily available. In these countries, the amortization period ranges between 20 and 40 years, and mortgage rates are typically in the single digits. Moreover, a variety of mechanisms subsidize the capital cost for private provision of affordable rental housing. By contrast, in Latin American and Caribbean countries, access to long-term mortgage loans is limited. Where such loans are available, the amortization period is considerably shorter and the interest rate is considerably higher than in developed countries. The average real mortgage rate in Latin America and the Caribbean reaches 11.4 percent (see chapter 3).

For example, in Uruguay, financial institutions offer onerous financing plans with amortization periods shorter than 18 years, interest rates well above 10 percent, and a maximum amount to be financed of 70 percent of the assessed property value (Marcello 2010). This pattern repeats itself in other Latin American and Caribbean countries, where the financial system has not developed financing schemes targeting rental builders. As such, rental investors are forced to take commercial loans or "free-investment" loans, which are short-term and carry significantly higher interest rates than the special credit lines offered to traditional building companies. In Colombia, for instance, an individual who wants to build a new rental project could be required to pay a real interest rate of 12.7 percent over a period of 15–20 years (Torres 2011).

Learning from Developed Countries

Since the end of World War II, public interventions in developed countries have impacted both the supply and demand sides of the housing market, particularly in the rental sector. These interventions vary and have included taxation, direct or indirect subsidies, and changes in the regulation of the rental market. In the aftermath of World War II, rental housing grew considerably to solve the war-caused shortage. Since the mid-1970s, however, in most industrialized countries the size of the rental sector, and more particularly the size of the private rental sector, has gradually declined (Van der Heijen and Boelhouwer 1996; Whitehead 1996). Austria, Germany, and Japan are exceptions (Pomeroy, Lampert, and Mancer 1999). Many factors underlie this contraction in rental markets, including demographic changes, shifting demand levels and consumer preferences, greater affordability of home ownership due to declining interest rates, the relative financial viability of ownership versus rental options, and importantly, the regulatory, taxation, and subsidy regimes in each country (Van der Heijen and Boelhouwer 1996; Whitehead 1996; Pomeroy, Lampert, and Mancer 1999).

Initially, policies concentrated on supply side interventions, first in the form of public housing and then through subsidies to private providers of rental housing in the form of rent assistance, preferential tax treatment, and preferential financing. In the 1990s, the focus changed to demand side interventions, such as housing vouchers. Nowadays, developed countries combine these different policies with initiatives to improve the flexibility of rent regulations (Turner and Whitehead 2002).

Public Housing

Public housing is generally managed by local housing authorities subject to the rules of the national government, especially as related to rent restrictions. Rents are usually capped at 30 percent of the recipient's income. The importance of public housing has been decreasing but it still represents a considerable proportion of rental units. In the United States, for instance, public housing represented 21 percent of the stock of assisted housing in the 1990s: some 1.25 million units (Newman and Schnare 1997). Public housing can increase the supply of housing (Sinai and Waldfogel 2005), guarantee high-quality housing units (Olsen 2001), and produce positive externalities in the form of higher property values for the surrounding community (Ellen et al. 2001; O'Sullivan 2008). It also tends to be expensive, is often poorly managed and tends to deteriorate over time, provides no choices to recipients, and is often located in poor and distressed areas (Newman and Schnare 1997; O'Sullivan 2009).

Tax Incentives

Preferential tax treatment includes programs that provide tax abatements for the construction, acquisition, and rehabilitation of affordable rental units. The tax treatment of the rental housing market has played a vital role in the development of a vibrant private rental investment in Australia, Canada,[3] France, Germany, the Netherlands, New Zealand, and the United States (Pomeroy 1998; Pomeroy and Godbout 2011). Most of the tax measures allow deduction of depreciation and other costs to reduce taxable net income.

The US Low-Income Housing Tax Credit (LIHTC) program, introduced in 1986, is widely regarded as an effective way to produce affordable housing. The LIHTC provides tax incentives for investors in affordable housing, reducing upfront capital costs in exchange for measures to make units more affordable. The main purpose of the tax credit is to encourage the production of rental housing and ensure that rental units remain affordable for low-income households over a long period of time. In the United States, "the program has engendered an industry of special for-profit and non-profit developers, syndicators, investors, and consultants. It is now the nation's primary program for the production of subsidized rental housing" (JCHS 2010, p. 28). According to the US Department of Housing and Urban Development (HUD 2011), between 1987 and 2009, some 33,777 projects and over 2.2 million units were placed in service, making it the "most important resource for creating affordable housing in the United States."[4]

Preferential Funding

Subsidized housing through preferential funding encompasses a wide range of mechanisms to stimulate private investment in the rental market, as well as direct funding to support the development and expansion of the community-based rental housing market. Subsidies typically take the form of preferred (below-market) interest rates (Canada, Germany, Japan, Sweden, and the United States), loan forgiveness, and direct grants (Canada and the Netherlands). In most cases, this support has involved some form of agreement to maintain rents at some defined affordable level over a certain period of time (Germany and the Netherlands).

Demand Subsidies

OECD countries have used two main program structures to subsidize the demand for affordable rental housing: rent supplements and housing allowances. Rent supplements represent a contractual arrangement with landlords to support low-income households. In the United States, they are portable and can be used at any rental facility. In Canada, they can be used only for a specific rental address. Households pay a partial rent based on 30 percent of their income, and the program pays the difference. Various programs may establish a cap on the government's contribution.

Rent assistance programs can be interpreted as a form of rent supplements. Households pay the "affordable rent" (usually defined as 30 percent of income), and governments cover the difference from the "fair market rent." Since this intervention allows property owners to supply affordable units by financing the operational deficit (the costs not covered by rent revenues), it encourages the private production and management of low-income housing. In the United States, this intervention is implemented by HUD, mainly through the Section 8 program, and it currently reaches 1.2 million units (Landis and McClure 2010).

In contrast, a housing allowance does not involve a direct contract with a landlord. Instead, recipients are free to choose where they live. The government's contribution is a specified percentage of the difference between the total rent and a specified percentage of household income (usually 30 percent). Most programs also place a cap on the government's contribution. Often, minimal conditions or size standards are put in place to ensure that the program is not supporting poor-quality housing.

In Austria, Denmark, Finland, Germany, Norway, and Sweden, these two structures coexist. The coverage of rent assistance programs varies among the OECD countries, from approximately 18 percent of the population in Great Britain to less than 1 percent in Spain and Italy (Andrews, Caldera Sánchez, and Johansson 2011). In the United States, 2.2 million low-income households currently receive rental vouchers (Landis and McClure 2010). These programs are usually recommended because they provide greater flexibility to households and can improve the distribution of wealth. In the United States, households receiving vouchers tend to locate in areas with less poverty and higher incomes than households in public housing or subsidized private units (Newman and Schnare 1997). However, if not well designed, vouchers can have limited impact, as landlords tend to capture part of the subsidy through rent increases (Laferrère and Le Blanc 2004; Andrews, Caldera Sánchez, and Johansson 2011).

In conclusion, the experience of many developed OECD countries shows a balanced approach that focuses on both supply and demand through a variety of strategies, including direct provision, rent assistance, preferential tax treatment, subsidies for capital improvements, and rent allowances.

How to Expand the Rental Housing Market

To expand the rental market, Latin American and Caribbean authorities must rebalance the region's housing policies. This will broaden families' choices for securing housing services and will produce a more effective and equitable agenda for the twenty-first century, particularly for low-income groups. First, the authorities must reduce or eliminate policies that favor home ownership so as to provide an even playing field for the overall housing market. Providing subsides for rental housing similar or equivalent to those provided for ownership would represent a big step in this direction. Based on the experience of OECD countries, other policy options for the region to explore include eliminating favorable tax treatment of capital and the imputed income earned through home ownership.

Second, policymakers must provide a regulatory framework for the rental market that better balances the rights and obligations of tenants and landlords, including the elimination of rent control. This would increase the supply of rental units, as investors would be attracted to a more balanced and transparent market, and potentially produce the added benefit of reducing rental rates in the long run. To overcome potential opposition, policymakers could promote community-based rental housing projects managed by the same residents or by nongovernmental organizations (NGOs) (see box 4.1 on Habitat for Humanity's project in Buenos Aires).

Box 4.1 The Potential for Rental Housing: Habitat for Humanity in Buenos Aires

Habitat for Humanity is a nonprofit organization whose primary objective is to assist poor families living in bad housing or experiencing homelessness to make decent shelter a matter of conscience and action. Founded in 1976, it has helped more than 2 million people around the globe.

Habitat for Humanity has a strong presence in Latin America and the Caribbean, working in 17 countries in the region. Habitat for Humanity Argentina (HFHA) began operations in 2002 and has helped more than 540 families access housing solutions and more than 1200 families improve their current living conditions. HFHA's methodologies include technical assistance and training for families in need, progressive home improvements, recycling and renting homes at affordable costs, as well as traditional home construction.

In 2011, HFHA's project "Developing Real Estate for Squatters and Tenants of the City of Buenos Aires" won the Ashoka Sustainable Urban Housing Award. The project is part of two HFHA programs—"Assisted Rents" and "Recovering Urban Homes"—that restore run-down unutilized urban buildings in Buenos Aires and help families overcome the legal and social obstacles of obtaining a decent rental home.

The project for squatters and tenants is designed to serve families that are currently informally renting inadequate overcrowded rooms in tenancy buildings within the city limits (and paying close to the formal market rent). These families do not meet the requirements of the formal rental market (they lack a formal job, a deposit, or property, or assets that could serve as a guarantee).

The project proposes the concept of "fair rental" (1 percent of the property value per year). Families pay the formal market rate rent and deposit the difference between that amount and a fair rent in a savings account for two years. At the end of that period, families can use the deposit to move into sustainable housing offered by the private sector. Housing is energy efficient and constructed with environment-friendly materials. The fair rent scheme ensures a return on the investment that will be reinvested in such sustainable housing units.

While the buildings are managed through a co-op, HFHA is the owner, acts as manager and guarantor of the rental contract, and controls its execution. While the program is in its initial stages, 5,000 families in the neighborhood of La Boca and 9,000 more in the southern area of the city will benefit over time.

Sources: Habitat for Humanity Argentina (2011) and Habitat for Humanity International (2011).

Providing rental assistance and vouchers could also help mitigate initial concerns about the effects of deregulation on affordability, especially in low-income areas.

Third, to expand access to serviced land, governments should continue exploring ways to improve funding for infrastructure. These efforts can include increasing property tax revenues through better cadastral systems and charging adequate rates, as well as using value capture tools and other mechanisms to finance infrastructure expansion through the land revalorization that it produces. To encourage land with good urban services to be made available for rental units, policymakers could follow the example of some cities that have recently implemented differential property taxes, increasing rates for underutilized parcels. In addition, preferential zoning and tax treatment for high-density developments could help achieve a more efficient use of the urban space.

Finally, to expand access to mortgage financing, policymakers could explore the introduction of preferential tax treatments, soft loan programs, or mortgage insurance mechanisms. In addition, they could reduce the risks associated with this type of investment for rental properties, introducing rental assistance programs, and thereby guaranteeing investors/owners coverage of operating costs when they build affordable rental housing.

The combination of these policies, adjusted to the particular conditions and circumstances of each country, could expand the rental housing market in the region. This would alleviate the quantitative and qualitative housing deficits in the region. It would also create significant welfare gains by expanding families' choices, allowing them to decide whether to buy or to rent, improving labor mobility, increasing efficiency in land use patterns, and reducing financial risks and exposure.

5

Digging up the Truth about Land Markets

Formal serviced land in Latin America and the Caribbean is too expensive and is, therefore, responsible for a number of ills that plague the housing sector—or is it? Unfortunately, many of the voices decrying high land prices lack data to support their opinions. Writing on land markets in the region's cities, Smolka and Mullahy (2000) stress that "there are many misconceptions in the form of myths, prejudices and misinformation that distort seriously the views of well meaning participants in the debate on land policy" (p. xxv).

Putting aside the misconceptions and passion surrounding the debate about land in urban areas, three essential questions remain regarding how well land markets function in the region. First, are land market outcomes contributing to the overall housing gaps in cities in Latin America and the Caribbean? Second, what is conditioning these outcomes, and more specifically, what is the role of regulation? Third, what public policies are needed to improve both the functioning and the outcomes of land markets in the region?

How Do Land Markets Work?

Urban land development is usually driven by demographic and economic growth. Increases in population, changes in household composition, and shifts in economic activity drive the demand for land upon which to locate residential, commercial, industrial, and other activities. By contrast, the demand for agricultural goods drives the demand for rural land.

The price of land is strongly influenced by transportation costs (both monetary and time costs). In the case of land used to produce goods or services that are sold to others, the location of production affects transportation costs. Even where the use is residential, transportation costs affect land prices. Residential users must make trade-offs between housing prices and transportation costs. Households living in remote areas pay higher transportation costs, and consequently offer lower prices for housing and land. Land or plots located closer to central business districts, activity centers, or transit stations typically have higher land prices, other things being equal. Increases in transportation efficiency (faster and more reliable travel) typically boost land values.

As land prices increase, less profitable land uses, such as low- and moderate-income housing, are either pushed to the periphery of cities (where transport costs reduce bids) or foster very high-density slums, where residents' payments (rents) are large enough in the aggregate to overcome other bidders.

Finally, in the absence of zoning, potential users of land can adjust the amount of built area per plot (their capital-to-land ratios) to increase the amount they bid for land. In cities without strict zoning regulation, this routinely results in higher commercial and residential densities in city centers.

Overall, the demand for land derives from the demand for the activities that are built on it. If population and economic growth increase rapidly, land prices also rise as demand for residential, commercial, and industrial activities expands. For cities located on a featureless plain with ubiquitous infrastructure service, urban land use may extend outward in all directions until agricultural activities outbid urban ones. Over time, as the population and economic activity of the city increases, the urban land area of the city increases as nonagricultural users outbid agricultural ones. The city will also experience "densification" as land values increase and developers hike floor area ratios to offset these higher land costs. Many cities, including Bogota, follow this strategy (Dowall and Treffeisen 1991).

As residential land supply expands outward and prices in the city center rise, the density of residential development increases and more dwelling units are provided. This supply response, however, depends on available infrastructure, enabling land regulation, property rights that are easy to exchange, and topography (Quigley and Swoboda 2007). Regulation plays a very important role. Land use regulations, development impact fees, subdivision regulations, complexity of the development review and approval process, property rights, and titling all constrain urban land supply.

Even in an expansive and flexible urban land market (unlimited space, ubiquitous infrastructure, and easily accessed property titles), low- and moderate-income households have problems gaining access to well-located, accessible housing. The poor still need to compete with higher-income residential bidders as well as commercial and industrial users. Prices of land for housing are affordable for upper- and middle-income households, but those at the bottom of the income distribution continue to face difficulties.

Is Land Too Expensive?

Trying to gauge whether land is too expensive in Latin American and Caribbean cities is a difficult task. Systematic land price data are very scarce for most cities, with notable exceptions. Even when data are available, an appropriate yardstick to compare land prices is needed. A natural measure is income. Land prices can also be measured relative to overall housing costs: that is, what percentage of the cost of a finished house does land represent? Different types of land also need to be considered: formal urban serviced or developed land that enjoys access to all essential basic services—including utilities, schools, health centers, and transportation—and that complies with existing regulations regarding zoning, subdivision, and the like; formal urban raw land; informal or irregular urban land; and rural land.

Construction costs, land, basic infrastructure, and administrative expenses make up the cost components of a privately built dwelling. According to data collected in the periphery of different cities in Latin America, the incidence of land prices on overall housing costs averages 14 percent. Even though the share of land costs is a little higher than the infrastructure component of a finished dwelling (12 percent), it is significantly less than the share of construction, administrative, and regulation costs (table 5.1).

Average land prices in most Latin American cities have risen in recent decades. Many claim that this increase has caused a scarcity of supply of urbanized land at prices that low-income households can afford. Information about the evolution of price components of social housing is available for Chile between 1994 and 2004. Table 5.2 shows that the price of land spiked in ten years, reaching almost 20 percent of the value of a finished dwelling in 2004, up from 7 percent in 1994. Even though costs have increased for the other components, clearly, in the case of social housing in Chile, land has increased the most. Moreover, the increase in urbanized, serviced land (which went from 36UF[1] in 1994 to 120UF in 2004) absorbed 67 percent of the increase in the cost of social housing dwellings in Chile between 1994 and 2004, as total housing cost increased by 126UF during that period (see Brain and Sabatini 2006).

Table 5.1 Housing Cost Components in Latin American and Caribbean Cities, 2010 (Percent of Price)

City	Price component					
			C. Construction costs			
	A. Land	B. Infrastructure	Materials	Labor	Total	D. Administrative
Buenos Aires	6	12	44	30	74	8
Guadalajara	15	20	n.d.	n.d.	50	15
Guayaquil	10	15	40	20	60	15
Ilheus	7	4	42	30	72	17
Jequie	16	6	40	35	75	4
Kingston	6	22	63	3	67	5
Mexico City	18	6	n.d.	n.d.	59	16
Montevideo	45	5	23	22	44	6
Ribeirao Preto	9	12	39	26	66	14
San Salvador	10	20	35	15	50	20
Santiago	16	4	n.d.	n.d.	80	n.d.
Sao Paulo	9	n.d.	34	21	55	36
Tijuana	11	20	n.d.	n.d.	50	19
Valledupar	13	13	38	19	57	17
Cities' average	*14*	*12*	*40*	*22*	*61*	*15*

Notes: Argentina (Buenos Aires), Brazil (Ilheus, Jequie, Ribeirao Preto, and Sao Paulo), Chile (Santiago), Colombia (Valledupar), Ecuador (Guayaquil), El Salvador (San Salvador), Jamaica (Kingston), Mexico (Guadalajara, Mexico City, and Tijuana), and Uruguay (Montevideo).

Construction Costs data for Guadalajara, Mexico City, Santiago, and Tijuana are not divided between components.

For Santiago, construction costs include some administrative costs.

n.d. = no data.

Source: Authors' calculations based on Artiga de Soundy et al. (2010).

Table 5.2 Chile: Evolution of Housing Cost Components in Social Housing Programs, 1994–2004

	Policy periods					
	1994		1998–1999		2002–2004	
	Average (UF)	Percent of housing price	Average (UF)	Percent of housing price	Average (UF)	Percent of housing price
Total housing cost	238	100	335	100	364	100
Construction costs	200	84	237	71	236	65
Land	17	7	58	17	72	20
Urbanization	19	8	34	10	48	13
Infrastructure	n.d.	n.d.	2	1	6	2
Other costs	2	1	4	1	4	1
Size (square meters)	41.6		43.2		41.5	

n.d. = no data.
UF = unidad de fomento (unit of account indexed to consumer price inflation); 1UF = US$35 approximately.
Source: Brain and Sabatini (2006).

However, land prices have risen in tandem with two other factors that have substantially boosted demand for land: city population and income. Therefore, before drawing conclusions about the increase in land prices and its impact on housing affordability, changes in family income in recent years must also be taken into account.

Land Prices and Housing Affordability

This study examines a sample of cities, and compares land costs in the urban fringe with household income. Two main methods are used to estimate land affordability. The first is based on average land prices in the urban fringe at the city level. The second is an in-depth analysis of land affordability that looks at the distribution of the supply of land in the urban fringe in five cities and compares it with the distribution of income in the city.

The first estimate uses land prices for a subset of cities from the Inter-American Development Bank (IDB) database on land and housing

Figure 5.1 Land Prices and Income for 18 Latin American Cities

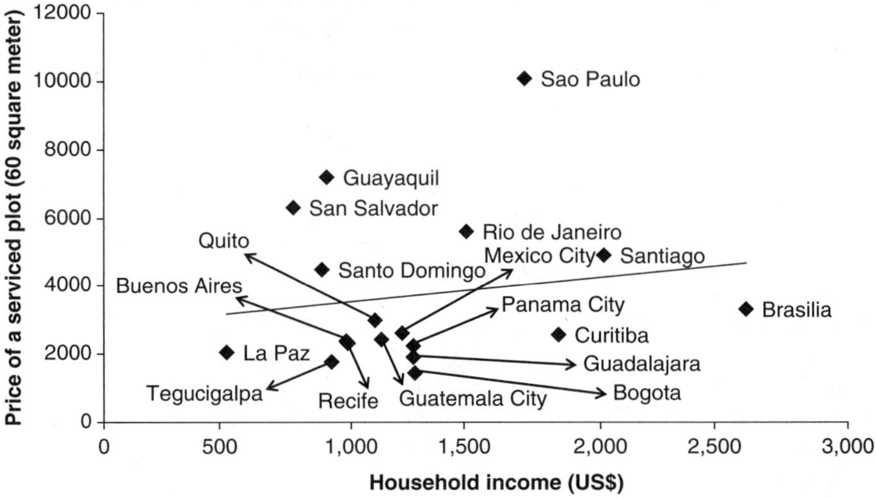

Note: Argentina (Buenos Aires), Bolivia (La Paz), Brazil (Brasilia, Curitiba, Recife, Rio de Janeiro and Sao Paulo), Chile (Santiago), Colombia (Bogota), Dominican Republic (Santo Domingo), Ecuador (Guayaquil and Quito), El Salvador (San Salvador), Guatemala (Guatemala City), Honduras (Tegucigalpa), Panama (Panama City), Mexico (Guadalajara and Mexico City).
Source: Authors' calculations based on Bouillon and Medellin (2011).

indicators (for details, see Bouillon and Medellín 2011). For cities for which information is not available, land prices are imputed using a statistical model that considers city-level variables that affect land prices, such as income, inequality, city size, and informality levels. As in chapter 3, plot and dwelling size are standardized to a basic unit of 40 square meters of built area and 60 square meters of land. Figure 5.1 shows land prices and income for 18 Latin American cities.

How do current land prices affect housing affordability? Compared to the housing affordability gap due solely to low income (which assumes land costs per standardized dwelling of US$4,000 for a total dwelling cost of US$15,000, as in chapter 3), current land prices increase affordability problems by more than 5 percentage points in Sao Paulo, San Salvador, Guayaquil, and Lima, in that order (see figure 5.2a). In the case of Sao Paulo, the percentage of households unable to afford a dwelling increased from 7 percent to 15 percent due to high land prices. If the plot size increases to 100 square meters, the number of cities with an affordability gap due to land prices that jump more than 5 percent increases to ten (see figure 5.2b).

Figure 5.2 Effect of Land Prices on Housing Affordability by Plot Size, Select Latin American and Caribbean Cities

a. 60-Square-Meter Plot Size

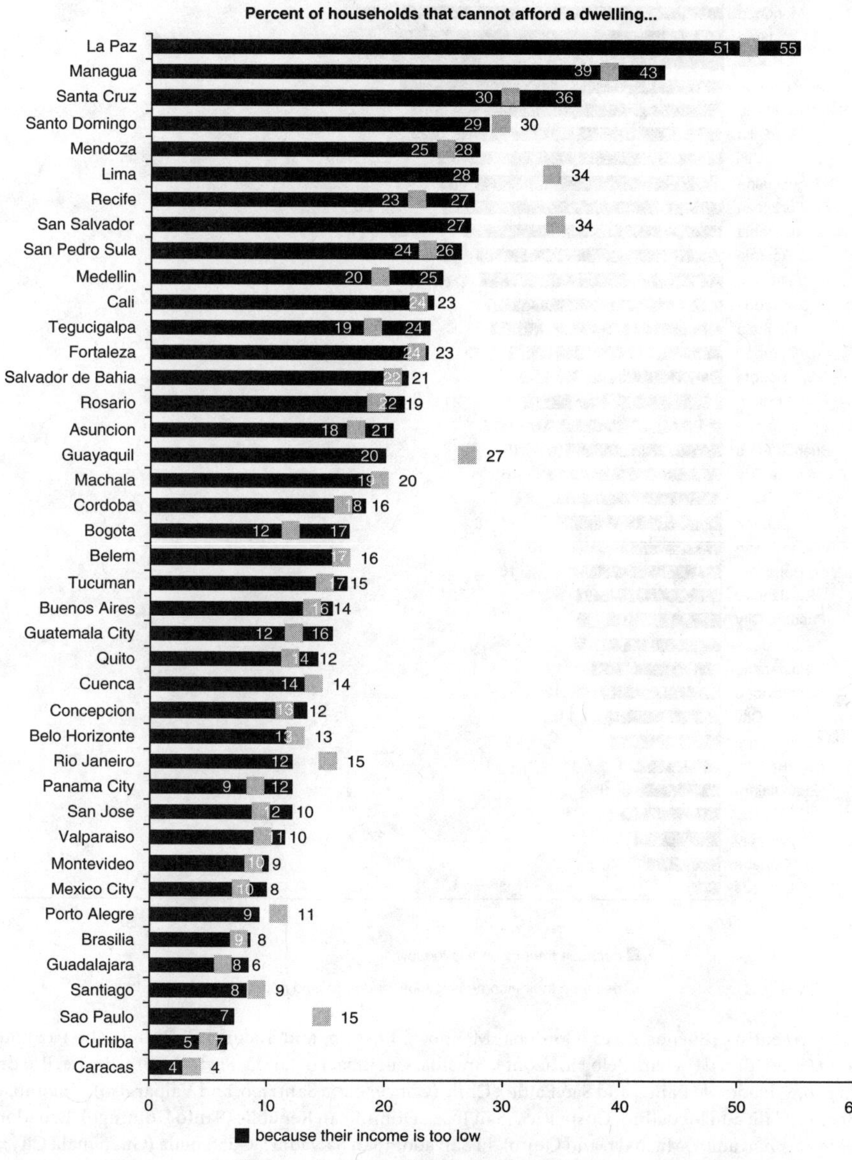

Figure 5.2 Continued

b. 100-Square-Meter Plot Size

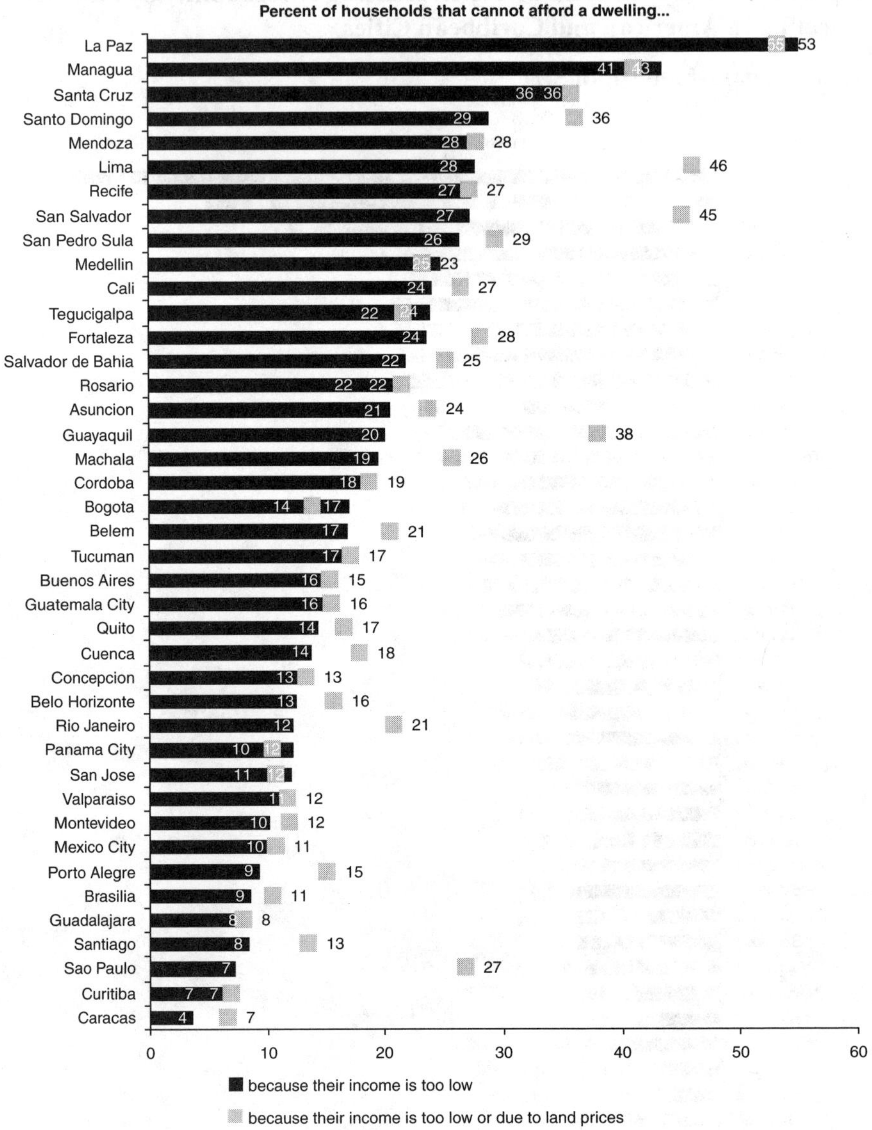

Note: Argentina (Buenos Aires, Cordoba, Mendoza, Rosario, and Tucuman), Bolivia (La Paz and Santa Cruz), Brazil (Belem, Belo Horizonte, Brasilia, Curitiba, Fortaleza, Porto Alegre, Recife, Rio de Janeiro, Salvador de Bahia, and Sao Paulo), Chile (Concepcion, Santiago, and Valparaiso), Colombia (Bogota, Cali, and Medellin), Costa Rica (San Jose), Dominican Republic (Santo Domingo), Ecuador (Cuenca, Guayaquil, Machala, and Quito), El Salvador (San Salvador), Guatemala (Guatemala City), Honduras (San Pedro Sula and Tegucigalpa), Mexico (Guadalajara and Mexico City), Nicaragua (Managua), Panama (Panama City), Peru (Lima), Paraguay (Asuncion), Uruguay (Montevideo), and Venezuela (Caracas).

Source: Authors' calculations based on Bouillon and Medellin (2011).

For instance, for the four cities mentioned earlier, the percentage of households not able to afford a dwelling due to land prices increases to around 20 percent. Other cities where the land price magnifies affordability problems are Rio de Janeiro, Santo Domingo, Machala, Porto Alegre, Santiago, and Fortaleza.

For the second estimate, comprehensive land prices of plots in the urban fringe are collected for five cities in Latin America (Buenos Aires, Cordoba, and Rosario in Argentina; Rio de Janeiro, Brazil; and Santiago, Chile). Those prices are used to estimate the land costs of a 60-square meter plot.[2] To estimate the affordability impact of these prices, following the methodologies developed in chapter 3, the maximum amount that families can pay for a finished house is compared to the cost of the serviced plot of land. Construction costs are assumed to be US$11,000, or three times serviced land costs, whichever is higher.

The simulation compares the distribution of the supply of housing derived from the observed land prices with the distribution of the population in the city ordered by the maximum capacity to pay for a finished home (with access to credit). The data for the population distribution according to the maximum value of land that families can afford come from each country's households surveys.

This estimate compares not only the percentage of the population that can afford the minimum priced plot, but the extent to which affordability is an issue for each price level of a formal, serviced 60-square meter plot of land with a standard dwelling.

Figure 5.3 shows the distribution of both supply and capacity to pay at different land prices.

Figure 5.4 shows the distribution of the supply over the different income deciles.

Three Cities in Argentina

In the case of Argentina, if a poor family saved every cent after paying for the basic needs required to survive, it would take them 33 years to purchase a formal, serviced 250-square meter plot—the minimum size plot required by regulation (Casazza et al. 2011b). Strict regulations make the formal land market more costly. Legal plots cost 10 percent more than illegal ones since they require the signature of a notary and the developers to provide several types of services on the land. Excessively strict land use regulations put formally developed land out of the reach of middle- and lower-income households, which have no other choice but to turn to informal solutions, claim Dowall (1992a) and Duranton (2008). However, others argue that the informal solutions "created" by the strict regulations

Figure 5.3 Housing Supply and Population Distribution Arranged by Land Cost and Family Capacity to Pay in Select Cities in Latin America

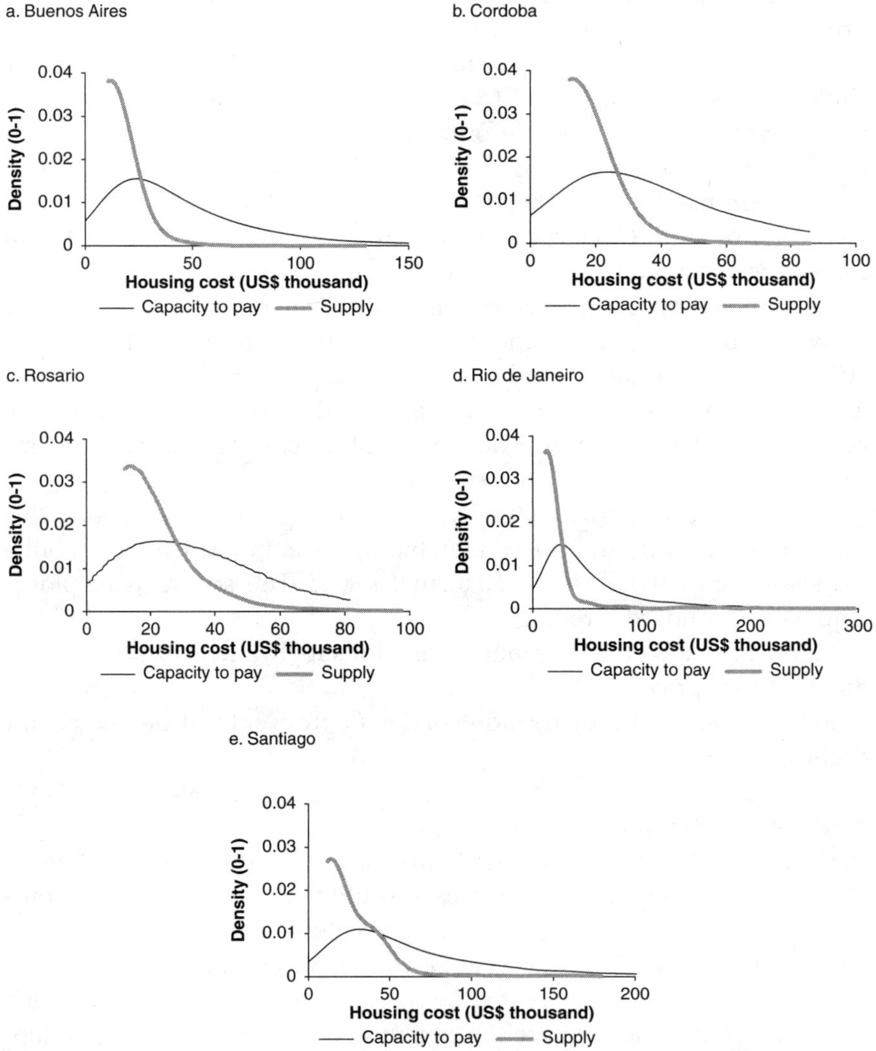

Source: Authors' calculations based on Casazza et al. (2011a).

Figure 5.4 Housing Supply by Income Deciles in Select Cities in Latin America

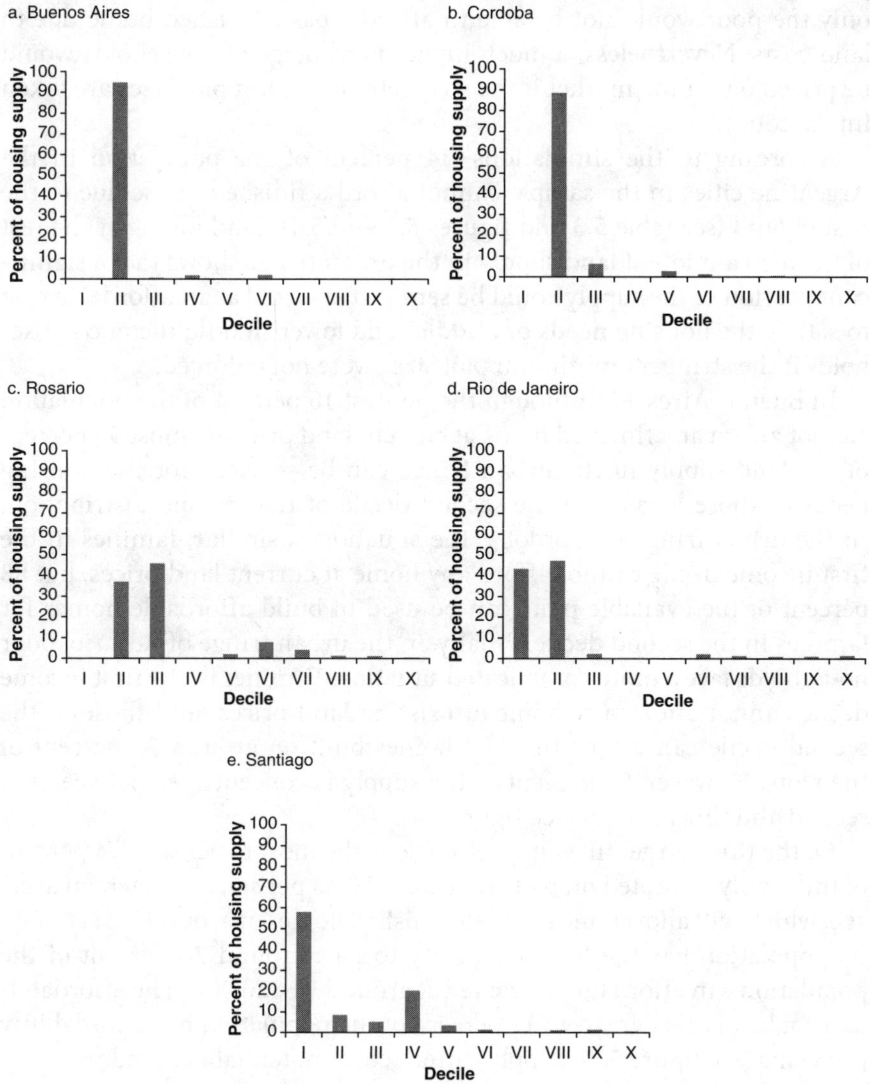

Source: Authors' calculations based on Casazza et al. (2011a).

in turn generate a negative externality that over time reduces the price of land in those jurisdictions.

Is land cheap or expensive in Argentina? The short answer is that land seems not to be expensive in the urban fringe of the cities. At current land prices per square meter and assuming no minimum plot size regulation, only the poor would not be able to afford a basic finished home due to land costs. Nevertheless, a much higher percentage of households would be priced out of the market if the stringent minimum plot sizes are taken into account.

According to the simulations, 14 percent of the population in the Argentine cities in the sample cannot afford a finished house due to the cost of land (see table 5.3 and figures 5.3 and 5.4). But looking at the rest of the distribution of land supply in the urban fringe shows that a significant portion of the supply could be serviced and sold at an affordable cost to satisfy the housing needs of middle- and lower-middle-income households if the stringent minimum plot sizes were not enforced.

In Buenos Aires, even though the poorest 10 percent of the population cannot afford any finished home at current land prices, almost 95 percent of the land supply in the urban fringe can be serviced for the housing needs of those located in the second decile of the income distribution. In the urban fringe of Cordoba, the situation is similar; families in the first income decile cannot afford any home at current land prices, but 88 percent of the available plots can be used to build affordable homes for families in the second decile. Finally, in the urban fringe of Rosario, poor households face a more complicated situation. Families in the first income decile cannot afford any home at existing land prices, and those in the second decile can afford finished homes built on around 37 percent of the plots. However, 83 percent of the supply is concentrated between the second and third deciles (see figure 5.4).

Of the three Argentine cities, Rosario is the most expensive (74 percent of the supply is located on plots that cost US$53 per square meter, on average, which will allow building basic finished homes of around US$14,000). Its population has the lowest capacity to pay: around 78 percent of the population can afford homes valued at around US$20,000. The affordability problem is also greatest; 17 percent of the population has affordability problems (see figure 5.3); supply cannot cover potential demand.

Rio de Janeiro and Santiago

Rio is a city of great socioeconomic contrasts. Some of the most expensive real estate in the planet can be found on Avenida Atlantica, with views

Table 5.3 Land Affordability in Select Cities in Latin America

		City				
		Buenos Aires	Cordoba	Rosario	Rio de Janeiro	Santiago
Value of a standarized dwelling (US$ thousand) based on land prices in the periphery	Minimum	11	12	12	11	12
	Maximum	166	86	98	295	206
	Average	13	14	18	18	25
	Median	12	12	13	13	13
Value of land (60 square meter plot - US$) in the periphery	Minimum	185	960	1,032	225	791
	Maximum	33,163	17,156	19,504	59,027	41,260
	Average	1,345	1,888	3,205	2,655	4,461
	Median	885	1,200	2,160	1,564	1,852
Affordability	Percent of population that cannot afford cheapest plot	12	14	17	5	8
	Percent of the supply serving the first 40 percent of the income distribution	97	95	83	93	92
Supply	Value of bulk of dwelling supply (US$ thousand)	12	13	14	13	14
	Value of land of bulk of dwelling supply (US$)	1,252	1,960	3,189	1,944	3,021
	Percent of dwellings at bulk of supply	89	85	74	79	58
Capacity to pay	Percent of population at bulk of supply	3	4	3	2	2
	Value of bulk of demand (US$ thousand)	24	24	20	26	30
	Percent of population at bulk of demand	81	79	78	60	72

Source: Author's calculations based on Casazza et al. (2011a).

of Ipanema Beach, yet a famous *favela* shares the same view, and *favela*s crowd the city. Some experts argue that Brazil suffers from a paradox in its urban housing market; expensive housing lacks both basic infrastructure and common areas (Dowall 2007). But, as most new housing springs up in the expansion areas of cities, it is important to determine the extent of the increase in land prices in Rio and how expensive land is in the outskirts.

To answer these questions, this study conducts the same exercise it did for the three cities in Argentina. The analysis shows that 5.4 percent of the population cannot afford the cheapest available plot on the outskirts of the city, and that 43 percent of land supply can be developed for affordable housing for the poorest 10 percent of the population (see figure 5.4). Most families in the city can afford a US$26,000 finished home. Land supply on the fringe of the city is affordable for most of these families. The bulk of land supply on the outskirts (79 percent) is priced at around US$32 per square meter; at this land price, finished homes for US$13,000 can be developed.

In Santiago, land prices have also increased substantially. In the last 15 years, the average real price of land has grown at an annual rate of 15 percent (Brain and Sabatini 2006; Trivelli 2010). Some studies find that land prices have increased the most in relative terms on the edge of the city, particularly in areas where social housing has historically been concentrated, but where houses are now being built for households with higher incomes. They claim that this process has contributed to the scarce supply of cheap land for poor families (Celhay and Sanhueza 2011).

Santiago follows Rosario with the second most expensive land plots on average among the five cities analyzed based on listing prices for land plots in the outskirts of the city. But Santiago also boasts the population with the best capacity to pay for a home. Only 8 percent of the population cannot afford the cheapest plot available, which is significantly less than for the Argentine cities (see figure 5.3). A significant share (92 percent) of the available land supply in the city is priced at or below US$138 per square meter and can be developed to serve the basic housing needs of families in the first 40 percent of the income distribution (figure 5.4). Notably, in Santiago almost 60 percent of land supply is affordable enough to be developed for families in the first decile of the population, which is higher than for any other city in the sample.

On the demand side, Santiago's population also appears to be the best off. Most households can afford finished homes that cost around US$29,600 (72 percent of the population's maximum affordability values are centered around those home values). On the supply side, most land

(60 percent) costs an average US$50 per square meter, which can be developed to supply basic homes at US$14,000.

Conclusions from the Five-City Analysis

Table 5.3 summarizes the findings for the five cities analyzed in this section. Contrary to popular belief, on the urban fringe, land is relatively affordable for most city dwellers. Even though a percentage of the population of each city cannot afford even the cheapest plot available, and the supply of cheap plots is not sufficient for an additional part of the population given their capacity to pay, on average not more than 12 percent falls into these categories. As shown in chapter 3, the overall affordability gap in Latin America and the Caribbean (combining restrictions related to income, interest rates, inability to document income, or housing prices) ranges from 29 percent to 80 percent—which is significantly higher than the affordability gap generated by land prices.

Families that opt either to buy cheap serviced land on the urban fringe or to develop it irregularly are trading location for distance to city center and time costs. Housing solutions on the periphery of cities inflate the cost of commuting to work and make it more difficult to access the social and labor network that can be found in more urbanized territories (Celhay and Sanhueza 2011). Therefore, such opportunity costs should be factored into any assessment of whether this land is expensive or cheap in the long run. As discussed, transportation costs influence land prices; plots closer to the central business centers of the cities will carry higher prices than plots further away.

In theory, higher labor force participation rates and better labor outcomes should be expected in places where there are more jobs. Therefore, people usually face a trade-off between living in cheaper locations further away from job opportunities and living closer to jobs, but paying more for housing. A study conducted in Santiago reveals that the persistence of slums in the city responds to location preferences. Low-income populations are willing to bear the cost of informality in order to have better employment opportunities, access to social services, and transportation systems (Celhay and Sanhueza 2011).

A Necessary Evil? Land Regulation

As cities extend outward, demand for land grows. Most newly urbanized land will be needed to house the poor. A number of factors likely explain the difficulties that poor people confront in affording a finished home or in building incrementally on a legal plot of land, as seen in chapter 3. One of these factors relates to land standards, which may reduce the incentives for developers to service land and floor space for low-income housing—even if raw land is not expensive. This pattern, in turn, can lead to informality.

Studies of land markets in the United States conclude that excessive regulation has caused price increases across cities and in turn generated a scarcity.[3] Standards and regulations are often crudely set. Moreover, they impose extra costs, including costs for inspections, permits, and appealing permit decisions.

Therefore, even though the evidence presented in the previous section suggests that serviced formal land on the urban fringe can be affordable, in city neighborhoods closer to the center, this is likely not the case. These plots cost more since they are better located. In addition, regulation—in the form of zoning requirements and restrictions, minimum plot sizes, or floor-to-area ratios (FARs), which regulate how much floor space can be put in a plot of land—may make them even more expensive. This is especially true for residential redevelopment for mixed socioeconomic uses. Land use and building regulations also respond to the interests of wealthier households already living in the area who want to protect their property values and fence in their neighborhoods against more socioeconomically mixed redevelopments.

In relation to standards, most developing countries have adopted industrialized urbanization models and standards oriented to the middle- and upper-income housing ideals of the 1950s and 1960s, such as the suburban subdivision models. Residential regulatory measures can be grouped roughly into five categories (Deakin 1989):

- Limits on and geographic preferences for the density and intensity of development;
- design and performance standards for lots and buildings;
- cost shifting from the locality to the developer;
- withdrawal of land from developable supplies; and
- direct and indirect controls on growth, applied to buildings and population.

These general categories can be expanded to incorporate specific regulatory tools (Quigley and Rosenthal 2005), as shown in table 5.4. The rationale for using any or all of the instruments is the promotion of economic efficiency by reducing the harmful effects (externalities) of certain land uses and of land development that is too rapid or disorganized. The most common form of controlling for externalities is to segregate land uses so

Table 5.4 Categories and Instruments for Land Use Regulation

Categories	Instruments
Residential development	Building permit cap
	Population cap
	Floor area ratio limit
	Down-zoning to open space/agricultural use
	Reduction in permitted residential density
	Referendum for density increase
	Supermajority in legislative body for density increase
Commercial/industrial development	Square footage cap (commercial)
	Square footage cap (industrial)
	Rezoning to lower intensity
	Height reduction
Land planning	Growth management element
	Moratoria
	Urban growth boundary
	Tiered development
	Subdivision controls
	Other growth control
Adequate public facilities requirements	Roads, highways, transit, and parking
	Water supply
	Water distribution
	Sewerage collection
	Sewerage treatment
	Flood control
	Other
Service capacity restrictions	Roads
	Water supply
	Water distribution
	Wastewater collection/treatment capacity
	Wastewater treatment quality
	Flood control
Development impact fee coverage	Administration
	Traffic mitigation
	Mass transit
	Parking
	Water: Service and treatment
	Sewer systems
	Flood control
	Parks and open spaces
	Natural resources
	Schools
	Libraries and arts facilities
	Other

Source: Quigley and Rosenthal (2005).

that incompatible land use activities remain separate: for example, keeping industrial activities out of residential districts. Such segregation maximizes land values and enhances efficiency (Bailey 1959).

On the other hand, zoning is and has been used to achieve social and economic segregation. If communities rely on property taxes based on property values to support service provision, higher-income communities have incentives to exclude low-income households, since their property values are lower and they will contribute less in property taxes (see Courant 1976; Hamilton 1978; Cooley and LaCivita 1982; and Fischel 1985).

Restrictive residential zoning can hurt poor families by limiting the supply of land for development and increasing prices for residential land. However, existing residents stand to gain, as the effect of the supply constraint places upward pressure on existing housing prices. If cities have monopoly power, they can use zoning and other land use regulations to limit the supply of land for residential development and drive up the price of existing housing (Thorson 1996).

Land use planning controls such as urban density controls, urban growth boundaries, greenbelts, and growth management practices can effectively limit the supply of urban residential land and housing. While the effects of these tools will vary according to how thoroughly they are implemented and enforced, they can lead to increased land and housing costs. In turn, these effects significantly impact the poor.

Subdivision regulations—which govern plot sizes, minimum frontage requirements, developer set-asides for streets, sidewalks, and public facilities—also affect residential land and housing prices. A higher cost of development reduces the price the developer is willing to pay for land, which reduces the housing supply and pushes up prices. A complex or slow regulatory process can also adversely affect urban land prices. If developers or builders are burdened with complex approval procedures, they often develop real estate in other cities or regions. In some instances, complex regulations foster monopolies, which provide one or a few developers who know how to navigate the system with pricing power and the ability to exclude competition (Quigley and Rosenthal 2005). In cases where enforcement is weak, developers and builders resort to informal or irregular development.

Unraveling the Red Tape

In most Latin American cities, land was incorporated by laying out widely spaced allotments and keeping the lands between these allotments unoccupied for land speculation. Low-income families tend to settle in the outskirts of cities, generating urban sprawl. Illegal settlements have sprung up on the urban peripheries, beyond the limits of urban regulations and often ignored by both public and private investors.

Starting in the 1950s, urban migration became unstoppable in many cities of the region, generating the need for regional planning. The few master plans drawn up at that time (for instance, in Buenos Aires, Bogota, Caracas, and Rio de Janeiro) failed to solve existing urban problems. Obstacles included absence of control of land use, limited capacity of local governments, and limited financing.

Since the 1960s, the region has benefited from technical assistance to strengthen planning capacity, leading to improved participatory planning and budgeting, squatter regularization, planning as part of natural disaster management, development of bottom-up processes, and decentralization. Those concepts form part of the new framework for the coming years. A summary of the current planning framework for various countries in the region is presented in table 5.5.

Even though the countries of the region have national planning frameworks that cover land uses and building specifications, many regulations are determined by local governments. Table 5.6 lists specific land regulations in 15 Latin American and Caribbean cities.

Note that the average FAR is two, meaning that on the average property a building two times the total plot area can be constructed. FAR restrictions reduce supply and thus increase demand, which boosts land prices in central areas. This, in turn, may encourage families to build their houses themselves in the areas where regulation is not enforced (often the outskirts of the city), causing urban sprawl.

Moreover, some cities mandate minimum plot size as high as 300 square meters, with no exception for social housing. This increases the land costs for low-income households willing to purchase land in formal markets. For instance, in Buenos Aires and Rosario, the minimum plot size of 300 square meters can impact housing affordability considerably. The percentage of households that cannot afford a house when the minimum plot size increases from 60 to 300 square meters at current land prices soars from 19 to 40 percent in Rosario, and from 14 to 31 percent in Buenos Aires (see figure 5.5).

Table 5.7 illustrates the wide gap between prices of developed land and raw land in the region. This gap highlights the substantial costs that regulation and infrastructure provision impose when raw urban land is converted into subdivided land with access to basic services. On average, raw

Table 5.5 Urban Planning Systems in Latin America, Select Countries

Country	Authority	Instruments	In practice
Argentina	No planning authority at the national level. Provincial administrations have the authority for land use planning. Local authorities are responsible for regulating urban land use. The provincial constitutions make it possible to create metropolitan areas.	Master plans, planning, and building codes.	Administrative levels not coordinated. Very few administrative bodies have planning units. Public participation starting to develop.
Bolivia	The Ministry of Sustainable Development and Environment is in charge.	The executive plan and the regulatory plan for urban issues, and the territorial organization plan for regional issues.	Top-down decision-making process. Difficulties in implementing participatory planning.
Brazil	The federal, state, and municipal levels are autonomous. At the federal level, the Ministry of Cities is responsible for urban affairs.	The federal constitution makes spatial planning compulsory. City planning is an obligation of the state to be implemented by the municipalities of over 20,000 inhabitants. Participation included in planning process.	Municipalities are responsible for controlling urban land use but capacity is limited.

Chile	Planning responsibility delegated to the regional and communal level.	Normative prescriptions for building activities and the subdivision of land into urban plots (plot sizes, intensity of occupation, building location and construction conditions, land and building uses).	Land evaluated in terms of building conditions. Communal plans and ordinances lack control.
Colombia	Planning and development are the responsibility of the municipalities.	Three types of plans based on number of inhabitants: more than 100,000; between 30,000 and 100,000; and less than 30,000.	Law 388/97 takes into account urban improvement in determining the value of land. Appropriate legislation is lacking to have it fully implemented.
Guyana	Responsibilities shared between the Central Housing and Planning Authority (CH&PA) and the Guyana Lands and Surveys Commission (GLSC).	Regional planning is being developed. Current planning instruments are development control standards. Land use plans and town plans are being prepared.	Concurrent jurisdiction of different institutions for regional planning. Implementation is challenging as enforcement capacity is limited.
Paraguay	The Technical Planning Secretariat and the Environmental Secretariat are in charge of the national plans and applying environmental regulations. The provincial governments are responsible for formulating plans in accordance with the national plans.	No specific national physical planning system. Plans are often produced to deal with economic and social issues, as well as to initiate dialogue with external financial assistance agencies.	Plans are not used as a management tool. Their implementation is partial.

Continued

Table 5.5 Continued

Country	Authority	Instruments	In practice
Peru	The National Land Use Agenda is responsibility of the Vice-Ministry of Urban Development of the Ministry of Housing, Construction, and Sanitation. Regional governments develop regional land development plans. Provincial and district municipalities develop municipal land use planning.	Planning instruments include: regional plans (regional land uses), local comprehensive development plans, local framework plans (for guiding urban expansion), and local development plans (for urban districts).	The planning system is complex. A variety of authorities is involved, which can cause confusion in practice.
Uruguay	The National Directorate of Planning of the Ministry of Housing, Planning, and Environment is in charge of the National and Regional Plans. Master plans are the responsibility of the departments.	The only formal planning instruments are master plans. Only building regulations control private development.	Spatial planning practice is not used systematically for territorial administration. The city of Montevideo is the only administration that has the technical capacity to implement its planning tools.

Source: Ryser and Franchini (2008).

Table 5.6 Land Regulations in 15 Latin American and Caribbean Cities

Country	City	Minimum plot size (square meter)	Floor-to-area ratio (FAR) for apartment buildings (square meter)	Minimum plot size used for social housing (square meter)	Land development permit delay (months)	Saleable area (percent of plot size)	Legal cost of land development (US$ per square meter)	Legal cost of a residential apartment building development (US$ per sqaure meter)
Argentina	Buenos Aires	300	2	300	24	60	2	94
Brazil	Sao Paulo	125	3	60	36	65	n.d.	57
	Guaruja	125	3	72	18	65	n.d.	n.d.
	Ribeirao Preto	125	5	n.a.	36	75	n.d.	73
	Ilheus	125	2	40	6	65	23	860
	Jequie	125	1	102	6	65	1	606
Jamaica	Kingston	372	Plot sizes controlled by residential density	112–560	3	70	0.4	n.d.
Uruguay	Montevideo	300	n.d.	250	4	70	12	13
Ecuador	Guayaquil	100	1.6–2.2	72	12	70	22	33
El Salvador	San Salvador	125	1.54–2.0	63	13	67	6	12
Mexico	Tijuana	180	2	120	2	79	18	57
	Guadalajara	90	2	90	2	85	35	59
	Mexico City	60–90	1	62.57–90	3	10–18	60	78
Chile	Santiago	120	3	120	39	56–62	0	5
Colombia	Valledupar	45	n.d.	35–120	0	50	14	17
Cities' average		*161*	*2*	*127*	*14*	*68*	*16*	*151*

n.d. = no data; n.a. = nonapplicable

Source: Authors' calculations based on Artiga de Soundy et al. (2010).

Figure 5.5 Plot Size Effect on Affordability, Cities with Minimum Plot Size Regulations

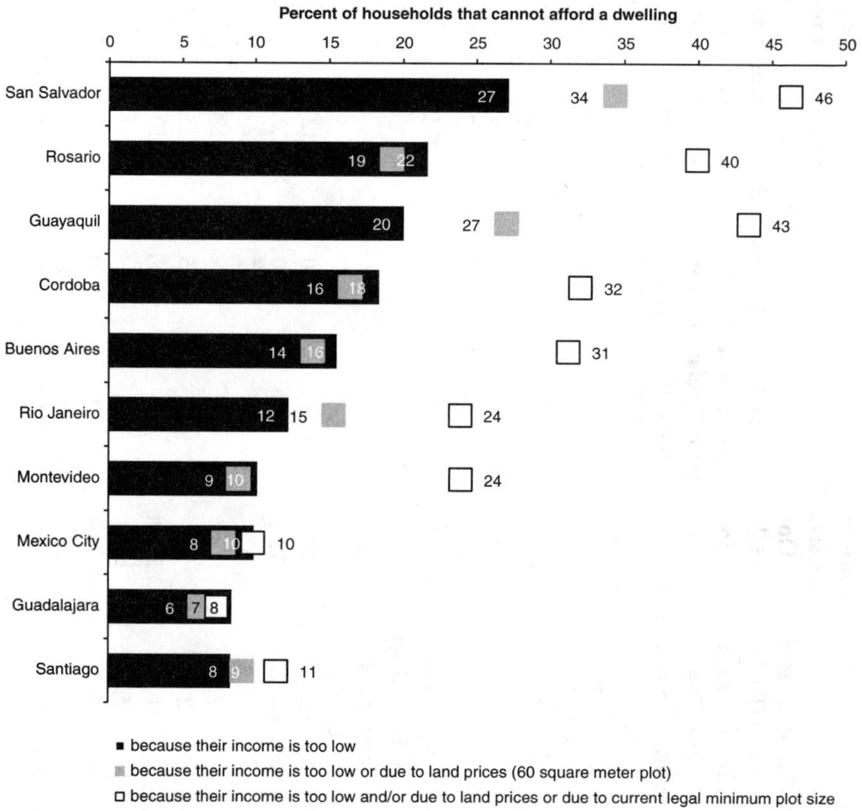

Note: Argentina (Buenos Aires, Cordoba, and Rosario), Brazil (Rio de Janeiro), Chile (Santiago), Ecuador (Guayaquil), El Salvador (San Salvador), Mexico (Guadalajara and Mexico City), and Uruguay (Montevideo).
Source: Authors' calculations based on Bouillon and Medellin (2011).

urban land is 5.6 times the price of rural land, and developed urban land is another 5 times the price of raw urban land. However, the costs vary substantially across cities. In Guayaquil, the cost of serviced land is 8 times that of raw land, while in Santiago, serviced land costs only 1.3 times more than raw land.

Even though table 5.6 presents land regulations for a small sample of Latin American and Caribbean cities, many authors argue that regulatory complexity and unclear land titling and registration are systemic

Table 5.7 Developed and Urban Land Premiums, Select Cities in Latin America and the Caribbean

Country	City	Developed land premium (price of urban raw land/ price of urban developed land)	Urban land premium (price of raw land in urban areas/price of rural land)
Argentina	Buenos Aires	6.5	3.7
Brazil	Sao Paulo	6.0	1.7
	Guaruja	6.0	n.d.
	Ribeirao Preto	12.5	4.0
	Ilheus	n.d.	n.d.
	Jequie	1.5	17.0
Jamaica	Kingston	1.9	13.8
Uruguay	Montevideo	15.0	2.0
Ecuador	Guayaquil	8.0	2.1
El Salvador	San Salvador	2.6	1.4
Mexico	Tijuana	1.6	2.6
	Guadalajara	2.4	4.0
	Mexico City	3.1	3.3
Chile	Santiago	1.3	10.4
Colombia	Valledupar	1.9	6.0
Cities' Average		*5.0*	*5.6*

n.d. = no data.
Source: Authors' calculations based on Artiga de Soundy et al. (2010).

problems in most cities in the region. The World Bank/International Finance Corporation's *Doing Business* survey collects a property registration indicator that is directly related to how cumbersome land regulations are in a country. The indicator

> records the full sequence of procedures necessary for a business (buyer) to purchase a property from another business (seller) and to transfer the property title to the buyer's name. The property of land and building will be transferred in its entirety. The transaction is considered complete when the buyer can use the property as collateral for a bank loan. (World Bank 2011b)[4]

Figures 5.6–5.8 present data from the survey on the time and cost to register property in the region.

As these figures reveal, Latin America is a relatively difficult place in which to register property. The property registration process in most Latin American countries is complex, time-consuming, and, relative to income

Figure 5.6 Time to Register Property in Latin American and Caribbean Countries, 2010

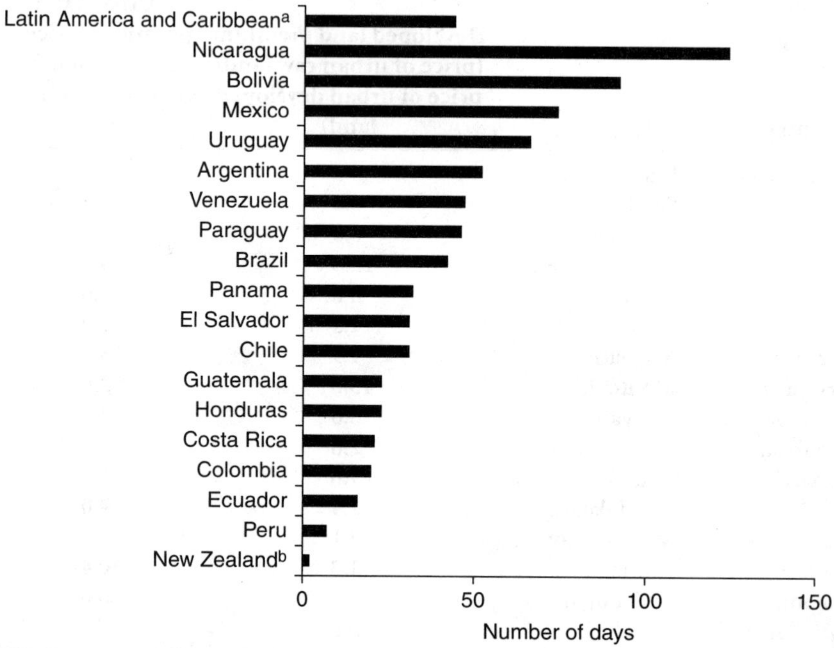

[a] Country's average in the figure.
[b] Country with the fewest days is the benchmark.
Source: World Bank (2011b).

per capita, expensive. Regulation imposes an extra burden, particularly for low-income families, contributing to the current deficiencies in the housing situation in the region.

Genesis of a Slum

Low- and lower-middle-income households seek out land to build homes themselves in informal settlements and slums as an alternative to more expensive, and, for some of them, unaffordable formal housing produced in the private sector. In the case of squatting, households occupy vacant public lands (such as excess rights of way, or land set aside for the future construction of public facilities, such as school sites or parks). However, not all squatting takes place on public land; some occurs on private land

Figure 5.7 Cost to Register Property in Latin American and Caribbean Countries, 2010 (Percent of Property Values)

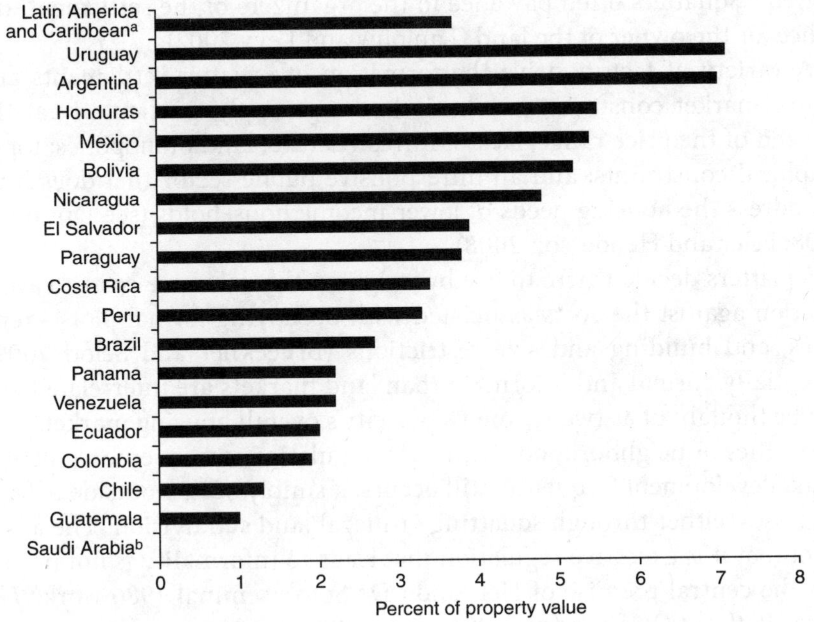

[a] Country's average in the figure.
[b] Country with the fewest days is the benchmark.
Source: World Bank (2011b).

Figure 5.8 Cost of Registering Property (Percent of Property Value) and Income Per Capita around the World, 2009

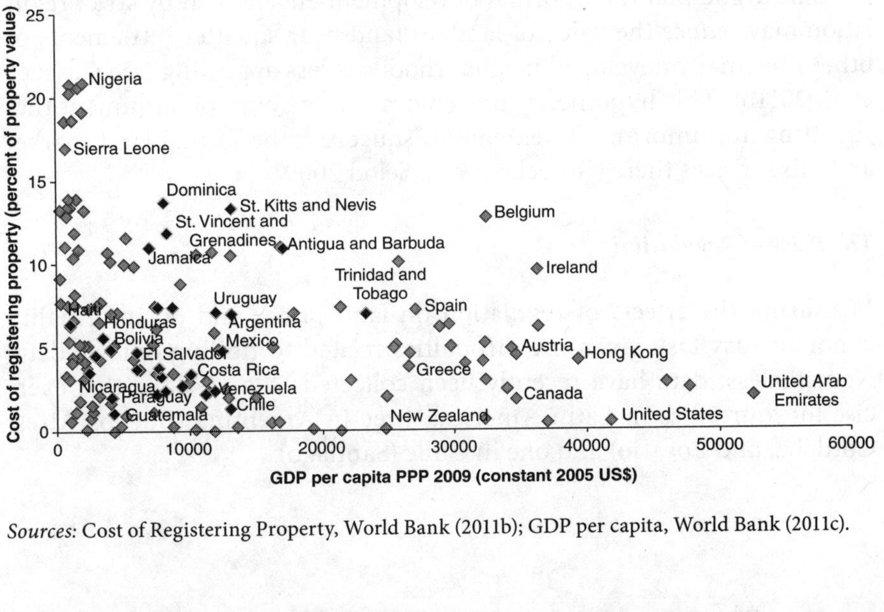

Sources: Cost of Registering Property, World Bank (2011b); GDP per capita, World Bank (2011c).

as well.[5] Squatters often pay a fee to the organizers of the settlement, the police, or the owner of the land (Lanjouw and Levy 2002).

A variety of factors drive the formation of squatter settlements and slums: market constraints; inelastic housing supply, particularly at the low end of the price range; lack of infrastructure; land monopolies; topographical constraints; and an unresponsive public sector that does little to address the housing needs of lower-income households (see Duranton 2008; Feler and Henderson 2008).[6]

Squatters decide where to live by weighing the defensive costs to avoid eviction against the costs associated with occupying formal plots—rent, taxes, and building and size restrictions (Brueckner and Selod 2009). Essentially, formal and informal urban land markets are interrelated and can be thought of as two segments of a city's overall housing market.

In cities or neighborhoods with strict regulations where enforcement is weak, development frequently still occurs; it simply occurs outside of legal processes, either through squatting or illegal land subdivision. The argument that it is excessive regulation that leads to informality is not new; it was the central premise of Hernando De Soto's seminal 1986 work, *The Other Path* (*El Otro Sendero*). Excessively strict land use regulations push the costs of formally developed land out of the reach of middle- and lower-income families, who then resort to informal solutions.[7]

Land regulation in Argentina, which requires developers to provide several services in new developments, helps explain the growth of irregular settlements in the periphery of Buenos Aires, as it makes formal housing developments too costly for lower-income groups, argues Reese (2009).

Some argue that the informal development engendered by strict regulation may *reduce* the value of land, as land near squatter settlements or other informally developed neighborhoods is less appealing (see Casazza et al. 2011b). This hypothesis runs contrary to a common argument that squatting and informal development "squeezes" the formal land market and raises prices there (Brueckner and Selod 2009).

The Price of Regulation

Measuring the effects of regulation on land prices and on informality is not an easy task given the difficulties related to finding reliable data. Nevertheless, data have recently been collected to undertake this exercise for four cities in Latin America: three in Argentina (Buenos Aires, Cordoba, and Rosario) and one in Chile (Santiago).

Three Cities in Argentina

The standards required for urbanization have multiplied in cities in Argentina. Local governments require developers to provide complete infrastructure. The requirements for land donations for green space and land reserves for community facilities have also risen. The regulations favor construction at the periphery, with relatively high minimum lot sizes, which result in large low-density areas and higher infrastructure costs. In Rosario, for example, the responsibilities associated with urban development that fall to the land owner or developer of a project include providing public works corresponding to secondary networks of household services (fresh water, drainage ditches, sewers, electricity, and telephone lines) as well as the land donations for parks and green areas, vehicle transportation, pedestrian spaces, and community facilities. Table 5.8 presents results from a survey of land developers in three cities in Argentina aimed at identifying the main factors that limit land development for low-income households.

Registration costs matter for land prices in Argentine cities. Plots with legal title cost around 10 percent more than those without title (Casazza et al. 2011b). The titling premium for squatters in Buenos Aires ranges between 13.8 and 18.5 percent (Galiani and Schargrodsky 2010). Plots located in areas where compliance with regulations is higher (that is, where a higher share of households have a legal title and where a lower share of households have illegally occupied the land) are more expensive.

Land regulation also affects land prices. In the three Argentine cities surveyed, the most restrictive FAR is 0.07 and the most flexible is 2.0 (see table 5.9). Having a higher FAR makes a plot more expensive. A 10 percent increase in the FAR is associated with a 1 to 2 percent increase in the price per square meter. Moreover, plots are more expensive when they are located in areas where the other lots have lower (that is, more restrictive) FAR values (Casazza et al. 2011b). Therefore, flexible land use regulation commands a premium, particularly if the other plots in the district have stricter regulations.

Not surprisingly, plots with more infrastructure services are more expensive in Argentina. For each additional element of infrastructure (running water, sewerage, town gas, drainage system, electricity, street lighting, and paved street), the price of the plot increases by about 10 percent (Casazza et al. 2011b). Plot size also matters for land prices. The larger the size of the plot, the lower the price per square meter.

Table 5.8 Factors That Reduce Private Investment in Land Development Targeted at Low-Income People in Argentina

Factors that reduce private investment in land development (1= least important; 12 = most important)	**Buenos Aires**	**Cordoba**	**Rosario**
The permitting and approvals process for subdivision entails many bureaucratic delays at the municipal level and is very expensive. There is uncertainty over obtaining legal permission to subdivide.	12	12	7
Regulatory requirements in terms of infrastructure networks cannot be met as they require too much investment. Moreover, there are no basic services in these peripheral areas.	11	7	9
The permitting and approvals process has many bureaucratic blockages in the province and is thus too expensive. There is uncertainty over how to obtain the legal subdivision permission.	10	4	6
Demand is not reliable as households are not solvent and have unstable incomes. This makes the business of selling lots in installments risky.	9	5	12
Middle- and low-income households can obtain cheaper informally subdivided lots and they do not require legal papers as they know the authorities will not question their tenure status and will regularize their land eventually.	8	1	11

There is not much supply of large parcels to subdivide. Landowners are better off leaving the land vacant to wait for it to increase in value rather than going through the subdivision process.	7	11	6
Difficulty in financing the project. Construction finance for required infrastructure work is either nonexistent or too expensive.	6	10	9
Profitability of this business is low, as the time to obtain permits investment in works and overall effort is not compensated.	5	9	4
High cost of credit in the medium and long term for paying the monthly installments of lots, and reduces demand.	4	2	10
Landowners tend to demand high profits that raise final land prices.	4	6	3
Legal requirements for land donations for streets, green space, and community facilities are too high.	2	3	1
Legal requirements for minimum lot size are difficult to meet, as smaller lots are demanded.	1	8	2

Source: Casazza et al. (2011b).

Table 5.9 City-Level Subdivision Regulations in Three Cities in Argentina

Subdivision regulation	Buenos Aires	Cordoba	Rosario
Minimum lot size	300 square meters	250 square meters	300 square meters
Minimum width of streets	15 meters	12 meters	18 meters
Minimum share of plot allocated to green areas	10	10	10
Minimum share of plot allocated to social areas	4	5	5
Floor-to-area ratio	0.15–1.80	0.30–2.00	0.07–1.00
Minimum provision of infrastructure	Running water Sewerage Drainage system Paved street Street lighting Electricity	Running water Sewerage Drainage system Paved street Street lighting Electricity Town gas	Running water Sewerage Drainage system Paved street Street lighting
Does the law include exceptions to the above thresholds when the subdivision is for low-income people?	Yes, but very hard to obtain	Yes and relatively easy to obtain. It allows lots of 162 square meters and less infrastructure	Yes, but very hard to obtain

Note: Empty cells mean no requirement.
Source: Casazza et al. (2011b).

The distance to the city center and to amenities (such as schools, hospitals, bus stops, parks, police, etc.) is negatively correlated with prices. Conversely, the distance to dis-amenities (such as shanty towns and garbage) is positively correlated with prices. Moreover, plots located in areas with higher socioeconomic status (that is, fewer poor households and more gated communities) are more expensive. These variables explain more than half the variation in land prices (Casazza et al. 2011b).

Finally, the evidence from Argentina suggests that in countries with low enforcement capabilities, stringent regulations and complex procedures promote informality and reduce the value of land because more affluent people dislike residing in those areas. Casazza et al. (2011b) find that more stringent regulations governing infrastructure provision, bureaucratic complexity, and urban requirements go hand in hand with lower levels of formality and lower prices.

Santiago

The same exercise to estimate the effects of regulation on land prices undertaken for the three cities in Argentina was conducted for Santiago, with less conclusive results. Trivelli (2010) estimates the impact of the regulatory regime, distance to local centers, access to basic trunk services, and infrastructure on the raw urban land-rural land price premium and the serviced urban land-raw urban land premium. In the case of the premium between raw urban and rural land, the exercise found that neither infrastructure nor regulation had much of an impact. Only one factor—provision of water—increased the price of land, and distance to city center decreased it, as expected.

On the other hand, for the premium between serviced urban land and raw urban land, the estimates show no effect for infrastructure but a positive effect for regulation. Regulation enforcement appears to increase the price of serviced urban land compared to raw urban land. Water and distance to the local center have the same effects as with the raw urban land-rural land price premium.

Attacking the Slum Problem: Before or After?

Slums and irregular settlements generally spring up because low-income families cannot afford a private market solution for their housing needs. Thus, slums and irregular settlements are symptoms of poor functioning land and housing markets.

Land speculation has a perverse effect, as well. Increasing land values encourage owners and investors to retain serviced land in the hopes of reaping greater profits in the future (future valorization). As a result, cities live a paradox in which serviced land is undersupplied in the market but vacant land is abundant. For instance, between 30 percent and 40 percent of the urbanized land in Brazilian cities was vacant in the 1990s (Fernandes 1997); 32 percent of the area of Buenos Aires and 26.6 percent in Guadalajara were empty at the beginning of the 2000s (Smolka 2002). In Bogota, more than 5,255 hectares—almost 16 percent of the total urban area—is classified by the Cadastral Department as "urbanized but not built" (UAECD 2008). Of this total, the Department estimates that at least

1,035 hectares, divided in 1,187 lots, were "fattening lots": vacant parcels being held off the market for speculative purposes (SDP 2009).

In many cases, local governments are the owners of those vacant premises. By keeping those plots underutilized, local governments miss the opportunity to generate land-based revenue. Land-based revenue instruments are an important source of revenue, particularly in the developing world, since they neither increase public debt nor are affected by any restriction on borrowing (see box 5.1).

Box 5.1 A Virtuous Circle: Financing Basic Infrastructure with Land-Based Revenue

Land assets are potentially one of the most important sources of revenue for local governments in the developing world. The revenues that could be generated by selling land nearly equal the governmental borrowing needed to finance capital investment in various developing countries (Peterson and Kaganova 2010). Direct sales of land are the clearest example of land financing. However, land can also be used as collateral for borrowing in order to finance urban investments. Local governments can also sell the development rights of underutilized land in order to generate fiscal revenue for investment without increasing municipal deficits or debts. For the city of Sao Paulo, for example, the total revenue generated from the sale of development rights between 2006 and 2011 is estimated to have been around US$300 million (Vetter and Vetter 2011). Land-based financing reduces the need for long-term credit, which is usually hard to obtain in the developing world.

Most municipalities in Latin American and Caribbean cities underutilize land-based revenue instruments to finance infrastructure investments. These instruments include: real estate property and transfer taxes[a]; impact fees for new development[b]; betterment levies[c]; sale of development rights; sale of underused public land and buildings; land readjustments; and urban concessions. None of these instruments would increase public debt or be affected by any restrictions on borrowing (Vetter and Vetter 2011).

Raising rates and improving collection on real estate taxes and fees could generate significant fiscal space for local investments. For example, just raising the ratio between the real estate property tax and GDP to the developing world average of 0.6 (Bahl and Martínez-Vázquez 2007) for a sample of Brazilian municipalities (selected on the basis of creditworthiness, financial performance, and economic potential) would increase total annual municipal revenue by over US$700 million, and entail an average annual per capita real estate property tax increase of only US$24. Additionally, as municipalities grow and provide new infrastructure, they create new real estate value as well. This value can then be captured in part by land-based instruments that could be used to finance new infrastructure or social housing.

Federal programs that allocate part of the annual share of credit that they give to municipalities based on performance criteria could generate more land-based revenue at the local level (Vetter and Vetter 2011). To help municipalities achieve that goal, technical assistance is needed to improve real estate taxes collection systems and to put land-based instruments into operation. The result could be a virtuous circle created by land financing.

[a] A transfer tax is a tax on the passing of property from one person (entity) to another.

[b] An impact fee is a fee that is implemented by a local government on a new or proposed development to help pay for a portion of the public costs of the new development. They are a charge on new developments to help fund and pay for the construction or needed expansion of offsite capital improvements.

[c] A betterment levy is a "compulsory charge imposed by a government on the owners of a selected group of properties to defray, in whole or in part, the cost of a specific improvement or services that is presumed to be of general benefit to the public and of special benefit to the owners of such properties" (Borrero Ochoa 2011, p. 14).

Sources: Bahl and Martínez-Vázquez (2007), Borrero Ochoa (2011), Peterson and Kaganova (2010), and Vetter and Vetter (2011)

Even though there is plenty of room in Latin American cities where poor households could settle, strict unrealistic regulations, along with public failure to provide trunk infrastructure and develop serviced land, have forced many of them to live as squatters in the many slums that have sprung up around the region. Transforming raw urban land to serviced land is a costly process that many developers are not willing to bear if profits will be small—which is likely if the potential clients are moderate- and low-income households.

Even though most governments have no policies directed specifically at the causes of the development of informal settlements and slums, they do have programs to assist families already settled in irregular land developments such as titling programs and slum upgrading. These policies have great potential to accelerate household investments in their homes, which positively impacts household well-being (see Galiani and Schargrodsky 2010).

Slum upgrading can be classified into three types: improving core basic services, regularizing tenure, and upgrading slums comprehensively. Improving core basic services involves upgrading roads (rights of way, rationalizing the road network of the community, leveling and compacting most roads, and paving main roads); basic sanitation (septic tanks, pit latrines, and connection to drainage networks); street lighting; communal water (standpipes); and drainage. The maximum cost per household for core basic service programs typically ranges from US$250 to US$1,200.

Land regularization programs focus on achieving secure tenure—a prerequisite for upgrading. Costs vary widely, depending on the complexity of the situation.

Comprehensive slum upgrading secures tenure and lifts slum communities to the same level as the formal city (rationalized paved road network, individual water connections, individual sewerage connection, drainage, public illumination, and full legal title). It includes key social services (child care and community centers/sports fields) and a strong participatory process. It is the typical approach in Latin America, pioneered and most developed in Brazil. A classic example is the *Favela-Bairro* slum upgrading project in Rio de Janeiro. The total maximum cost per household of comprehensive slum upgrading in middle-income countries typically ranges from US$3,000 to US$7,000.

Table 5.10 shows the cost of providing infrastructure in both a regular land development and in a slum upgrading program. Clearly, upgrading and regularization is not an efficient way of providing basic infrastructure

Table 5.10 Costs of Providing Housing Infrastructure in Regular Land Development and Slum Upgrading Programs

	Regular land development	Slum upgrading (normal)	Slum upgrading (complex)
		Percent	
Water	10.6	6.0	7.4
Sewerage	19.9	20.1	17.7
Drainage	10.0	24.2	29.6
Paving	47.1	31.3	18.4
Retaining structures	n.a.	11.5	25.2
Electricity	3.6	5.9	1.7
Lighting	8.8	1.1	0.2
Total	*100*	*100*	*100*
Total (US$)	1,667	4,143	12,757
Cost relative to land developing dwelling (times)		2.5	7.7

n.a. = not applicable.
Source: Abiko et al. (2007).

to poor households in the long run. Providing infrastructure through a slum upgrading program is almost 2.5 times more expensive than providing it through a regular land development program. The multiple increases to almost 8 times if the slum upgrading program is complex. Seen in this light, it makes sense for local and national governments to develop strategies and subsidy programs to increase the supply of affordable urban land (given that there is plenty of vacant land in the region) and prevent the formation of slums, instead of urbanizing the existing ones.

The most effective and sustainable approach to enhance the efficiency and efficacy of urban land and housing markets in developing countries is likely to be an enabling approach (World Bank 1993; Dowall and Clarke 1996; Angel 2000). Such an approach promotes the expansion of serviced urban land, provision of infrastructure, access to credit for construction and purchase, realistic land use regulations that reflect willingness and ability to pay for housing, and access to building materials and construction services. Most countries have focused their housing policies and programs on either direct provision or subsidies to buy finished homes. With few notable exceptions, they have forgotten interventions and regulation reform that would improve the functioning of land markets (see chapter 9).

Trying to solve the problem of informal housing once it is established is more complex and more expensive than preventing it. Neighborhood and slum upgrading programs are still necessary to tackle the current stock of informality. But the agenda of those responsible for improving the urbanization of the region should include policies aimed at preventing the formation of slums.

In Need of a Policy Overhaul

The evidence suggests that land in the periphery of many Latin America cities can be developed to provide affordable housing for low-income groups. This implies a trade-off for households between accessibility and location for cheaper housing. To ease the burden of distance on the poorest households, good public transportation systems and roads are needed. Public investments have a strong role to play in potentially lowering the transportation costs that low-income households must pay to live in the periphery of cities. Investments in mass transit systems, good roads and arteries, and good city planning are key to ensuring that distance does not become a burden for middle-and low-income households in growing Latin American cities.

Current land regulations are constraining the supply of developed urban land and the use of vacant land in more central city locations. Innovative programs are needed to create incentives for land developers to create mixed-use spaces, such as the Macroproyectos program in Colombia, where high-quality and affordable houses are provided on a large scale, along with access to services such as education facilities, hospitals, and green spaces (see box 5.2).

Box 5.2 Colombia's Macroproyectos: A Successful Case of Low-Income Housing in a Mixed-Use Setting

The government of Colombia established the Macroproyectos de Interés Social Nacional (MISN) program to enhance access to low-income housing in Colombia through a public-private model for land and housing development. The objective is not only to overcome the country's quantitative housing shortage, but also to provide high-quality dwellings and surroundings in a nonsegregated urban environment. By 2014, 1 million homes are expected to be built as part of the MISN.

Macroproyectos are big urban projects that provide affordable housing with access to running water, electricity, proper sewage, and other infrastructure, and that is close to schools, libraries, hospitals, parks, sports facilities, community centers, and public transportation. Macroproyectos also offer an opportunity to stimulate the development of manufacturing and retail industries in new areas, and to generate new employment opportunities for the residents of the projects.

A total of 30 Macroproyectos are planned; 13 are in the identification stage, 7 are ready to begin, and 10 are underway in the cities of Barranquilla, Buenaventura, Cali, Cartagena, Manizales, Medellín, Neiva, Pereira, and Soacha. As of September 2011, Macroproyectos had urbanized 181 hectares of land (of the 1,800 that will be urbanized through the first 10 projects) and built 11,000 homes (of the 23,000 planned). The target of the 10 projects currently underway is 127,000 homes, of which 60 percent will be targeted toward low-income families.

The biggest Macroproyecto in the country is Ciudad Verde in Soacha in Bogota. It plans to urbanize 328 hectares of land: 50 percent will be used for social housing; 17 percent for nonsocial housing (adding up to nearly 42,000 new homes); 22 percent for retail and services; and 11 percent for private and public uses (schools, libraries, hospitals, and sports facilities). There will be 57 hectares of green space, more than 170,000 square meters of paved streets, and 9 kilometers of bike lanes.

Between 2006 and 2007, the private owners of the 26 parcels of land that currently constitute Ciudad Verde joined together and accepted the offer of one of the most important construction companies in Colombia (Amarilo S.A) and eight allied firms to put together an MISN there. The land was underutilized back then. However, its privileged location (in the metropolitan area of Bogota) and the housing shortage in Soacha provided the right incentives for the private sector to become interested.

Instead of using the land to establish high-income housing solutions and retail only, Amarilo S.A. decided to develop the land through an MISN. By opting for an MISN, the developer benefits from an expedited procedure to convert rural land into urban land, significantly reducing the time and number of steps needed to develop it. An MISN requires that the project service land to build at least enough social housing units to house 1 percent of the households in the municipality where it is established. In the case of Ciudad Verde, the private owners of the land transferred their parcels to a trusteeship, which includes Fondo Nacional de Vivienda (FONVIVIENDA). In turn, they receive a percentage of the profits of the project, in accordance with their participation. Ciudad Verde also includes some public land that Amarilo S.A. bought from the municipality of Soacha. However, those areas can be used only for public amenities that the residents would otherwise not be able to enjoy.

The Macroproyectos model relies on large-scale production and profitable mixed uses for the land. It combines social housing with retail, industry, and private investments through cross-subsidies between final land users. It would have been virtually impossible to provide affordable social housing in Ciudad Verde (where the cheapest new home costs a little less than US$20,000) with high-quality surroundings had the project been entirely residential. However, thanks to the location of retail, industry, and services, which are more profitable land uses compared to social housing, private sector investors can be attracted to develop the projects and include the construction of low-cost dwelling units in a desirable location.

Sources: Ciudad Verde (2011), Henao Padilla (2011), Ministerio de Ambiente, Vivienda y Desarrollo Territorial (2011), and Presidencia de Colombia (2011).

Many governments are still focused on treating the symptoms rather than the causes of the poor housing outcomes of the region. An example of this is to respond to irregular land development with titling and slum upgrading programs, instead of confronting the regulation failures, lack of investment in trunk infrastructure, and constraints to credit and enforcement problems that attract or push households toward informal land developments. Both a well-functioning housing sector and an appropriate institutional, legal, and regulatory framework that govern the sector are essential to prevent slum formation (Acioly 2009).

Addressing the regulation problems that the region faces requires citizen engagement, compromise, and political will to put the needs of the ones that have less first. Countries need to strengthen the regulatory and technical advisory role of higher levels of government. In Latin America and the Caribbean, land and construction regulation are strongly influenced by local governments. Local elites or wealthier neighbors often exert influence on local governments to enact regulations that restrict land and housing supply for low-income households. National housing ministries need to act in the interest of all people and play an active and constructive oversight and advisory role in the enacting of land and building codes.

6

A Construction Industry in Need of Remodeling

The supply of housing units for low-income households is limited in Latin America. In many cases, families located at the bottom of the income distribution cannot find an affordable housing solution in the private market. In many cities, the bulk of new homes are sold to the wealthiest socioeconomic segments of the population. In six of nineteen cities surveyed, the cheapest dwelling costs far more than what low-income households can afford: more than US$35,000, on average. In three of those cities (Buenos Aires, Caracas, and Santiago), the average price is higher than $40,000 (see chapter 3).

The distortion of the housing market has been driven by failures of both land and capital markets, as well as problems in the building sector (see chapter 3; and Lizarralde and Root 2008). This chapter focuses on the construction industry. It examines the extent to which the organization of the construction industry, as well as the evolution and incidence of construction costs and technologies, make houses unavailable to or unaffordable for low-income groups.

Forces affecting both housing supply and demand drive the private sector's willingness and ability to deliver low-income housing. Demand for privately built inexpensive houses may be lacking in countries where low-income groups do not have access to mortgages. Moreover, the high social value of owning a home in Latin America might encourage the less fortunate to turn to informal housing, mainly by building or adding to their homes gradually (Ferguson and Smets 2010). These constraints on demand lower the scale of production to the point that contractors and developers have little incentive to serve that segment of society. To make matters worse, regional or local characteristics in each country conspire against the development of construction technologies capable of providing cheap housing solutions. The pattern of and preference for conventional construction techniques, power of the cement/concrete industry, availability of capital, relative returns of different housing market segments, and macroeconomic situation hamper innovation in the construction sector. Such innovation, in turn, could lower costs enough to provide the incentives needed for businesses to serve the poorest sectors. Thus, solutions that address both housing supply and demand are needed to provide affordable housing units for low-income groups.

Construction Costs

The cost of a privately built dwelling has several components including construction costs, land, basic infrastructure, and administrative expenses. Construction costs (materials and labor) are one of the main determinants of the overall dwelling cost, since they are more sensitive to the ups and downs of the local economy than other components such as administrative expenses or the provision of basic infrastructure.

Construction costs constitute the main component of housing costs.[1] Almost two-thirds (61.3 percent) of the sales price of a new private dwelling can be attributed to construction costs: 39.8 percent for materials and 22.1 percent for labor (see chapter 5).

Obviously, construction costs vary according to the type of home, ranging from social housing with bare-bones basic finishes, to average-income houses with standard finishes, to lavish high-income housing with luxury finishes. Table 6.1 shows the relative construction costs of a single family dwelling with either luxury or standard finishes compared to an economical model for selected cities in Latin America.

Luxury finishes cost 2.2 times more than economy finishes, on average. The difference between standard finishes and economical ones is greatest in Brazilian cities.

How do construction costs affect housing affordability for low-income households? Begin by considering the share of construction costs in the total price of the cheapest dwellings offered by the private sector (see figure 6.1). On average, construction costs for economical finishes account for almost 70 percent of the price of the cheapest housing solution offered by the private market. Clearly, construction costs can price a home beyond the reach of many low-income households.

Another way to analyze the impact of construction costs on affordability is to examine them as a percentage of city median income (table 6.2). Construction costs for social housing (by square meters with

Table 6.1 Construction Costs by Type of Finishes in Select Cities (Economical Finish Type = 100)

Country	City	Finish type	
		Standard	Luxury
Argentina	Buenos Aires	113	144
Brazil	Sao Paulo	127	173
	Ribeirao Preto	77	110
	Ilheus	249	337
	Jequie	249	337
Chile	Santiago	118	200
Colombia	Valledupar	109	152
Ecuador	Guayaquil	149	205
El Salvador	San Salvador	195	305
Jamaica	Kingston	115	127
Mexico	Mexico City	136	204
	Guadalajara	133	224
	Tijuana	157	320
Uruguay	Montevideo	125	220
Latin America and the Caribbean[a]		*147*	*218*

[a] Simple average of select cities.
Note: Data are for a single family dwelling.
Source: Authors' calculations based on Artiga de Soundy et al. (2010).

economical finishes) account for about 5 percent of the median annual income in a sample of Latin American cities; they range between almost 18 percent in Kingston, Jamaica to less than 1 percent in Ilheus and Jequie, Brazil.

Since construction costs are the main component of housing costs in Latin America, understanding their evolution in both absolute and relative terms is important to determine the impact they might have on housing affordability for low-income groups. An increase in construction costs not only increases the price of finished dwellings (Potepan 1996) but also reduces residential construction (Somerville 1999).

Figure 6.2a reflects the change in real construction costs in some cities and countries in Latin America from 1990 to 2010. Construction costs rose by 13 percent at the city level and 5 percent at the national level from 2000 to 2010 in real terms.[2] Those increases came from a boost in both real material and labor costs, which rose 8 and 14 percent between 2000 and 2010 at the city level, and 15 and 9 percent at the country level, respectively

Figure 6.1 Construction Costs as a Share of the Total Price of the Cheapest Housing Solution, Select Cities, 2010 (Percent of Total Price)

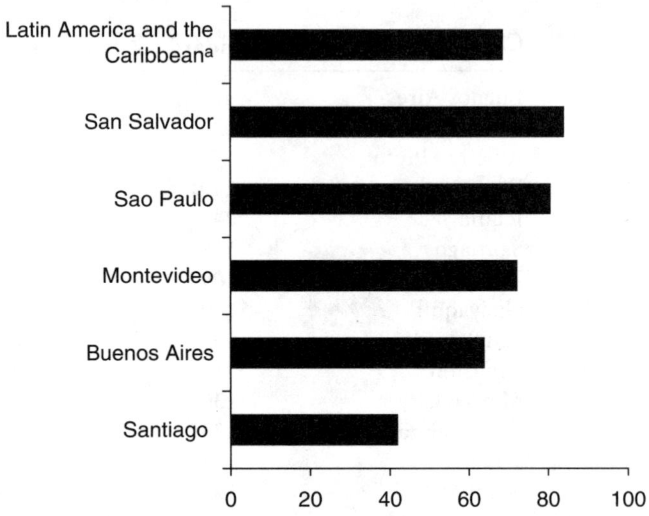

[a] Simple average for selected cities.
Note: Argentina (Buenos Aires), Brazil (Sao Paulo), Chile (Santiago), El Salvador (San Salvador), and Uruguay (Montevideo).
Source: Authors' calculations based on Artiga de Soundy et al. (2010).

(see figures 6.2b and 6.2c). Real construction costs rose in most of the countries and cities in the sample. In Brazil, construction costs ballooned almost 20 percent (material costs rose by 23 percent, and labor costs by 15 percent). In Buenos Aires, costs soared by 76 percent.

This increase in real construction costs occurred as the region was growing rapidly. The especially steep rise in construction costs in Argentina (Buenos Aires) and Brazil is in line with the belief that they are two of the emerging economies at greatest risk of overheating. This belief is borne out by the emerging market overheating index prepared by the *Economist* based on inflation, GDP growth, unemployment, credit growth, real interest rates, and change in current account balance. Argentina ranks first and Brazil ranks second in terms of greatest risk.[3]

Rising construction costs in the region over the last 10 years have contributed to the affordability gap in housing, particularly in countries or cities where construction costs have outpaced wages, such as Buenos Aires. The ratio between the two provides a measure of how many square

Table 6.2 Construction Costs and Household Income, Select Cities, 2010 (Construction Costs by Square Meter for a Dwelling with Eonomical Finishes, Percent of Household Annual Median Income)

City	Materials	Labor	Total
Kingston	n.d.	n.d.	17.8
Valledupar	8.8	1.7	10.5
Tijuana	n.d.	n.d.	4.7
Buenos Aires	3.4	2.6	6.0
Montevideo	2.3	2.2	4.5
Guaruja	n.d.	n.d.	n.d.
Sao Paulo	2.4	1.5	3.9
Guadalajara	n.d.	n.d.	3.6
Mexico City	n.d.	n.d.	3.4
San Salvador	1.4	0.8	2.2
Guayaquil	1.9	0.9	2.8
Ribeirao Preto	4.2	1.0	5.2
Santiago	n.d.	n.d.	1.8
Ilheus	0.5	0.1	0.7
Jequie	0.4	0.1	0.5
Latin America and the Caribbean[a]	*2.8*	*1.2*	*4.8*

[a] Simple average for select cities.
n.d. = no data.
Notes: Data are by square meter for a single family dwelling. Argentina (Buenos Aires), Brazil (Ilheus, Jecquie, Sao Paulo, and Ribeirao Preto), Chile (Santiago), Colombia (Valledpuar), Ecuador (Guayaquil), El Salvador (San Salvador), Jamaica (Kingston), Mexico (Guadalajara, Mexico City, and Tijuana), and Uruguay (Montevideo).
Source: Authors' calculations based on Artiga de Soundy et al. (2010).

meters can be bought with one month's wage. Data showing the average wage purchasing power in terms of housing is available for Buenos Aires from 1993 to 1998 and from 2003 to 2009. On average, construction costs have increased more than income during the last 10 years. The purchasing power of formal workers in terms of housing decreased 24 percent; for informal workers, the decline reached 47 percent (Cristini, Moya, and Bermúdez 2011).

Given the relatively high and increasing construction costs, innovations in construction techniques that allow houses to be built more quickly, economically, efficiently, and in a more environment-friendly

Figure 6.2 Construction Costs in Select Latin American and Caribbean Cities and Countries (Base Year 2000 = 100)

a. Overall Costs

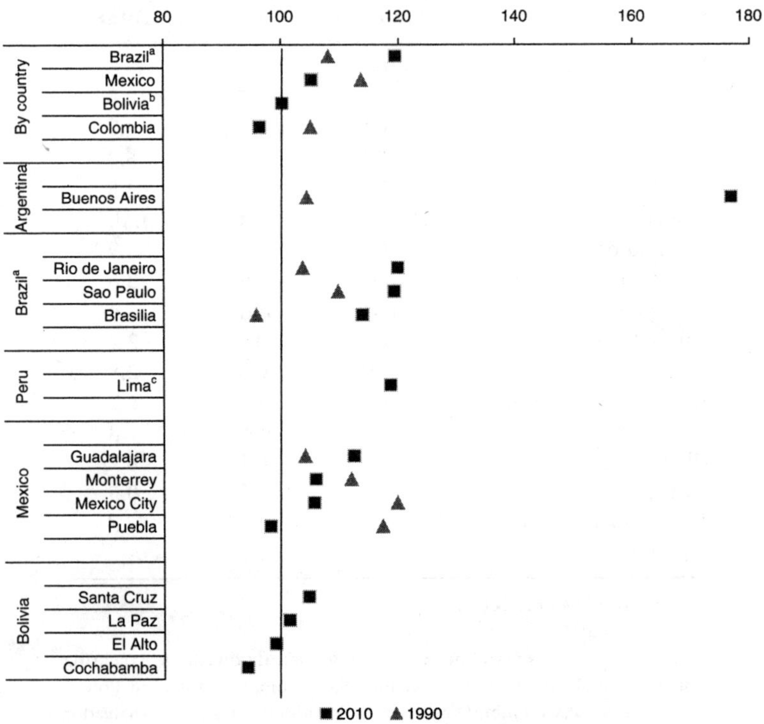

[a] The last year available for Brazil is 2009.
[b] Data for Bolivia are for 2002 and 2007.
[c] Data for Lima are available from 1999 onward, with 1994 = 100.

manner have great potential to ease housing affordability constraints in the region. Conventional construction techniques (using bricks, concrete, or cement blocks as materials and having workers on site) must give way to new, innovative technologies that use greener materials and can be prefabricated. The transition is not expected to be easy given the trends in traditional construction. In the majority of countries, even in social housing, the traditional construction technique is the most common. In Chile, Honduras, and Peru more than 60 percent of social housing is built with traditional construction techniques. In Colombia and Guatemala, around 70 percent of social housing is built using structural masonry. In Mexico

Figure 6.2 Continued

b. Material Costs

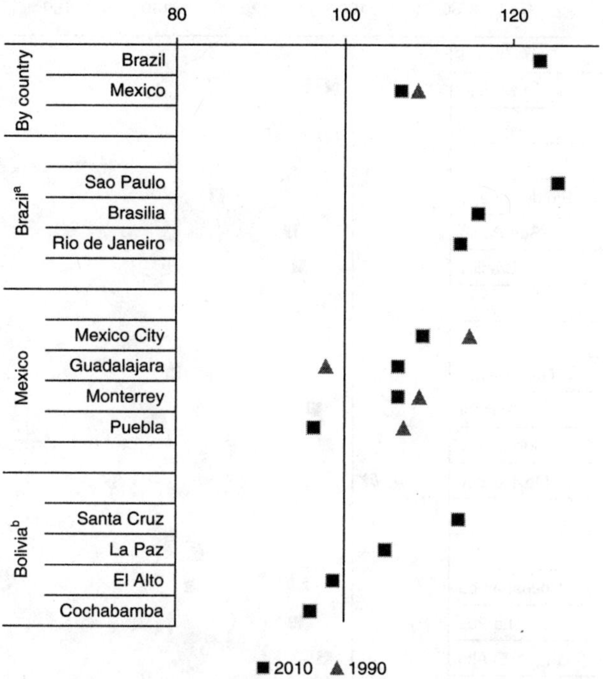

[a] Separations of costs by components for Brazil are available from 1994 onward. The last available data is for 2009.

[b] Data for Bolivia are for 2002 and 2007.

and Costa Rica, on the other hand, an average of 60 percent of social housing is preconstructed (Torres and Torres 2009).

The Nuts and Bolts of the Construction Sector in Latin America

The construction sector in the region displays some peculiarities that affect the private sector's willingness and ability to provide low-income housing. The main characteristics that compromise the provision of low-income units are the size of the businesses that make up the industry, its labor intensiveness, and its openness to global markets and technological

Figure 6.2 Continued

c. Labor Costs

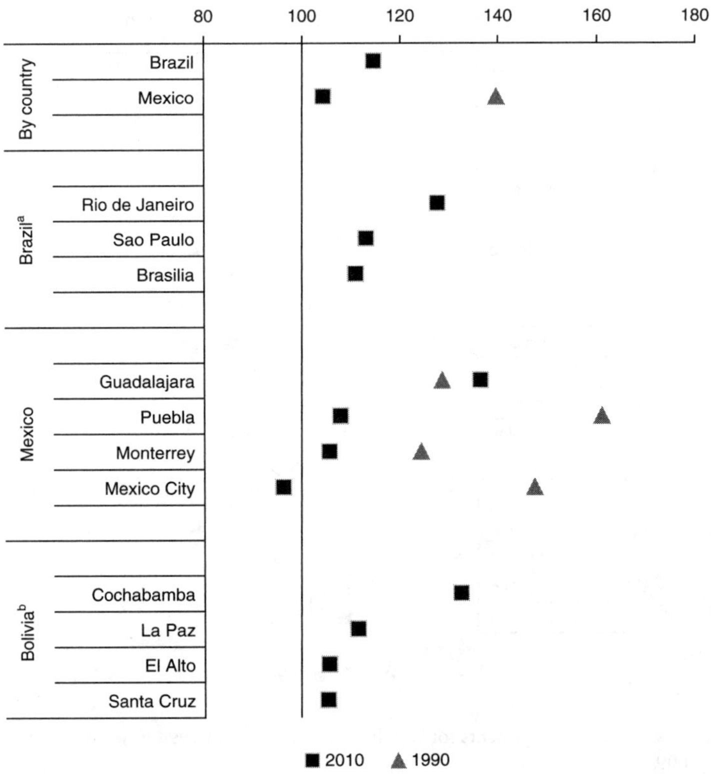

[a] Separations of costs by components for Brazil is available from 1994 onward. The last available data is for 2009.

[b] Data for Bolivia are for 2002 and 2007.

Sources: Authors' calculations based on national construction statistics. Argentina (INDEC 2011); Bolivia (INE 2011); Brazil (IBGE 2011); Colombia (DANE 2011); Mexico (INEGI 2011); and Peru (INEI 2011).

innovation. Table 6.3 summarizes the characteristics that distinguish the construction industry.

While many industries are becoming more globalized, the construction sector is not. The building industry remains essentially local, and the labor that it employs is still driven by local legislation and institutions (Mayagoitia 2009). This feature makes the industry more vulnerable to the ups and downs of the local economy than other sectors.

Table 6.3 Special Characteristics of the Construction Industry

Nature of the projects	Characteristics of the industry	Challenges that it faces
They are unique and cannot be duplicated They are not permanent They are restricted by time, cost, and quality Their development involves different players, usually in conflict Many decisions about their execution are solely based on the experience of those in charge	Fragmented with many specialties Competitive and with high failure indices Easily affected by recession periods Low investment in R&D Participants do not share information Slow to adopt new technologies Local	Increase in environmental and safety regulations New materials and technologies Limited budget and time but high quality demand Increase in costs Lack of skilled workers

Source: Mayagoitia (2009).

There is strong substitution between capital and labor in the sector. Construction is more labor-intensive in developing countries than in developed countries because of the relative costs of capital and labor. While high-income countries account for 77 percent of the total world production of the construction industry, they employ only 26 percent of the workers in the industry (Mayagoitia 2009).

Developing countries depend heavily on the practice of hiring labor through intermediaries. In Latin America, developers in the housing sector usually hire an intermediary or subcontractor who recruits the workers who actually work on the project. The developer has no direct relationship with the workers. This arrangement provides flexibility for firms. By hiring workers through a subcontractor, firms need not incur the fixed costs of paying wages when there is no project in place, and can avoid the costs of complying with labor legislation such as providing vacation time and social security payments. This practice has led to extensive fragmentation of the industry. In most countries in the region, the field of residential construction is made up of small companies (in terms of the number of workers employed) that do not stay in business more than five years. In Colombia, for example, 50 percent of firms stay in the market for less than two years, and 70 percent stay for less than five (Torres and Torres 2009). On average, micro or small companies account for more than 70 percent of the businesses in the industry (Suárez 2011). The sales value of firms is also quite small. In Colombia, 70.9 percent of the businesses have sales values of US$500,000 or less (Torres and Torres 2009).

Small and medium businesses not only lead the sector as sources of employment but also as drivers of demand for construction materials. In Mexico, for instance, small construction companies and self-builders consume some 60 percent of the cement produced for the domestic market (Mayagoitia 2009). In Argentina, small companies with an average of 3 workers employ 20 percent of the construction workforce; medium-sized ones (with between 10 and 100 workers) employ another 50 percent (Cristini, Moya, and Bermúdez 2011). In Brazil, companies with fewer than 10 workers employ 13.2 percent of the construction workforce, and firms with between 10 and 50 workers employ another 25.5 percent.

Small companies usually build apartment buildings and suburban subdivisions, and independent contractors build detached houses (Cristini, Moya, and Bermúdez 2011). On the other hand, large building companies, in general, have shifted from residential construction to public infrastructure or commercial construction. In many countries, those companies have also switched from providing goods to providing services. They look for clients and business opportunities that are later serviced by the small companies that they subcontract.

To understand the structure of the sector in the region, it is important to look at the concentration and the dispersion of the construction industry. Table 6.4 shows both indicators for a sample of cities from Latin America and the Caribbean. Industrial concentration is defined as the percentage of new housing units in the formal sector built by the five largest developers (public or private). Industrial dispersion is defined as the number of residential construction companies registered in the city per thousand inhabitants. In the largest cities in the sample, such as Buenos Aires, Santiago, and Sao Paulo, industrial concentration is relatively low, with less than 30 percent of homes produced by the five largest firms, on average. That is not the case for the smaller cities.

In terms of industrial dispersion, there are on average 0.3 residential construction companies per thousand inhabitants. These figures clearly set a lower bound, since informality in the construction sector remains very high in Latin America. Many small companies or independent contractors are not formally registered. In Argentina, for example, in 2004, firms in the informal sector that did not have permits or licenses produced 40 percent of total housing (Cristini, Moya, and Bermúdez 2011).

Table 6.4 Concentration and Dispersion of the Construction Industry in Select Cities in Latin America and the Caribbean, 2010

City	Industrial concentration[a]	Industrial dispersion[b]
Buenos Aires	15.2	0.9
Guadalajara	36.2	0.1
Guayaquil	70.0	0.7
Ilheus	65.0	0.0
Jequie	18.9	0.5
Kingston	78.3	0.2
Mexico City	40.3	0
Montevideo	n.d.	0.1
Ribeirao Preto	n.d.	1.9
San Salvador	21.3	0
Santiago	19.8	0
Sao Paulo	26.1	0
Tijuana	71.3	0.1
Valledupar	93.1	0
Latin American and Caribbean cities[c]	*46.3*	*0.3*

[a] Percent of new housing units in the formal sector built by the five largest developers.
[b] Number of residential construction companies registered in the city per thousand inhabitants.
[c] Simple average of select cities.
n.d. = no data.
Note: Argentina (Buenos Aires), Brazil (Ilheus, Jequie, Ribeirao Preto, and Sao Paulo), Chile (Santiago), Colombia (Valledupar), Ecuador (Guayaquil), El Salvador (San Salvador), Jamaica (Kingston), Mexico (Mexico City, Guadalajara, and Tijuana), and Uruguay (Montevideo).
Source: Authors' calculations based on Artiga de Soundy et al. (2010).

Moreover, as noted, in many cases large companies are legally responsible for a project, but they end up subcontracting the actual work to different smaller companies or independent contractors.

As for the workforce, in general, construction workers have low levels of education. In Mexico, for example, around 10 percent of the workers have no formal vocational training, and around 55 percent have only a primary school education (Mayagoitia 2009). Around 95 percent of the workers in the developing world acquire their building skills informally. Even though professional schools exist, many workers and developers still see formal instruction as an unnecessary expenditure. This presents a problem, because as clients demand higher-quality housing products and as market demands shift the way construction processes are carried out, it becomes hard to find qualified labor.

Both workers and developers have good reasons for not investing in training. For workers, their high rotation from job to job, which usually translates into lack of stability and a high risk of unemployment, discourages them from spending time and money on training. Similarly, developers worry that workers may leave for another job or another employer. Moreover, in the short run, training costs money, which could harm their competitiveness in a market that is highly competitive at the bottom.

To sum up, the construction sector is highly labor-intensive. Workers have little formal training. The sector is also fragmented at the bottom. Small companies make up the largest share of the sector in many countries. Many firms are informal. These characteristics hamper both productivity and innovation in the sector (see IDB 2010a). Evidence for the region shows that between 1990 and 2005, average annual labor productivity growth in the construction sector (which includes residential and nonresidential constructions) was lower than for the majority of other sectors. Labor productivity in the construction sector grew on average 1 percent per year compared to 5 percent for the mining sector, a little more than 4 percent in public utilities, around 3.5 percent for agriculture and a little less than 2.5 percent in manufacturing. Within countries in Latin America, average annual labor productivity in the construction sector also grew slower than in most of the other sectors of the economy (the only exception being Peru). In fact, in Bolivia, Colombia and Mexico, annual labor productivity growth was negative for the period 1990–2005 (IDB 2010a).

Tied Up in Red Tape

Regulation has a strong role to play in the construction industry to protect health and safety, maximize positive externalities and minimize negative neighborhood externalities, guarantee minimum housing and neighborhood standards, and provide incentives for green housing. However, excessive regulation and red tape can multiply costs for the formal construction industry, reducing the profitability of low-margin projects—such as small-scale low-income housing—and the affordability of those developments for low-income households. The time it takes to get a construction permit and the cost related to obtaining a legal dwelling are sometimes the tipping point at which the less fortunate decide to go to the informal market for a housing solution.

Table 6.5 presents the legal costs associated with the construction of a single detached dwelling as a percentage of the property value, as well as the time (in months) that it takes to secure a construction permit,

Table 6.5 Legal Costs and Time Needed to Obtain Construction Permits, Select Latin American and Caribbean Cities, 2010

City	Legal cost (percent of dwelling price)	Construction permits time (months)
Buenos Aires	1.0	6.0
Guadalajara	8.0	1.1
Guayaquil	6.4	4.0
Ilheus	3.5	1.0
Jecquie	3.2	1.0
Kingston	7.3	5.0
Mexico City	5.6	1.5
Montevideo	12.7	0.3
Ribeirao Preto	9.2	1.0
San Salvador	2.0	3.0
Santiago	0.5	1.3
Sao Paulo	7.9	1.0
Tijuana	7.5	1.5
Valledupar	3.3	n.d.
Latin American and Caribbean cities[a]	*5.6*	*2.1*

[a] Simple average of select cities.
n.d. = no data.
Note: Argentina (Buenos Aires), Brazil (Ilheus, Jequie, Ribeirao Preto, and Sao Paulo), Chile (Santiago), Colombia (Valledupar), Ecuador (Guayaquil), El Salvador (San Salvador), Jamaica (Kingston), Mexico (Mexico City, Guadalajara, and Tijuana), and Uruguay (Montevideo).
Source: Authors' calculations based on Artiga de Soundy et al. (2010).

for a sample of Latin American cities. On average, legal costs represent almost 5.6 percent of the property value, and it takes 2.2 months to land a construction permit. The legal cost is highest in Montevideo (almost 13 percent of the property value), but it takes less time to get a construction permit there (less than one week if all the documentation is in order). On the other hand, it takes the longest to secure a construction permit (6 months) in Buenos Aires, but the legal costs of constructing a house are not even 1 percent of the property value.

Table 6.6 shows the cost of dealing with construction permits in terms of time and relative to per capita income in the region. Comparable international data are available only for commercial buildings, and are used as a proxy for residential construction. Regulation costs are measured as the number of procedures that must be followed to build a warehouse legally and the time (in days) and cost required to complete each procedure (as a percentage of per capita income). The average cost for the region is almost

Table 6.6 Effort, Time, and Money Required to Obtain Construction Permits in Latin American and Caribbean Countries, 2009

Country	Number of procedures	Time (days)	Total cost (percent of annual income per capita)
Antigua and Barbuda	10	134	26
Argentina	25	365	182
Belize	17	181	33
Bolivia	8	91	17
Brazil	14	249	96
Chile	17	469	47
Colombia	17	155	95
Costa Rica	10	79	484
Dominica	20	189	210
Dominican Republic	9	165	13
Ecuador	14	216	124
El Salvador	16	128	269
Grenada	33	157	172
Guatemala	8	123	28
Guyana	19	202	638
Haiti	8	195	44
Honduras	9	1,179	599
Jamaica	14	107	291
Mexico	8	145	387
Nicaragua	11	138	474
Panama	16	218	537
Paraguay	18	128	123
Peru	12	291	333
St. Kitts and Nevis	11	139	4
St. Lucia	7	125	29
St. Vincent and the Grenadines	8	112	6
Trinidad and Tobago	17	297	4
Uruguay	27	234	107
Venezuela	10	381	345
Latin America and the Caribbean[a]	*14*	*227*	*197*

[a] Simple average of select countries.

Source: World Bank (2011a, c).

Figure 6.3 Cost of Construction Permits and Income Per Capita, 2009

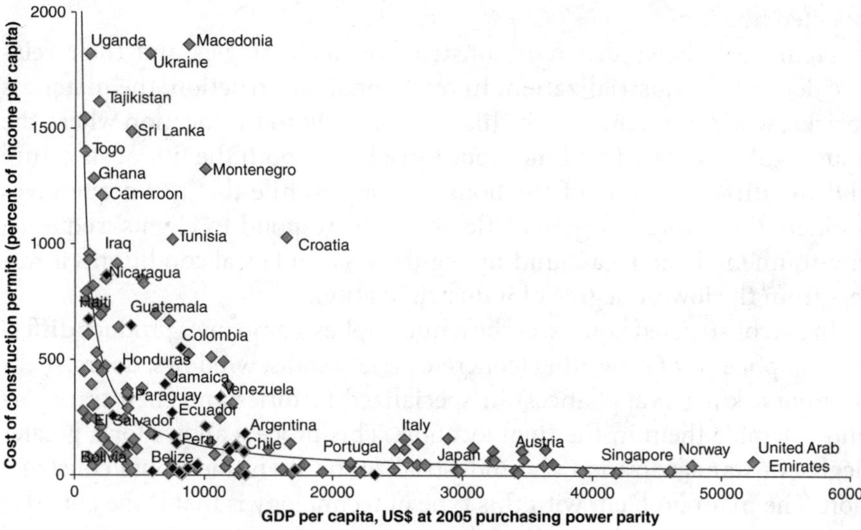

Source: World Bank (2011a, c).

2 years of per capita income. Guyana suffers the highest cost for construction permits; obtaining a permit there requires almost 6 years of per capita income. Figure 6.3 shows the relationship between the cost of construction permits (as a percentage of income per capita) and GDP per capita in 2009 for countries around the world. In nearly half of the countries in Latin America, the costs of construction permits exceed what would be expected given their income level. Some of the countries with the highest costs for construction permits given their GDP per capita, such as Ecuador, Nicaragua, and Venezuela, have made the least progress in terms of correcting the quantitative deficit in housing (see table 2.5).

An Alternative to Bricks and Mortar

One promising method whereby the housing industry can correct deficiencies, reduce costs, and increase productivity and scale is by industrializing construction. In taking such steps, housing would be following in the footsteps of the manufacturing sector. Industrialized construction ranges from the construction of readymade complete dwellings or rooms that can later be transported and assembled in a particular location, to the production of different dwelling elements that can then be assembled with other prefabricated elements and conventional materials on site (preconstructed houses).

Figure 6.4 shows different construction technologies and their relative degree of industrialization. In traditional construction, the materials (bricks, wood, cement, and the like) are brought to the location where the house will be situated and the labor force builds both the initial structure and the different units of the house on site. While this technique gives builders the greatest degree of flexibility to respond to clients' requests, environmental and local building regulations, and local conditions, it suffers from the lowest degree of industrialization.

In preconstructed houses, as the name implies, companies produce different components of a dwelling (concrete panels, walls, windows, doors, bathroom and kitchen appliances) in specialized factories and then transport and assemble them in the final location. This process allows for a greater degree of standardization and industrialization than traditional construction. The main problem with this type of technology is that if the concrete panels are not assembled in the right way on site, then the quality of the final product suffers. This technology offers lesser flexibility; producers must stick to standard designs since it is quite costly to change the machinery

Figure 6.4 Construction Technologies

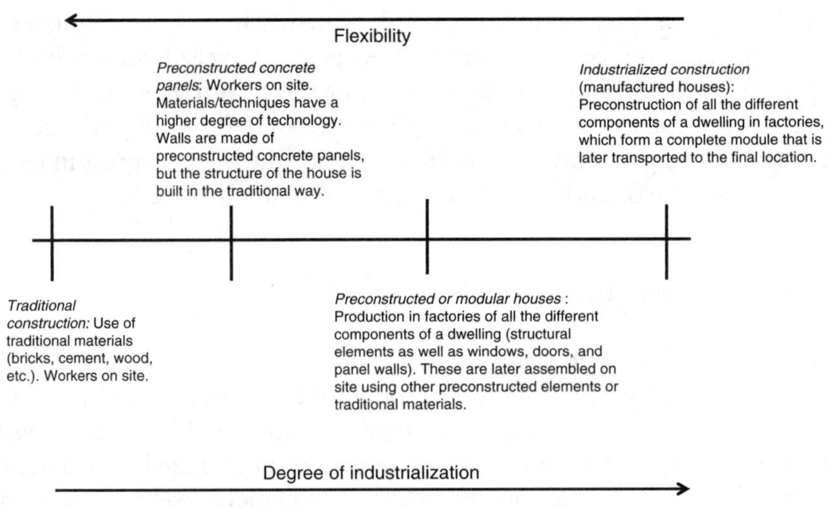

Source: Authors' compilation.

that produces the components. Therefore, consumers lose in terms of variety and flexibility, but gain in terms of costs. Other benefits of this method include greater production speed, better quality, and less waste.

The highest degree of industrialization occurs with manufactured construction. Entire units are fully prepared in factories using wood, concrete panels, or steel. They are then pieced together on site. Even though some processes must be performed on site such as digging and pouring the foundations, connecting to basic services, and the actual placement of the house, the construction time and the number of workers on site are greatly reduced, thereby saving money.

As with any other process or technology, industrialized construction offers both advantages and disadvantages (see table 6.7). The advantages of industrially manufactured houses include the high speed of construction, better control of the process, larger-scale production (which reduces the cost of labor and materials), lower financing costs, and a lower environmental impact of construction (Duffau 2011). Disadvantages include the inflexibility of the project, the inability to modify modules once they have been produced, the higher risk associated with the fixed costs of running the factories where the components are constructed, higher transportation and R&D costs, and the potentially negative effect on future property values because of the inflexibility of some designs.

Table 6.8 highlights the differences between traditional construction and modern industrialized construction for civil construction in the developing world. Differences include dissimilarities in materials, labor, equipment, capital, and transportation of components, as well as type of production and organization of the process.

Modern technologies are relatively more complex. Each dwelling part is produced separately in different production lines. Each production line has its own group of technicians and production times. Therefore, the need to control and administer the different processes to keep up with market demand is higher.

Baby Steps for Industrialized Construction in Latin America

Producing houses with industrial processes is still in its infancy in Latin America. Very few, if any, social housing dwelling projects have been based entirely on innovative technologies; in general only select parts are

Table 6.7 Advantages and Disadvantages of Industrialized Construction

Advantages	Disadvantages
Faster speed of construction: The production of components is fast since they are mass-produced using a production line instead of being built in stages on site.	*Construction of materials could be more rapid than plot preparation:* It might take longer to service the plot or comply with local regulations that complete production of the dwelling components.
Reduced exposure to weather conditions: Factories where the different components are produced are not exposed to weather or terrain conditions.	*Inflexibility of the project:* Once the modules are produced in the factories, it is impossible to modify them. A poor specification at the initial stages of the construction process will have unintended consequences for all the houses produced with that component, thereby increasing the costs.
Better control of processes: Industrialized construction allows for better control of inventories and therefore reduces costs related to waste of materials and storage of unused materials. Quality checks are also cheaper since the processes by which the different components are produced are standard.	*High fixed costs and business risk:* The construction industry is highly volatile; the effects of that volatility are higher in industrialized construction than in traditional construction due to the fixed costs of permanently running the factories.
Low labor cost and increase in productivity: Industrialized construction requires fewer workers on site and on the production lines.	*Higher expenditure in R&D*
Lower cost of materials: The higher scale of production increases the negotiating power of individual developers for the cost of inputs.	*Availability of labor force:* In countries where the availability of workers in the construction industry is high, there might be an incentive to keep building in a traditional way.
Lower financial cost: As construction times are lower, the period for which credit is needed (to pay for wages, equipment, etc.) is lower as well.	*Higher transportation costs:* There is a tradeoff between lower labor costs associated with construction of components in factories in lower-wage regions and the cost to transport those modules to the final location.

Lower probability of accidents *Lower environmental impact:* Materials waste and emission of carbon dioxide are lower on site. *Rationalization of constructive processes:* This new method requires a better planning strategy and reduces improvisation, which in turn increases efficiency. *Community impact:* There is less impact on local residents during construction.	*Limited focus on consumers' taste:* The uniform mass production of houses (necessary to decrease construction costs) makes their design less attractive to potential consumers. *Quality and regulation:* To regulate the standardization of the products and to guarantee their quality, strict rules must be followed by the different agents of the production process. *Higher financial cost in the acquisition of a finished house:* Mortgages to buy a manufactured or preconstructed house usually carry a higher interest rate and shorter terms since financial institutions believe that those houses have a shorter life span and think buyers generally have lower incomes. *Effect on property values:* The experience in the United States shows that the resale market for manufactured houses is still weak. Moreover, the maintenance and expansion costs are higher for manufactured houses than for traditional ones, which decreases the property value at the time of sale.

Sources: Authors' compilations based on Duffau (2011) and Parliamentary Office of Science and Technology (2003).

Table 6.8 Differences between Traditional and Modern Construction Technologies

Aspect	Construction technologies: Traditional	Construction technologies: Modern/industrialized construction
Materials	• Simple	• Sophisticated
	• Raw materials are acquired or produced locally	• Raw materials come from different locations and are produced off-site
	• Use of a few elements	• Preconstruction of components
Labor	• Intensive	• Partially substituted by equipment
	• Self-construction or small contractors	• Outsourced
Energy use	• Limited	• Intensive
	• Not commercialized and local	• Commercialized
Capital use	• Limited	• Intensive
Equipment	• Simple tools	• Specialized tools
Transportation	• Men and animals	• Specialized machines
Production	• Small scale	• Large scale
	• Monitored by the user	• Monitored by specialists
	• Individual decisions	• Centralized decisions
Organization	• Simple	• Complex, partially done on the premises

Source: Abiko (2003).

industrialized, not the whole process. Moreover, projects that use this type of technology do not invest in R&D but rather copy the methods used in other parts of the world.

Yet the approach offers significant advantages. In Argentina, in the city of Barrenqueras, in the province of El Chaco, a pilot study shows that prefabricating a dwelling using wood easily found in the region would cost only 75 percent the cost of building with traditional construction. Industrialization of the construction process would reduce the cost in materials and labor by 8 percent, and reduce direct and indirect costs by 76 percent. It would also reduce the construction time (from 6 months to 1.5 months), and be more environmentally friendly (reducing the consumption of energy all year long) (Carballo et al. 2001). While the set-up costs of such a system are significant, the reduction in costs compared to traditional construction methods would be even higher once production is scaled up.

In Chile, industrialized manufacturing techniques are primarily used to add or improve second floors on existing dwellings constructed with conventional methods. In 2006, 28 percent of homes in Chile were built with covered partition panels made out of wood or another material (which can be thought of as a proxy for industrialized houses). Meanwhile, conventional or traditional dwellings account for 53 percent of the housing market (Duffau 2011).

Social dwellings in Chile (built incrementally by families themselves with government support for the initial site or for an initial core unit, or built entirely under a public housing program) represent almost 40 percent of the houses at the national level. They are mainly located in urban areas. About two-thirds (67 percent) of them are built with conventional materials; another 22 percent are industrially manufactured houses. In contrast, 48 percent of privately built houses are built with conventional methods, and almost 32 percent with industrialized methods (Duffau 2011).

Colombia has made a few attempts to industrialize the construction of houses for low-income people (Vargas Garzón 2007). Some examples are the Torres de San Agustín in Cali, and the Torres de Monterrey in Bucaramanga. While these developments were easy, cheap, and clean to build, some quality problems emerged (bad acoustics between apartments and cracks between panels).

With the exception of Chile, industrialization in construction is minimal and has been targeted to individual solutions rather than being part of national housing policies. The poor quality of some early projects tarnished the reputation of the technology for some. But these problems of poor quality have been absent in the more recent examples of industrialized housing.

Is Industrialized Construction Worth It?

When does it make economic sense to adopt industrialized construction technologies? A cost-benefit analysis (CBA) of industrialized construction in Latin America could help answer this question. A CBA compares the benefits (net of costs) of each building technology (traditional and industrialized) to quantify the potential gains of switching from one technology to the other. However, given the limited penetration of industrialized construction in the region, not much information about the potential monetary costs and benefits exists.

The available information allows a partial comparison of some of the costs of traditional construction methods and preconstructed houses. Information about fully industrialized construction compared to traditional construction can be found for countries outside the region such as Spain and the United States (see table 6.9). On average, industrialized construction cuts overall construction costs by 11.8 percent compared to traditional construction. However, the range of potential saving is wide. On the one hand, there are examples in the Unites States, Spain, and Argentina where the cost of construction with a high degree of industrialization is lower than with any other construction technique. But some examples in the United Kingdom and Argentina suggest the opposite. Nevertheless, many times costs appear to be high because some benefits, such as better-quality houses or fewer accidents, are not reflected in project accounts (Parliamentary Office of Science and Technology 2003). Moreover, evidence for the United States indicates that construction costs for manufactured houses increase at a slower pace than costs for traditional construction: 1.6 percent real growth versus 2.9 percent between 1990 and 2000 (Apgar et al. 2002).

Stumbling Blocks to Industrialized Construction

Although low-income housing is potentially a market niche for industrialized residential construction and for the implementation of new cost-saving building techniques, there seems to be no private sector interest in filling that niche or in innovating. Even when governments take an active role in social housing—which is the case in many countries in the region—they have not been able to incentivize construction firms to penetrate the lowest sectors or to implement newer technologies. For example, in Peru, the social housing program Techo Propio stagnated during its initial years because the private construction sector was not interested in building houses for low-income groups (Fernández-Maldonado and Bredenoord 2010).

Some argue that lack of demand and low profits explain why the private building sector does not serve low-income groups. Lack of demand is likely one of the culprits. The simulations presented in chapter 3 show that around 9 percent of households would not be able to afford a dwelling at current prices offered by the private sector.

Table 6.9 Savings of Industrialized Construction

Comparison	Country	Savings		Source
		As percent of total construction costs	In construction time	
Manufactured vs. traditional	United States	42	n.d.	NAHB Research Center, Inc. (1998)
	Spain	Between 24 and 31	n.d.	Taranilla (2009)
	United Kingdom	Between −7 and −10	n.d.	Parliamentary Office of Science and Technology (2003)
	Argentina	−13.80	n.d.	Pizarro, Michelini, and Maldonado (2003)
Manufactured vs. preconstructed	Chile	3[a]	50 (from 70 to 35 days)	Mayagoitia (2009)
Manufactured vs. preconstructed	United States	32	n.d.	NAHB Research Center, Inc. (1998)
Preconstructed vs. traditional	Argentina	25	75 (from 6 to 1.5 months)	Carballo et al. (2001)

[a] Savings in percent of labor in total cost

n.d. = no data.

Source: Authors' compilations.

As in any other sector, businesses in the construction industry look for opportunities to maximize profits. Construction firms earn limited profits per unit for building houses for low-income groups. Delivering units in large numbers to obtain economies of scale can increase the profitability of the sector. This is not easy to achieve in Latin America, where housing construction is focused on small-scale projects. Figure 6.5 shows the scale of construction of new social housing for some countries in Latin America. With the exception of Chile and Peru, single detached dwellings are the most common constructions (making up between 70 and 100 percent of social housing).

Two possibilities exist for construction firms to improve profitability and still provide high-quality dwellings at an affordable price. The first is through innovation in the way they build houses. The second is negotiating with input providers to reduce their costs (Mayagoitia 2009). This last possibility seems hard to achieve in Latin America given the structure of the sector. Cement production is extremely concentrated, residential construction firms are small and fragmented, and there is a popular belief that the relative simplicity of the process does not require collaboration among developers, providers, and subcontractors.

Large firms have a higher propensity to invest in innovation than small and medium ones. Large firms can distribute the high fixed costs

Figure 6.5 Type of Construction for New Social Housing in Select Latin American Countries (Percent)

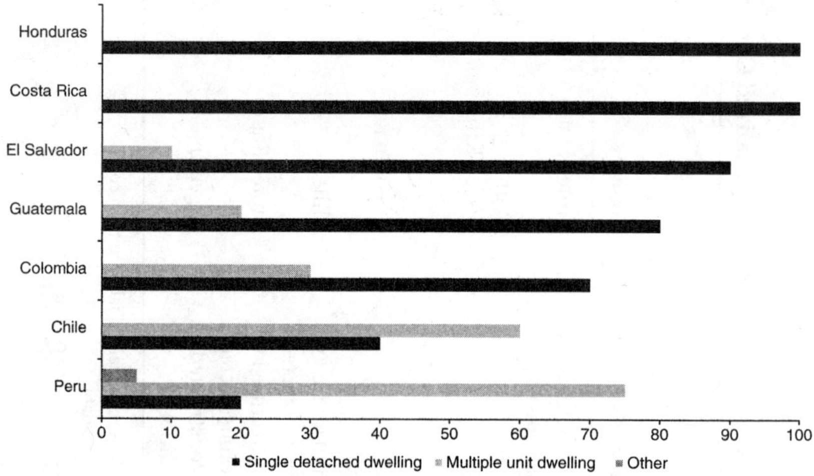

Source: Torres and Torres (2009).

of innovation across a larger volume of sales and have better access to financial resources, technology, and specialized human capital markets. Residential construction firms are usually small, do not coordinate with other firms, have different economic interests, and have only a small influence in generating new construction methods. Thus, the current construction process does not favor an integrated industrialized scheme (Mayagoitia 2009).

Financing constraints and the inability of firms to wait for long periods before recovering investments further discourage construction firms from investing in innovation (IDB 2010a). The risks of failing in industrialized construction are extremely high, particularly for small enterprises, due to the fixed costs of not only establishing the factories and the production lines but also running the whole process. Risky investments are hard to finance everywhere, but particularly in Latin America, where there is a shortage of financial intermediaries to encourage private sector innovation.

Finally, the lack of potential demand is a constraint. The market for manufactured homes is not as stable as the market for other manufactured products such as cars. The main reasons for the lack of stability include variations in land prices and availability of basic infrastructure for land development, access to mortgages to generate demand, and fluctuations in consumption patterns. Mayagoitia (2009) highlights the lack of demand as the main reason why in Latin America industrialization has been confined to preconstructed houses.

People might resist using this new form of construction in their houses. Low-income Chileans, for instance, value the materials used to build their house more than any other factor when choosing a new home (89 percent consider them the most important aspect). In particular, only 4 percent would choose a prefabricated house; 77 percent prefer a house built with bricks and cement, and 19 percent prefer a house made out of wood. Even the size of the dwelling does not sway people's opinions. People who prefer a conventional dwelling are indifferent between a 55-square-meter house made out of traditional materials and a 70-square-meter prefabricated one (Duffau 2011).

The common perception is that manufactured houses do not provide the quality or durability that traditional construction methods provide, and that the life span of a manufactured house is shorter. Duffau (2011) reports that for social houses in Chile, 12 percent of the units built with industrialized construction show serious deterioration compared to just 3 percent for a traditionally built house. For houses that present an acceptable quality over time, those figures are 31 and 14 percent, respectively. These findings might make buyers reluctant to purchase a manufactured dwelling.

Families might not want to buy a prefabricated dwelling because of the potential loss in property value. Duffau (2011) uses the hedonic price approach to compare the effect of an industrialized dwelling on property value with that of a conventional home. She finds that, all other characteristics remaining constant, a house built with industrialized techniques is worth less than a traditional one (negative marginal valuation). In 2006, for households that receive subsidies, industrialized houses had a negative marginal valuation of around US$1,800 compared to traditional houses made out of bricks. For households that did not receive subsidies, the negative marginal valuation increases to US$2,200.

Even if consumers are willing to buy an industrialized house, banks and other financial institutions might not be willing to extend the credit necessary to buy it. In the United States and the United Kingdom, credit institutions extend credit with a higher cost and a lower repayment period to buyers of industrialized or prefabricated houses in comparison to traditional construction ones (Duffau 2011).

Another reason why the construction sector might not readily implement innovative measures is that consumers provide little feedback. Moreover, the sector's capacity to learn is constrained by the high rotation of its labor force and the lack of uniformity in the production process since every project is unique.

Government incentives to innovate are also lacking. The potential of traditional construction methods to generate massive employment for low-skilled workers does not create the perfect environment for technological proposals that use capital intensively instead of labor. However, if the government seeks to generate employment, it can do so in other sectors besides simply construction. The efficiency of what is being built must be weighed against the employment the sector generates. This is particularly important considering the jump in labor costs in the region in the last ten years. Additionally, the current scarcity of an adequately qualified level of workers that some countries in the region experience also shows the need to develop technologies that rely less on labor. In Brazil, for example, in 2010, 62 percent of developers had concerns about the lack of adequate workers for their projects[4] (Brazil Real Estate Partners 2011).

The current state of the transportation sector represents another barrier to implementing industrialized construction in the region. The new technology requires moving the finished dwelling components to the final location, which can drive transportation costs higher than conventional construction (Mayagoitia 2009). Moreover, in Latin America, transportation is usually inefficient and very expensive, which might boost the final dwelling price even more and counteract the benefits of industrialized construction in providing affordable housing.

The characteristics of the cement/concrete industry in Latin America may create another barrier. The cement/concrete industry supplies the main input of traditional construction, and could be seriously damaged if the building sector begins using either new materials or less cement in projects (manufactured houses can be made out of wood or steel, for example, or concrete panels, all of which require lower quantities of cement than a house made out of bricks). The cement/concrete industry is highly concentrated. In Mexico, for example, just six firms make up the entire market (Kumaran and Martínez González 2008). The situation is similar in other countries. Given that the construction sector accounts for an average of 5.42 percent of the GDP of Latin America (Torres and Torres 2009), and that the main input in residential construction is cement, no doubt it is an industry with considerable negotiating power. The reluctance of the cement/concrete industry to shift into industrialized construction could be a barrier for the implementation of the new method.

Laying the Building Blocks for Innovation and Industrialized Construction

Both the construction industry and government can take action to facilitate innovation in the residential construction sector. Firms need to develop a better understanding of what consumers want. They also need to focus on their production processes to decrease costs and possible failures. To that end, they could take several steps. First, develop a deep understanding of the needs of the market, and try to align demand with production, as in the automobile industry. Second, strive to increase the aggregated value of the final product. This can be done by increasing choices for the client without losing the concept of standardization and mass production. To this end, companies can offer more diverse and flexible prototypes, and incorporate greater functionality and comfort into the housing units they market. Third, establish a construction system based on an efficient use of the labor force. Fourth, establish production processes that allow different lines to be integrated and that result in a high-quality final product. Finally, establish new business alliances to facilitate integration (Mayagoitia 2009).

For its part, government can also pursue several options. The power of the state can be used to affect market incentives (through subsidies, regulations, and the like), which in turn affect outcomes. The choice of the policy depends on both the flexibility and resources available in the current market (IDB 2010a). Some economists believe that industrial policy has the potential to solve specific bottlenecks in a focused way and may facilitate structural transformation. However, it is critical that the state concentrate its efforts on industries with sufficient productive potential.

Lately, the main focus of industrial policies in the region has been public financing to develop new industries and strengthen existing ones. This approach addresses the lack of long-term credit for new initiatives in countries with very incomplete financial markets (IDB 2010a). One way the state could incentivize the formation of a manufactured housing industry would be to extend public financing to that sector.

Moreover, the state can protect industrialized construction as an infant industry that has the potential to become an important one. In Japan, for example, the government realized in 1955 that home building was relatively sluggish considering the need for reconstruction after the war (Mayagoitia 2009). It promoted the use of standardized systems and concrete panels to meet demand. Even though at the time the incentives did not work, they were the basis for the industrialization process that started a couple of years later and continues today. In the United Kingdom, the social housing regulator for England and Wales, the Housing Corporation, requires that a quarter of the new houses that it funds be built with industrialized construction methods.

Finally, the government can also provide the information and training necessary for firms to shift toward more industrialized and innovative construction techniques; for example, in the United Kingdom, where the government-sponsored programs encourage the use of industrialized methods by promoting best practices and providing information, such as the Rethinking Construction Program and the Promoting Off-site Production Applications.[5]

Painting the Housing Sector Green

In addition to cutting the time and cost it takes to produce a finished unit, the residential construction sector in the region also faces the challenge of reducing its negative impact on the environment. Environmentally friendly or "green" housing has become increasingly important in housing markets. Energy-efficient investments in construction and other environmentally friendly investments, such as low water usage toilets and grey water recycling, tend to pay for themselves in terms of lowering energy (or other utility) costs and reducing the carbon footprint of households.

Homes are long-lived durables; once built, they tend to lock in energy demand for long periods of time. Energy-intensive homes will tend to remain energy intensive over their lifespan, which can be 50 years or more, implying that carbon emissions will also tend to be fixed to a certain extent (Rosendahl and Strand 2009; Shalizi and Lecocq 2009; Costa and Kahn 2010).

Energy efficiency and energy consumption play a role in a building in at least two different ways: heating/cooling consumption (including hot water) and power (lighting services and appliance usage). Each of these uses, in turn, can be viewed in terms of its energy efficiency and intensity.[6] Both heating/cooling and power usage are determined by the characteristics of the building. Insulation and other construction techniques are key variables determining demand for heating/cooling, while access to natural light can lower demand for artificial light.

Energy-Efficient Construction: The Economic Case

When it comes to household energy use, energy markets present both market failures and behavioral failures that generate inefficiencies and justify policy interventions (Gillingham, Newell, and Palmer 2009). Households and consumers commit one of the biggest behavioral failures by underinvesting in energy efficient appliances, thereby slowing the adoption of energy efficiency innovations. Consumers either do not know or misunderstand the benefits of energy-efficient investments. They tend to apply unreasonably high rates to energy-efficiency investments and thus do not buy energy-efficient appliances or demand energy-efficient construction technologies. Moreover, some changes to become more energy efficient actually increase total energy consumed. This phenomena caused by energy-efficient appliances is called the "rebound" effect. By reducing the cost of consuming the same amount of energy, it provides incentives to consume more energy until the cost of the energy consumed matches the previous level.

There are, however, promising initiatives. Implementing a program of refrigerator efficiency standards in Central American countries may have important energy savings and avoid considerable emissions of CO_2. If the policy proposed in one study (McNeil, Van Buskirk, and Letschert 2006) had been implemented in 2005, fifteen years later, by 2020, projected energy savings would range from 39 gigawatt hours in Costa Rica (the lowest savings) to 205 gigawatt hours in El Salvador. Avoided emissions in Costa Rica would be 2 kilotonne (CO_2) and as much as 76 kilotonne (CO_2) in Guatemala. While retail prices of the different refrigerators in the different countries would have increased by between 5 and 25 percent, the electricity savings would be around 30 percent. This translates into mean aggregate savings of US$50 to US$100 over the lifetime of refrigerators.

Studies have also found positive return rates for other energy-efficient investment. For example, in the United States, the Energy Star Program has generated considerable residential energy savings for consumer electronics (CE) and miscellaneous electronics (ME) such as desktops, laptops, videogames, VCRs, audio equipment, monitors, top boxes, dehumidifiers, and ventilation fans (Sanchez, Brown, and Homan 2008). Cumulative savings from 1998 to 2007 were 108 terawatt hours, which is roughly 6 percent of the reference case consumption of that period and about 25 percent of total EPA Energy Star electricity savings from product labeling (both residential and commercial savings) over the same period.

Overall, there is mixed evidence regarding the impact of energy-efficient products and investments on energy efficiency and conservation. Nevertheless, there are behavioral and principal-agent problems[7] that might complicate the achievement of positive impacts from adopting energy-efficient technologies (see box 6.1).

Box 6.1 Energy Efficiency in Barbados

Barbados has been piloting several renewable energy initiatives for households and small businesses, taking steps to make them more viable and affordable. Small-scale renewable Distributed Generation (DG)[a] with solar photovoltaic (PV) panels is already viable in Barbados, thanks to concessional financing provided by the government with the support of the Inter-American Development Bank (IDB). The electric utility Barbados Light & Power (BL&P) has recently begun offering a pilot Renewable Energy Rider (RER) at avoided cost, with limited eligibility, and net billing.[b] The government is working with the regulator and the electric utility to put in place a sustainable energy framework (SEF) in the electric sector, also with support from the IDB (Gischler and Janson 2011). Generation costs and tariffs are high in Barbados, which is a concern for the government as well as households and businesses.[c]

A Smart Fund Program focuses on the design and implementation of key financial mechanisms needed to jump-start the renewable energy and energy-efficiency market in Barbados, targeting small and medium enterprises (SMEs), as well as the residential sector, with loans, grants, and rebate mechanisms. Figure B6.1 shows that thanks to the program, DG with PV is viable. The gray bar shows the original long-run marginal cost. The black bar shows the effect of the Smart Fund. Solar PV systems have a long-run marginal cost of US$0.20 per kilowatt hour.[d] Moreover, 2-kilowatt systems for residential and small business purposes are not far from being viable.[e] Larger decreases in capital costs (from

Figure B6.1 Viability of Renewable Distributed Generation (DG) in Barbados (US$ per kilowatt hour)

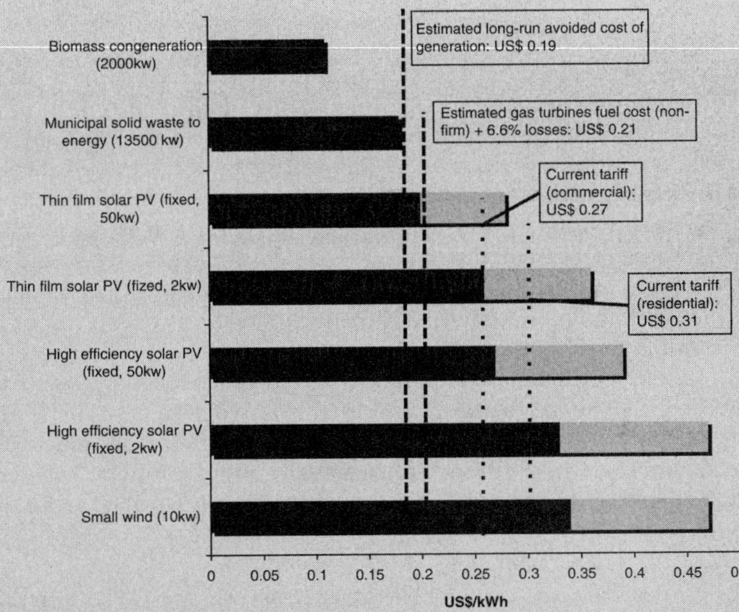

Notes: The gray bars show the original long-run marginal cost; the black bars show the effect of the Smart Fund Solar with solar photovoltaic (PV).
Source: Authors' calculations based on IDB (2011a).

US$6,000 to US$3,000) would be needed for small-scale wind power to become viable.[f]

BL&P has also been proactive in exploring how small-scale renewable DG could help save fuel costs. Since 2010, BL&P has provided a pilot renewable energy rider (RER) that lets customers develop grid-connected small PV and wind (BL&P 2010b). The RER's main features are:

- Term: Two years.
- Eligibility: Cap on individual systems (maximum installed capacity 5 kilowatts for small customers, 50 for large customers), as well as on total systems eligible (1.6 megawatt, approximately 1 percent of peak demand, or 200 systems—whichever occurs first).
- Feed-in tariff rate: Short-run avoided cost of generation, with a floor (US$0.16, or 1.8 times the fuel clause adjustment, which covers fuel costs—whichever is highest).
- Metering arrangement: Net billing, using bidirectional meters to separately measure and bill the electricity bought and sold.

The RER is well designed in that individual and total capacity is capped, the rate is set at avoided cost, and the metering arrangement used is net billing. The recently approved RE policy calls for further improvement in this framework by the following means:

- Extending the term of the RER: Two years is too short compared to the useful lifetime of systems.
- Developing a disaggregated, cost-reflective tariff structure: Many electricity tariffs in Barbados bundle different services together in the same rate (US$ per kilowatt hour): energy supply, connection to the distribution grid, and provision of back-up and stand-by capacity to assure electricity even when intermittent distributed RE is not being generated. Some solar PV systems are already commercially viable (costing less than the tariff), although not economically viable (costing more than avoided cost of generation). Therefore, the current tariff structure may give customers (particularly residential ones) an incentive to self-generate, such as with solar PV, to avoid paying the tariff. However, by not paying that tariff (which includes services other than energy supply), they would be enjoying services provided by the utility, without actually paying for them. Thus, other customers that do not have a system would ultimately pay the cost for those other services.

The SEF also encourages the use of energy-efficient (EE) appliances in residential and commercial buildings, particularly the tourism sector, which is the main source of income in Barbados. The IDB and the government of Barbados prepared

Figure B6.2 Average Power Consumption by the Hotel Sector in Barbados

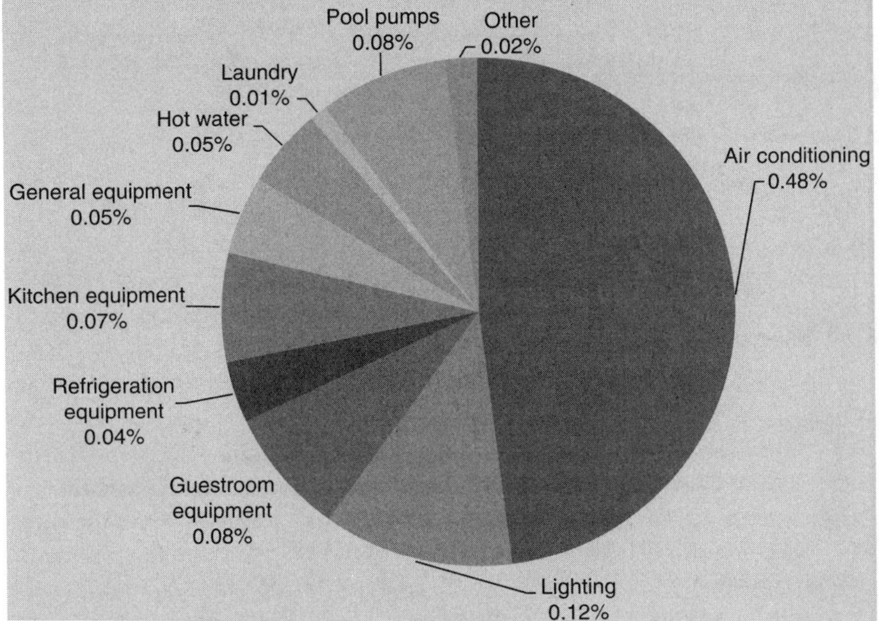

Source: IDB (2011c).

a program called the Caribbean Hotel Energy Efficiency Action Program (CHENACT) to assess the power consumption and potential savings of the hotel industry in that country.

Figure B6.2 shows the disaggregated power consumption of an average hotel and, hence, the potential energy savings particularly in air conditioning, lighting, pool pumps, appliances in the hotel room, and hot water.

Figure B6.3 shows the commercially available EE appliances in Barbados. All appliances with a long-term marginal cost lower than the avoided cost of the utility would reduce the power consumption of residential and commercial buildings.

The promotion of these technologies and the enactment of building codes that encourage steps to save energy will generate energy savings of 21 percent (compared to the baseline of 2009). Both the renewable energy policy and the energy efficiency policy will help reduce Barbados's fossil fuel dependence by at least 30 percent.

Figure B6.3 Cost Effectiveness of Energy-Efficient Appliances in Barbados

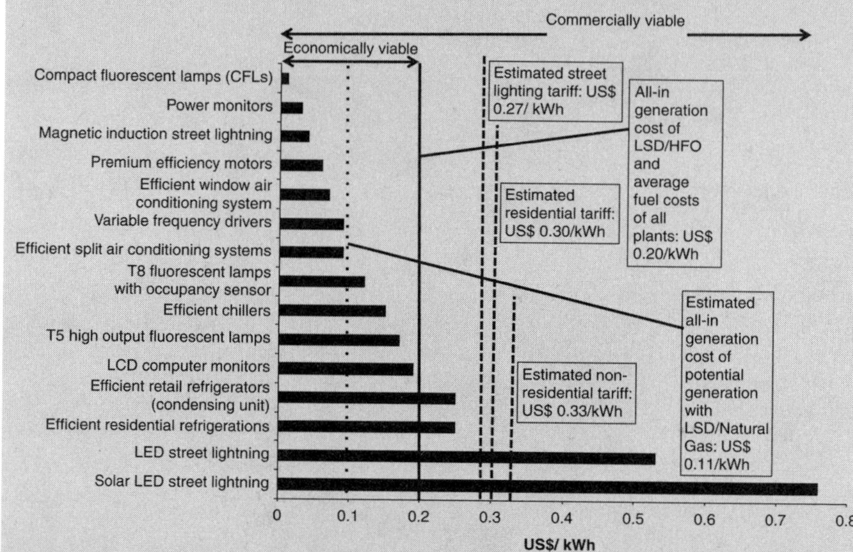

Source: IDB (2011a).

[a] Distributed Generation (DG) generates electricity from many small energy sources.

[b] "Avoided cost" refers to the marginal cost for a public utility to produce one more unit of power. "Net billing" refers to what remains after the deduction of any energy outflows from metered energy inflows.

[c] The estimated avoided variable cost of diesel-fueled plants was US$0.21 per kilowatt hour in 2010, while the estimated long-run marginal cost of low-speed diesel plants was about US$0.19 per kilowatt hour, assuming oil prices of US$100 per barrel. The residential tariff was estimated at about US$0.31 per kilowatt hour; the commercial tariff was estimated at US$0.27 per kilowatt hour (IDB 2010b).

[d] Assuming a capital cost of US$4 per watt installed, a capacity factor of 21 percent, and a 5 percent discount rate.

[e] Assuming capital costs of US$5 to US$6 per watt installed. They would become viable once costs are in the range of US$4 per watt installed.

[f] This is because small-scale wind power in Barbados has lower capacity factors (about 20 percent), compared to larger-scale wind power (about 30 percent).

Policies to Promote Energy Efficiency

Several types of policies have proven to have an important impact on energy savings and energy efficiency in the building sector. Nevertheless, not all countries in Latin America will be able to implement energy-conservation policies and keep growing sustainably (Chang and Soruco Carballo 2011).[8]

As a result, some countries must make a difficult trade-off between sustainable growth and environmental conservation.

The Importance of Building Codes

Building codes are important to promote rational energy use, as California's experience deftly illustrates. While per capita use of electricity in the United States has grown 50 percent since 1973, and residential retail electricity sales per housing unit increased 60 percent between 1970 and 2007 (Costa and Kahn 2010), per capita consumption in the state of California has remained flat and retail electricity per housing unit has increased only 24 percent. California can thank more stringent building codes for its more moderate electricity consumption as the average house in California becomes ever more energy efficient. Building and appliance codes have been effective in keeping the consumption curve in California's electricity demand flat, especially after 1983 (Costa and Kahn 2010). Homes built in the 1990s consume 15 percent less electricity than those built between 1978 and 1983.[9]

Home renovations are not the answer, as home renovations tend to increase energy consumption between 1.4 percent and 5 percent, depending on the type of renovation.[10] Only new roofs seem to reduce electricity purchases by about 1.6 percent.

Other empirical findings lend further credibility to the hypothesis that building codes encourage energy efficiency and are good for the environment and consumers alike (see Jacobsen and Kotchen 2010). Increasingly stringent requirements are associated with a 4 percent decrease in electricity consumption and a 6 percent decrease in natural gas consumption. Consumption of electricity for air conditioning in summer and natural gas for heating in winter fell. The private payback period for the average residence is 6.4 years. Moreover, the social payback period, which accounts for the avoided costs of air pollution emissions, is 3.5 years, if benefits associated with lower CO_2 are taken into account.

The impact of changing building codes to promote energy efficiency in Latin America and the Caribbean may be limited since most houses are built without following construction codes. In part this occurs because codes are unrealistic and increase construction costs, deterring households from implementing them. Interestingly, in Chile, one of the areas in which households have made the least progress when expanding or improving the core houses that they start with is with thermal insulation (Greene 2011). Adapting building and land development codes to the needs of low-income households is one of the most pressing regulatory changes needed to improve housing markets.

Taxes versus Subsidies

Taxes and subsidies can also be used to increase energy efficiency. A study of the cost-effectiveness of different policy options to replace certain home appliances (refrigerators, washing machines, boilers, and light bulbs) with more energy-efficient ones in four countries of the European Union (Denmark, France, Italy, and Poland) found that subsidies, in most cases, were less cost-effective than energy taxes in improving energy efficiency (Markandya et al. 2009). However, the peculiarities of each country make it difficult to recommend a general policy option for all appliances from the perspective of cost-effectiveness. Tax credits on some appliances (such as boilers) appear to be an attractive option for some cases (Denmark and Italy), while subsidies on compact fluorescent light bulbs (CFLs) seem to be a better policy in France and Poland.

Construction at a Crossroads

Latin American cities suffer from a lack of private sector interest in building low-income housing. Private builders do not appear to have either the incentive or the demand to build for less fortunate households. If public policies in the housing sector aim to incentivize developers to serve that segment of society, they must promote innovations that decrease construction costs (which have been rising in the region) and produce dwellings on a larger scale. Industrialized construction shows potential to achieve these objectives. While it has some disadvantages, it can produce houses in a faster, cheaper, and more environmentally friendly way. However, the characteristics of the construction industry and specific local conditions have stunted the development of industrialized construction. The challenge for the region is to sort out those difficulties while simultaneously easing the factors that constrain the demand for these homes.

Tackling carbon emissions produced by the housing sector in Latin America and the Caribbean requires reducing overall energy demand, which will rise with income and urban sprawl as cities grow and lower-income households acquire larger housing units and more appliances. Well-functioning land markets with incentives for mixed and intensive land use are essential to control sprawl and reduce cities' carbon footprint.

As more efficient appliances spread, especially in the form of newer heating/cooling technologies, and more stringent codes are enforced, the energy demand growth curve could "bend" significantly, meaning demand would decline and stabilize at a lower level. The evidence suggests that increases in energy-efficient investments generate positive returns as an economic investment.

Energy-efficient building codes appear to lower energy consumption significantly. In contrast, remodeling does not appear to reduce energy demand. This is an important finding in Latin America and the Caribbean, where residents build on to existing homes in stages. The way the house is originally built tends to lock in energy demand for long periods of time. Thus, policy should focus on conditioning new construction rather than adapting already existing structures. More stringent energy and building codes make up part of such a policy package, but unless they are properly enforced, the impact will be limited.

The construction industry in Latin America and the Caribbean is at a critical crossroads. Industrialized construction and greener housing mark the path toward a different future while bricks and mortar lead the industry down the same old trail.

7

Too Small to Thrive: The Housing Finance Market

A country's housing finance system can help or hinder the provision of adequate housing. Access to financial markets influences the capacity of households to buy formal finished dwellings. A more developed mortgage market system can offer reasonably priced mortgage loans to a broad range of families. Financial markets are also essential to providing working and investment capital to land developers and builders, as houses take time and resources to build, and significant upfront resources are required to buy and develop serviced land.

Housing finance systems in Latin American and Caribbean countries, with the exception of Chile and Panama, are tiny relative to those in other countries, but the systems in the region have at least two positive features. First, home prices in Latin America and the Caribbean have been less volatile than in most other emerging economies in the 2000s (figure 7.1). As a result, while some much larger systems experienced a meltdown during the global financial crisis, the region's housing finance systems fared relatively well. Given the importance of financial stability, the region's countries should be congratulated on this score.

Moreover, the fact that home ownership rates in many Latin American and Caribbean countries are as high as anywhere in the world (see chapter 4) might suggest that housing finance systems, while small, are adequate. Unfortunately, this is not the case. The region's high home ownership rates more likely reflect decades of lax enforcement of land regulation and failure to adhere to building codes, both of which make it easy to own an inadequate house with small upfront costs. Consistent with this hypothesis, many Latin American and Caribbean countries are still grappling with substantial housing deficits: some actual (people lack any form of adequate shelter); some qualitative (shelter exists, but it is substandard). Moreover, a substantial portion of the population lives in slums (see chapter 2).

Figure 7.1 An International Comparison of House Price Levels (Constant Prices)

a. Advanced Economies and Emerging Economies, 1990–2010

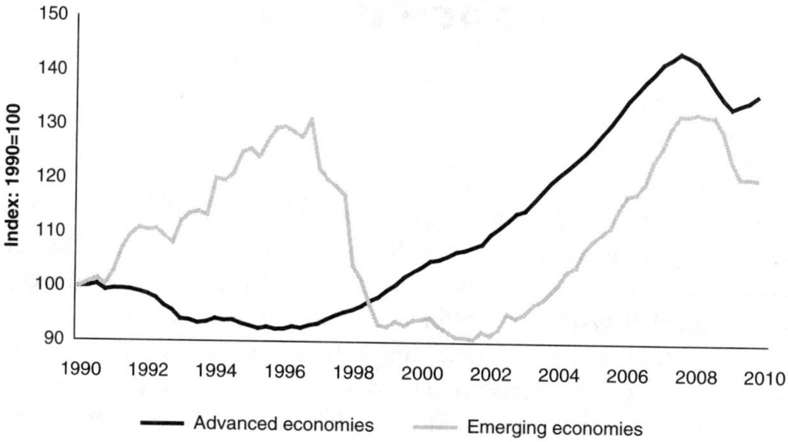

b. Select Developing Countries and Regions, 2000–2010

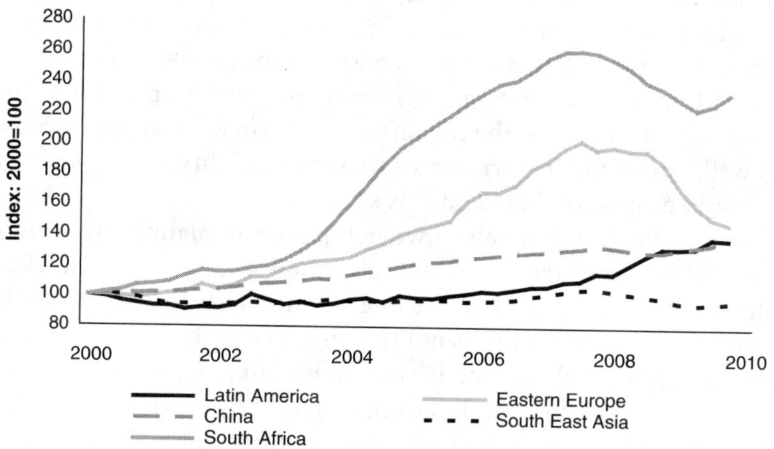

Source: Cesa-Bianchi (2011).

The substantial housing deficits pervasive in the region cannot be addressed through small improvements to existing housing and housing finance policies; they demand more fundamental changes. A housing finance system that facilitates and encourages more private sector financing for housing could be one step toward alleviating the housing deficits in the region. Furthermore, the widespread prevalence of incremental housing[1] in the region is prima facie evidence that well-functioning (and larger) systems of housing finance would be desirable.

Housing finance systems in Latin America and the Caribbean are small but government involvement (and hence government spending) is substantial, ranging from a large presence of public banks in the banking sector (table 7.1) to an array of subsidy programs and other schemes to facilitate access to housing finance by low- and middle-income households (see IDB 2004).

Table 7.1 Market Share of Government-Sponsored Credit Institutions in Real Estate Lending in Select Latin American Countries (Percentage Points)

	2005	2006	2007	2008	2009	2010
Residential real estate lending						
Argentina	43.4	48.1	45.0	53.4	59.1	61.8
Brazil	74.4	72.9	61.8	59.5	67.1	65.9
Chile	n.d.	n.d.	25.3	24.9	25.5	24.1
Colombia	0.8	0.6	0.6	0.5	0.5	0.4
Mexico	67.2	66.6	65.5	65.0	64.6	65.4
Other lending						
Argentina	30.8	26.6	27.3	29.6	34.9	34.0
Brazil	10.7	9.9	9.1	8.9	13.8	11.7
Chile	n.d.	n.d.	11.6	10.2	13.5	12.8
Colombia	5.2	4.1	3.8	4.4	5.6	5.1
Mexico	22.7	20.1	14.6	15.8	17.8	10.9
Total lending						
Argentina	32.2	27.6	29.3	32.5	37.7	36.6
Brazil	17.1	16.7	15.4	14.7	22.0	20.3
Chile	n.d.	n.d.	14.8	13.7	16.6	15.8
Colombia	4.8	3.7	3.5	4.1	5.1	4.7
Mexico	35.7	35.3	31.6	31.9	33.4	30.4

n.d. = no data.

Source: Calculations based on Bureau Van Dijk (2011).

The two main questions this chapter asks are: Why are the region's housing finance systems so small? And what can governments do to enable and promote the development of sustainable private systems?

International Benchmarks: How the Region Measures Up with Others

As measured by the ratio of mortgage debt outstanding to gross domestic product (GDP), housing finance systems in Latin America are small. Size, however, is not an optimal measure of how well a housing finance system functions. The size of mortgage markets can be influenced by price dynamics and tax considerations. For example, favorable tax treatments for mortgages in countries such as the Netherlands and the United States tend to result in a larger stock of mortgage debt. Moreover, in some countries, mortgage markets are arguably too large or are growing too quickly, which might contribute to macroeconomic instability. Housing bubbles require larger housing finance markets (all else being equal), and sometimes these bubbles burst and lead to financial meltdowns. Besides size, other dimensions to gauge how well a housing finance system functions include access (the portion of households that has access to appropriate housing finance products), product range (the range of financing products available), and stability (the extent to which housing finance systems impact macroeconomic fluctuations).[2] Any measure—whether size, product range, or stability—will have drawbacks.[3]

Nonetheless, size as a measure has two important qualities: it can be constructed for a wide range of countries, which provides an important point of comparison and benchmarking, and it may be a proxy for other important aspects of housing finance systems. For example, all else being equal, larger housing finance markets are likely to reach a greater proportion of the population.

Figure 7.2, from Warnock and Warnock (2011), shows mortgage debt as a percentage of GDP for over 50 countries, as an indicator of the relative size of each country's mortgage market.[4] The panels are separated by region; each has the same scale (0–100 percent) for ease of comparison across regions. Housing finance systems in Latin America and the Caribbean tend to be quite small. Chile and Panama have the largest mortgage markets, with debt averaging 20 percent of GDP. Other countries in the region have much smaller markets (Mexico, 9 percent; Brazil, 3 percent; Argentina, 2 percent). The region as a whole has a GDP-weighted average mortgage debt that is 5.5 percent of GDP. In contrast, mortgage

Figure 7.2 Mortgage Debt as a Percent of GDP, 2009

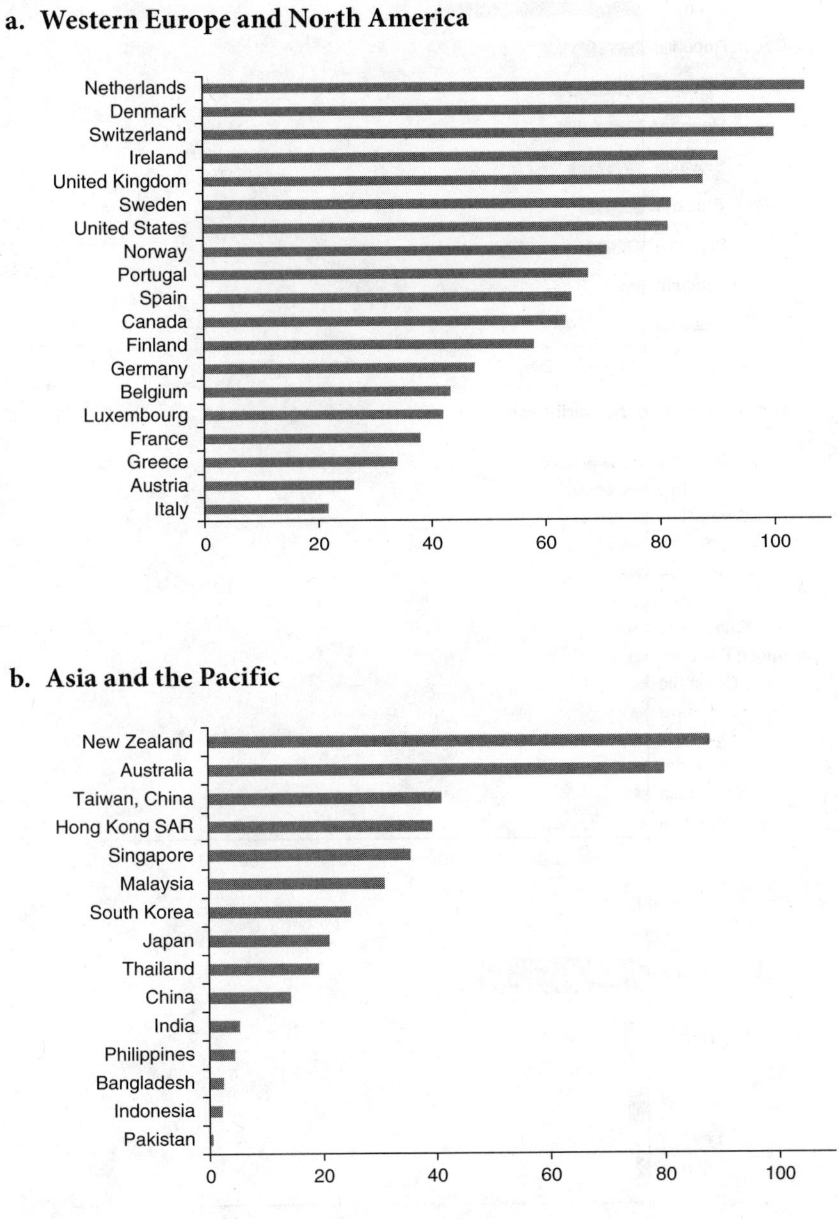

Figure 7.2 Continued

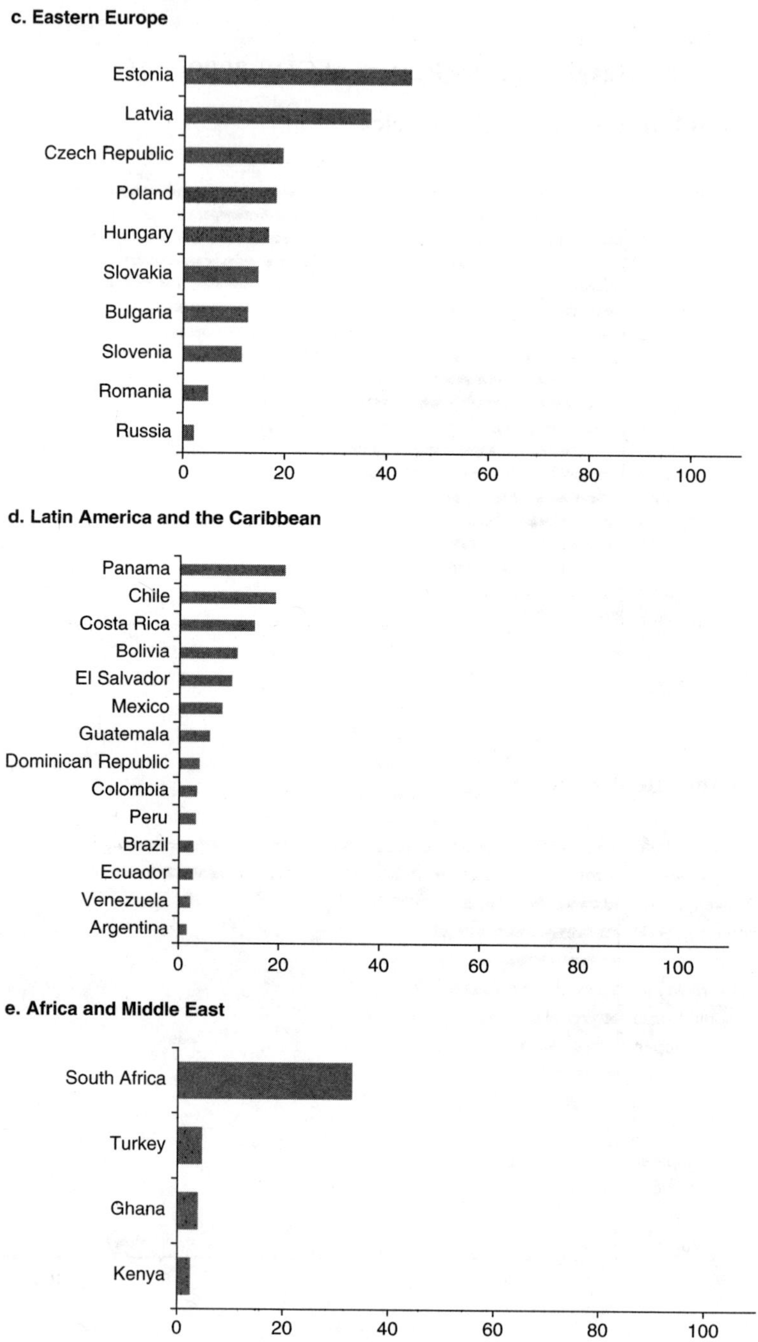

Source: Warnock and Warnock (2011).

markets in Asia, while not enormous, are somewhat larger as a share of GDP, with mortgage debt averaging 12.4 percent for the region and including Malaysia at 31 percent and Thailand at 19 percent. Mortgage market debts average roughly 60 percent of GDP in advanced economies, with some countries (Denmark, the Netherlands, and Switzerland) at roughly 100 percent; some (Australia, New Zealand, and the United States) average around 80 percent, and others (Japan and Korea) around 20 percent.

Bigger mortgage markets are not always and everywhere better, but it is important to understand what is holding back the development of mortgage markets in Latin American and Caribbean countries. To do so, the simple supply and demand framework developed by Warnock and Warnock (2008; 2011) is useful for understanding cross-country differences in the size of mortgage markets. In that framework, demand for housing finance derives from the demand for home purchases, which in turn depends on the rate of household formation, income levels, interest rates, and the ease of purchasing (and registering) property.[5] In addition, for affordability reasons, housing finance should be longer term in nature, as housing costs are typically a multiple of annual income.

On the supply side, housing finance can be split into two components: the provision of housing finance by a lender that has ample funds on hand; and the mobilization of funds within an economy so that lending institutions have access to funds. For a lender with adequate funds, the decision to allocate some portion to long-term housing finance hinges on several requirements. Lenders need *information about the borrower* (information about the creditworthiness of prospective borrowers can help lenders determine the probability of default and, hence, price the loan appropriately). Lenders also need the *ability to value the property* (from, for example, a mandatory property registry that maintains detailed information about housing transactions, including data about the sales price and relevant features of the home such as location, size, quality, and age). Lenders must have the *ability to secure collateral* in case of default. Finally, lenders need *macroeconomic stability* (if inflation is volatile, the lender would incur substantial interest rate risk or, if passed on to the borrower, default risk).

If the conditions for long-term lending are in place, lenders must have ample access to funds to lend. One *source of funds* can be the primary market (for example, deposit-taking institutions, such as banks). However, the inherent maturity mismatch would tend to produce housing loans that are short-term or feature variable rates, the risk of which might prove difficult for consumers to gauge. Lending would also tend to be geographically concentrated.[6] Another source of funds is the secondary market, which buys the loans from the primary market and finds ways to mobilize long-term matching funds[7] (see box 7.1). At times, housing finance systems require *additional sources of liquidity*, such as a governmental liquidity window (in case of temporary liquidity crunches).

Box 7.1 Securitization and Mortgage Financing in Latin America and the Caribbean

Securitization is the process by which individually illiquid assets are pooled so that they can be repackaged and sold as interest-bearing securities. These securities carry different grades of risk depending on their seniority, with the most senior tranches in the securitization typically bearing the lowest risk. Their payoff profile depends on the underlying assets and cash flows pledged as collateral, and not on the overall financial strengths of the originator.

Experience with securitization of mortgage financing is limited in Latin America and the Caribbean. In addition to the inherent complexities of this technique and the housing challenges faced by the region, mortgage securitization has traditionally suffered from the absence of a homogeneous and structured legal and regulatory framework. Latin American and Caribbean governments began to fill this gap by promoting assorted initiatives. Among the regional experiences in housing financing securitization, three cases can be identified: Chile, Colombia, and Mexico.

Three Experiences in the Region

Chile

In the case of Chile, securitization was formally introduced in 1994. In the specific case of mortgage finance, the instruments are subject to prudential rules and regulations dictated by the Superintendencia de Bancos e Instituciones Financieras (SBIF). The Chilean securitization model is a rather simple one. Commercial banks and other financial institutions act as originators by offering loans and generating a financial asset in their portfolio that will later be transferred to institutional investors through securitizing companies.

Notwithstanding the existence of a legal framework and good market practices, the mechanism for structured finance has not reached significant volumes in Chile. The current total stock of securitized bonds backed by mortgages to October 2008 was equivalent to just over 1 percent of the total stock of residential housing mortgages granted by the banking system. Among the reasons that

Figure B7.1 Securitized Mortgages as a Percent of Total Mortgage Portfolio

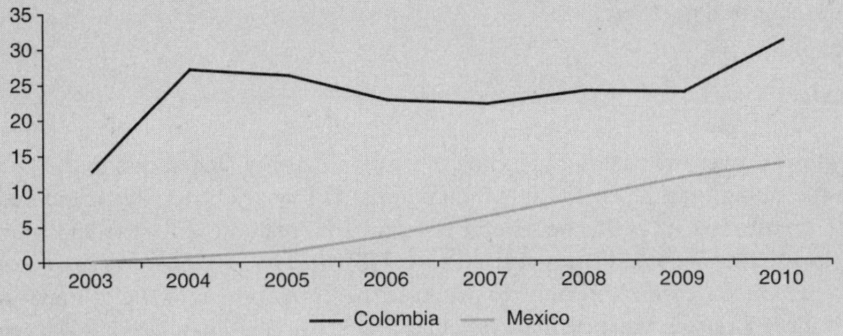

Source: Authors' calculations based on statistical agencies.

volumes have remained so low is the scant interest of market players because of the abundant sources of long-term funding for Chilean commercial banks, including in the domestic bond market. The securitization process has also been slowed by the high demand for refinancing underlying loans in these instruments during periods in which market interest rates were historically low (prepayment risk). Moreover, the international financial crisis has increased the relative risk aversion of international investors and consequently increased the cost of capital for mortgage backed securities (MBS), which imposes a new restriction to securitization.

In contrast to the low volumes in Chile, the levels of securitized mortgages have increased more markedly in Colombia and Mexico in the past decade (see figure B7.1). Although still in its infancy, securitized mortgages now represent 30 percent of total mortgage financing in Colombia and 10 percent in Mexico.

Colombia

In Colombia, securitization started in 1999 when the government approved the Ley de Vivienda (Law 546) to generate additional resources for housing finance through capital markets. To reduce the cost of funding, the government designed an incentive mechanism by which investors were exempted from paying income taxes on returns from mortgage securities. After the modest but positive response of capital markets, home financing became more adequately regulated in 2001 and the first entity specializing in securitizing mortgage loans, the Titularizadora Colombiana, was created.

Since then, the securitized mortgage portfolio as a percentage of the country's GDP has progressively grown. Banks act as direct originators of mortgage loans and the risk is concentrated on banks and debtors more than on the market.

Current standards prevent the origination of subprime loans. Colombian issuing banks keep part of the loan's risk on their balance sheets. Titularizadora Colombiana selects good-quality loans and verifies the conditions for the totality of the acquired portfolio.

Mexico

In Mexico, over the past decade, the government has boosted access to the housing financing market for the low-income population, traditionally considered a high credit risk. In 2001, the federal government created the first federal mortgage bank, the Sociedad Hipotecaria Federal (SHF). The SHF operates as a second tier "national credit institution" to promote the development of the primary and secondary housing finance markets. The SHF's primary mandate is to develop the mortgage securitization market by issuing guarantees and standardizing the practices of initiation and administration of mortgage loans.

Since 2003, Mexico has used mortgage securitization as a tool for developing the market for housing financing and to complement traditional mechanisms of funding. The mortgage portfolio portion of GDP has grown from 7.4 percent in 2003 to 9.2 percent in 2010; during that time, the share of securitized mortgages increased considerably, from 0.1 percent to 13.6 percent of total mortgages.

Mortgage securitization took off in Mexico, with investors gobbling them up enthusiastically, once these securities were perceived as providing a good risk-return profile. Nonetheless, the positive trend of the past decade came to a halt with the global economic recession, when the levels of securitization of financial intermediaries fell drastically due to a combination of demand and supply side factors. Job losses, real income contraction, and lower consumer confidence caused the demand shrinkage. On the supply side, the crisis dried up liquidity and reduced the capacity of Sofoles and Sofomes—the Mexican financial institutions specialized in housing. Only INFONAVIT and FOVISSSTE managed to remain active in the securitization process during the crisis.

Reforms and Challenges Ahead

After the financial crisis in 2008–2009, several reforms aimed at improving the regulatory standards applied to market participants in the securitization chain process. The G-20 has taken the lead in guiding postcrisis reforms. One of the most significant improvements was the strengthening of risk management captured by the Basel capital framework, including enhancements to the capital treatment of securitizations, off-balance sheet exposures, and trading book activities. The Basel Committee for Banking Supervision has also enhanced disclosure requirements related to securitizations. To improve the risk management process, banks are now required to exercise more effective due diligence over structured products and securitized assets; originators are required to retain a portion of the securitized portfolio in order to internalize part of the risk; and individual compensation incentives must be better aligned to risk management objectives. Despite these efforts, resuming securitization remains challenging and may require further action

A successful securitization process and market is a likely ingredient of an effective housing finance system in Latin America and the Caribbean. Although several industry initiatives are under way to standardize terms and structures, reduce complexity, and enhance transparency, the official sector ought to provide a regulatory framework that balances incentives for growth investment opportunities with the needed discipline in the securitization market.

To make this framework operational and measurable, comparable information for the aforementioned factors is needed. For most of these factors, data are available from the World Bank's Doing Business reports.[8] *Legal Rights for Borrowers and Lenders* is an index that ranges from 0 to 10, with higher scores indicating that collateral and bankruptcy laws are better designed to expand access to credit. For a mortgage lender to be comfortable lending long term, it needs to be able to secure collateral against the loan; in turn, this ability hinges on being able to seize the collateral (the property) in the case of default.[9] *Credit Information* measures the depth of lenders' access to standardized and informative sources of credit information on potential borrowers. The index ranges from 0 to 6, with higher values indicating greater availability of credit information.[10] An additional measure is *Ease of Registering Property*, a combination of three components: the number of procedures, the amount of time, and the official costs necessary for a buyer to purchase a property and to transfer the property title so that it can be used, sold, or posted as collateral.[11] Warnock and Warnock (2011) recast the World Bank's ranking of this component into a variable that ranges from 0 (very difficult and costly to register property) to 10 (easy and inexpensive). The final measure is *Inflation Volatility*, which is related to the interest rate risk that can impede lending. It is measured as the standard deviation of quarterly consumer price index (CPI) inflation rates (from the IMF International Financial Statistics database) over the period 2000–2009. When inflation volatility is high, long-term lending is not sustainable.[12]

Regression analysis in Warnock and Warnock (2008; 2011) suggests that mortgage markets, whether scaled by GDP or private credit, are larger in countries with stronger legal rights for borrowers and lenders, deeper credit information systems, greater ease in registering property, and less macroeconomic instability. Table 7.2 presents regional averages of these measures. The Doing Business dataset presents country-by-country data on the *Legal Rights*, *Credit Information*, and *Ease of Property Registration* variables.

Compared with other regions, Latin America and the Caribbean scores well only on the depth of its credit information systems. The depth of credit information does not vary much across countries, suggesting that as a cross-sectional variable it will not be very informative. Part of the problem with the credit information system score is that it does not take into account the percentage of the adult population that is covered. For example, Brazil rates very well, scoring five out of six. But only 27 percent of adults are included in its public credit registry. While the private credit registry covers a broader set of the population (54 percent of adults), it does not maintain both positive and negative information about borrowers, making it very difficult to create an informative credit score. That said, at least by the Doing Business measure, the credit

Table 7.2 Factors Favoring the Provision of Housing Finance (Regional Averages)

Measures	Advanced economies	Emerging economies	Latin America and the Caribbean	Emerging Asia	Eastern Europe
Mortgage debt as GDP percent	61.4	9.4	5.4	12.4	8.3
Legal rights[a]	7.2	5.5	4	6.3	5.1
Credit information[b]	5.6	4.5	5.2	4.2	4.8
Ease of property registration[c]	7.4	6.2	4.4	6.6	7.1
Inflation volatility[d]	1.14	3.34	4.1	2.3	4.4

[a] Legal rights index ranges from 0 to 10, with higher scores indicating that collateral and bankrupcy laws are better designed to expand access to credit. Credit information index ranges from 0 to 6, with higher values indicating the availability of more credit information.

[b] Credit information index ranges from 0 to 6, with higher values indicating the availability of more credit information.

[c] Ease of property registration ranges from 0 to 10, with higher scores indicating easier and lower scores more difficult registration.

[d] Inflation volatility is standard deviation of quarterly CPI inflation rates over the period 2000–2009.

Notes: Averages are GDP-weighted. Data pertain to the latest year available.

Sources: Warnock and Warnock (2011) and World Bank (2010).

information systems in Latin America and the Caribbean are as good as anywhere in the world, as most countries in the region score five or six out of six.[13]

On *Ease of Registering Property*, while many Latin American and Caribbean countries score well enough, three large countries—Argentina, Brazil, and Mexico—score quite poorly. Registering property is crucial for the assets that back mortgages to be used as collateral. An adequate property registry allows potential lenders to evaluate the track record and the liens that rely on the properties they would finance, and hence, by increasing transparency, enhance the value of mortgage-backed assets.

On *Legal Rights for Borrowers and Lenders*, there is much more variation, with most Latin American and Caribbean countries scoring five or below (out of ten), and many countries in other regions scoring much better. The lack of legal protection for creditors has been identified as the single most important regulatory limitation for the development of credit markets in the region.[14] Regarding housing finance, crucial weaknesses in most countries include the duration of legal proceedings in protecting creditor rights, which can take more than three or four years, the excessive number of appeals allowed on behalf of the debtor during the process, and the lack of political will to protect such rights (Rojas and Masci 2007).

For *Inflation Volatility*, lower volatility (that is, greater stability) is associated with larger mortgage markets. On this measure, Latin America and the Caribbean scores well enough—certainly much better than in the 1980s or 1990s. While maturity and currency mismatches pinpointed in previous work on housing finance (IDB 2004) have greatly decreased, memories of macroeconomic instability may persist, suggesting that for many countries in the region a much longer period of macroeconomic stability is needed to further support private sector mortgage lending.

The interaction of the aforementioned factors is also crucial to promote the development of housing finance. The recent case of Argentina, studied in detail in Auguste, Bebczuk, and Moya (2011), provides a good example of how these factors interact.[15] The mortgage market, though small, grew steadily up until Argentina's 2001–2002 crisis, when the market collapsed. Before the crisis, housing finance was deeper in states where the protection of creditor rights was stronger. After the macroeconomic shock, and regardless of the degree of protection of creditor rights, mortgage markets have yet to recover. Nonetheless, real estate is perceived as a safe asset and a store of value, and families continue to purchase housing assets despite the lack of mortgage loans. A survey designed for the study confirmed this trend and found that 80 percent of homeowners in Buenos Aires did not use any type of loan to finance their home purchase. The authors note that the lack of mortgage credit has negatively affected the quality of real estate purchased.

To summarize, the preceding analysis suggests that mortgage markets in Latin America and the Caribbean are small because the region lags in legal rights for borrowers and lenders—and on ease of registering property, at least for some of the largest countries. The road ahead is a long one. Reforming regulations to strengthen creditor rights is a difficult endeavor from a political standpoint. Regarding mortgages, the most pressing needs lie in streamlining the legal procedures for foreclosures in a way that enables greater lending but does not violate debtors' rights. Policymakers throughout the region have considered steps to limit the number of appeals. Reforming property registries is another task required in many countries—one that entails building extensive and nationwide information platforms that allow the owner of an asset to be identified efficiently and all types of contracts in which the asset has been pledged as collateral to be tracked. Countries should also strive to continue to improve the quality of credit information available, which would support the development of adequate scoring models. Finally, preserving macroeconomic stability is another top priority for the development of mortgage finance. Lenders and borrowers alike do not soon forget a history of macroeconomic imbalances.

Drafting a Blueprint for Governments: Examples from Four Countries

Despite improvements in some of the dimensions noted earlier, developing mortgage markets has not been an easy task in the region. In many countries, the macroeconomic imbalances that restricted the development of their housing finance systems in the 1970s, 1980s, and 1990s have been alleviated, but sizeable housing finance systems have been limited to a few countries such as Chile and Panama. In other cases, such as Brazil, several years of macroeconomic stability and the development of deeper information sharing mechanisms have not resulted in much improvement.

Substantial housing deficits in many Latin American and Caribbean countries and the need to implement fiscal stimulus in response to the global crisis have prompted some countries in the region to attempt to support housing finance markets by implementing a variety of policies. These include using public banks to finance mortgages, earmarking funds in private institutions for mortgage funding, implementing different types of subsidy and credit guarantee schemes to promote mortgage lending, and supporting the development of securitization agencies, despite their mixed record (see IDB 2004 for a historical review of these programs). The following discussion examines experiences with some of these alternatives.[16]

Chile: A Well-Equipped Toolbox

By many accounts, Chile has one of the best housing finance systems in the region. Its mortgage market is the largest in South America, at almost 20 percent of GDP, and housing outcomes have improved dramatically over the past few decades. Chilean authorities have used a wide range of instruments to promote the housing credit market, ranging from subsidies to channeling large amounts of credit through their public first-tier bank. The authorities recently strengthened these programs as part of the recent government stimulus package, but also in response to the devastating earthquake in 2010. The combination of brisk private sector–led financial development and policies supporting housing finance has led to a relatively deep market with wide access, especially to lower-income populations.

But even in the case of Chile, these policies pose challenges and risks. As Micco et al. (2011) point out, mortgage lending boomed between 2000 and 2008, but by 2010, about a quarter of all outstanding mortgages issued by Banco Estado, a state-owned commercial bank that focuses on lower-income segments, were nonperforming. Although part of the rise in nonperforming loans might be due to the international crises that hit Chile, the region, and the global economy, funneling countercyclical policy to counteract these shocks through the state-owned lender raises questions about the appropriateness of stimulating low-income borrowing to this extent.[17]

The use of public banks to fuel mortgage markets can be a valuable catalyst. However, this policy needs to be supported by strong institutions at the levels of both the public bank and the financial regulators and supervisors. Strong governance of the public bank is crucial to avoid political use of credits. Further, a strong financial safety net is necessary to develop prudential mechanisms to cope with the rising financial risks associated with serving vulnerable groups, as well as avoiding financial market bubbles.

Brazil: Earmarking Funds for Housing Finance

In Brazil, earmarking is the main force behind private sector mortgage lending. Interest rates fell dramatically after inflation—which raged well over 1,000 percent in the late 1980s and early 1990s—declined significantly, first with the Real Plan of 1994 and then with the adoption of the inflation targeting model in 1999. Inflation has fluctuated around 5 percent (sometimes a bit higher, sometimes lower) in the past five years. But even with increased macroeconomic stability and some improvement on the legal front, the Brazilian housing finance system has not grown much. Martins, Lundberg, and Takeda (2011) show that almost all of the recent growth is due to government involvement either directly (through public lenders, which make up 40 percent of the market) or through its "earmarking" rule for housing funds.[18] The "earmarking" rules in Brazil are such that for every *real* that banks receive in deposits in savings accounts, they must direct 65 centavos to housing finance.[19] This sets a lower bound on funds available for home loans at roughly 65 percent of the savings in the country's banks.

One feature of this Brazilian policy is that the amount of earmarked funds can be linked to the monetary policy rate. That is, there could be a negative relationship between the overnight policy (SELIC) rate and the amount of savings. This is possible because savings accounts earn a quasi-fixed return (of 6 percent plus the Brazilian central bank's "reference rate," known as TR). Moreover, alternative stores of value, such as fixed income instruments and certificates of deposit (CDs), have returns that are highly correlated with the SELIC rate. Thus, increases in the SELIC rate make savings accounts less attractive and decreases make savings more attractive. As expected, when the SELIC rate is reduced, the amount deposited in savings accounts increases, thereby generating an increase in funds for housing finance as "earmarked" funds grow. Similarly, when authorities need to tighten policy, this automatic mechanism leads to a contraction of both deposits and mortgage lending funds.

The downside is that private lenders do not seem willing to fund more home loans than required by regulation. As figure 7.3 shows, the increase in private lenders' home loans has moved in lock-step with requirements through the earmarking rule. While public lenders have more flexibility, for private lenders the amount of funds in savings accounts drives the

Figure 7.3 Brazil: Net Requirements and Total Housing Loans by Private Lenders

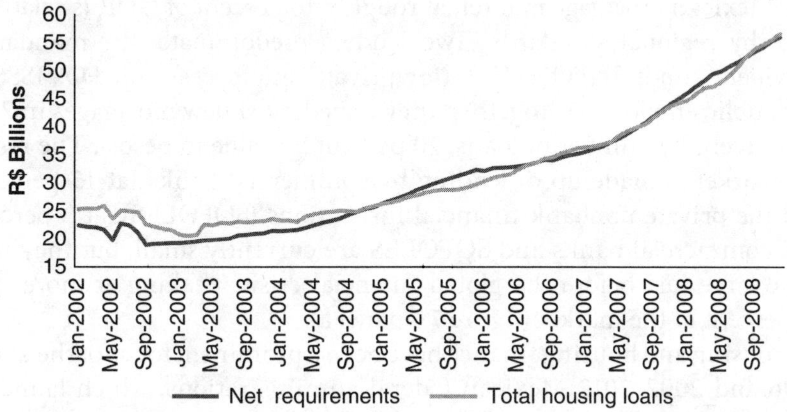

Source: Martins, Lundberg, and Takeda (2011).

amount they are willing to lend into the housing market because of the 65 percent earmarking rule.

A fundamental question to ask is this: Why are private lenders unwilling to commit any more funds to housing finance than they are required by law? The global benchmarking discussed earlier in this chapter suggests two reasons: Brazil scores three out of ten on the protection of legal rights for borrowers and lenders, and scores the same in ease of registering property. Were Brazil to improve on these two dimensions—were it just to reach the average scores in emerging Asia—the regression analysis suggests its mortgage market would be as large as Chile's.

The authors note at least one potential pitfall of this system. Because the "earmarking rule" is essentially a cross-subsidization scheme to funnel funds toward housing finance, it could eventually lead to an oversupply of housing funds. If such oversupply were to occur, riskier loans would be funded, thereby increasing the likelihood of future default and financial and macroeconomic stability. While there is no evidence that such risks have materialized, this possibility highlights the need to have a strong institutional framework to monitor the implementation of the earmarking strategy, to regulate the amount of the target, and avoid financial risks. To exploit the full potential of this policy, a framework that enables strong creditor rights is also needed.

Mexico: Promoting Housing Finance, Construction, and Ownership

The Mexican mortgage market, at roughly 10 percent of GDP, is relatively large by regional standards. Two lenders predominate: the mandatory provident funds INFONAVIT (for private employees) and FOVISSSTE (for public employees). Together, they issued most new mortgages in 2009 (82 percent by number of loans, 70 percent by value in pesos). The rest of the market is made up of lending by commercial banks (at 15 percent), and the private nonbank financial institutions (SOFOLES), at 3 percent. The commercial banks and SOFOLES are currently small, but they were quite large just before the global financial crisis, peaking at more than 40 percent of the market (figure 7.4 panel a).

Housing and housing finance have been a prominent focus of the 2000–2006 and 2007–2012 Mexican federal administrations, which launched (and maintained) a comprehensive policy package geared toward promoting housing finance, construction, and ownership. The largest public-sector mortgage bank, INFONAVIT, has implemented changes that have enabled it to boost mortgage issuance while greatly reducing its nonperforming loan rate and increasing the share of loans to the poor; encourage new private sector mortgage issuers; establish a mortgage-backed securities market; and implement a large-scale grant program for the acquisition of affordable housing, especially for low-income families. The results have been impressive. The number of housing mortgages issued each year almost tripled from 2000 to 2009 (figure 7.4 panel b). Annual grants for the purchase of affordable housing reached 340,475 units in 2009, and financial institutions have issued mortgage-backed securities for seven years.

Empirical analysis by López-Silva et al. (2011) focuses on a key element of Mexico's housing policy: CONAVI's large subsidy program ("Esta es tu Casa"). It provides a subsidy of approximately US$3,000 to low-income families that use a mortgage to acquire a house. Upfront grant programs such as CONAVI's, explicitly designed to enable relatively poor applicants (with lower job stability and thus potentially higher default rates) to obtain a mortgage and purchase a house, could potentially imply significant financial costs to mortgage banks. The upfront subsidies may affect repayment behavior, as borrowers who receive such assistance risk losing less of their own money in case of a foreclosure.

To identify whether borrowers who received subsidies exhibit different repayment behavior than comparable borrowers who did not, López-Silva

Figure 7.4 Mexico: Evolution of Loan Origination by Main Participants

a. Percent of Mortgage Loans

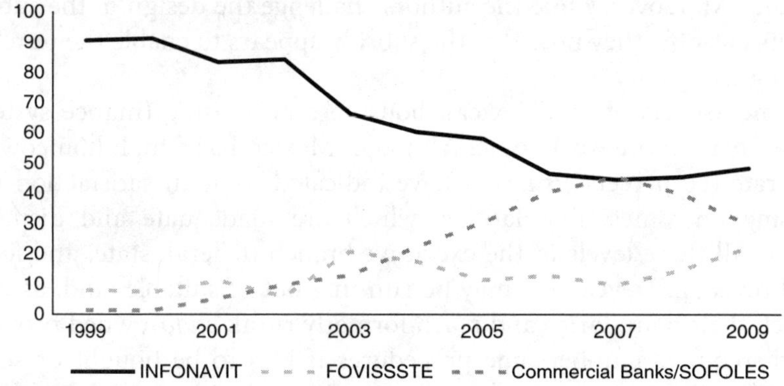

b. Number of Mortgage Loans

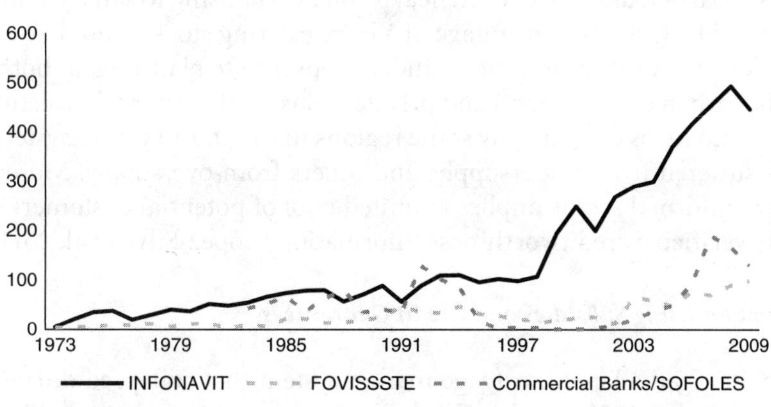

Source: López-Silva et al. (2011).

et al. (2011) analyzed a database containing information on INFONAVIT's mortgage operations over the last few years. Focusing on mortgage recipients who left the formal sector, became self-employed, or lost their jobs,[20] they use a propensity score matching technique to show that those with a subsidy miss a lower percentage of monthly payments (about 1.8 percentage points less) and wait about 1.7 months longer before missing a payment. Thus, the authors argue that the large subsidy programs currently in operation do not have negative financial implications for mortgage institutions; the subsidy appears to improve repayment behavior among workers, especially among those who have lost their formal employment. Better repayment behavior is important, as INFONAVIT offers lower rates the lower the borrower's income, so there is no buffer against higher defaults. Moreover, while the authors challenge the design of the subsidy and its cut-offs, they note that the subsidy appears to enable the purchase of a higher-quality home.

Some aspects of the Mexican housing and housing finance systems, however, are more worrisome. Although Mexico has a high homeownership rate (80 percent), surveys have indicated some dissatisfaction with housing outcomes. Regulations, which are inadequate and dispersed among all three levels of the executive branch (federal, state, and local), need revision. Developers may be running out of suitable land, as cities stretch their boundaries and reach formerly rural, *ejido*-owned property, which requires cumbersome procedures if it is to be bought or sold.[21] Investment protection needs to be significantly improved, as foreclosure procedures can take two or even three years in some Mexican states. Market participants have relied heavily on new housing to satisfy demand, and tried little to take advantage of a large existing stock of used housing. A lack of relevant information hinders appropriate planning, at both the public (urban development) and private (housing finance and investment) levels, and helps explain why some regions in the country have systematically suffered from undersupply, and others from oversupply. Moreover, a large informal sector implies a limited pool of potential customers with easily verifiable creditworthiness information (López-Silva et al. 2011).

Colombia: Using Subsidies and Credit Guarantees

Colombia had a large mortgage market system that collapsed during the crisis of the late 1990s and has just started to recover. The recent combination of policies followed by authorities has received much attention. In the early 1970s, spurring construction activity was the cornerstone of the country's development strategy.[22] Housing savings corporations (CAVs) were formed by decree. Their assets were limited to mortgage loans and their liabilities were expressed in an inflation-adjusted unit (the UPAC). A fund at the central bank (the FAVI fund) enabled CAVs to alleviate their inherent maturity mismatch by transforming CAV deposits into longer-term UPAC loans. Early on, savings migrated to CAVs; their UPAC accounts were popular savings vehicles because the real rates on other accounts were negative, with low nominal rates more than outstripped by inflation. While the CAVs likely promoted housing construction, they were highly procyclical.[23] In good times, they expanded credit rapidly (knowing they had access to FAVI liquidity), but in bad times, excess deposits at CAVs were parked at the central bank in the most profitable investment vehicle (UPAC), thereby reducing lending. CAVs were successful in attracting funds because of an implicit subsidy (their ability to offer UPAC rates and get maturity transformed through FAVI). But when market interest rates increased, this advantage lessened and the CAVs contracted.

The CAVs eventually ran into liquidity problems, and the calculation of the UPAC was modified several times to provide CAVs with an advantage that would help keep them afloat. But eventually (in the early 1990s), FAVI was eliminated and CAVs lost their special advantages.

During the financial crises of 1997–1998, mortgage payments remained tied to UPAC (now inflation plus an interest rate component). Meanwhile, Colombian nominal interest rates spiked. A crisis ensued, and in the end the government moved liabilities onto its books. Mortgage lending declined[24] and did not recover until 2005. The recovery, while weak, has been linked not only to improved macroeconomic stability but also to a combination of subsidies and guarantees implemented by the government that have proved successful, especially by promoting the development of mortgage markets for lower-income earners during the mortgage credit recovery.

Arbeláez, Camacho, and Fajardo (2010) explore the effectiveness of housing finance policies aimed at lower-income segments of the Colombian housing market, the so-called social interest housing (or VIS).[25] The authors note that the housing deficit in Colombia is high, at 36.4 percent, and also show that social mortgages are a small but not inconsequential portion of the overall mortgage market (see figure 7.5).

The study focuses on the impact of a social housing subsidy, a one-time direct subsidy created in 1991 to partially fund the purchase of affordable housing. It finds that between 2003 and 2008, the percentage of subsidy beneficiaries belonging to the three lowest income quintiles increased from 65 percent to 80 percent, although in 2008 only one-third of the subsidy beneficiaries were classified as poor, according to the Index of Unsatisfied Basic Needs (UBN).

This suggests that although the targeting was adequate in terms of reaching the vulnerable, it was not effective enough to reach the poorest of the poor. To reach such populations, housing solutions may require vehicles other than credit, since the very poor usually lack sufficient collateral and income to gain support through credit. Where the authors see headway is in the impact of housing subsidies and credit on the quality of

Figure 7.5 Colombia: Mortgage Disbursements for Social and Nonsocial Housing

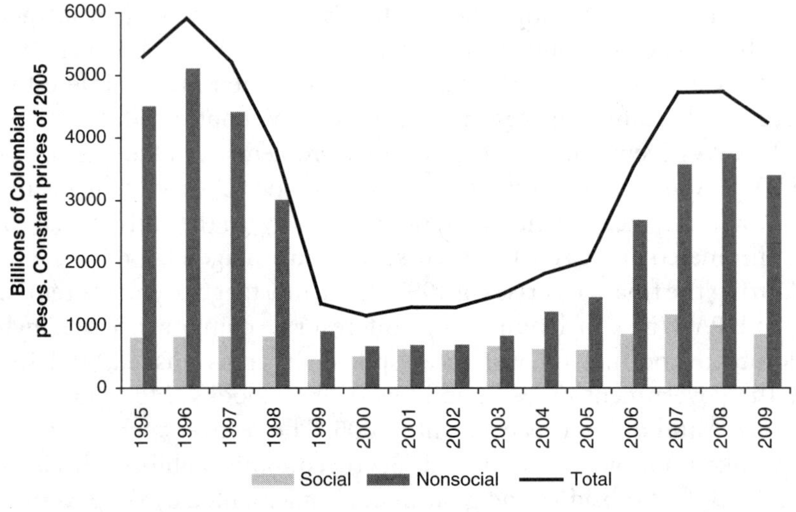

Source: Arbeláez, Camacho, and Fajardo (2010).

dwellings and quality of life. Using propensity score matching and data from Quality of Life Surveys, they find that the social housing subsidy and housing credit improve the quality of the dwellings and the quality of life of its beneficiaries.

The key institutional element in the case of Colombia has been the adoption of a properly stated rule to define social housing. This rule has been widely accepted. Through that mechanism, certain levels of the lower-income population have been reached, the subsidy has become better targeted, and mortgage financing has been promoted.

In addition to the VIS subsidy, Colombia has an interest rate subsidy. The subsidy, originally implemented in 2009 during the global financial crisis as a countercyclical policy to boost the construction sector during the recession, covers up to 5 percentage points of the agreed interest rate for a seven-year period. Hofstetter, Tovar, and Urrutia (2010) have analyzed this subsidy. They show that for nonsocial interest housing, the subsidy led to a 38 percent increase in mortgage loans. For social interest rate housing, it led to a 36 percent increase. The authors view both estimates as lower bounds. After controlling for other relevant determinants, real mortgage interest rates (that is, the interest rate agreed between the bank and the customer before the government rebate, adjusted for inflation) did increase—by 1.09 percent—suggesting that, as with any subsidy, banks were able to capture part of the revenues by charging a higher interest rate. Another way to look at this result is that the estimated pass-through of the subsidy to customers was between 65 percent and 74 percent. Banks benefit by capturing part of the subsidy, but consumers benefit too. While this policy has been useful in promoting mortgage lending, it draws on scarce fiscal resources. The authors question whether a government that persistently runs a budget deficit can continue to finance such a stimulus.

Arbeláez, Camacho, and Fajardo (2010) also explore the use of another government program, the partial credit guarantee for social housing loans. This was implemented in 2004 and was aimed at addressing the obstacles of lack of collateral and costly collateral recovery. While they find evidence that the policy has helped develop the mortgage market for social housing, they also conclude that these credits have a higher delinquency rate than those not covered by the guarantee, suggesting that moral hazard is a crucial element to consider in the design of housing market policies.

Overall, the experience of Colombia suggests that well-designed public policies can help expand the mortgage market. However, in the absence of deeper reforms such as strengthening protection of creditor rights, the gains of direct interventions by the public sector may remain limited.

Building a Better Mortgage Market

Housing finance markets in Latin America and the Caribbean are small and underdeveloped. As shown in this chapter, many countries in the region have made significant efforts to promote information sharing mechanisms and to strengthen their macroeconomic policies that are important to the development of mortgage markets. In order to reach a stage of mortgage market development consistent with the income level of the countries in the region, reforms are needed that foster the protection of creditor rights, enhance property registries, and strengthen the institutional framework to enable their use. These reforms, supported by an adequate prudential policy that promotes proper risk valuations and equivalent risk provisions for borrowers, are the cornerstones of well-functioning and stable private mortgage markets worldwide.

Several Latin American and Caribbean countries have undertaken a new series of government interventions to promote mortgage markets. Some of the instruments that have been tested throughout the region include the use of public banks to allocate credit; interest rate and direct subsidies; and financing schemes based on earmarked funds. The fact that strong private sector–led mortgage market development has not responded suggests that without deeper reforms, the effectiveness of these types of initiatives will be limited. The case studies show that with proper institutional adjustments, countries could see some gains from cautious design and implementation of government-supported intervention schemes. But until more is done to strengthen the legal, information, and regulatory environment, especially the protection of creditor rights, private sector–driven mortgage market development will likely be muted, despite policy interventions to stimulate it. And until the private sector steps up its participation, housing finance markets will continue to underserve potential home buyers in the region.

8

Doing It Yourself

Doing things yourself is not necessarily bad. Things tend to cost less when you do them yourself and are more tailored to your tastes and preferences. But sometimes doing things yourself can take too much time, can cost more than you expected if you make mistakes, and can be dangerous if you don't know what you're doing. Unfortunately, many times you don't have a choice. If you don't have money to hire a professional to paint your house, you still can have that special new color on your bedroom wall if you are willing to spend your free Sunday painting it yourself. If you're lucky, the hardware store will give you some painting tips, and the paint store will let you use your credit card so you can pay for your paint over time.

Many low-income and lower-middle-class households in Latin America and the Caribbean build their houses themselves. They do it over time. In many countries, more than half of households are their own "builders." They do it on their own, without much help and few if any handy tips, and they do it without much outside financing, because they can't get credit.

Doing it yourself is a perfectly rational response by households to the limitations they face and the failures they must cope with in the housing market. If they can't get a mortgage—because lenders won't give them one—they rent, or if they can't rent, they scrounge around to find what housing they can. If they don't have a lot of money for home improvements—and lenders won't give them a loan—they build in small stages over time. If they can't get title to land, they squat, and wait until it looks like they can stay on their lot and in their house—and then they invest in home improvements. If they can't afford to move, they stay put, and make the improvements they can, over time.

But while this behavior is rational for individual families and households, is it rational for society as a whole? Are there things that can be done to address the problems and failures that led to the improvised behavior—doing it yourself—in the first place? Are there things that can be done—by government, the private sector, nongovernment organizations (NGOs), and alliances among them—in the short and medium term to make housing better for the millions of households that have to build for themselves? This chapter addresses those questions.

The Long and Winding Road to Building a Home

Adequate housing includes legal security of tenure, availability of basic services and infrastructure such as power, water and sewerage, affordability, habitability, accessibility, location, and cultural adequacy. In reality, all these conditions are seldom met at the same time, especially for low-income families.

Market Failures in the Value Chain of Progressive Housing

Poor and lower-middle-income households face adverse conditions along various stages of the progressive building process, from access to land and services to financing (see figure 8.1). Obtaining land with secure tenure, which occurs at the beginning of the value chain, is a crucial obstacle for lower-income households. Even if households can build a dwelling by themselves, the very basic fact that they are investing limited resources in an illegal settlement and incurring the risk of being evicted is a major concern. Access to services is also limited for illegal households. Suppliers of services such as water and electricity often refuse to serve illegal dwellings for legal reasons.

In the middle of the value chain, households face the challenge of building their homes, and improving them over time. To do so, they need low-cost homes, and simple designs that can be added to over time. They need low-cost building materials. And they need know-how if they are to build or improve their homes themselves: not just in construction techniques, but in obtaining titles, organizing communities for successful redress of housing and community problems, and obtaining basic services.

At the end of the value chain lies financing. Traditional mortgage finance institutions have typically lacked the low-cost, community-based systems necessary to lend to the low-income market. Microfinance institutions have stepped into this financing niche (see discussion at the end of this chapter).

Figure 8.1 Critical Market Failures along the Low-Income Housing Value Chain

Access to land and services	Construction materials	Construction	Delivery Channels	Financing
- High cost of urban land	- Most companies are focusing on product innovations that are not relevant to low-income individuals or that need larger solutions	- Self-construction and limited construction skills (safety issues)	- Limited formal distribution	- Lack of collateral
- Inefficient/ inappropriate property rights system			- Small individual transactions	- Lack of regular and verifiable salary
- Illegal settlements				- Limited outreach of housing microfinance
- High cost of infrastructure				

Source: Drayton and Ashoka (2008).

Step by Step: Incremental Housing

How do all these gaps play out for millions of households in the region? Consider a relatively successful outcome, Ciudad Nezahualcoyotl (Ciudad Neza) in the state of Mexico. Ciudad Neza was built on the drained bed of Lake Texcoco. Once the draining was completed, in the early twentieth century, the government sold the land to private owners. Two things happened. First, plots lacked basic utilities (they were unserviced), failing to comply with state regulations. Second, plots were sold and resold, creating confusion about the status of tenure. By the 1960s, 600,000 people lived in the area.

In the 1970s, local residents' associations mobilized and protested against the actions of land developers and the general living conditions. The federal government stepped in, which resulted in the creation of a trust (and later a state government organization) in charge of managing the regularization of properties.[1] By the late 1990s, tenure was unresolved for only 12 percent of the plots. Public services were introduced in the early 1970s, and by 1980 the area had street lighting, paved roads, water, and drainage. Today, Ciudad Neza is dotted with trees, banks, shops, offices, libraries, schools, universities, cinemas, a cathedral, and an Olympic sports stadium (UN-HABITAT 2003a).

Building a home—much less a community—is a long process. In the case of Ciudad Neza, the consolidation of the area took 30 years, from 1950 to 1980. For Mexico, overall, the median time to complete a home is 16 years (Prahalad 2005).

Accelerating the process by which families build their houses themselves requires some degree of land tenure security. In Ciudad Neza, once homeowners had a reasonable expectation that they would not be removed, they proceeded with improvements. That behavior has repeated throughout the region, as observed in a 40-year longitudinal case study of incremental housing in El Salvador (Gattoni, Goethert, and Chávez 2011).

In most cases in which families build their homes themselves, governments need to step in to provide infrastructure and services, as households cannot effectively access land and provide trunk infrastructure and services (Wakely and Riley 2010). The lack of basic services was the main trigger for the protests in Ciudad Neza in the 1970s that ushered in the government's involvement (Ward 1986).

Informal land development generates a series of planning issues for the long run. In Ciudad Neza, the original developers envisioned a number of housing blocks surrounding a central open space with public amenities. However, as demand for housing accelerated, these central areas became occupied and, in some cases, no open space was left (Castillo 2006).

Successful experiences of families building their own homes (especially for the lowest-income households) involve communities that provide mutual support and community organizations to address common issues (Gattoni 2009). For instance, in the case of Ciudad Neza, the associations led the protests in the 1970s that pressured the government into becoming involved.

Incremental Building 101

The process by which families build their homes has three phases: initial access to land; construction of a basic housing nucleus or core house; and home improvement (Greene and Rojas 2008).

Phase One: Gaining Access to Land

The pressure on land for housing in Latin America and the Caribbean is enormous. Cities need to develop two to four times the amount of land that is currently being used to accommodate the next two generations (see chapter 2). The growing number of households adds to the pressure. Newly formed families, young couples that decide to live together and then get married, or multiple families that used to live in the same dwelling and face the challenge of building their own house all need concrete, cost-effective solutions to build a dwelling.

The pressure on many cities is immense, as city budgets are insufficient to develop land with infrastructure and services, which in turn forces illegal settlements to spread. From the government's point of view, the issue is to provide basic trunk infrastructure and incentives for new developed land for mixed and intensive use to control urban sprawl (see chapter 5). From the point of view of new families that want to start building a home, the issue is to find a piece of land relatively close to work opportunities or with access to an efficient transportation system, with a reasonable level of land security.

Three conditions for tenure security are key (Brown et al. 2006). First, the level of political commitment must be high. Second, the agency in charge must have jurisdiction over the land it regulates. Third, the long-term strategy should be flexible; a variety of instruments can be used to provide tenure security such as titling, zoning, and urban planning.

Tenure security does not require titling: rather, the feeling of security is the first condition for any housing investment (Gattoni, Goethert, and Chávez 2011). As Angel (1983) explains, "Tenure security, whether backed by documents, by promises, or by hopes, is fundamentally subjective. The feeling of security is an expectation. If such expectations are high, people can safely invest in their houses without running the risk of losing their savings" (p. 112). Payne (2001) concurs and points out, "Where people feel secure, they are likely to invest what they can afford in improving and extending their homes and environment" (p. 1). A variety of measures, including freedom from eviction by the government, recognition of intermediate rights, or recognition of the legality of the neighborhood, can transmit a feeling of security.

Affordable and flexible land development is essential to improve the process by which families build their own homes. However, most developing countries adopted industrialized urbanization models and land development standards geared toward the middle- and upper-income housing ideals of the 1950s and 1960s (such as suburban subdivision models), which limit land affordability and use for low-income families. These standards usually lead to wasteful and inefficient land use, expensive infrastructure that in most cases must be provided by land users, and the need for long-term maintenance. In addition, unrealistically high or inappropriate official standards render the settlements and houses typically built by the poor illegal. Finally, private informal contractors tend to bypass the costly standards by selling small lots without services in "illegal subdivisions" at prices affordable to the poor (Gattoni 2009).

What can make lots more accessible and more affordable for lower-income families? Four factors influence the cost of land plots: plot frontage (less frontage reduces cost), block length (bigger blocks reduce land requirements for other needed uses), reduced street width, and infrastructure standards. Cities often issue guidelines for land use. Typical categories and percentages include: 10–15 percent for land for circulation (streets and sidewalks), 20–35 percent for land for public uses (parks, schools, hospitals, and the like), and 45–60 percent for land for private use (for housing). The higher the percentage of private land use, the lower the cost per square meter of salable land. Also, the lower the percentage of public land, the lower the cost of public maintenance of those areas. Therefore, layouts should maximize private land uses and reduce public land uses.

Another measure to consider is the ratio of the linear length of infrastructure (power lines, and water distribution network, for instance) to the number of lots served. For low-income models, the linear length of networks per lot should be reduced.

In summary, an efficient low-income model includes mixed land uses, land use percentages that reduce circulation area and increase residential area, reduced infrastructure length per lot, and low public land maintenance responsibility (Dowall 1992a).

Phase Two: Building a Basic Unit (Core House)

Successful incremental processes start with a good basic unit (core house) on serviced land. The core house is designed to very low-cost, basic standards so that beneficiaries can immediately move into the house. As its name implies, the core house is not a full house. It provides the basis for future adjustments. For families, it offers an inexpensive starting point. For policymakers and planners, it can be viewed as a combination of financing and technical instruments to jump-start the incremental process (figure 8.2).

The specifications for core houses depend on the local and national context of each country. However, common features include access to basic infrastructure and a single room (including a cooking and bath area), with possibilities for expansion. Average size varies from 15 to 40

Figure 8.2 Basic Starting Options for a Core House, Guyana Incremental Housing Program

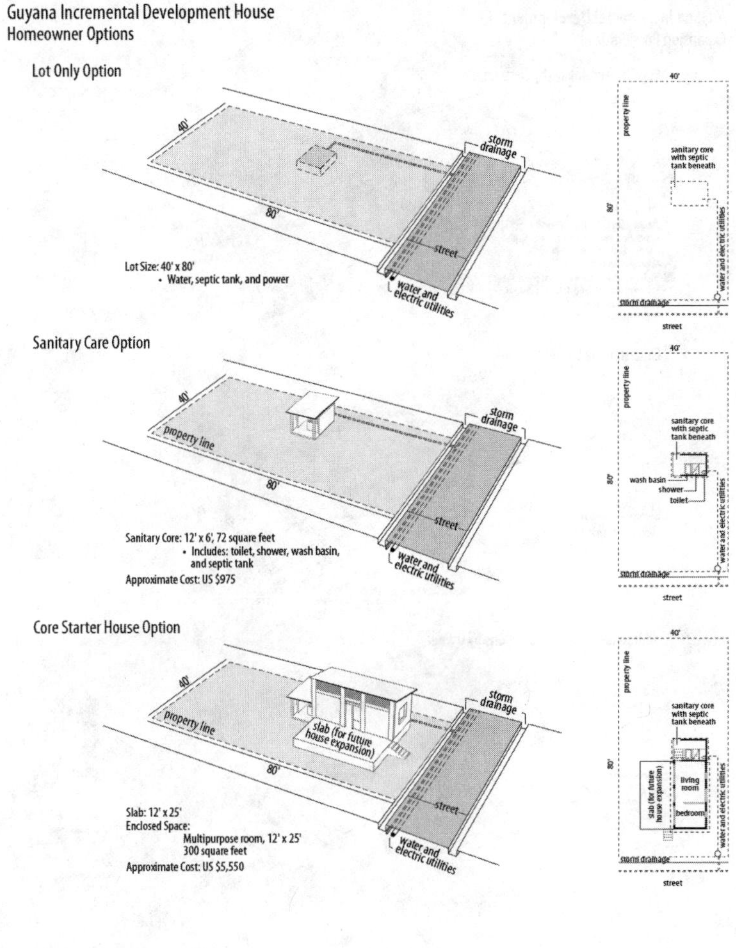

Source: IDB (2008).

square meters. Core houses have thrived in sites and services programs. More recently, they have been a common way to rebuild in the aftermath of natural disasters (as after the earthquake in Haiti), as they allow low-income families to recoup from the loss of their assets. In all cases, "building it yourself" is seen as part of the solution to the housing needs for low-income families (Turner and Fichter 1972).

Successful core houses must offer both lower costs and conditions for future expansion. Here, good design can help. The kitchen and bathroom

Figure 8.3 Expansion Possibilities for a Core House, Guyana Incremental Housing Program

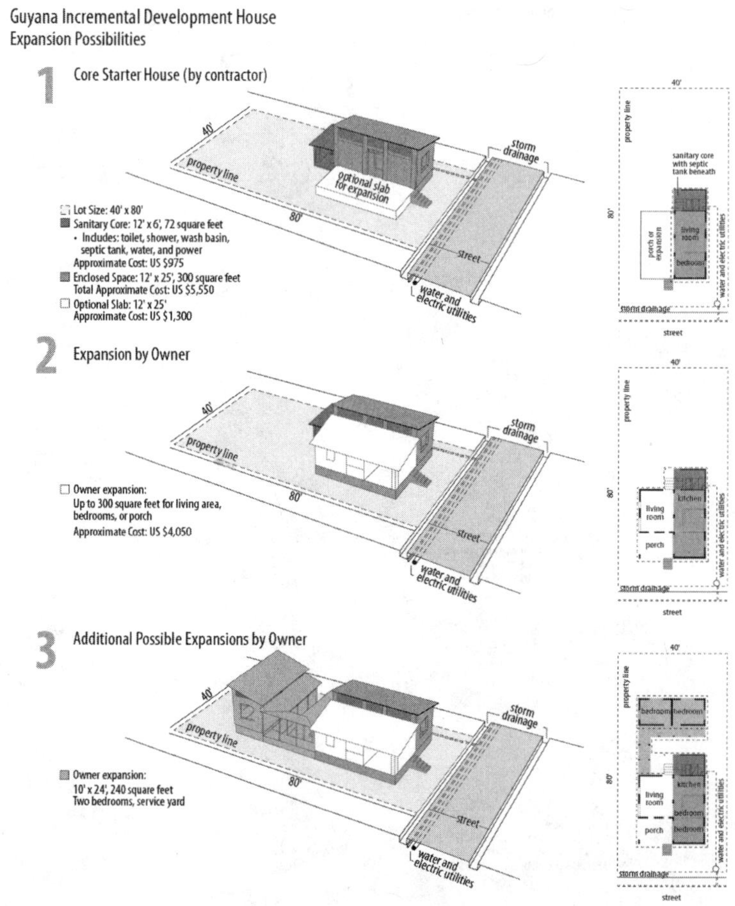

Source: IDB (2008).

should be next to each other to minimize the cost of pipelines. Moreover, a series of core houses should be built as mirror images so that street manholes can be used economically.

Ideally, expansion can occur while maintaining a relatively harmonious façade on the street. The shape of the core house, as well as the basic structure, can facilitate expansion.

Incremental housing programs offer different starting options that accommodate different household preferences and budget restrictions. For example, in Guyana, the government's Low Income Settlement Program offers three core unit options for low-income families when they apply for a subsidy to buy a lot sponsored by the program (see figure 8.2). Different extensions to that core unit are possible from the outset (figure 8.3). Together, figures 8.2 and 8.3 illustrate what the incremental process is about.

The lot-only option is the most accessible to the lowest-income families (figure 8.2). However, it suffers from numerous shortcomings, including the basic fact that a lot alone is not a home. Moreover, it generates lot occupancy issues: for instance, maintenance of the investments in basic infrastructure, and difficulty for the beneficiaries who are already renting to save enough to be able to build their home. When working with the lot-only option, designers should take into consideration such factors as land subdivisions, key elements of basic infrastructure (streets, water, power, street lighting, and storm drainage) at the time lots are allocated, and community facilities (community centers, police stations, playing fields, and bus shelters, for instance). In the case of Guyana, the lot-only options offered by the low-income housing program took pains to place the new sites next to ones that had been previously developed to limit off-site investment costs, and better coordinate designs to consider drainage needs and the planning of streets and lots.

The sanitary core option adds an improvement, as it enables beneficiaries to move into the lot (figure 8.2). A sanitary core or "utility" wall contains the connections to water, drainage, sewerage, and electricity. This option was not popular. Instead, households preferred the core house.

Figure 8.3 shows the various options for expansion, based on the plan used in Guyana. Rooms (gray areas) can be added to the side and back of the unit and a porch can be added to the front or back. The original idea was to design a construction credit pilot mechanism, including a phased approach based on the final project envisioned. The three designs were supposed to be the three options for financing.

To succeed, the incremental process should be part of a package by which a lot plus basic services and shelter come along with the instruments that allow low-income households to expand the starting option. Technical assistance and credit are the key instruments for a successful expansion of core units.

The choice of materials can also make the house more affordable (and possibly, energy-efficient and sustainable). Materials vary, depending on local conditions. For instance, in Guyana, timber has replaced concrete for the beams, and blocks with rebar and concrete infill have replaced concrete piers. Concrete blocks are the preferred material in Latin America thanks to their association with modernity, social mobility, and security.

New materials, such as prefabricated materials, and new construction techniques could lower costs and expedite construction in incremental housing processes (see chapter 6). Until recently, technological innovation played a small role in housing construction in developing countries. Norms for high-cost building, zoning, and subdivision regulations also discouraged creativity (Bertaud and Lucius 1989). Recently, however, soaring energy costs have made new technologies for homes and communities more cost effective and are turning green housing into something of a growth industry. An explosion in new technology for affordable housing construction and basic services (such as potable water, solar electricity, and off-grid electrical) are rapidly changing the potential for truly low-cost, affordable, high-quality housing units. However, major impediments for its application in the region remain and must be solved (see chapter 6).

Phase Three: Improving the House

The third step in the incremental process is the improvement phase. In all types of settlements (illegal, legal, and those specifically designed to support incremental housing), residents expand and improve their houses over time. The pace is different depending on each settlement type. Illegal settlements (slums and nonconforming subdivisions) generally take longer to receive utilities, and residents' incomes are oftentimes irregular. As a consequence, these tend to start up slowly.

Households' contribution to the self-help process is substantial, regardless of the initial subsidy. In Chile, in the case of three housing programs—Programa de Mejoramiento de Barrios, (PMB, Neighborhood Improvement), Programa de Vivienda Progresiva (PVP, Progressive Housing), and Programa de Vivienda Basica (PVB, Basic Housing)—families invested between half and three times the initial cost of the home: from about US$10,500 to US$14,600 (US$14,000 in the case of sanitary core). The lower the initial subsidy, the higher the amount of the families' investment (see table 8.1).

Investment levels are similar in El Salvador, averaging approximately US$11,300 (Vance 2011) but priorities for improvement vary. In El Salvador, families have focused on adding an extra bedroom and securing the house for safety. In Chile, the priority is on finishing the dwelling and expanding, so that the dwellings reach an average of 60 square meters.

Table 8.1 Residents' Own Investments in Housing Improvements in Chile's Progressive Housing Programs

Program	Starting cost (US$)	Family investments (US$)	Final house value (US$)	Family investments over starting costs (ratio)
Programa de Mejoramiento de Barrios (PMB)	5,010	14,668	19,678	2.9
Programa de Vivienda Progresiva (PVP)	8,743	10,496	19,239	1.2
Programa de Vivienda Basica (PVB)	18,218	10,705	28,923	0.6

Source: Authors' calculations based on Greene (2011).

In El Salvador, beneficiaries tend to improve the quality of materials (for instance, upgrading from wood to concrete block). In the case of programs that were jump-started with a core or complete house, improvements focus on adding rooms or second and third stories, and upgrading services. Households undertook more improvements in houses in incremental programs than in other forms of self-construction (see table 8.2).

The level of household income figures prominently when deciding whether to improve and expand and sets the time and pace of improvements. In all types of settlements, there is a direct correlation between household income, discretionary income, and the amount of expansion/improvements. The lower the household income and the larger the number of family members, the fewer the improvements (El Salvador). Income affects access to financing and construction costs (taking into account preference for materials).

Low-income families are vulnerable to the availability and cost fluctuations of construction materials, as they influence when and to what extent to invest. External factors such as building booms (following a natural disaster, for instance) or economic overheating create shortages and push up wages for skilled labor. In addition, low-income families tend to be do-it-yourself homebuilders, and so buy materials in small quantities. This also tends to push up costs.

Table 8.2 Household Housing Investments by Type of Initial Housing Solution, El Salvador (Percent of Total)

Initial program	Fundamental[a]	Consolidated[b]	Improved[c]
Site and services core houses	38.3	31.7	30
Upgraded settlement	36.7	36.7	26.7
Illegal, not upgraded	50	50	0
Private land, no services	46.7	53.3	0
Public, complete house	40	43.3	16.7
Private, complete house	36.7	46.7	16.7
All houses in the sample (average)	*41*	*41.9*	*17.1*

[a] Fundamental: Only minor improvements undertaken.
[b] Consolidated: Homes expanded and completed.
[c] Improved: Homes expanded and services upgraded.
Source: Authors' calculations based on Gattoni, Goethert, and Chávez (2011).

Green housing can also inflate costs—at least, up-front costs. This is a challenge for the region as it attempts to mainstream green housing for lower-income households (the majority) and to attain long-term sustainability goals. Waste also boosts costs. Families can waste time, materials, and money when they build their houses themselves. In Mexico, for instance, families that build their homes spend 30 percent in unnecessary construction materials (Kellogg School of Management 2011).

The need to bring in specialists, such as plumbers and electricians, if owners lack certain skills also adds to costs. More broadly, how should technical assistance be brought in? The most difficult problem for communities is how to cooperate with governments and technical professionals, such as architects and planners. Incremental housing represents a new area for many architects. As one architect noted, "My architecture training had only equipped me to help the 3–5 percent of the world who could afford my skills and the technology that they were designed to use; the remaining 95 percent had to make do without professional skills" (Anzorena 1993, p. 122).

New Partnerships and New Packages of Services

Solutions to the problems all along the housing value chain lie in new forms of partnerships between the private sector, government, and nongovernmental organizations. For instance, suppliers of construction materials are awakening to the potential of low-income families as consumers and their willingness to build their houses themselves. Technical assistance programs, as well as better distribution platforms, are becoming available throughout the region.

Three examples illustrate the possibilities and show how the improvements can be supported.

Fundasal

FUNDASAL in El Salvador was one of the first institutions to develop the incremental sites and services concept. Its mission is to help individuals and communities develop their potential and to overcome the impact of poverty. The broad objective of this NGO is social change, and its housing program constitutes a means to that end. The institution concentrates on removing barriers to accessing land, credit, and houses. FUNDASAL functions as an intermediary between the informal and formal sectors. By keeping production cost per unit low (by means of higher land density, smaller plot sizes, and high cost recovery, and by applying the incremental process), FUNDASAL demonstrates that government and private developers can join forces to produce housing and subdivisions in an affordable way.

Patrimonio Hoy

Conceived by the Mexican-based global building materials company CEMEX in 1998, Patrimonio Hoy organizes low-income families into self-financing cells that facilitate and expedite self-help home building. The program started in Mexico and spread to Colombia, Costa Rica, Nicaragua, and Venezuela. CEMEX and its network provide the products needed, as well as the technical assistance, including an architect. To date, more than 150,000 families have benefited. The success of Patrimonio Hoy derives from its recognition that the social norms and economic habits of households differ from those of its usual clients. For instance, Patrimonio Hoy has improved the *tanda* practice, which consists of people in the community joining money-pooling groups. *Tanda*s last ten weeks and usually involve payments of $100 per week, with weekly distribution of the pot. The *tanda*s offered by Patrimonio Hoy include club membership, technical advice, and credit for members during a 35-week period, and serve as the basis for a 70-week building materials program (see more about Patrimonio Hoy in box 8.1).

Box 8.1 Patrimonio Hoy

The Patrimono Hoy (PH) program of CEMEX, the giant Mexican cement-maker that ranks third in the world, serves do-it-yourself homebuilders who account for 40 percent of the consumption of cement in Mexico. CEMEX market studies show that low-income homebuilders in Mexico take four years to complete one room, and thirteen years to complete a four-room house; households also typically waste one-third of their expenditures. This slow rate and high cost largely reflect the lack of formal support. Many households join informal savings clubs (*tanda*) in which each family pays US$10/month to a pool and one member is selected each week by lottery until all have received money. However, such informal methods have big drawbacks: building materials dealers often sell these households poor-quality materials left over from large projects; households who lack construction skills often waste materials by buying too much or too little; families hoard these materials, which deteriorate due to the weather or are stolen; home design and construction is often poor quality; savings sometimes are spent on parties rather than on construction.

The Patrimonio Hoy program addresses these problems with the business goals of elevating the profile of the CEMEX brand and increasing sales in the self-help market. PH first organizes groups of three families who commit to a 70-week saving program. As *tanda*, each group's members take turns collecting payments and playing the role of enforcer. To ensure that savings are spent on construction materials, families receive raw materials rather than cash. Deliveries start after only two weeks, before families have saved much, and subsequent deliveries are made each ten weeks. PH, in effect, advances microcredit to these families in the form of building materials at a rate of 16 percent per annum—far below microcredit and consumer credit rates in Mexico. PH operates by establishing "cells"—four-member offices—located in low-income communities. These cells arrange with local building materials distributors to deliver high-quality products including not only cement but other building materials and provide technical assistance to households in planning and construction. Rather than advertise, CEMEX hires local "promoters"—98% of them women—to market the program, screen potential clients, and resolve communication/payment problems.

Over the past ten years, PH has assisted 250,000 Mexican households to add bedrooms, saving these families an average of one-third of total costs and finishing construction in one-quarter of the time of unassisted incremental building. PH's operations have proved profitable, although at somewhat lower rates than CEMEX as a whole. These profits come from a variety of sources beyond the sale of cement including a margin on other building materials, a membership fee, and microcredit. While cement and building materials sales for large-scale formal development projects have fluctuated greatly with the macroeconomy and the real estate industry, PH sales and profits have proved more stable. CEMEX has now expanded PH to a number of other Latin American countries, including Colombia, Costa Rica, Nicaragua, and Venezuela.

PH has received many awards. As one of the first and the best-known "Base of the Pyramid" (BOP) corporate affordable housing initiatives, PH has ignited great interest throughout the multinational corporate world. Other global and regional cement manufacturers (for example, Holcim, LaFarge, Portland Cement, etc.) and building materials manufacturers/retailers have now started similar enterprises. Thus, the demonstration effect of PH has begun to transform the housing industry in emerging countries.

Hogar de Cristo

Hogar de Cristo is a Christian charity in Ecuador that specializes in supplying cheap bamboo/wood houses to low-income families. It provides interest-free loans to families for a period of three years. Houses sell at cost and Hogar de Cristo does not make a profit. In 1970, Hogar de Cristo installed a 15,000-square-meter sawmill and began to build bamboo houses at a rate of two a week. Today, production has reached 50 houses a day. The principal material consists of bamboo panels assembled on site. Hogar de Cristo received the 1995 United Nations World Habitat Award for its work.

These three stories show that beyond technical assistance, potential beneficiaries look for a package of services including intermediaries between the informal and formal sectors, provision of materials, proximity, and knowledge of the local culture. FUNDASAL, Patrimonio Hoy, and Hogar de Cristo have been successful in offering those services.

The Missing Link: Money

Incremental housing is often financed from a variety of sources, including individual and group savings, windfalls, fabrication of building materials, sweat equity, small loans from neighborhood money lenders, barter arrangements, communal self-help, and remittances from family living abroad. These sources of funding share a common problem: they remain unconnected to formal institutions and markets (Ferguson 1999). Microfinance offers a solution, providing not only funding, but also technical assistance and new partnerships that can improve the quality of housing solutions.

Filling a Niche: Microfinance

Microfinance institutions were pioneers in the region in offering credit to poor households that do not qualify for loans from other financial institutions and lack the key requirements for mortgage finance—given their labor market informality and thus their lack of a stable income stream, paychecks, or collateral.

The series of small, short-term loans that allow households to buy building materials to build and improve a housing unit progressively are known as "housing microfinance." Commonly, the loan is a nonmortgage type of credit ranging between US$500 and US$2,500 with a term of two to five years. The amount varies considerably across countries and across microfinance institutions. For example, housing microfinance for new construction typically has a longer term, five to fifteen years, and ranges from US$3,000 to US$7,000.

Housing microfinance encompasses a broad range of services, including purchase of a lot, title regularization, adding rental units to the homeowner's property through horizontal or vertical expansion, and funding individual and communal infrastructure. Microfinance can be linked to land regularization in successful public-private partnerships (see box 8.2).

Housing microfinance has expanded significantly but can still meet only a small fraction of the demand for loans. The region's low-income housing market is estimated to be about US$300 billion and this may be on the low side given the difficulties in collecting data on low-income and informal households (Hammond et al. 2007). By way of comparison, the entire microfinance industry, serving about 50 million clients around the world, meets only about 5–10 percent of the demand for loans (Schmidt and Budinich 2006). The market for housing microfinance is even smaller, but has strong potential to grow.

The aspiration to own or build a house has proved to be one of the main motivations for families to save in both developed countries (where "savings and loan" societies have traditionally linked these functions) and emerging economies (where savings clubs and housing cooperatives have emerged for the same purpose). Hence, adding a home-improvement credit as well as savings products makes sense for microfinance institutions seeking to take deposits and become regulated financial institutions. Thus, housing microfinance fits well with the business strategy of many microfinance institutions.

Many public programs and housing finance agencies in the region have attempted to reach low-income families through subsidies to stimulate housing solutions and make them affordable. In particular, demand-side subsidy programs have successfully increased affordability, stimulated financial institutions to develop lending products, and fueled a commercial

Box 8.2 Market-Based Slum Upgrading: Terra Nova in Brazil

André Albuquerque, a lawyer specialized in conflict mediation, created Terra Nova (TN) in 2001 to regularize the ownership status of squatter families' land in Brazil's major cities. The company is in the process of regularizing 20,000 families. It has tested its methods of land regularization and conflict resolution in eight cities in four Brazilian states. In contrast to heavily subsidized government slum upgrading programs—the norm in Brazil—TN charges households for the cost of regularizing property title and community projects, making slum upgrading much more sustainable and empowering households.

TN provides an urban and environmental screen and urban plan, organizes community associations, negotiates with stakeholders, formalizes title, underwrites household payment capacity, compensates the original landowners, relocates families from environmentally sensitive areas, advocates and ensures the provision of infrastructure by local authorities, and spreads community activism to other areas. TN works with community associations to prorate the cost of improvements and land regularization among households.

What does TN Do?

1. Performs diagnostics using government housing metrics: land measuring, assessment, community sensitizing.
2. Negotiates agreements: between landowner and squatters on sales price of parcel, with municipality on local infrastructure and services to be provided—sewer system, drainage, electric lines, and roads.
3. Registers title to individual lots.
4. Establishes a price for community projects and works with community organizations to prorate the cost of loans for purchasing land and community projects among individual households.
5. Underwrites and negotiates payment terms with individual household.

Loan term to households is typically eight years, after which families receive full legal title to their lot from TN after making the last payment.

Costs:

TN charges a minimum total service fee of US$3,300. Depending on the community, different percentages of the sales price go to TN, a clearance fund for projects within the community, and to the original property owner. The effective annual interest rate of TN loans to families is (TR) 1.8 percent + 12 percent; in comparison, consumer finance for purchasing building materials (widespread in Brazil) typically costs over 60 percent per year.

The company assesses the family's job and income, and conducts interviews to evaluate payment capacity and term. The majority of households are informally employed. The default rate is being evaluated more robustly only now (the current estimate is 12.8 percent). After five months of nonpayment, the contract is rescinded and TN typically enters into a new accord with occupant. In the event of unwillingness to pay after renegotiation, TN can take back the lot. The market value of the land typically increases from US$41 per square meter before regularization and upgrading to US$107 per square meter afterward.

The company encourages family relocation from protected areas such as national parks, near waterways, or terrain prone to mudslides and floods. The economic feasibility of upgrading depends upon several factors including the number of families that must move and their willingness to migrate. The family's agreement plays a major role in the future of the project.

The total cost to the family—including the US$3,300 TN fee plus landowner indemnification—can vary from US$6,000 to US$9,400; the higher amount encompasses upgrading with urbanization projects such as community centers. In comparison, government slum upgrading subsidies average US$5,000 per household for basic services (and increase up to US$15,000 per family in difficult slums); public slum upgrading also depends upon the initiative of government agencies, which act slowly. Government slum upgrading has fallen far behind slum formation throughout Brazil. Illegal subdivisions on the urban fringe constitute the main method of urban development while central-city slums increasingly breed physical violence and drug trafficking, creating enormous social and economic problems.

TN's model potentially makes slum upgrading a much faster and more financially sustainable process that empowers the community. The company has improved its outreach by placing a community agent in each neighborhood that determines and resolves payment issues. TN has also adopted Banco Santander's microcredit methods and their IT system. TN's future plans include expansion in Sao Paulo and Rio de Janeiro because of their market size and higher-income profiles. However, the model presents considerable financial challenges today. Although a client pays in about eight years, the company has to pay up front the cost of land and upgrading in less than two years. TN has used temporary high-cost bridge loans from Banco Santander to fund this mismatch, which is manageable at low volume, but has become a hindrance to its ability to grow. Alternatives to finance the receivables are under negotiation and will significantly impact the firm's ability to scale its operation.

home building industry for middle-income families in such countries as Chile, Colombia, Ecuador, El Salvador, Honduras, Mexico, and Peru (Ferguson, Rubinstein, and Domínguez Vial 1996). Unfortunately, the experience in Latin America indicates that government provision of housing subsidies induces developers to build and financial institutions to lend only to middle-income households, excluding the poorest households that lack income history. Government subsidy programs have proved insufficient to persuade financial institutions to finance and developers to create a supply of low-cost housing solutions for low-income and informally employed households. Microfinance can help fill this niche.

Small sequential credits to households to buy building materials to improve their homes began expanding a decade ago. By then, roughly 200 microfinance institutions worldwide had become commercially viable (Robinson 2001). Increasing competition had caused microenterprise loan markets to tighten in some countries, such as Bolivia. Diversifying into home-improvement lending and savings products seemed useful next steps for leading microfinance institutions and their networks.

Housing microfinance is a promising financial tool to help lower-income households build their housing units. Three alternatives involving microfinance have sprung up: public sector housing programs, subsidies, and interventions; private sector business models; and a hybrid of public and private sector initiatives, which may or may not include the participation of NGOs and other citizen groups. In Paraguay, a joint venture involving international, national, and local nongovernmental organizations provides both credit and technical assistance for low-income housing (see box 8.3).

Box 8.3 A Joint Venture to Foster Low-Income Housing in Paraguay

The government of Paraguay has enacted a series of policies to guarantee the constitutional right of citizens to access decent housing, starting with the establishment of the Instituto Paraguayo de Vivienda y Urbanismo (Paraguayan Institute of Housing and Urbanism) in 1964. Until 1971, the government tried to fulfill the role of housing developer, builder, and financier. In the 1970s and 1980s, the government promoted housing financing mechanisms through the newly created Banco Nacional de la Vivienda (National Housing Bank). However, both initiatives had a limited impact on improving housing finance in Paraguay. In 1992, with the creation of the Consejo Nacional de Vivienda (CONAVI), housing subsidies were introduced, which required that beneficiaries match the subsidy with a loan. However, this initiative was ineffective, as the private sector did not have the risk appetite to provide the required financing.

In 2009, the Agencia Financiera de Desarrollo (AFD) launched the mortgage credit and home improvement program "Mi Primera Casa" (My First House), targeting low-income families earning between one and five times the minimum wages (the minimum wage is equivalent to US$316). Loans have a term of up to 20 years, finance new home construction up to US$40,000, and are funded by commercial banks willing to assume the specific risk. To date, the program has primarily benefited young families earning between four and five times the minimum wage that are looking to buy their first home. Hence, low-income families, most of which already own a substandard home, remain without access to credit to fund necessary home expansions and improvements.

An Innovative Business Model

To address the lack of long-term financial housing products for low-income families, the Inter-American Development Bank (IDB), Citibank, and two non-governmental organizations, Vision Banco and Habitat for Humanity, launched an innovative project combining credit and technical assistance specifically for home improvements and expansions.

The program aims to reach up to 2,500 microentrepreneurs with combined family incomes of between one and four times the minimum wage. It will support new construction, progressive building, and home rehabilitation, improvement, or expansion. Vision Banco will screen and select the beneficiaries, assuring that they belong to the target income group, that they meet the eligibility criteria, and that they can repay their debt. Habitat for Humanity will assess their current housing conditions and needs for improvement or expansion and assign an architect, who together with the beneficiary, will budget the costs and prepare a design for the proposed construction.

Habitat will also conduct financial literacy workshops for the beneficiaries to help them manage their financial affairs, including their creditworthiness and thus their prospects for future credit. Families that attend financial education workshops learn how to live within their means, prioritize expenses, create budgets and follow savings plans for future home improvements. All participants must complete the introductory training before they can receive the loan. Once Habitat verifies the costs of construction and the beneficiaries' participation in the workshop, Vision will prepare the loan contract, which will be signed during a second financial literacy workshop.

In addition, beneficiary families must invest some of their own labor in the construction of their home. Families also must attend Habitat's self-construction workshops, where they will be instructed in the processes and skills required to safely, efficiently, and effectively implement their home designs. Habitat will also help families hire local plumbers and electricians to connect the homes to the local network of basic services. Vision will supply the resources for Habitat to fund the technical assistance. Habitat will supervise the construction of the homes to insure that they meet Paraguay's safety and construction codes.

Affordable housing in emerging countries has become one of the major market opportunities of the twenty-first century. So is housing microfinance. Major private banks might be reluctant to expand business to the base of the pyramid. Although large commercial banks have the technological know-how and infrastructure such as branch networks, they lack the willingness to become involved with low-income and financially uneducated consumers (Martin 2008). The successful business models of housing microfinance also include technical assistance. Business innovation for the bottom of the pyramid markets focus on hybrid solutions and blending old and new technologies (Prahalad 2005). This dual approach has intensified in recent years and has supported the creation of inclusive housing business models.

Affordable housing programs are high-value products that continue to be relevant for the bottom of the income pyramid, the BOP market. A recent study indicates that in Mexico and in the other countries in the region where Patrimonio Hoy has initiated operations, there is still an enormous untapped potential demand for support for financial and non-financial services for progressive and incremental improvement of affordable housing (Vance 2010).

The Role of Remittances

The huge flow of remittances into the region offers another possibility for housing finance. There is an unexploited potential to combine remittances with microloans to scale up housing microfinance. This is especially true for Central American countries, including El Salvador and Honduras. In El Salvador, one-fourth of households receive remittances, and most of the recipient households are low-income. Currently, only a small percentage of remittances are spent on housing. Official statistics from the Encuesta de Hogares de Propositos Multiples (EHPM) survey 2005 indicate that 76 percent of remittances are used on consumption, 9 percent on education, 6 percent on savings, and 1 percent on housing expenses (Vance 2011). However, it is likely that the reported expenditures in housing are undervalued due to significant flows of cash and goods sent as remittances via informal channels. This small percentage could increase if a business model that combines technical assistance is put in place.

While allocations of remittances for housing construction and improvement are small, they are significant. Families that receive remittances invest, on average, seven times more than those without remittances: US$5,736 compared to US$773 (McBride 2009) (see table 8.3).

Government Support for Housing Microfinance

Seeking to meet ambitious production goals, government housing agencies have frequently given in to the temptation to extend small subsidized

Table 8.3 Comparative Investment Patterns of Households That Do and Do Not Receive Remittances

Description	Nonremittance households	Remittance households
Households that made improvements over the last ten years (percent)	35	76
Amount spent per household (US$)	773	5,736
Paid for hired labor (percent)	40	81
Purchased land (percent)	13	31
Purchased new homes (percent)	10	30
Home additions (built extra rooms; percent)	16	27
Improved roofs (percent)	6	27
Improved floors (percent)	9	28

Source: McBride (2009).

credits directly to families for low-cost housing solutions. These government "housing microcredits" usually become grants and cover only a small share of eligible households. Such publicly provided subsidized housing microfinance can hinder the development of private housing microfinance markets. Moreover, public housing microfinance imposes numerous requirements on borrowers, the waiting period to receive finance is long, and the supply is limited. There is substantial unsatisfied effective demand, which may be sufficient to fuel a private sector industry offering competitive market rates.

Private, market-rate housing microfinance can potentially improve greatly the efficiency, targeting, and scale of government housing finance policy and programs. Currently, many Latin American governments raise huge sums through mandatory salary contributions to provident/housing funds[2] that extend mortgage finance at below-market rates, mainly to construct and purchase new developer-built housing. These provident/housing funds account for the bulk of mortgage finance in most of the region, fuel a commercial homebuilding industry, and fund the development of many new communities with full infrastructure and services. However, they are costly (averaging $5,000 dollars to $15,000 per household in subsidies),[3] suffer from low coverage, and have other problems.

In contrast, the government can support access to housing microfinance at lower cost. For example, in Mexico, the Sociedad Hipotecaria Federal (SHF) grants a subsidy of US$1,500 to US$2,000 to households to complement its liquidity to first-tier lenders for housing microfinance credit. Most private housing microfinance involves no government subsidy. In particular, a well-functioning housing microfinance system can make public programs to upgrade slums and informal settlements more sustainable and larger scale. Government can focus public subsidies on communal infrastructure and service provision, and leave financing the structure of the house and individual services (such as connection to water distribution lines and septic tanks) to families.

Government support of housing microfinance can take various forms. These include provision of debt and equity funding, grants to complement housing microfinance credit, and creation of an appropriate regulatory environment. More broadly, government can balance its enormous support for mortgage-financed, developer-built housing suited to the middle class by building a system for delivering progressive housing at scale to low-income households that joins microcredit, urban land, and progressive communal infrastructure.

Division of Labor in Incremental Housing: Government, Communities, and Families

It is relatively easy to document how households build their homes themselves (see methodologies detailed on http://web.mit.edu/incrementalhousing/). But it is not easy to design effective policies and assign roles and responsibilities to governments, communities, and households themselves.

Should incremental housing be part of national housing policies to address low-income housing needs? Some observers note that incremental housing already is national policy through slum upgrading programs, which are common in the region. Indeed neighborhood programs provide secure tenure and essential, basic infrastructure services to existing low-income settlements and their residents.

Others argue that a "national aided self-help housing policy" is a contradiction in terms, emphasizing top-down decision-making instead of grassroots empowerment. As Turner and Fichter (1972) put it, "The urgency of a basic shelter problem cannot be ignored; but neither the shelter problem nor the manifold social problems of which it is part can be solved by bureaucratically administrated, politically imposed programs" (p. 8, quoted in Bromley 2003, pp. 289–290).

That said, low-income families continue occupying land closer to work opportunities, despite a lack of tenure security, infrastructure, and services. As a consequence, the stock of inadequate housing keeps growing. What can the government do to facilitate self-help/progressive/incremental processes in the sector?

Reforming regulations and providing public subsidies for basic infrastructure should be key components of the incremental option for low-income households. Policies to assist poor households should include the following: Political commitment for the long run to deal with landowners and define processes; better coordination between actors for planning purposes; and flexibility when offering solutions that adapt to the different needs of families (from new urban migrants to existing residents and from those in the informal sector to those in the formal one).

A plot alone does not solve the shelter problem of low-income households in the short run. Site and services programs need to be complemented with additional services at the outset, including social and community services, as well as access to financing and technical assistance. The option of a starter (or core) house helps households move to their plots and begin the home improvement process. However, adopting the core house option is not easy, as this often means that the neighborhood will not look attractive for a number of years. That said, once the core house approach is chosen, policy should determine its acceptable size. In Chile, two recommendations for successful homes are that the minimum space per person be ten square meters and that the steps toward incremental growth be completed within approximately seven years. In other countries, the tendency is to start with smaller houses, as promoted by various NGOs. The next challenge would be to gather and reconcile those stand-alone experiences to gauge whether they can be turned into comprehensive housing policies.

Another area to foster is for-profit development businesses that have identified the low-income markets as a primary future opportunity. The best-known example is the Grameen Bank, a microfinance institution in Pakistan. These businesses are profitable and are gaining a strategic advantage. Joint public-private enterprises such as FONAVIPO in El Salvador also offer a promising alternative (see box 8.4).

Box 8.4 A Public-Private Partnership for Low-Cost Housing in El Salvador

El Salvador has developed a unique and sustainable financial business model that mobilizes resources from both the public and private sectors, including commercial banks and multilateral institutions, to enable low-income consumers to buy a lot, improve their housing, or expand their homes over time. The program addresses two important barriers facing low-income households. The first is the lack of access to housing finance, which has been curtailed by microfinance institutions in favor of the short-term productive credit. The second barrier is the lack of an effective mechanism for helping low-income households meet the requirements for obtaining subsidies or housing finance, such as how to complete all necessary paperwork, how to document the legal status of a property, how to submit an estimated construction budget, and how to obtain registry documents.

The program increases the lending resources of the state-owned National Low-income Housing Fund, Fondo Nacional de Vivienda Popular (FONAVIPO). FONAVIPO is a second-tier financial lender to microfinance institutions, including cooperatives and other nongovernmental organizations. It operates under a different set of rules than regulated, commercial banks, and administers a government subsidy program that provides less-affluent households with grants of up to US$3,000 to buy a lot or build/upgrade a home.

FONAVIPO has earned a reputation for combining rigorous financial practices, including an innovative risk assessment model, and sustainable lending policies for consumers at the bottom of the economic and social pyramid. FONAVIPO provides both technical assistance and new financing to microfinance institutions, which in turn offer loans and support to 2,300 low-income families. A key ingredient for the success of the program is technical assistance. This includes the establishment of an information and advisory center and mobile administrative units, which help low-income homeowners or potential homeowners submit the proper documents and complete the required paperwork and technical and financial documents to qualify for loans and subsidies. Training is also offered to personnel of the participating microfinance institutions to improve customer service and lending methods and to expand the client base.

Source: IDB (2011b).

To encourage their development, policy should create favorable conditions, such as making their presence in low-income neighborhoods attractive. Examples include tax relief, stimulus to encourage client growth (subsidies for improvement, for instance), and grants to encourage the identification and development of new businesses to benefit low-income households (Letelier, Flores, and Spinosa 2003). In the area of housing microfinance, regulatory reform, complementary public goods (such as consumer credit registries), and provision of second-tier capital are options to consider.

The Importance of Autonomy

A key concept of the self-help process is autonomy, which can be defined as the issue of "who decides" (Turner 1976). The rationale is that owners are best suited to define and implement their expectations.[4]

As novelist V. S. Naipaul (1959) noted in his haunting account of a street in Port of Spain, Trinidad and Tobago, "A stranger could drive through Miguel Street and just say 'Slum!' because he could see no more. But we who lived there saw our street as a world..." (p. 63). The residents are indeed the ones who can say what is needed. This is the root of the social organization processes.

In the case of incremental housing, this can take a variety of forms, such as mutual help, a social and technical process in which families work together in groups building their own houses. During the mutual help stage, families can be trained for different building, organizational, and social tasks. By working in groups together, without knowing which house would be assigned to each family, the beneficiaries get to know one another and develop an organizational structure that will help when addressing social issues in the future (Stein 1990).

Fostering the conditions for community creation and consolidation is the most challenging feature of the incremental process. Perhaps the key here is to associate incremental processes with progressive development (as FUNDASAL has done). The incremental process of building is associated with the development of the individual, family, and community—meaning helping to organize the residents into self-sustaining community organizations, programs for household and group participation, and mutual help.

In a bottom-up approach, beneficiaries lead to the solution. This can take the form of consultative/participative processes (which tend nowadays to be included in every program design), community-driven initiatives (famous ones in the region include the creation of Casa Melhor/PAAC's "Better Home and Program of Support for Self Building," in Fortaleza, Brazil), or representative organizations or federations formed by the urban poor to work with governments to address their needs (not very common in Latin America, but growing in Asia and South Africa).

The government's role in this process is to foster autonomy and deal with the bottlenecks along the way. Alliances among private sector partners, NGOs, and government also offer promise. As the various successful innovations in the region have demonstrated, no single organization can do it all.

For government and policymakers in the region, the challenge is to enable and promote the scaling up of these innovations, jump-start or assist the process when needed, and address some of the regulatory and institutional failures that corner lower-middle-income households into building their houses themselves.

9

Hammering Out a Housing Policy That Works

The challenge for the region's housing sector is clear: to eliminate existing quantitative and qualitative shortages while catering to the needs of newly formed households. The key question is: How do we do it? Should governments intervene in the housing sector? If so, how? Is there a combination of public policies and programs that can generate better housing outcomes?

Many justifications exist for government intervention in the housing sector. One, based on market failures, argues that imperfect information, lack of access to credit, and externalities (location externalities, externalities between different types of land use—industrial, residential, commercial, etc.) lead the market to offer an inadequate supply of housing in terms of both quantity and quality. This insufficiency, in turn, reduces individual and social welfare (Stafford 1978).

There are also ethical arguments. Housing is considered a merit good by many, especially legislators and policymakers, as revealed in the constitutions of 18 countries in the region (see table 9.1). Many legal frameworks argue for government intervention in the housing sector based on its classification as a basic right.

The various constitutional provisions imply varying levels of public intervention in the housing sector. Those that declare housing a right emphasize two public sector roles: governments must guarantee all citizens access to a decent and proper home (*vivienda digna*; Argentina and Ecuador), or they should promote social housing programs for low-income and vulnerable households (all other countries).

Another justification for government intervention is rooted in housing's many links to economics. Housing construction provides an important source of demand for unskilled labor and a driver of economic

Table 9.1 Constitutional Provisions Concerning Housing in Select Latin American Countries

General principle	All persons have the right to live in adequate housing		Housing is a merit good	No mention of housing or no government commitment
Means	The state will provide social benefits, including housing. The state will guarantee access to a decent and proper house for all	The state will promote social housing programs through adequate financing mechanisms, with a focus on low-income, rural, and vulnerable households	The state will facilitate the construction of houses and development of financing mechanisms accessible to the largest possible proportion of households, with priority for low-income households	
Countries	Argentina Ecuador	Bolivia Brazil Colombia Costa Rica Dominican Republic Guatemala Honduras Mexico Nicaragua Paraguay Peru	El Salvador Panama Uruguay Venezuela	Chile

Source: Authors' compilation.

activity. Governments often use public expenditure in housing as a means to jump-start stalled economies. According to the Seventeenth Session of the Commission on Sustainable Development (ECLAC 17), countries in Latin America and the Caribbean used investment in housing as one of the measures to reactivate their economies after the 2008 financial crisis (ECLAC 2009).

There is general consensus that adequate housing conditions play a vital role in the well-being of individuals and the economies of countries (chapter 1). There is also consensus that well-functioning housing markets play a key part in assuring good housing and that governments should take the lead through both regulation and public housing programs to promote better functioning markets and better access to quality housing for low-income households. However, there is no consensus on how to achieve these objectives, and in particular on the scope and nature of the public interventions that should be implemented.

Which Housing Programs Work? An Unfinished Policy Debate

The countries of Latin America and the Caribbean have implemented a vast array of housing policies and programs. Public concern for urban housing issues began in the 1960s with accelerating urbanization, which led most governments to directly build, finance, and distribute houses for low-income households. Most of these housing programs proved difficult to sustain and target. Most institutions implementing the programs were financially unsustainable, the houses built were expensive and cost recovery was weak. Under these circumstances, most housing programs became a heavy burden for governments and leveraged very few resources from beneficiaries. Furthermore, as the housing sector as a whole seemed oriented toward serving higher-income segments, the dwellings produced by the government for the poor were attractive to middle-income households, This, in turn, put pressure on governments to relax the targeting of housing programs, effectively crowding out the initial intended beneficiaries (Rojas 1995).

In the 1990s, the debate over government intervention in housing reached a turning point with the birth of the "enabling markets" approach to housing. Based on the premise that markets are more efficient than governments in constructing and distributing houses, this approach suggested that governments should focus on facilitating the functioning of housing markets while moving away from direct provision and financing of houses. The approach was pioneered by Chile in the late 1970s and proposed by the United Nations (UN) as a good strategy to face housing issues (UN 1988). In turn, the World Bank and the Inter-American Development Bank (IDB) adopted the approach in the early 1990s. Specifically, the approach identifies seven instruments for public intervention in the housing sector, as presented in table 9.2.

The premise of the enabling markets approach fit the economic climate of the time by supporting a reduced role of the state and fiscal austerity. Thus, in the 1990s, several countries—Bolivia, Colombia, the Dominican Republic, Ecuador, El Salvador, Mexico, Panama, and Peru—joined the pioneers, Chile and Costa Rica, in moving toward policies and programs that facilitated private sector participation in the housing market.

In the ensuing years, Latin American and Caribbean countries have followed different paths and experimented with a wide variety of housing programs. On one end of the spectrum, policymakers believe that housing markets should operate freely with little or no intervention. They favor a government that relies on the private provision of housing and limits its interventions to eradicating informal settlements and helping households that cannot afford housing. At the other end, some policymakers suggest that the public sector should actively control housing agencies, housing supply, and access to credit, with the authority to fully regulate markets (Lansley 1979). Somewhere in the middle lies the view that the government should take on a key role in setting standards, providing subsidies, and strictly narrowing direct provision to very low-income groups.

In most countries, governments implement a range of interventions in housing markets. These policies and programs range from those considered very interventionist (such as directly providing housing) to those considered market-oriented (reforming regulations, investing in trunk infrastructure such as roads and electrical lines, and boosting the availability of mortgage financing). These measures are described in table 9.3, with the most direct interventions on the left and those involving a more limited public commitment on the right.

The presence of programs supporting both types of policy options (direct provision and market facilitation) in almost all countries indicates that no country has fully embraced the instruments advocated by the enabling markets approach. However, most countries have followed some of its "dos and don'ts." While some countries have eliminated

Table 9.2 Dos and Don'ts of the Enabling Markets Approach to Housing

Instrument	Do	Don'ts
Developing property rights	· Regularize land tenure · Expand land registration · Privatize public housing stock · Establish property taxation	· Engage in mass evictions · Institute costly titling systems · Nationalize land · Discourage land transactions
Developing mortgage financing	· Allow private sector to lend · Lend at positive market rates · Enforce foreclosure laws · Ensure prudential regulation · Introduce better loan instruments	· Subsidize interest rates · Discriminate against rental housing investment · Neglect resource mobilization · Allow high default rates
Rationalizing subsidies	· Make subsidies transparent · Target subsidies to the poor · Subsidize people, not houses · Subject subsidies to review	· Build subsidized public housing · Allow for hidden subsidies · Use rent control as a subsidy
Providing infrastructure	· Coordinate land development · Emphasize cost recovery · Base provision on demand · Improve slum infrastructure	· Allow bias against infrastructure investment · Use environmental concerns for slum clearances
Regulating land and housing development	· Reduce regulatory complexity · Assess costs of regulation · Remove price distortions · Remove artificial shortages	· Impose unaffordable standards · Maintain unenforceable rules · Design projects without links to regulatory institutional reforms
Reorganizing the building industry	· Eliminate monopoly practices · Encourage entry of small firms · Reduce import controls · Support building research	· Allow long permit delays · Institute regulations inhibiting competition · Continue public monopolies
Developing a policy and institutional framework	· Balance public-private roles · Create a forum for managing the housing sector as a whole · Develop enabling strategies · Monitor sector performance	· Engage in public housing · Neglect the role of local government · Retain financially unsustainable institutions

Source: World Bank (1993).

Table 9.3 Housing Programs in Latin America and the Caribbean

Approach	State guarantees access to good housing						Government facilitates the operation of housing markets			
Type of program	Direct public intervention in the housing sector ←						→ Promarket interventions			
Country	Direct provision of finished houses by the government	Direct provision of incremental houses by the government	Government provision of serviced land for residential uses	Government provision of subsidized housing finance	Settlement upgrading and tenure regularization	Housing upgrading	Housing vouchers	Government financing for incremental housing	Regulations to facilitate the subdivision of land for residential use	Interventions to expand private housing finance
Argentina	X			X	X	X				
Barbados	X				X	X				
Bolivia	X			X			X			
Brazil	X			X	X		X			X
Chile	X	X			X	X	X			

Colombia			X	X	X	X	X			X
Costa Rica						X	X			X
Dominican Republic		X	X				X		X	
Ecuador					X	X	X	X		
El Salvador					X		X		X	X
Guatemala						X	X	X		
Guyana			X	X			X			
Honduras					X	X	X			X
Jamaica	X		X	X	X				X	
Mexico		X		X	X	X	X		X	X
Nicaragua						X	X	X		
Panama				X	X	X	X	X		X
Paraguay	X				X		X			
Peru		X		X	X		X		X	X
Suriname				X			X			
Trinidad and Tobago	X			X	X			X	X	
Uruguay		X		X	X	X	X		X	X

Source: Authors' review of housing programs in the country.

implicit subsidy schemes and implemented demand-side subsidy programs (Ecuador, Guatemala, and Peru), they have not implemented other reforms, such as those focused on improving property rights or on reducing restrictive zoning and building regulations, or they have not made much progress in lifting barriers to deepen financial markets and promote private sector participation. A number of countries still stick mostly to direct provision and financing of houses through public programs (Argentina, Barbados, Jamaica, Trinidad and Tobago, and, to a lesser extent, Venezuela). Brazil still maintains substantial interest rate subsidies for moderately priced houses. With the exception of Colombia and Guyana, most countries do not implement programs to improve the provision of residential land.

Most of the programs that focus on supporting housing demand, particularly those combining savings, upfront subsidies, and a loan (also called ABC programs, after the program's Spanish language name, *Ahorro, Bono y Credito*) do not reach households at the bottom of the income distribution. The need to obtain a loan, an eligibility requirement, tends to exclude much of the low-income population (Gonzales Arrieta 1998; Angel 2000; Rojas 2001; Coady, Grosh, and Hoddinott 2004; Ruprah 2010c). On the other hand, there is a fairly established consensus that neighborhood upgrading programs—which fall on the interventionist side—do benefit the poor, and significantly impact the well-being of the population (Brakarz, Greene, and Rojas 2002; Rojas 2010).

Housing policies in Latin America favor home ownership and pay little attention to renting as a useful form of tenure. This is a shortcoming that is discussed by UN-HABITAT 2003b, who argues forcefully for a change in outlook, pointing out the many advantages of rental housing and advocating for its promotion, or at least for adopting a tenure-neutral shelter policy (see chapter 4 on the rental market). UN-HABITAT advocates a more proactive position on the part of the government concerning the development of rental markets, given the central role those markets play in well-functioning housing markets (UN-HABITAT 2011b).

In addition, and in line with the bias toward home ownership, most governments in the region favor the production and delivery of new, finished housing units over improving the quality of the existing housing stock or supporting incremental housing construction (Greene and Rojas 2008).

Why do countries implement a mix of direct intervention and pro-market programs? How do they choose which mix to apply? Are these approaches mutually exclusive? Is there a mix of instruments and programs that can close all gaps, for all income levels? Last but not least, how do countries better target the poor? There is little detailed analysis about the processes that lead governments to choose a given combination of housing policies and programs. Perhaps the need to target all income groups has led governments, over time, to develop a mix of interventions and delivery options to fulfill their multiple objectives for the sector. Only a detailed country-by-country analysis of housing policy and program choices can shed light on this question (Ruprah and Marcano 2007; Marcano and Ruprah 2008).

Pragmatic Responses or Policy Prescriptions? A Tale of Three Countries

In an attempt to respond to the previously posed questions, this section details the housing policies and outcomes in three countries: Argentina, Chile, and Colombia.

Argentina, Chile, and Colombia were selected for several reasons. First, all three share a sustained interest in the housing conditions of their populations, expressed in a long history of public investment programs in housing. Second, their approaches toward housing policies and programs differ. While Chile adopted market-oriented interventions early on, Argentina stuck firmly to policies and programs based on the government directly supplying housing and financing. In the last decade, Colombia has moved toward the enabling markets approach, including efforts in the area of residential land development.

A third factor in the choice of these three countries derives from the very different results housing policies have had in each. As noted in chapter 2, housing conditions in Chile—particularly the quality of dwellings and access to infrastructure—have improved in the last 15 years in accordance with the country's economic development. By contrast, housing conditions in Argentina are worse than what would correspond to its income level. The quality of the housing stock has stagnated in terms of overcrowding and building materials, while problems related to tenure have increased. Housing quality in Colombia is better than what could be expected from its income level, but results are mixed: the quantitative housing shortage has shrunk significantly, but drawbacks remain in improving access to infrastructure and security of tenure.

In the second half of the twentieth century, concern for the poor housing conditions of the majority of the population prompted the governments of the three countries to provide housing directly. In Argentina, financing provided by the National Housing Fund (Fondo Nacional de la Vivienda, FONAVI) supported housing construction and financing programs by the provincial governments. In Chile, the Ministry of Housing and Urban Development (Ministerio de Vivienda y Urbanismo, MINVU) directly implemented housing construction and financing programs. In Colombia, the national government supported housing schemes financed and executed by the Territorial Credit Institute (Instituto de Crédito Territorial, ICT). Lessons learned from these experiences, along with changes in the political and institutional circumstances—notably, the fiscal crisis and the emergence of the enabling markets approach—led Chile and Colombia to change their approach. Argentina clung to policies and programs that support the direct provision of housing.

The Evolution of Housing Policies: Change versus Stagnation

The military regime that governed Chile from 1973 to 1989 favored a smaller government in all aspects of the economy. In housing, Chile transferred more responsibility to households to solve their shelter problems. The country pioneered the introduction of up-front housing subsidies to complement household savings (ABC programs), making mortgage financing more available to middle- and low-middle-income households. Colombia followed a similar approach in 1991 when it established the National Institute for Urban Development (Instituto Nacional de Desarrollo Urbano, INURBE), which replaced the failed Institute for Territorial Credit, and adopted programs with the same up-front approach to housing demand subsidies. Over the years, both countries have significantly altered their original up-front schemes, adjusting to changing circumstances and incorporating the lessons learned during implementation. For its part, Argentina introduced few changes in the way the federal government finances and builds houses (see Rojas et al. 2010 for a detailed analysis of the evolution of housing policies and programs in these countries).

Argentina

Argentina has relied continuously on private contractors to directly provide houses financed by the government. Mortgage finance is available at subsidized rates through the Housing Institutes (Institutos de Vivienda, IPV), which operate in all provinces and some municipalities. This approach underlies the two major housing programs: the National Housing Fund (FONAVI), and the more recent Federal Housing Programs (Programas Federales de Vivienda, PFV). Figure 9.1 describes the evolution of housing policies and programs in Argentina in the last 20 years.

Both FONAVI and PFV provide housing in a context where for the last three decades (except for a brief period) most of the population has lacked access to long-term financing from the private sector. The more recent Federal Programs are playing the same role as earlier FONAVI, although their launching was motivated more by the desire to introduce dynamism into an economy that stagnated after the financial crisis of 2000.

These direct provision programs tend to be fairly rigid in terms of the product supplied (mostly finished houses), their location (usually in the peripheries of cities, where land is less expensive), and the conditions of

Figure 9.1 Housing Policy in Argentina: Approaches and Trends

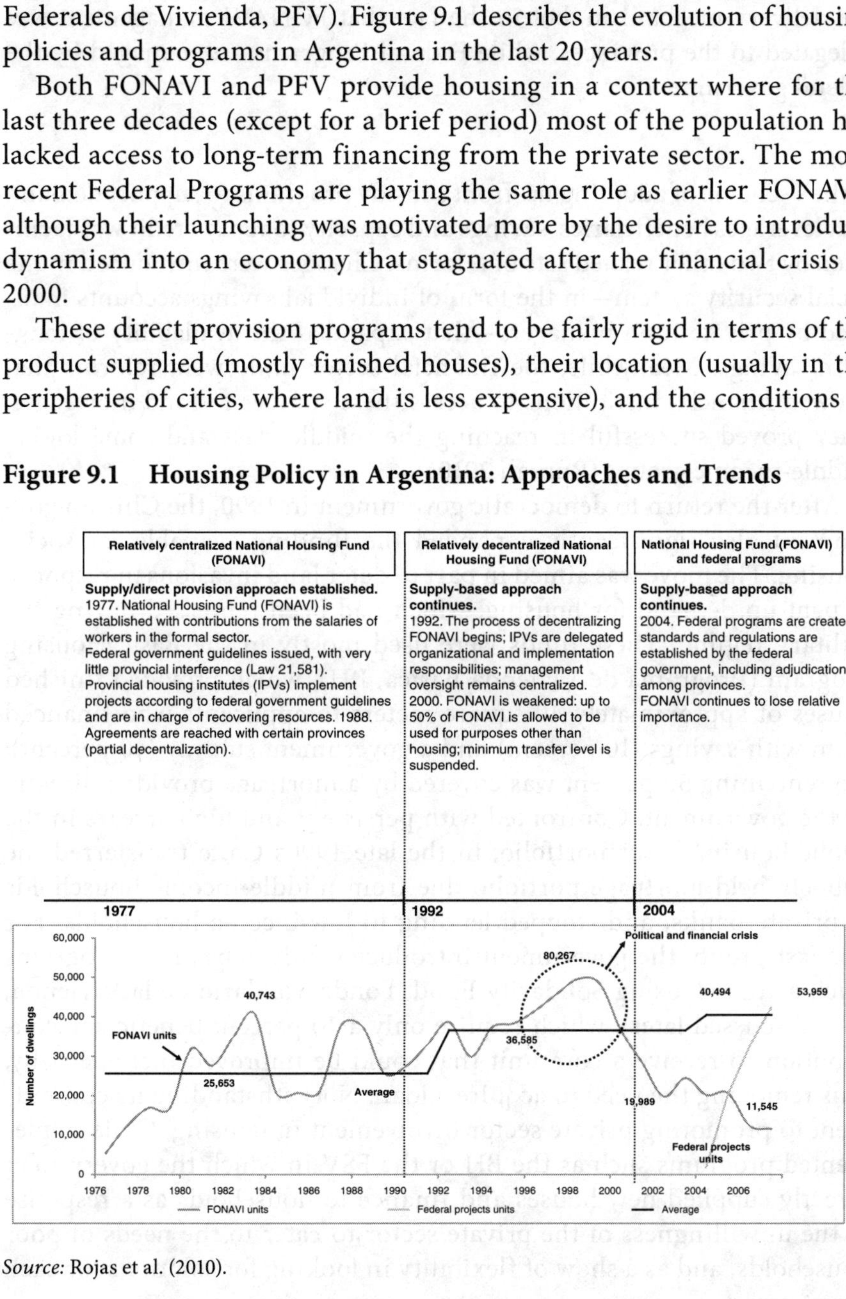

Source: Rojas et al. (2010).

access (often requiring payment of the houses under subsidized schemes run directly by the government housing institutions).[1] They differ not in the delivery mechanism, but in the fact that FONAVI management was delegated to the provinces, while Federal Programs are managed by the federal government.

Chile

Chile's scheme of adopting up-front subsidy programs to support demand that leverages beneficiaries' savings and capacity to repay credit was facilitated by two other related sets of reforms. Changes were introduced in the social security system—in the form of individual savings accounts managed by private fund managers—that expanded the availability of long-term savings. Meanwhile, the financial sector underwent reforms that allowed financial institutions to access these sources to fund mortgages. They proved successful in reaching the middle-class and some lower-middle-income groups (Ruprah 2010c).

After the return to democratic government in 1990, the Chilean government also significantly expanded the funding available for social housing. The move was aimed in part to deter land invasions in response to pent-up demand for housing, which had been repressed during the military regime. These funds were used mostly in the Basic Housing Program (Programa de Vivienda Básica, BH), which provided finished houses of approximately 40 square meters to applicants who financed them with savings (10 percent) and a government subsidy (40 percent); the remaining 50 percent was covered by a mortgage provided directly by the government. Confronted with persistent and high arrears in the public housing loans portfolio, in the late 1990s Chile transferred the publicly held mortgage portfolio due from middle-income households to private banks, and stopped lending to low-income households. For this last group, the government introduced fully subsidized programs (such as the Housing Solidarity Fund, Fondo Solidario de la Vivienda, FSV, discussed later), which require only a 10 percent beneficiary contribution to receive a core unit that could be improved incrementally, thus removing the need to acquire a loan. Notwithstanding its commitment to promoting private sector involvement in housing, Chile implemented programs such as the BH or the FSV in which the government directly supplied new houses and finance to households as a response to the unwillingness of the private sector to cater to the needs of poor households, and as a show of flexibility in looking for solutions for each target group.

Other changes present further proof of a flexible approach. For instance, to expand the involvement of beneficiaries in choosing the location or type of houses built with FSV financing, the Fund finances projects proposed by communities of between 10 and 50 households and helps them purchase the land, as well as contract the construction of the houses and the services of a technical cooperation firm. The FSV also allows contributions from third parties (municipalities, charities, corporations, the beneficiaries) to improve the core house and neighborhood amenities. To encourage densification and avoid gentrification in inner city areas, in addition to the upfront subsidies, Chile recently introduced a location subsidy that benefits households willing to purchase houses in inner city areas.

The usefulness of some of these programs has been questioned. For example, some experts argue that the location subsidy may push land prices up, and that the quality of the core dwellings provided by the BH program has deteriorated rapidly in some areas (although the quality of incremental housing solutions in Chile has held over time, as shown in chapter 8). However, the array of programs provides proof of the

Figure 9.2 Housing Policy in Chile: Approaches and Trends

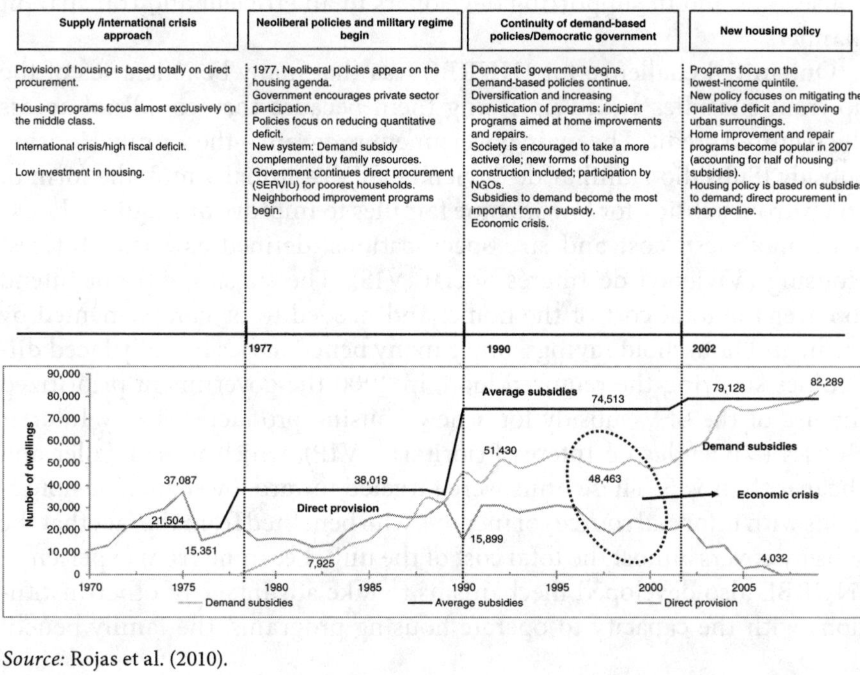

Source: Rojas et al. (2010).

willingness of Chilean governments to address emerging issues with structured responses, regardless of the general noninterventionist principle of its approach to housing policy. Such an approach, combined with a sustained commitment to address the housing affordability problem by leveraging private resources, along with maintaining macroeconomic stability, has helped create a stable investment climate in a sector characterized by long-maturing projects—a factor generally credited as a key contribution to expanding the involvement of the private sector in the production and financing of houses. Figure 9.2 traces the evolution of policies and public sector involvement in Chile in the last 20 years.

Colombia

Housing policy in Colombia has also relied on a mix of programs and instruments to address emerging issues and incorporate lessons learned. During the 1990s, the government changed the focus of its main housing programs from the direct supply of houses by public institutions such as the ICT toward programs addressing the affordability problem of the ABC-type approach—but not without difficulties. The government created the INURBE to manage public housing funds. From the start, INURBE confronted challenges in allocating housing subsidies to households and in supporting developers in an efficient and transparent manner.

One initial challenge for INURBE was that many beneficiaries of the up-front subsidies ended up losing them because they could not access the required credit. The main government program—the Family Housing Subsidy (Subsidio Familiar de Vivienda, SFV)—initially took the form of an up-front subsidy for low-income families to improve or acquire a house with maximum cost and size specifications, defined as Social Interest Housing (Vivienda de Interés Social, VIS). The subsidy did not intend to cover the total cost of the home, and needed to be complemented by credit and household savings. Since many beneficiaries initially faced difficulties securing the required loan, in 2000 the government prioritized the use of the SFV subsidy for a new housing product, Priority Interest Houses (Viviendas de Interes Prioritario, VIP), which were smaller and cheaper than VIS. These units were targeted toward lower-income households with informal sources of income, who benefited from the fact that the subsidy covers almost the total cost of the unit. Learning from experience, INURBE also developed mechanisms to take advantage of other institutions with the capacity to operate housing programs: the family benefit funds, or Cajas de Compensación Familiar (CCF); social benefits associations linked to specific industries or guilds; and the National Housing Fund (Fondo Nacional de la Vivienda, FONVIVIENDA). VIS units are produced and effectively targeted to lower-middle-income households with a delivery mechanism managed mostly by the CCF, which caters to formal workers. Informal workers benefit from the SFV subsidy provided by FONVIVIENDA; if they cannot access a loan, they acquire a VIP with no credit. At present, the CCFs also administer the delivery of FONVIVIENDA's subsidy to informal workers. Colombia's refinement of the delivery system for housing subsidies and the involvement of the CCFs in administering subsidies for part of the eligible households illustrates the changes introduced to improve delivery and leverage resources from beneficiaries.

In 2009, the government created the Voluntary Contractual Savings Program (Ahorro Voluntario Contractual, AVC), managed by the National Savings Fund (Fondo Nacional de Ahorro, FNA), to respond to the challenges that self-employed workers and those working in the informal sector face in accessing mortgage financing. As seen in chapter 3, income informality prevents between 10 and 15 percent of Colombian households living in the major cities from qualifying for a mortgage to purchase a basic house. The AVC program creates a savings program for these groups and screens beneficiaries with irregular incomes to test their capacity to repay a housing loan.

Colombia is one of the few countries in the region that has tackled the problems created by the private sector's lack of incentives to develop land for low-income housing. Through the Macroproyectos initiative, the central government cofinances land development schemes of urban residential plots in the major cities of the country. Macroproyectos land developments provide infrastructure and subdivided plots in partnership with landowners for mixed-income housing developments. Through cross-subsidies, the cost of servicing lots for low-income households is offset with the benefits of the lots for higher-income housing (see box 5.2 in chapter 5).

Other examples of Colombia's comprehensive approach to the housing sector in the last decade include a variety of tax incentives to promote savings for housing by middle-income households, along with incentives for developers to invest in new housing construction and financing. Figure 9.3 traces the evolution of policies and public sector involvement in Colombia in the last 20 years.

Figure 9.3 Housing Policy in Colombia: Approaches and Trends

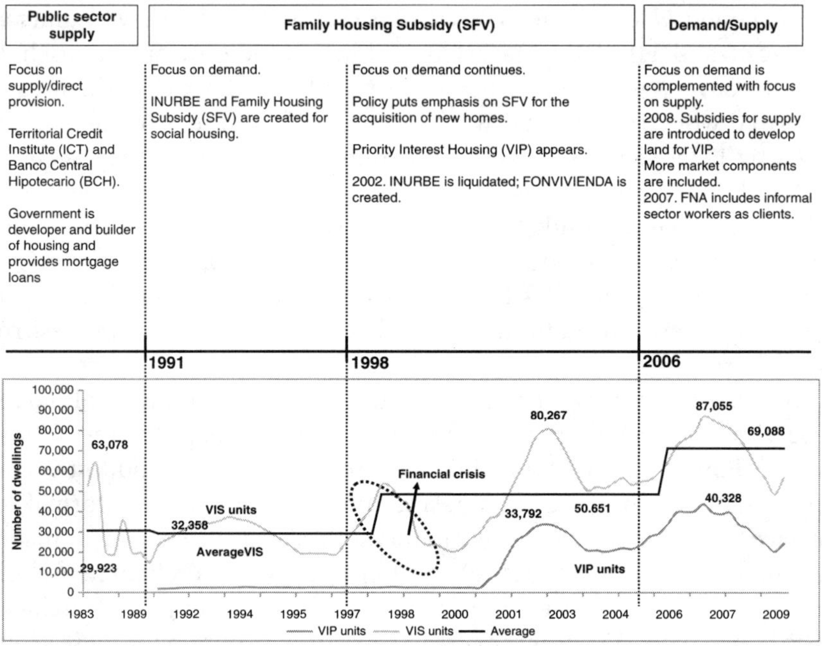

Source: Rojas et al. (2010).

Caught in an Economic and Political Web

Objectives not related to housing, which originate in most cases from broad social and political circumstances, have also shaped housing policies and programs in the region. In Argentina, most of the changes in housing programs can be attributed not so much to objectives linked to the efficient and equitable distribution of public resources for housing as to the evolution of the complex revenue sharing system within the Argentine federal system and the management of economic crises. For instance, the decentralization of the FONAVI fund in 1992 was more the result of a negotiation between the federal government and the provinces concerning revenue sharing than a measure to increase efficiency in housing spending. Although the funds were allocated through a formula based on the housing needs of the population and originally were earmarked for housing, the rules allowed the provinces ample leeway in selecting housing types and beneficiaries. The restriction on their use was lifted after the 2000 crises, allowing the provinces to use the resources for general purposes to cover short-term revenue shortfalls. The Federal Housing programs introduced in 2001 also illustrate this point; they were created to recentralize resources devoted to housing so they could be used to reactivate the economy after the crisis. The stated objective of these programs was to generate employment by reactivating the construction sector. To date, Federal Programs have been significantly larger than the FONAVI and represent the main housing initiative in the country.

Similarly, in the last decade the government of Colombia charged its housing programs with the task of providing shelter in the cities to the population displaced from rural areas as a result of guerrilla activities. Targeting eligibility was changed to include displaced households, which are not necessarily the best tenants of new permanent houses since they consider themselves—and behave like—temporary occupants of the houses, do not have stable income to maintain them, and maintain no ties with the local community.[2]

Along the same lines, the Chilean government currently gives priority in the allocation of FSV benefits to vulnerable groups such as the elderly, handicapped, and teenage mothers. In pursuit of this objective, houses are often assigned to individuals who cannot take care of them, resulting in empty and deteriorated houses.

The evolution of housing programs and policies was also dictated by the economic crises of the 1980s, which significantly reduced government budgets and forced corresponding cuts in housing programs. Housing production has been volatile, with several peaks and downturns in the total number of houses produced in all countries studied. The downturn of economic cycles impacted total housing production less in Chile than in Argentina and Colombia, in part due to the private sector's greater involvement in producing and financing houses in Chile, along with the larger role of public housing programs in Argentina and Colombia. As economies rebounded in the 2000s and padded government budgets, several countries in the region used investment in housing as part of their strategy to face economic downturns (ECLAC 2009).

Have Housing Programs Worked?

The success or failure of government interventions in housing can be gauged by the evolution of housing sector outcomes—in particular, by the volume of formal housing production in relation to needs, as well as the quality of the housing stock in terms of access to basic services, transportation, the size of houses, and the quality of building materials.

Over the last 15 years, total housing production in Argentina and Colombia has failed to cover the needs of newly formed households. As a result, a significant proportion of houses are produced by the informal sector: 56 percent in Colombia, and 37 percent in Argentina. Chile not only covered these needs, but even generated a small annual surplus to cater to the quantitative housing shortage (Rojas et al. 2010) (see figure 9.4 and table 9.4).

Matching these outcomes with the housing conditions presented in chapter 2 suggests that Argentina faces a significant challenge in improving the quality of its housing stock, particularly access to urban infrastructure by low-income households. In Colombia, the challenge is different: to

Figure 9.4 Housing Sector Results, Household Formation, and Formal Housing

a. Argentina

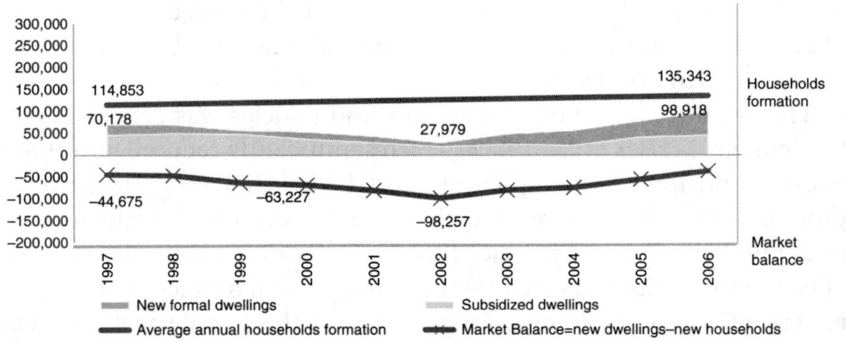

b. Chile

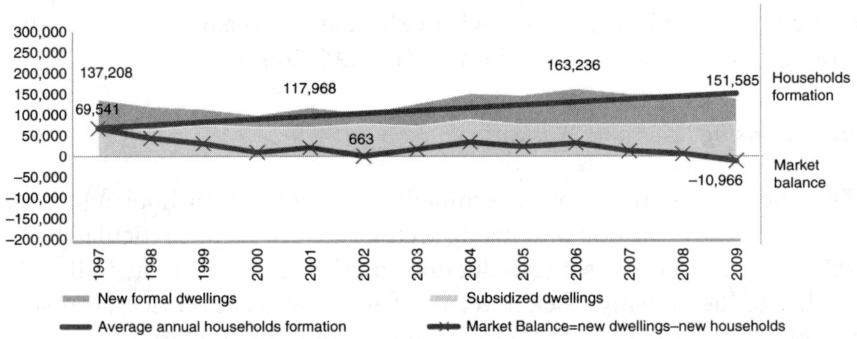

c. Colombia

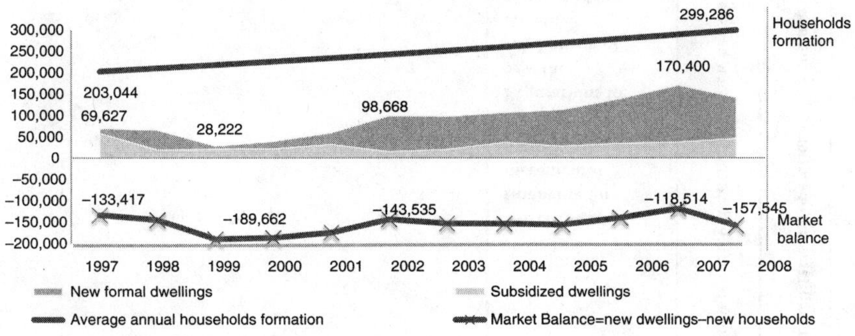

Source: Rojas et al. (2010).

Table 9.4 Annual Housing Production in Each Submarket in Argentina, Chile, and Colombia

Housing market segment	Argentina (2007)		Chile (2008)		Colombia (2008)	
	Housing units	Percent of total	Housing units	Percent of total	Housing units	Percent of total
Private formal market	104,000	42	72,647	48	75,000	24
Publicly supported formal market	53,000	21	78,264	52	60,000	19
Informal market	93,000	37	n.d.		175,000	56
Total	*250,000*	*100*	*150,911*	*100*	*310,000*	*100*

n.d. = no data.
Source: Rojas et al. (2010).

attain sufficient scale in the production of houses to address the needs of the growing urban population. In Chile, the government faces the challenge of helping the housing sector adjust to the demands of a population with higher incomes and more diversified housing demands, and to rehabilitate a large stock of low-quality housing in remote locations, most of which was provided by past public programs. The sustained focus of the Chilean programs on building new houses is hampering its capacity to address widespread housing issues—the quality of the existing housing stock, the deterioration of neighborhoods containing social housing,

Table 9.5 Housing Programs in Argentina, Chile, and Colombia

Approach	State guarantees access to good housing ⟵						⟶ Government facilitates the operation of housing markets			
Program type	Programs supporting the supply of housing						Programs supporting the demand for new houses			
Country	**Direct provision of houses by the government**	**Direct provision of incremental houses by the government**	**Government provision of serviced land for residential uses**	**Government provision of subsidized housing finance**	**Settlement upgrading and tenure regularization**	**Housing upgrading**	**Housing vouchers**	**Government financing for incremental housing**	**Regulations to ease the subdivision of land for residential use**	**Interventions to expand private housing finance**
Argentina	Federal programs for construction, Stage I			National Housing Fund (subsidized credit)	Neighborhood upgrading (PROMEBA)	Federal program for housing improvement (Live better)				
	Reactivation I and II			Federal programs (subsidized credit)	Housing solidarity					
	National Housing Fund (finished housing)				Program for basic sewage in vulnerable areas (PROSAC)					
					Program for the provision of drinking water, social help, and basic sewage (PROPASA)					

	Housing solidarity		Program for the social development of border areas (PROSOFA)		
	Emergency housing		Program for neighborhood upgrading and basic infrastructure (PROMHIB)		
			Rosario Habitat		
Chile	Basic housing	Dynamic social housing without debt (VSDsD)	I love my neighborhood	Family assets protection program (PPPF)	Unified general subsidy
	Free-choice Basic housing			Housing maintenance SERVIU	Special program for workers
	Solidarity fund (I and II)				Urban rehabilitation subsidy (DS40)
					Housing leasing
					Social integration subsidy
					Location Subsidy

Continued

Table 9.5 Continued

Country	Direct provision of houses by the government	Direct provision of incremental houses by the government	Government provision of serviced land for residential uses	Government provision of subsidized housing finance	Settlement upgrading and tenure regularization	Housing upgrading	Housing vouchers	Government financing for incremental housing	Regulations to ease the subdivision of land for residential use	Interventions to expand private housing finance
Colombia			Macroprojects	Subsidized interest rate credits	Titling of municipal land	Healthy housing	Familiar housing subsidy (FONVIVIENDA)		Macrojects	Voluntary contractual savings program (AVC)
					Neighborhood improvement		Familiar housing subsidy (Family Benefit Funds)			Tax exemptions to promote social housing (VIS) financing Tax exemptions to promote social housing (VIS) renting

Source: Rojas et al. (2010).

the transportation issues faced by beneficiaries of social housing built far from employment and service centers, and the need to improve the supply of serviced land for low-income households.

These results suggest that direct government interventions play a significant role in the evolution of the housing sector, not only in Argentina, where publicly financed housing represents almost half the total formal housing production of the country, but also in Colombia, where government interventions expand the supply of serviced land for low-income households. The combination of policies and programs implemented by Chile has contributed to this country's capacity to close most housing gaps.

Argentina, Chile, and Colombia have programs in which the government intervenes directly in housing markets. These programs represent a significant portion of the public funding for housing provided by their central governments. Chile and Colombia's programs explicitly target low-income households (the lowest two quintiles in the income distribution structure). Program targeting in Argentina is more widely defined, as it seeks to benefit the entire 80 percent of households in the country that cannot access financing to obtain a home (see table 9.5 for an inventory of programs in Argentina, Chile, and Colombia).

Do Public Housing Programs Reach the Poor?

When assessing whether a public program reaches the poor, four factors should be taken into account. *Targeting* refers to who receives public funding. *Coverage* assesses the scope of the government's effort in relation to the size of the target population. *Impact* measures whether the program achieved its intended development objectives. *Satisfaction* measures beneficiaries' perception of how these programs improved their quality of life.

Targeting

Housing programs employ different mechanisms to select beneficiaries. Federal programs in Argentina use lax targeting systems, while programs in Chile and Colombia use stricter ones. Given the latitude the federal government gives to the provinces and municipalities in Argentina to devise their own systems to select beneficiaries, this section focuses on those systems implemented by two municipalities in the Buenos Aires Metropolitan Area (see table 9.6). They were selected because their beneficiary selection criteria are representative of the most commonly used programs in Argentina. For Chile and Colombia, the discussion focuses on national data.

Table 9.6 Features of the Most Important Housing Programs in Argentina, Chile, and Colombia

	Argentina	Chile	Colombia
Features	**National Housing Fund (FONAVI) and Federal programs**	**Housing Solidarity Fund (FSV)**	**Family Housing Subsidy (FONVIVIENDA)**
Price cap on the dwelling	Not defined	480 Unidades de Fomento[a] (UF) (US$18,019)	Less than 70 minimum wages
Subsidy varies	No	Fixed for two different subprograms; marginalized regions receive more subsidy (vulnerable and marginalized households can apply for additional subsidy)	Subsidy size increases according to vulnerability of households
Subsidy size	Not applicable	FSV I: 320 Unidades de Fomento (UF) (US$12,013) FSV II: 410 Unidades de Fomento (UF) (US$15,392)	4–22 minimum wages (US$922–5,070)
Credit	Yes, public	No	Yes, private
Savings	Not defined	FSV I: 10 Unidades de Fomento (UF) (US$375) FSVII: 30 Unidades de Fomento (UF) (around US$1,130)	At least 10 percent of the dwelling's value (not compulsory for households with income below 2 minimum wages, relocated from high-risk places or displaced by violence)

Continued

Table 9.6 Continued

Features	Argentina National Housing Fund (FONAVI) and Federal programs	Chile Housing Solidarity Fund (FSV)	Colombia Family Housing Subsidy (FONVIVIENDA)
Income targeting	Wide. Varies across programs.	Narrow. Quintiles I and II (households with less than US$180 per capita, around US$630 per household)	Narrow. Household income less than 4 minimum wages (US$922)
Selection method (eligibility)	Multiple. Some programs use raffles, scoring methods, or others All municipalities include income in the scoring methods	Unified system. Scoring system includes proxy means testing (Ficha Protección Social) and housing vulnerability	Unified system. Scoring systems include proxy means testing (SISBEN l), housing vulnerability, social vulnerability (female-headed households, handicapped members, elderly) and other variables such as previous participation and saving levels (only those who obtain a credit can actually receive the subsidy)
Priority	Not specified	According to household score. For projects, other important factors include: vulnerability of the group, additional funds, feasibility and quality of the project	Higher scores are given priority, but only those who obtain a loan from a private institution can receive the subsidy

Continued

Table 9.6 Continued

Features	Argentina National Housing Fund (FONAVI) and Federal programs	Chile Housing Solidarity Fund (FSV)	Colombia Family Housing Subsidy (FONVIVIENDA)
Requirements	Vary across programs but usually include: • Age cap for the head of household • Not a home owner • Has not benefitted from a housing program before • Argentine citizen (provide ID) • Capacity to make monthly payments • Families only	• Not a home owner • Has not received a housing subsidy before • Foreigners must have a permanent resident status • Must complete savings requirements before submitting an application • No single-person households, except for elderly, handicapped, and victims of violence	• Not a home owner • Has not received a housing subsidy before • Works in the informal sector • Family income less than 4 minimum wages • No single-person households

[a] Unidad de fomento = Unit of account indexed to consumer price inflation.
Source: Rojas et al. (2010).

In Argentina, only 38 percent of beneficiaries belong to the poorest 20 percent of the population, compared to 76 percent in Colombia. Chile is in the middle, with 69 percent of beneficiaries in the first quintile of income distribution. More striking is that in Argentina, 18 percent of beneficiaries belong to the highest income quintile, while in Colombia and Chile no beneficiary is in this income segment (figure 9.5).

Figure 9.5 Percent Distribution of Beneficiaries of Select Public Housing Programs by Income

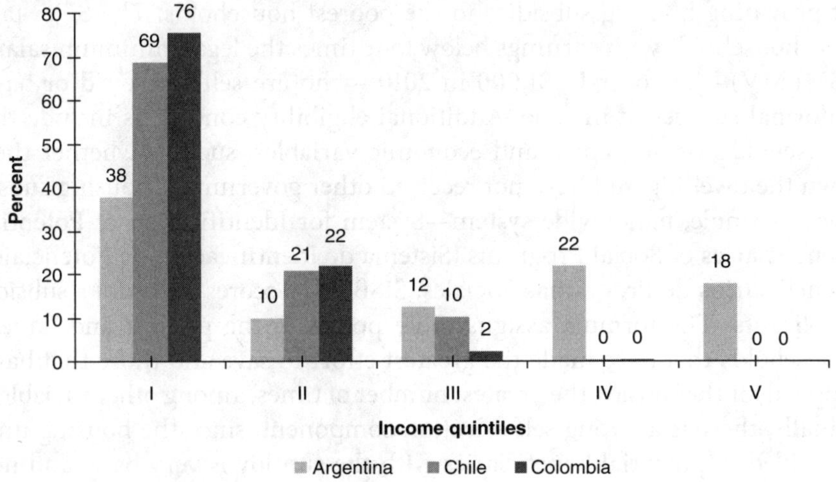

Source: Rojas et al. (2010).

Various factors explain these different targeting results, including differences in the stated objectives of each country's housing policy, the existence (or lack) of mechanisms that prioritize beneficiaries, and appropriate incentives for self-selection by beneficiaries. In Argentina, housing programs do not have the explicit objective of reaching lower-income households, so their eligibility criteria do not include an income cap. FONAVI focuses on households without access to mortgage credit—80 percent of the population—while Federal Programs originally aimed to stimulate the economy. When a family is deemed eligible, no standard nationwide process prioritizes these families and grants them subsidies. With the introduction of Federal Programs, some municipalities established point systems to select beneficiaries. In general, these systems use sociodemographic variables (such as age of head of household, and number of members of the nuclear family), along with other measures of the precariousness of construction materials or the lack of services in the currently occupied dwelling. Finally, in Argentina, few incentives exist for "self-selection" by beneficiaries, as the dwellings offered are relatively attractive in terms of quality, size, and access to urban services. In addition, many members of the middle class have unmet housing demands and consider public housing programs a good way to secure a better home; thus, many have applied for this type of housing. This situation is common in FONAVI projects cofinanced by trade unions or other organizations.

In contrast, Colombia's family housing subsidy (SFV) specifically aims at providing housing subsidies to the poorest households. The SFV[3] targets households with earnings below four times the legal minimum salary (SMLMV)—just over US$1,000 in 2010—who are self-employed or have informal sources of income. Additional eligibility conditions include the household's demographic and economic variables, such as whether they own the dwelling and have not received other government housing subsidies. A single, nationwide system—System for Identification of Potential Beneficiaries of Social Programs (Sistema de Identificación de Potenciales Beneficiarios de Programas Sociales, SISBEN)—scores and ranks subsidy applicants. The formula assigns more points to the poorest and largest households that have made the greatest effort to save and those that have applied for the subsidy the greatest number of times, among other variables. Finally, there is a strong self-selection component, since the housing unit provided to potential beneficiaries with the subsidy is very basic and not very attractive to the middle class. Unlike the union-administered funds in Argentina, Colombia's family benefit funds (Cajas de Compensación Familiar, CCFs) offer their own housing programs for formal workers that are not complemented by public subsidies. Recently, the CCFs have been administering the subsidies allocated by FONVIVIENDA for informal beneficiaries.

The experience with Colombia's Family Housing Subsidy does not suggest any leakage toward households that earn more than four times the minimum wage. Since 2005, the program has worked toward the goal of delivering 80 percent of subsidies to households with earnings equal to or less than two times the minimum wage. In practice, in 2007, practically all households (99 percent) that received the Family Housing Subsidy were at that income level (Rojas et aol. 2010).

Chile's main housing program, the Housing Solidarity Fund (FSV), targets groups considered vulnerable based on their income and their needs. Target groups are identified by their point score on the Social Protection Certificate (FPS), which is used to target the government's social programs. In the case of housing, this score is complemented by another one that measures housing need as a set of factors pertaining to the degree of precariousness of the dwelling where the potential beneficiary family lives. The program's target group consists of the two lowest income quintiles, as in Colombia. Although 90 percent of the beneficiaries are in the two lower quintiles, 10 percent of the households are in the third quintile and should not have received the subsidy. Also, 4 percent of households owned a dwelling when they applied for the subsidy. These leakages may result from the nonhousing objectives attached to this program, which also aims at benefiting other social groups at risk (the elderly, teenage single mothers).

Coverage

While no program sets the goal of covering its entire target population in a single year, it is useful to compare the number of housing solutions produced by the programs with the size of the intended beneficiary population in a given period.[4] Table 9.7 provides estimates for the three countries (Rojas et al. 2010).

Low coverage is a major shortcoming for most public housing programs in the region. Even the program with the best coverage—the Chilean FSV—will take more than a quarter of a century to provide a house to the entire target population, including new households that are formed during that time. These timeframes are neither reasonable nor socially sustainable. Given the current coverage of housing programs, closing the existing and forecasted housing gaps is going to be too slow, even when taking into account that income growth will help in closing them. The expansion of private lending for housing, paired with the right incentives and public-private partnerships for land developers, builders, and lenders to move down market, will be necessary, even if governments expand funding for effective programs.

Leveraging Private Sector Resources

One alternative to expanding the coverage of public housing interventions is to increase financing from beneficiaries and private sources. *Leverage* measures the amount of private funds (from households or other contributors, such as private enterprises and philanthropic institutions) mobilized by each unit of public spending. It is calculated by deducting the public subsidy provided for each housing solution from the final cost of the solution. The difference totals the amount provided by the beneficiaries' own resources through savings, credit, or by other nongovernment contributors.

In Colombia, beneficiaries of the national SFV program acquire a dwelling at an average sales price of US$10,600. The central government provides 51 percent of the financing. Other sources chip in the rest, often including 13 percent from municipalities. Consequently, leveraging of private resources totals 36 cents per public dollar invested. This level of

Table 9.7 Coverage of Housing Programs

	Number of eligible households in shortage (stock)	Average number of subsidies issued per year	Years to eliminate the stock of eligible households in shortage	Average number of eligible households formed per year (flow)	New eligible households as percent of the average number of subsidies	Subsidies available to reduce the stock after taking care of the flow	Years to eliminate the flow and stock of eligible households
Argentina	1,547,142	33,130	47	28,444	86	4,686	330
Chile	601,649	39,264	15	19,239	49	20,025	30
Colombia	986,472	36,630	27	29,991	82	6,639	149

Notes: The number of eligible households is calculated based on the criteria of each program.
For Argentina: Households with more than one person (except for elderly adults living alone), not homeowners, head of household under 60 years old.
For Chile: Households with more than one person (except for elderly adults living alone), not homeowners, up to the second quintile of per capita income, not having received any previous subsidy.
For Colombia: Households with more than one person (except for elderly adults living alone), not homeowners, income less than four times the minimum salary, not having received any previous subsidy.
Source: Rojas et al. (2010).

leverage exceeds the other programs studied, but it comes at a price; up to 25 percent of households eligible for the program end up not using the subsidies provided by the central government because they cannot obtain a loan to complete the financing (Rojas et al. 2010).

In Argentina, effective subsidy amounts are extremely high and complex to calculate because the solutions provided vary widely across provinces. Thus, it is hard to generalize about the amount of private resources mobilized per public dollar spent, or to determine a "typical" level of subsidy for a single type of housing solution. By design, Argentine programs should leverage a large proportion of private resources, since the beneficiary is supposed to pay back the entire cost of the home through a loan. However, numerous implicit subsidies ranging from interest rate subsidies to loan defaults by a third of beneficiaries effectively reduce the cost of the house.[5]

This situation reduces the coverage of programs and is highly inequitable. Argentina could greatly expand the coverage of its housing programs by improving targeting and leverage. With the large number of houses built and financed by the FONAVI and the Federal Programs, loan repayments could provide a significant part of the annual financing needed to ensure the continuity of the programs.

In Chile, the total value of the subsidy provided by the FSV ranges from US$12,600 to US$21,700, depending on the municipality where the dwelling is located and the type of project (houses in more remote municipalities are more expensive to build). The FSVI—which subsidizes the purchase of both new and existing homes—requires minimum household savings of US$450 and does not require complementary loans. Given the low income of its beneficiaries and the maximum and minimum amounts of possible subsidies, the FSVI actually leverages very little private money. At one end of the spectrum, a beneficiary could purchase a US$13,100 dwelling by providing only US$400, leveraging less than three cents per public dollar spent. At the other end, the highest possible subsidy plus the required minimum contribution would allow for the purchase of a US$20,000 dwelling, leveraging two private cents per public dollar spent. However, actual leverage of household resources may exceed this estimate since households must expand and improve on the core housing solutions provided by the SFVI.

Impact

What quality of life improvements do housing programs bring to their beneficiaries? There are few rigorous evaluations of the results attributable to housing programs in the region. Those available—such as Ruprah and Marcano (2007) and Ruprah (2010c)—deal with imperfect information. The results of housing programs are usually based on surveys in which beneficiaries are asked about the conditions of their housing before and after receiving the benefits of the programs; specifically, they are questioned about the quality of construction materials, the availability of public services, and access to urban amenities. In Argentina and Colombia, control groups were also established to isolate certain effects caused by other factors unrelated to the programs, such as macroeconomic conditions, better credit conditions, and local neighborhood improvement programs offered by municipal governments. While the surveys are not standardized and the results are not strictly comparable across countries, they show whether, according to beneficiaries, housing outcomes improved as a result of the programs.

In Argentina, based on the analysis of a representative sampling of beneficiaries for the Federal Programs and FONAVI in the Greater Buenos Aires area,[6] beneficiaries reported a significant improvement between the dwellings they lived in previously and the ones they received thanks to government programs (see figure 9.6). Access to public utilities such as

Figure 9.6 Argentina: Changes in Housing Conditions for Beneficiary Families Due to Housing Programs (Percentage Points)

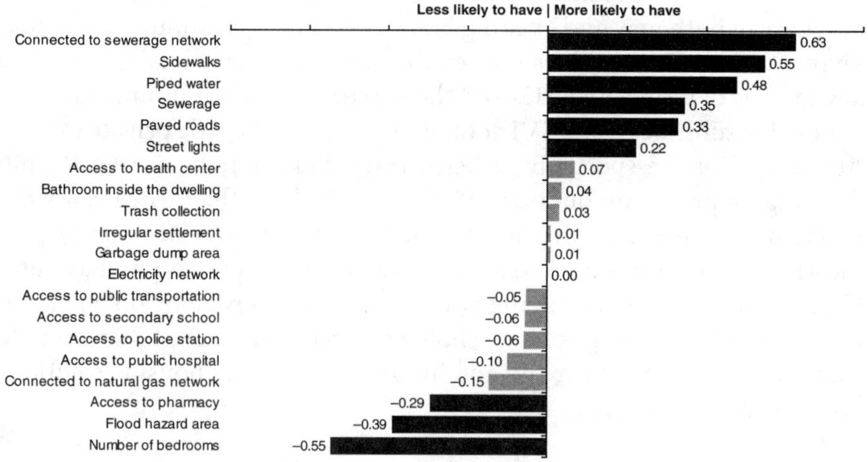

Note: The results correspond to a difference of means test that compares beneficiaries and a control group formed on the basis of INDEC (2001). Statistically nonsignificant results are shown in gray.
Source: Rojas et al. (2010).

water and sewerage (with the exception of natural gas) improved systematically as did street lighting and infrastructure such as paved roads and sidewalks. However, three components of good living conditions—access to education (access to a secondary school), health (access to public hospital), and security (access to police station)—remain deficient in the areas where new housing units have been built by government programs.

In Colombia, the results of the evaluation of the Family Housing Subsidy carried out by Centro de Estudios Nacionales, Cafeteros y Empresariales (CRECE)[7] show a positive and significant effect on the quality of the construction materials of the dwellings financed by the SFV. For example, there are no dirt or sand floors, no roofs are made of thatch or waste materials, and most walls are made of concrete blocks, brick, or stone. However, when compared to the control group, this effect is very small. In terms of public services, positive impacts were found in all services except landline telephones and paved roads (see figure 9.7).

However, the results show that in their new homes, beneficiaries live farther away from urban services. Often beneficiaries and households in the control group rented or shared a house with other households in more central locations than the beneficiaries, which explains the small positive effect of some of the indicators and the fact that they live farther from urban services (see figure 9.8).

Figure 9.7 Colombia: Changes in Housing Conditions for Beneficiary Families Due to Housing Programs (Percentage Points)

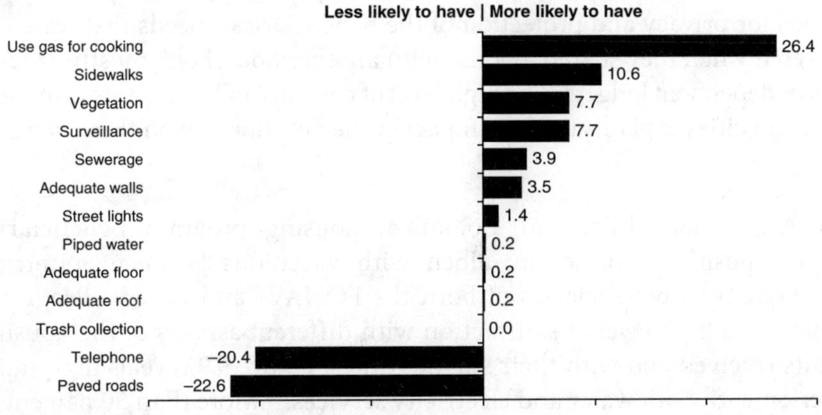

Note: Estimates are based on a parametric model of differences-in-differences (D-in-D).
Source: Rojas et al. (2010).

Figure 9.8 Colombia: Changes in Distance to Amenities for Beneficiary Families Due to Housing Programs (Percentage Points)

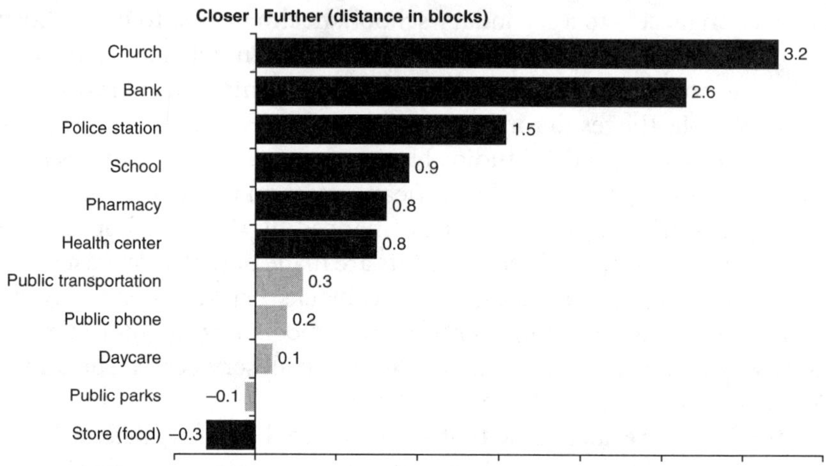

Note: Estimates are based on a parametric model of differences-in-differences (D-in-D). Statistically nonsignificant values are shown in grey.
Source: Rojas et al. (2010).

In Chile, the FSV housing program helped reduce the incidence of shared housing among beneficiary households (as shown by data from the National Urban Housing Evaluation project, DNEHU). Only 2.6 percent of beneficiaries reported sharing a dwelling with another household. Overcrowding (persons per room) also declined. These improvements clearly satisfy the needs for privacy and protection of the beneficiaries—needs that were not covered when they shared a house with another household, mostly as renters or dependent lodgers. The high level of coverage of basic services in most Chilean cities explains the low impact of the new housing on these items.

Satisfaction

In Argentina, Chile, and Colombia, housing program beneficiaries report positive satisfaction, albeit with variations between countries. In Argentina, beneficiaries of both the FONAVI and Federal Programs reported a high level of satisfaction with different aspects of the housing units received and with their surroundings. Figure 9.9 reveals high satisfaction with both water and electricity services."[8] More than 50 percent of households also reported satisfaction with the location of neighborhoods,

Figure 9.9 Argentina: Level of Satisfaction with Housing Programs (Percentage of Households)

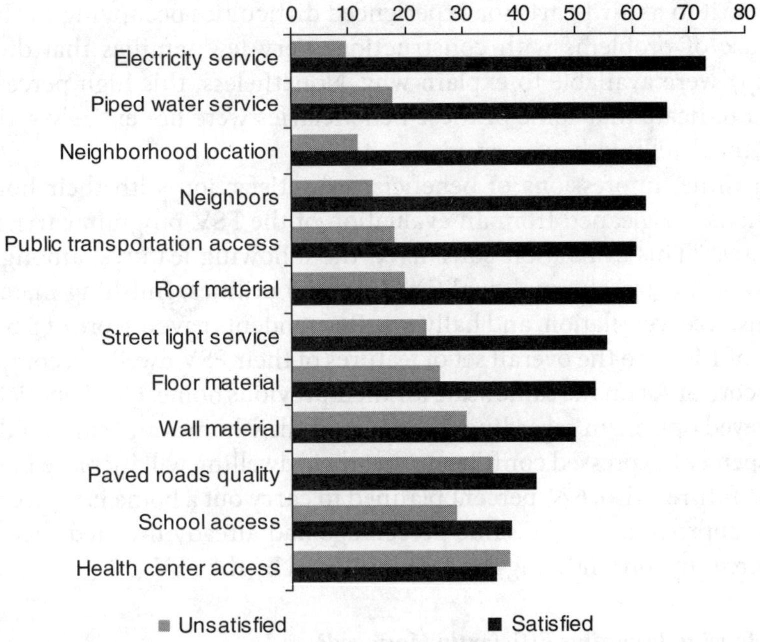

Source: Rojas et al. (2010).

immediate neighbors, availability of public transport, and roofing materials. A high percentage of households expressed satisfaction with their floor and wall materials, and with street lighting. Beneficiaries indicated less satisfaction with paved roads in their neighborhood, health centers, and availability of schools.

In Colombia, an assessment of the SFV program showed that it impacted positively on beneficiaries' perception of their home and their surroundings.[9] Beneficiaries were more satisfied with their own dwelling than with the state of their neighbors' dwellings or the condition of the neighborhood. This may reflect the conditions in which beneficiaries used to live: while they were satisfied with their old neighborhood and neighbors, they were not satisfied with their former dwelling. Overall, 91 percent of beneficiaries expressed highly favorable opinions of their new dwelling, neighborhood, and neighbors.

Interestingly, the original beneficiaries did not occupy 26.5 percent of the delivered dwellings. The alleged reasons for this phenomenon are called "special situations" in which the owner rented the property, decided to leave it to a third party, or experienced difficulties occupying the house because of problems with construction. Very few families that did not occupy were available to explain why. Nonetheless, this high percentage could indicate that some of these beneficiaries were not entirely satisfied with the dwelling they received.

In Chile, impressions of beneficiaries' satisfaction with their housing solutions are gleaned from an evaluation of the FSV program carried out in 2009.[10] This evaluation considered the following features, among others: acoustic and thermal qualities, installed utilities, finishing materials, rooms, size, ventilation, and hallways. Respondents gave a score of 5.5 (on a scale of 1 to 7) to the overall set of features of their FSV dwelling, compared to a score of 4.4 on the same scale for their previous home. FSV beneficiaries conveyed optimism regarding the future of their homes and surroundings; 70.8 percent expressed confidence that their dwelling will increase in value in the future. Also, 67.1 percent planned to carry out a home improvement, while approximately the same percentage had already invested their own resources in consolidating the asset provided by the FSV.

Are Housing Programs Efficiently Managed?

Housing programs to assist the poor are costly to implement. The range of costs to consider includes administrative expenses incurred in managing the programs, such as the costs of gathering and disbursing resources at both the central and local level. Some programs also include technical assistance. For instance, in Chile, the FSV finances organizations that provide services, such as assisting beneficiaries in obtaining subsidies or purchasing land, designing and contracting the construction of housing units, and supervising construction. Information about administrative expenses is limited and highly aggregated, so it is difficult to compare programs and draw comparative conclusions.

In Argentina, administrative expenses include payments for the management of the programs, an average 14 percent of total funds allocated to the program. The incidence of expenses to total resources varies widely among provinces, ranging from 1.8 percent in Santa Cruz to 22 percent in Tierra del Fuego to 28.3 percent in Neuquen.

In Colombia, estimates based on information about the allocations for the SFV in 2005 indicate that the direct administrative expenses of

FONVIVIENDA are approximately 11 percent. However, a more detailed study of the expenses incurred by the different actors involved in the subsidy allocation cycle (suppliers, CCFs, and households) indicates that costs can reach 27 percent. The costs are borne mostly by suppliers (10 percent) and the national government (11 percent), while households pay the least (6.5 percent). These high costs are not the result of administrative inefficiencies; rather, they reflect a system that has expanded controls to correct the irregularities of the past. Expenses have grown with the need to establish the stringent guarantees and safeguards required when funds are disbursed to developers to finance housing construction. The guarantees and safeguards are less stringent when funds are disbursed after the dwellings are built.

For Chile, there is little meaningful disaggregated information to estimate the administrative costs of the FSV. The available information suggests surprisingly low administrative expenses, equivalent to 3 percent of total resources devoted to the programs. Significantly, the FSV includes resources to assist households in accessing the program, either individually or as groups, for technical assistance to design and contract the construction of the housing units, and for the technical supervision of the construction. These expenses vary depending on the number of households involved, but can reach 6 percent of the total subsidy.

A Tool Kit for Better Housing Policies and Programs

Clearly, public intervention in housing is justified. Houses are produced and traded in a complex set of interrelated markets such as land, credit, building materials, and construction. Each individual market suffers from imperfections (information, externalities, monopolies, oligopolies, and the like) that can result in suboptimal social outcomes. Even when some of these flaws can be eliminated, the high levels of inequality in Latin American countries bode poorly for satisfactory results. These problems are not exclusive to housing markets, but the relevance of their outcomes for individual and collective well-being turns housing into a merit good, prompting sound government regulation and effective housing programs to ensure a minimum consumption of housing services by all households.

Even if there is consensus on the need for public intervention in the housing sector, differences arise when defining its type and scope. There are two extreme positions on the matter. One advocates a strong interventionist role for government that includes regulating and actively participating in housing provision. The other favors facilitating the operation of all markets related to housing. As discussed, these "pure" extreme positions are not often found in practice, since most governments implement both types of programs.

The in-depth analysis of Argentina, Chile, and Colombia provides no clear evidence that one position yields significantly better housing results than the other. In fact, the two approaches seem to complement each other. Since housing deficits faced by low-income households are so large in most Latin American and Caribbean countries, public resources should be complemented by private interventions. On the other hand, the role of the public sector as facilitator should not be interpreted as a mandate to retreat from the housing market.

Direct provision, with its high costs, high-quality housing standards, and high subsidies, has not been effective in expanding coverage and leveraging resources from households. However, when these interventions are well targeted to the poor and efficiently executed—as in the case of the FSV in Chile—they significantly improve access to services and reduce overcrowding, albeit at a high cost.

The ABC programs—commonly associated with the enabling markets approach—seem to have originated as a practical response to tackle the affordability issue and reduce the fiscal burden of housing policy. This was done in the belief that public subsidies would mobilize private resources, which would cover the cost of housing solutions while lowering costs to the state. However, since the underlying market failures that affect low-income groups were not resolved (mainly their low saving capacity and lack of access to credit), private financing was unavailable. Moreover, the private sector has remained reluctant to go downstream and supply low-income housing in the region, probably due to some combination of lack of demand, profitability concerns, overly stringent regulations, and the prevailing informality in land development and construction.

The Chilean case supports the mixed approach to housing policies. Even though Chile was a pioneer of the enabling markets approach launched in the 1970s, at present, its public housing program is bigger, and provides almost full subsidies to vulnerable and low-income groups.

Besides these general conclusions, certain issues must be addressed when putting together a tool kit to design sound public policies for housing.

- Countries need to adopt a comprehensive vision of the housing problems affecting all income groups, going beyond low-income groups to include lower-middle- and middle-income households that are underserved. Each group faces different challenges, so the instruments to support them should differ. Lower-income groups—particularly those with informal sources of income—need higher subsidies to afford a house of even minimum quality; land policies and regulation to ensure the supply of serviced land for their needs; and incremental construction approaches when appropriate. The middle class needs incentives to save and help with loans to increase the affordability of housing.

- There are significant trade-offs between quality, targeting, and coverage. High-quality standards not only raise the cost of houses but also make them attractive to higher-income groups that compete with lower-income households, thereby missing the opportunity for beneficiaries to "self-target" by choosing the type of housing designed for needier consumers. This obviously translates into lower coverage, as in the case of Argentina. This does not mean that quality should be disregarded or ignored to a point of extending coverage successfully with extremely low standards. When this has been the case, individual families end up having to spend too much to live in the houses and to benefit from the basic bundle of services they offer, leading them to abandon these houses. This has occurred in some cases in Chile and Colombia, mostly when the houses were built in remote locations or left unfinished.
- Public housing policy should not be rigid, but it should remain stable in its fundamental objectives. In the three case studies, policy objectives have been affected by economic downturns and sociopolitical conditions. In Argentina, housing programs became a means to reactivate the economy and create jobs in the 2001 crisis. In trying to generate employment, Argentina may have built more houses than actually needed in some localities and neglected the pressing needs for long-term improvement of the housing stock and access to infrastructure for low-income households. Similarly, in Chile, the haste to build houses in large quantities later created an urban problem that forced the government to spend additional public resources to upgrade low-quality neighborhoods. In Colombia, besides working anticyclically, housing policy has responded to diverse objectives, among them attending to the population displaced by violence, the "*desplazados*." Specially designed programs that take into account the potentially temporary nature of the problem and the beneficiaries' lack of integration to the local communities may better serve the objective of absorbing the displaced population in Colombian cities. All these changes to some extent alter the original rules and negatively affect the capacity to plan ahead. Such a longer-term capacity is fundamental for market development, especially to promote private sector participation. Arguably, the rigidness of Argentina's programs has crowded out private sector participation.
- A sustainable, long-term solution to existing housing gaps requires the mobilization of private resources. To this end, countries need to make full use of the instruments of the enabling markets approach designing programs that

promote savings and facilitate access to credit to middle- and low-income households. Part of the solution will also come from increases in per capita income, macroeconomic stability, and more developed financial markets that enable more households to be assisted by the private sector. Chile, for example, has implemented a number of reforms to expand housing finance since the 1980s: promoting long-term savings, encouraging financial products to channel these savings to housing, improving the security of transactions, and easing the execution of guarantees. As a result, 70 percent of the population can potentially access credit. The deeper involvement of the private sector in providing housing and credit in Chile has helped free up government resources to focus on lower-income groups and offer large subsidies. For its part, the government of Colombia is working to extend credit to the poor by supporting access to finance for informal workers through the Ahorro Voluntario Contractual (AVC) Program, operated by the Fondo Nacional del Ahorro (FNA). Though still new and limited in scope, the AVC is helping a considerable number of informal workers obtain access to mortgage finance.

- On the supply side, policy must encourage the production of low-income housing, promote competition among developers, and improve tools that support low-cost land development—a key issue in large cities. This last aspect is a weak point in most housing policies in the region, although Colombia has made some progress with the Macroproyectos de Interés Social Nacional.
- Housing policy in the region has focused almost exclusively on the construction of new housing units, which has led to good results in lowering the quantitative housing deficit. However, housing policy should diversify, not just to reduce costs but also to attend to the low quality of the existing housing stock, which affects the poor the most. To move in this direction, countries should adopt, continue, or expand options such as incremental housing programs, rental housing, and upgrading poor neighborhoods. For low-income households, group or community-based housing subsidy schemes present definitive advantages over the individually based housing subsidies that work for middle-income households under the ABC modality.
- Program implementation must be improved. Current high execution costs stem from the need to ensure targeting and avoid leakages. Linking eligibility to housing programs to social evaluation instruments, like the Social Protection Certificate in Chile or SISBEN in Colombia, represents a good first step to share the costs of screening applicants with other social programs. However, more needs to be done to reduce the costs of housing programs and home construction supervision and allocation. It may be possible to simplify procedures by enhancing transparency and more fully involving the community in supervising local elected officials. This development can occur more easily at the local level, creating an additional rationale for the decentralized execution of these programs.

- In finding a long-term sustainable solution to the housing needs of the population, the government in the short term should continue helping low-income households satisfy their housing needs. This has a high fiscal price, as proven by Chile's FSV—and more recently by Argentina's Federal Housing Programs. These programs target the poor much better than many of the past FONAVI projects, mostly because the housing solutions provided are smaller in size, of lower quality, and located in more remote locations than the average FONAVI home. This improvement in targeting suggests that it is easier to reach the poor by directly providing houses that are subsidized, but also of lower standards—which also cuts the cost to government and discourages middle-income groups from entering the programs. Low-income groups are riskier clients for the private sector because of their limited and potentially unstable capacity to pay, and the lack of information on their credit behavior. Even if the potential market for housing microfinance (HMF) is large,[11] the private sector is still reluctant to fully attend to such demand. Moreover, it is crucial to develop specific business models to serve low-income groups, which require longer repayment times, flexible collection schemes, technical assistance, and a staged approach to acquiring a house (see chapter 8, on incremental housing). Public intervention will be crucial to support the development of products and methodologies to tap this market, which is still in an embryonic stage in the region.

In this context, amid many successes, the three cases studied still face major challenges. Although the government of Argentina has made a significant contribution to the well-being of part of its population in terms of housing, it probably did so at a much higher cost than was necessary. Moreover, under this scheme, the government assumed a large financial burden that it has had difficulty honoring in times of crises. Most significantly, the modus operandi of the government directly providing houses has crowded out potential contributions that beneficiaries could have made to resolving their housing problems, thus reducing the volume of total (public plus private) resources flowing into the housing sector. This effect of public interventions, together with a poorly developed system of housing finance, explain Argentina's less-than-stellar housing outcomes when assessed in relation to its per capita income. Argentina should seek to mobilize more private resources, support the development of mortgage markets, and in time—once the private sector starts catering to the housing needs of the middle class—focus its interventions on lower-income groups.

Colombia faces a challenge in trying to improve the quality of its subsidized houses while maintaining strict targeting and coverage levels. For this purpose, it must reinforce its ABC program (SFV) to make more credit available to informal groups, while developing accessible urban land.

Even Chile, which has reached good levels of quality and coverage, should remedy problems generated due to bad policy decisions, especially regarding the distant location of social housing projects, or the delivery of complete houses to vulnerable groups that cannot maintain them.

There is no silver bullet to solve the complex maze of housing sector issues in the region. With an estimated 3 million new households springing up every year in the cities of Latin America, the shortfall in new houses produced and consumed in formal housing markets will force between 1.5 and 2 million households a year to obtain shelter in informal markets (Rojas and Medellín 2011). Under these circumstances, there is a pressing need to maintain and improve the housing delivery mechanisms that have arisen to take up the slack of houses not supplied and financed by the private formal markets.

The solution to the housing dilemma should be tailored to local needs, comprehensive, and attend to the different aspects of the problem. It should be pragmatic, rather than ideological, combining the best of the interventionist approach with market enabling techniques to attend to the housing needs of all people. Programs should focus on generating a new housing stock along with improving the existing one, taking into consideration the quality of materials, access to urban and public services, and property rights. Policy should simultaneously focus on short-term needs, without jeopardizing long-term sustainability. To this end, it is necessary to act on the root of the problem instead of focusing just on its symptoms. Otherwise, despite all the best of intentions, the region's housing policies and programs will continue to display considerable room for development.

Notes

1 Dirt Floors and Unpaved Streets: Why Housing Markets Matter

1. Three or more people per room is considered overcrowding.
2. Sites that increase the risk of vector-borne diseases: infections transmitted to humans and other animals by blood-feeding anthropods, such as mosquitoes, ticks, and fleas. Examples of vector-borne diseases include Dengue fever, viral encephalitis, Lyme disease, and malaria.
3. The Peabody Picture Vocabulary Test measures the receptive (hearing) vocabulary of children and adults. The test is an individually administered, norm-referenced, wide-range instrument.
4. Neighborhood effects are typically defined as community influences on individual social or economic outcomes.
5. Latin America was responsible for only 4.3 percent of global emissions in 2007 (UN-HABITAT 2011a, p. 15).
6. *Compactness* refers to the extent to which the city shape approximates an increasing circle.
7. Urban sprawl refers to cities that are low in density and dispersed. They are usually organized in polycentric patterns that feature single uses for land. For example, zones for housing are separated from zones for retail, office, and other types of development.
8. The countries are Argentina, Bolivia, Brazil, Chile, Colombia, Costa Rica, Ecuador, El Salvador, Guatemala, Honduras, Mexico, Nicaragua, Panama, Peru, Paraguay, Uruguay, and Venezuela. The data are for the years 2000, 2001, and 2003–2007.

2 Portrait of a Problem: The Housing Sector

1. Based upon historical poverty-GDP growth elasticity and real GDP forecasts.
2. In making these measurements, standards for "adequate" outcomes must be clearly defined.
3. Peer effect is the term used to describe an individual's potential change of behavior due to the presence or pressure of its peers. For a fuller description, see chapter 1. Poverty traps refer to any self-enforcing mechanisms that cause poverty to persist. For discussions, see Azariadis and Stachurski (2005).

4. Poverty is defined using the United Nations Economic Commission for Latin America and the Caribbean (ECLAC) food poverty line.
5. The costing exercise assumes US$11,000 in construction costs, US$3,000 in land costs, and US$1,000 in operational/administrative expenses.
6. In comparison, many East Asian countries have made much more rapid progress in housing and urban development.

3 Two Bedrooms, Two Bathrooms, and a Big Yard? Housing Demand in Latin America and the Caribbean

1. Indicators come from various sources compiled by the Research Department of the Inter-American Development Bank (details can be found in Bouillon and Medellín 2011).
2. Financial institutions usually adapt their mortgage products to the risk profile of the household. However, for modeling purposes, it is complicated to build a flexible model for the interest rate; thus, for this simulation the study used the reference mortgage rate estimated by the central banks or the national superintendence of financial institutions.

4 To Buy or Not to Buy: Expanding the Rental Housing Market

1. These costs are substantial. In the United States, e.g., they represent the sum of 3 percent of the value of a house and 4 percent of household earnings (Haurin and Gill 2002). This financial cost is aggravated by the time it takes to complete the associated transactions. These burdens are likely to be higher in Latin America and the Caribbean, where legal transactions take longer and are riskier.
2. The economic effects of rent control have been studied extensively. Studies include Arnott and Johnston (1981); Fallis and Smith (1984, 1985); Gyourko and Linneman (1989); Arnott (1995); Arnott and Igarashi (2000); Basu and Emerson (2000, 2003); and Glaeser and Luttmer (2003).
3. In Canada, the Multi Unit Residential Building (MURB) program was introduced in the mid-1980s but was abandoned in 1991.
4. Taken from http://huduser.org/portal/datasets/lihtc.html.

5 Digging up the Truth about Land Markets

1. UF stands for "unidad de fomento," which in Chile is a unit of account indexed to the consumer price inflation.
2. In some cases, this standardized plot is smaller than the legal minimum plot size allowed in some cities. For example, for cities in Argentina, the minimum plot size ranges between 250 and 300 square meters.

3. See Mayer and Somerville (2000); Green, Malpezzi, and Mayo (2005); Glaeser, Gyourko, and Saks (2005); Quigley and Raphael (2005); Gyourko, Mayer, and Sinai (2006); and Gyourko, Saiz, and Summers (2008).
4. Available at: http://www.doingbusiness.org/methodology/registering-property (accessed July 2011).
5. See Galiani and Schargrodsky (2004); Buckley and Kalarickal (2006); Flood (2006); and Di Tella, Galiani, and Schargrodsky (2007).
6. Feler and Henderson (2008) argue that there is clear evidence of explicit exclusionary policies in Brazilian cities in the 1980s, as cities underserviced infrastructure to low-cost settlements.
7. The argument has been put forward by several others (Dowall 1992a; Duranton 2008; Brueckner and Selod 2009) and included in the World Bank (1993).

6 A Construction Industry in Need of Remodeling

1. While there are differences among cities, IDB research found only one city—Montevideo—in which construction costs did not predominate.
2. Nominal construction costs adjusted by the consumer price index (CPI), the so-called construction cost real indices.
3. Argentina's index is 100, meaning that it is at the maximum risk of overheating. Brazil's index is a little above 80 (*The Economist* 2011).
4. Even though this figure comes from a civil construction poll, it reflects the situation of the construction industry as a whole, including residential construction. Brazilian building site workers are each day refusing more to accept a job that presents a tough working condition with a low paying level, particularly with the growing number of new opportunities that improving economic conditions present in other sectors.
5. For information about these programs, see http://constructingexcellence.org.uk/.
6. Total energy consumption will equal total hours of usage (intensity) times energy consumed per hour (efficiency).
7. Principal-agent problems arise in the context of incomplete and asymmetric information. Two characters are defined, a "principal" and an "agent." The principal enacts (or pays) the agent to act on his behalf or provide some service for him. As a result two problems arise: adverse selection and moral hazard. The first problem is generated when an agent acts opportunistically prior to engaging in a contract; the second problem arises when an agent acts opportunistically after doing so.
8. According to the authors, there is statistical evidence that only four countries in the region might be able to introduce energy-conservation policies without hampering economic growth: Argentina, Dominican Republic, Mexico, and Panama. Another twelve nations including Brazil, Chile, Colombia, Costa Rica, Ecuador, Honduras, Jamaica, Nicaragua, Peru, Paraguay, Uruguay, and Venezuela should instead focus on growth. For another four countries it was impossible to statistically determine the possible relation between energy and growth.

9. Interestingly, buildings built in periods when electricity prices are low are less energy efficient, which would imply that homebuyers to some extent factor in energy consumption in the demand for housing.
10. Costa and Kahn looked at the installation of new heating and cooling units and new kitchens, and the addition of square footage.

7 Too Small to Thrive: The Housing Finance Market

1. Incremental housing is the widespread practice of beginning with a core structure and gradually adding rooms, amenities, and upgrades as the owner's financial circumstances allow.
2. Across countries, mortgages vary in their typical length, loan-to-value ratios, and rates (whether they tend to be fixed or adjustable). Warnock and Warnock (2008) noted that as of 2005, long-term fixed rate mortgages were not widely available in any emerging market economy. Only a few—Malaysia, Thailand, and some transition economies in Eastern Europe—had typical maturities of 30 years. Another nonoverlapping subset of emerging markets tended to have fixed-rate mortgages. In contrast, many developed countries had mortgages with terms of 25 years or longer, and roughly half had predominantly fixed-rate products. Data on such characteristics were not complete or reliable enough to be included in Warnock and Warnock's (2008) empirical analysis. The authors note, however, that while in any economy it is not clear a priori whether lender or borrower preferences account for the prevalence of fixed or variable rate mortgages, within the set of developed countries, it appears that those with more stable inflation tend to have a greater share of fixed-rate mortgages.
3. The US housing finance crisis has shown that having too many mortgage products, especially when not well understood by borrowers, is also suboptimal.
4. Warnock and Warnock (2011) compiled mortgage data from Hypostat, Swiss National Bank, Titularizadora Colombiana, UN-Habitat, Bank of Ghana, and, for Asia, national sources as provided by BIS Asia.
5. The World Bank's Doing Business reports note that if the transfer of formal property is too costly or complicated, formal titles might become informal again, and that even if titles remain formal, the property market will not function effectively.
6. More generally, a well-developed housing finance system will typically have a diversity of lenders in the primary market (such as nondepository mortgage specialists, nongovernmental organizations, microfinance institutions, and contractual savings systems) and greater specialization in mortgage delivery.
7. One set of participants in the secondary market is mortgage securitizers, which bundle and repackage mortgages (or parts of mortgages) to create new securities, and investors in these mortgage securities. The securitizers can be public or private; the investors can be domestic or foreign institutions or individuals. Recent events in markets for mortgage securities notwithstanding, secondary mortgage markets can be an important part of a country's broader capital markets. In Latin

America and the Caribbean, securitization has become an important funding source in Colombia and, to a lesser extent, Mexico. See box 7.1 for more details.

8. See www.doingbusiness.org/MethodologySurveys/GettingCredit.aspx and http://www.doingbusiness.org/methodology/registering-property. Doing Business data are available at http://www.doingbusiness.org/data.
9. Specifically, *Legal Rights for Borrowers and Lenders* is composed of ten criteria, eight pertaining to collateral law and two to bankruptcy law. A score of one is assigned for each criterion that is present in the country, so the overall score indicates how many of the criteria are met.
10. Similar to *Legal Rights*, the *Credit Information* score is one point for each criterion that is met, although for this measure there are only six criteria.
11. This variable is more specifically about businesses, not households, but serves as a proxy for costs in real estate markets.
12. In the regression analysis, Warnock and Warnock (2008; 2011) use country size as a control variable, measured by a long-term average of PPP-adjusted nominal GDP from http://data.worldbank.org/. It can be argued that country size is exogenous, whereas per capita income might be endogenous, as it is influenced by financial sector development.
13. There is always a question of whether the type of credit information collected is informative about all segments of the population, but with vibrant microfinance sectors in many Latin America and Caribbean countries, appropriate information may be available even for the lowest-income segments.
14. See, e.g., Pagano (2001) and IDB (2004).
15. On the Argentine housing finance system prior to the 2001/2002 crisis, see also Cristini, Moya, and Powell (2001).
16. For a description of the case of Peru, Trinidad and Tobago, and some countries in central America, see Palomino and Wong (2011); Auguste, Moya and Sookram (2010); Cuevas, Lee, and Bonilla (2010); and Sancho, Rivera, and Rosales (2010), respectively.
17. There are many examples in which a surge in lending to the poor ended in crisis. See the recent subprime crisis in the United States. Another example is South Africa's small- and medium-size banking crisis from 1999 to 2003, which led to the liquidation of many of that country's banks and sparked the formation of a new national credit regulator (Mboweni 2004).
18. In their analysis, the authors also consider important new laws, some of which, such as Law 9154 (1997) and Law 10,931 (2004), reduced legal risks to lenders. However, they found that stronger protection of creditor rights is less important than the impact of the rule in explaining recent mortgage market growth.
19. It is somewhat more complicated than that, but the 65 percent rule is a good first approximation. See Martins, Lundberg, and Takeda (2011) for full details.
20. The authors argue that for those with uninterrupted work in the formal sector, monthly payments are automatically deducted from payroll, so an analysis of their repayment would not be critical.
21. An *ejido* is a small Mexican farm that is owned and operated by either individual inhabitants of a village or by a group collectively.

22. This historical description of the Colombian housing finance system is based on Hofstetter, Tovar, and Urrutia (2011).
23. In the early 1990s, UPAC added an interest rate component to its inflation component.
24. In addition to the macroeconomic crisis that reduced lending, mortgage loans were rewritten and the interest rate was reset either at a fixed nominal interest rate or with payments tied to inflation. This generated legal instability, which interacted with macroeconomic uncertainty and severely hurt the mortgage market.
25. VIS refers to houses with a purchase price below 135 monthly minimum wages (or about US$36,000 in 2010), with greater subsidies for houses priced at below 70 minimum wages (about US$19,000).

8 Doing It Yourself

1. Fideicomiso de Ciudad Nezahualcóyotl (FINEZA) and later the Comisión para la Regulación del Uso del Suelo del Estado de Mexico (CRESEM).
2. Contributions are 8 percent of formal payrolls for Fundo de Garantia do Tempo de Serviço.
3. The lowest-priced core expandable units in middle-income Latin American countries (Argentina, Brazil, and Mexico) sell for US$15,000 to US$20,000, after subtracting US$5,000 to US$15,000 in various types of subsidies provided by several levels of government (such as demand-side subsidies and interest rate subsidies funded by national government, and free or discounted land from the state or local government).
4. The importance of communities is highlighted by the higher levels of life satisfaction reported by families that live in more cohesive communities as shown, e.g., in a study for poor neighborhoods in Lima (Alcázar and Andrade 2010).

9 Hammering Out a Housing Policy That Works

1. These are not structural problems (as there are implementation strategies that can avoid them); however, they should be considered structural, as they appear in most schemes in which government institutions directly supply houses.
2. This government objective can probably be attained more efficiently and the target population better served by providing housing for rent that later can be transferred to city residents.
3. From 1991 to 2008, 597,080 subsidies were allocated, totaling US$4.12 billion on average, there were 33,000 beneficiary households per year with an annual expenditure of US$229 million.
4. Measurements used the two-way methodology suggested by Ruprah (2010c). First, the average number of housing units built in the past five years is compared with the number of eligible households. Second, the number of households formed is compared with the number of currently eligible households.

5. There are three main sources of unprogrammed subsidies. First, the dwelling is provided at lower cost than the full opportunity cost. (The provincial housing institutes are legally authorized to provide capital reductions of up to 20 percent. Moreover, costs are calculated at historic values.) Thus, there is a capital transfer. Second, financing is subsidized. (Interest rates on financing are charged at below-market rates; in many cases, the rate is set at zero.) Thus, a subsidy effectively accrues over the long term. Finally, some beneficiaries (approximately 30 percent) never make their payments. Consequently, there may be a partial or total transfer of capital.
6. A difference of means test was used first to make a comparison with the dwellings where the beneficiaries had lived previously and then to measure the difference of means between beneficiaries and a control group. The control group was formed on the basis of the 2001 Living Conditions Survey, using the propensity score matching (PSM) technique. The analysis is based on the survey of beneficiary households of government housing programs in the Greater Buenos Aires area (Encuesta de Hogares Adjudicatarios de Programas Estatales de Vivienda en el Gran Buenos Aires) carried out by Fundación de Investigaciones Económicas Latinoamericanas (FIEL) in 2009.
7. This evaluation was designed and financed by the IDB's Urban Social Interest Housing Program. Baseline surveys were conducted with a group of households that received the Family Housing Subsidy (SFV) to purchase a new dwelling in 2004, and with a control group. Two years later, the same groups were surveyed to measure the impact of the program. A differences-in-differences (D-in-D) parametric model was used. A total of 1,496 beneficiaries responded to the 2004 survey. In 2006, only 565 households were living in the dwelling they had bought with the subsidy; over half were not living in it because it had not been delivered.
8. Dissatisfied households responded with a one or two on a scale of one to five, while satisfied households chose four or five. Households that were neither satisfied nor dissatisfied chose three.
9. Programa de Vivienda de Interés Social Urbana. Operación de Credito BID-1483; Evaluación Final y de Impacto. Diciembre 2008. Realizada por CRECE (Centro de Estudios Nacionales, Cafeteros y Empresariales).
10. The National Urban Housing Evaluation (DNEHU) was requested by MINVU in 2009 and conducted by the External Services Department of the Faculty of Architecture, Design and Urban Studies of the Pontificia Universidad Católica de Chile. This study examined 2,067 cases, including beneficiaries of four current housing programs. To focus on the country's most vulnerable population, the study worked with a subsample of 1,048 cases in which the FSV provided a dwelling as an end product of the program. (It did not include beneficiaries of the location subsidy that complements the FSV, for example.)
11. This group could include that 40 percent of the households in the region that cannot afford a finished home produced by the formal housing sector and must build incrementally.

References

Abiko, A. 2003. Tecnologias apropriadas em construção civil. In W. J. Freire and A. L. Beraldo, eds., *Tecnologias e materiais alternativos de construção.* Campinas, São Paulo, Brazil: Editora da UNICAMP.

Abiko, A., L. R. de Azevedo Cardoso, R. Rinaldelli, and H. C. Riogi Haga. 2007. Basic Costs of Slum Upgrading in Brazil. *Global Urban Development* 3(1) November. Available at http://www.globalurban.org/GUDMag07Vol3Iss1/Abiko.htm. Accessed on November 13, 2011.

Abramo, P. 2006. *Ciudad caleidoscópica: una visión heterodoxa de la economía urbana* [Kaleidoscopic city: a heterodox vision of the urban economy]. La Coruña, Spain: Netbiblo.

———. 2007. O mercado de solo informal em favelas e a mobilidade residencial dos pobres nas grandes metrópoles: notas para delimitar um objeto de estudo para a América Latina [Informal Land Markets in Favelas and Residential Mobility of the Poor: A Contribution to a Research Agenda]. Instituto de Pesquisa e Planejamento Urbano e Regional, Rio de Janeiro, Brazil.

Acioly, Jr., C. 2009. Overcoming the Challenge of Informal Settlements in the Developing World: Slum Upgrading and Slum Prevention. Paper presented at the International Tripartite Conference on Urbanization Challenges and Poverty Reduction in African, Caribbean and Pacific Countries, June 8–10, Nairobi.

Alcázar, L., and R. Andrade. 2010. Influence of Individual, Urban, and Civil Society Spheres on Quality of Life in Metropolitan Lima, Peru. In E. Lora, A. Powell, B. M. S. van Praag, and P. Sanguinetti, eds., *The Quality of Life in Latin American Cities: Markets and Perception.* Washington, DC: Inter-American Development Bank and World Bank.

Altermatt, E. R., and E. M. Pomerantz. 2005. The Implications of Having High-Achieving versus Low-Achieving Friends: A Longitudinal Analysis. *Social Development* 14(1): 61–81.

Andrews, D., A. Caldera Sánchez, and A. Johansson. 2011. Housing Markets and Structural Policies in OECD Countries. OECD Economics Department Working Paper no. 836. OECD Publishing, Paris.

Angel, S. 1983. Upgrading Slum Infrastructure: Divergent Objectives in Search of a Consensus. *Third World Planning Review* 5(1): 5–22.

———. 2000. *Housing Policy Matters: A Global Analysis.* New York: Oxford University Press.

Angel, S. (with J. Parent, D. L. Civco, and A. M. Blei). 2011. *Making Room for a Planet of Cities.* Cambridge, MA: Lincoln Institute of Land Policy. Available at: https://

www.lincolninst.edu/pubs/dl/1880_1195_Angel%20PFR%20final.pdf. Accessed July 2011.

Angel, S., J. Parent, D. L. Civco, and A. M. Blei. 2010. The Persistent Decline in Urban Densities: Global and Historical Evidence of "Sprawl." Working Paper no. 10SA1. Lincoln Institute of Land Policy, Cambridge, MA.

Anzorena, J. 1993. Supporting Shelter Improvements for Low-Income Groups. *Environment and Urbanization* 5(1): 122–31.

Apgar, W. 2004. Rethinking Rental Housing: Expanding the Ability of Rental Housing to Serve as a Pathway to Economic and Social Opportunity. Working Paper no. W04–11. Joint Center for Housing Studies, Harvard University, Cambridge, MA.

Apgar, W., A. Calder, M. Collins, and M. Duda. 2002. An Examination of Manufactured Housing as a Community- and Asset-Building Strategy. Report. Ford Foundation and Joint Center for Housing Studies, Harvard University. Available at http://www.jchs.harvard.edu/publications/communitydevelopment/W02-11_apgar_et_al.pdf. Accessed on November 17, 2011.

Arbeláez, M. A., C. Camacho, and J. Fajardo. 2010. Social Housing Finance in Colombia. Inter-American Development Bank, Washington, DC. Unpublished.

Arbeláez, M. A., R. Steiner, A. Becerra, and D. Wills. 2011. Housing Tenure and Housing Demand in Colombia. IDB Working Paper Series no. IDB-WP-259. Department of Research and Chief Economist, Inter-American Development Bank, Washington, DC.

Arnott, R. 1995. Time for Revisionism on Rent Control? *Journal of Economic Perspectives* 9(1) Winter: 99–120.

Arnott, R., and M. Igarashi. 2000. Rent Control, Mismatch Costs and Search Efficiency. *Regional Science and Urban Economics* 30(3) May: 249–88.

Arnott, R., and N. Johnston. 1981. *Rent Control and Options for Decontrol in Ontario.* Policy Study Series. Toronto: Ontario Economic Council.

Arriagada, C. 2000. Pobreza en América Latina: nuevos escenarios y desafíos de políticas para el hábitat urbano. Serie medio ambiente y desarrollo no. 27. United Nations Economic Commission for Latin America and the Caribbean (ECLAC), Santiago, Chile.

Artiga de Soundy, E., N. Baltrusis, M. Bonilla, R. Casanova, Y. Gaete, P. McHardy, H. Menna Barreto, M. Perló, A. Sparacino, and P. Trivelli. 2010. Land and Housing Indicators Database in Selected Cities in Latin America and the Caribbean. Department of Research and Chief Economist, Inter-American Development Bank, Washington, DC. Unpublished.

Associated Press. 2011. Amendment Introduced to Help Homeowners Stay in Their Homes. March 29. Available at http://inslee.house.gov/press-release/amendment-introduced-help-homeowners-stay-their-homes.

Auguste, S., R. Bebczuk, and R. Moya. 2011. The Demand for Mortgages under Macro Volatility: The Argentine Case. Technical Note no. IDB-TN-284. Department of Research and Chief Economist, Inter-American Development Bank, Washington, DC.

Auguste, S., R. Moya, and S. Sookram. 2010. The Mortgage Market in Trinidad and Tobago. Inter-American Development Bank, Washington, DC. Unpublished.

Azariadis, C., and J. Stachurski. 2005. Poverty Traps. In P. Aghion and S. N. Durlauf, eds., *Handbook of Economic Growth*. Volume 1A. Amsterdam: North-Holland.

Bahl, R., and J. Martínez-Vázquez. 2007. The Property Tax in Developing Countries: Current Practice and Prospects. Working Paper no. WP07RB1. Lincoln Institute of Land Policy, Cambridge, MA.

Bailey, M. 1959. A Note on the Economics of Residential Zoning and Urban Renewal. *Land Economics* 35(2): 288–92.

Barata, M., E. Ligeti, G. De Simone, T. Dickinson, D. Jack, J. Penney, M. Rahman, and R. Zimmerman. 2011. Climate Change and Human Health in Cities. In C. Rosenzweig, W. D. Solecki, S. A. Hammer, and S. Mehrotra, eds., *Climate Change and Cities: First Assessment Report of the Urban Climate Change Research Network*. New York: Cambridge University Press.

Basu, K., and P. M. Emerson. 2000. The Economics of Tenancy Rent Control. *Economic Journal* 110(466) October: 939–62.

———. 2003. Efficiency Pricing, Tenancy Rent Control and Monopolistic Landlords. *Economica* 70(278) May: 223–32.

Belsky, E. S., and R. B. Drew. 2007. Taking Stock of the Nation's Rental Housing Challenges and a Half Century of Public Policy Responses. Working Paper no. RR07–1. Joint Center for Housing Studies, Harvard University, Cambridge, MA.

Belsky, E. S., N. P. Retsinas, and M. Duda. 2005. The Financial Returns to Low-Income Homeownership. Working Paper no. W05–9. Joint Center for Housing Studies, Harvard University, Cambridge, MA.

Bertaud, M. A., and D. Lucius. 1989. Land Use, Building Codes, and Infrastructure Standards as Barriers to Affordable Housing in Developing Countries. Urban Development Department, World Bank, Washington, DC. Unpublished.

Black, S. 1999. Do Better Schools Matter? Parental Valuation of Elementary Education. *Quarterly Journal of Economics* 114(2): 577–99.

BL&P (Barbados Light & Power Co., Ltd.). 2010a. *2010 Annual Report*. St. Michael, Barbados. Available at http://www.blpc.com.bb/photos/BLP%20REPORT.pdf. Accessed November 2011.

———. 2010b. *Renewable Energy Rider*. Available at http://www.blpc.com.bb/bus_energyrider.cfm. Accessed November 2011.

Boehm, T. P., and A. M. Schlottmann. 2002. Housing and Wealth Accumulation: Intergenerational Impacts. In N. P. Retsinas and E. S. Belsky, eds., *Low-Income Homeownership: Examining the Unexamined Goal*. Washington, DC: Brookings Institution Press and Cambridge, MA: Joint Center for Housing Studies, Harvard University.

Borrero Ochoa, O. 2011. Betterment Levy in Colombia: Relevance, Procedures, and Social Acceptability. *Land Lines* 23(2) April: 14–19.

Bouillon, C., and N. Medellín. 2011. Housing Affordability in Latin America. IDB working paper. Department of Research and Chief Economist, Inter-American Development Bank, Washington, DC. Forthcoming.

Brain, I., and F. Sabatini. 2006. Los precios del suelo en alza carcomen el subsidio habitacional, contribuyendo al deterioro en la calidad y localización de la vivienda social. Relación entre mercados de suelo y política de vivienda social basada en subsidios a la demanda: estudio en la Región Metropolitana de Santiago. *ProUrbana* [Pontificia Universidad Católica de Chile] 4 (May): 2–13.

Brakarz, J., M. Greene, and E. Rojas. 2002. *Cities for All: Recent Experiences with Neighborhood Upgrading Programs*. Washington, DC: Inter-American Development Bank.

Brazil Real Estate Partners. 2011. Brazil Real Estate and Land Investors 2011 Report. Brazil Real Estate Investment Guide. Available at http://brazilrealinvestment.blogspot.com/2011/01/brazil-real-estate-land-investors-2011.html Accessed November 2011.

Brennan, M. 2011. The Impacts of Affordable Housing on Education: A Research Summary. Insights from Housing Policy Research Brief. Center for Housing Policy and National Housing Conference, Washington, DC.

Bromley, R. 2003. Peru 1957–1977: How Time and Place Influenced John Turner's Ideas on Housing Policy. *Habitat International* 27(2) June: 271–92.

Brown, E., D. Dimitrova, D. Ehrenberg, J. Heyes, P. Kusek, G. Marchesi, V. Orozco, L. Smith, and E. Vilchis. 2006. Secure Tenure in Latin America and the Caribbean: Regularization of Informal Urban Settlements in Peru, Mexico and Brazil. Report. Woodrow Wilson School of Public and International Affairs, Princeton University, Princeton, NJ. Available at http://wws.princeton.edu/research/final_reports/f05wws591g.pdf. Accessed November 2011.

Brueckner, J. K., and H. Selod. 2009. A Theory of Squatting and Land-Tenure Formalization in Developing Countries. *American Economic Journal* 1(1): 28–51.

Buckley, R. M., and J. Kalarickal, eds. 2006. *Thirty Years of World Bank Shelter Lending: What Have We Learned?* Washington, DC: World Bank.

Bureau Van Dijk. 2011. Bankscope. Available at http://www.bvdep.com/kr/BANKSCOPE.html. Accessed November 2011.

Campbell, A. 1976. Subjective Measures of Well-Being. *American Psychologist* 31(2) February: 117–24.

Carballo, M. R., G. Jacobo, I. Presman, and D. Vedoya. 2001. Desarrollo de sistemas constructivos prefabricados en maderas del NEA para su aplicación en viviendas de interés social en el Chaco. Instituto de Investigaciones Tecnológicas para el Diseño Ambiental del Hábitat Humano (I.T.D.A.Hu.) and Facultad de Arquitectura y Urbanismo—UNNE, Chaco, Argentina. Available at http://www1.unne.edu.ar/cyt/2001/7-Tecnologicas/T-049.pdf. Accessed November 2011.

Casas-Arce, P., and A. Saiz. 2006. Owning versus Leasing: Do Courts Matter? Working Paper no. 06–21. Federal Reserve Bank of Philadelphia, Philadelphia, PA.

Casazza, J., R. Massena, P. Monkkonen, E. Reese, L. Ronconi, P. Trivelli, D. Vetter, and M. Vetter. 2011a. Land Price Indicators in Buenos Aires, Rosario, Córdoba, Rio de Janeiro and Santiago. Department of Research and Chief Economist, Inter-American Development Bank, Washington, DC. Unpublished dataset.

Casazza, J., P. Monkkonen, E. Reese, and L. Ronconi. 2011b. Regulations and Land Markets in the Peripheries of Three Argentine Cities: Buenos Aires, Córdoba and Rosario. Centro de Implementación de Políticas Públicas para la Equidad y el Crecimiento (CIPPEC), Buenos Aires. Unpublished.

Case, K. E., and M. Marynchenko. 2002. Home Price Appreciation in Low- and Moderate-Income Markets. In N. P. Retsinas and E. S. Belsky, eds., *Low-Income Homeownership: Examining the Unexamined Goal*. Washington, DC: Brookings Institution Press and Cambridge, MA: Joint Center for Housing Studies, Harvard University.

Castillo, J. M. 2006. The Informal Economy as a Way of Life. *Urban Age*, February. Available at http://urban-age.net/0_downloads/archive/Jose_M.C.Olea_2006-The_Informal_Economy_As_A_Way_Of_Life-Mexico_City.pdf. Accessed November 2011.

Cattaneo, M., S. Galiani, P. Gertler, S. Martínez, and R. Titiunik. 2009. Housing, Health, and Happiness. *American Economic Journal: Economic Policy* 1(1): 75–105.

Celhay, P., and C. Sanhueza. 2011. Location, Location, Location: Labor Outcomes in Urban Slums of Santiago-Chile. IPP Working Paper no. 3. Instituto de Políticas Públicas, Facultad de Economía y Empresa, Universidad Diego Portales, Santiago, Chile.

Cesa-Bianchi, A. 2011. Housing Cycles in the Global Economy. IDB Working Paper. Inter-American Development Bank, Washington, DC. Forthcoming.

Chang, C. C., and C. F. Soruco Carballo. 2011. Energy Conservation and Sustainable Economic Growth: The Case of Latin America and the Caribbean. *Energy Policy* 39(7) July: 4215–21.

Ciudad Verde. 2011. Online portal. Available at http://www.ciudadverde.com.co/. Accessed November 2011.

Clichevsky, N. 2006. Regularizando la informalidad del suelo en América Latina y el Caribe: una evaluación sobre la base de 13 países y 71 programas. Serie manuales no. 50. United Nations Economic Commission for Latin America and the Caribbean (ECLAC), Santiago, Chile.

Coady, D., M. Grosh, and J. Hoddinott. 2004. *Targeting of Transfers in Developing Countries: Review of Lessons and Experience*. Washington, DC: World Bank.

Coccato, M. 1996. Alternatives to Home Ownership: Rental and Shared Submarkets in Informal Settlements. Thesis, McGill University, Montreal, Quebec.

Cooley, T. F., and C. J. LaCivita. 1982. A Theory of Growth Controls. *Journal of Urban Economics* 12(3): 129–45.

Costa, D. L., and M. E. Kahn. 2010. Why Has California's Residential Electricity Consumption Been So Flat since the 1980s? A Microeconometric Approach. NBER Working Paper no. 15978. National Bureau of Economic Research, Cambridge, MA.

Courant, P. N. 1976. On the Effect of Fiscal Zoning on Land and Housing Values. *Journal of Urban Economics* 3(1): 88–94.

Cristini, M., R. Moya, and G. Bermúdez. 2011. Argentina's Housing Market in the 2000s. IDB Working Paper Series no. IDB-WP-262. Department of Research and Chief Economist, Inter-American Development Bank, Washington, DC.

Cristini, M., R. Moya, and A. Powell. 2001. The Importance of an Effective Legal System for Credit Markets: The Case of Argentina. In M. Pagano, ed., *Defusing Default: Incentives and Institutions*. Washington, DC: Inter-American Development Bank and Paris: Organisation for Economic Co-operation and Development.

Cuevas, M., S. Lee, and M. I. Bonilla. 2010. The Missing Foundations of Housing Finance: Incomplete Markets, Fragmented Policies and Emerging Solutions in Guatemala. Inter-American Development Bank, Washington, DC. Unpublished.

DANE (Departamento Administrativo Nacional de Estadística). 2008a. Censo de edificaciones. Bogotá. Available at http://www.dane.gov.co/index.php?option=com_content&view=article&id=155&Itemid=117. Accessed June 2011.

———. 2008b. Encuesta de calidad de vida 2008. Bogotá. Available at http://www.dane.gov.co/index.php?option=com_content&view=article&id=115&Itemid=66. Accessed June 2011.

———. 2011. Índice de costos de la construcción de vivienda—ICCV (Historic Database). Available at http://www.dane.gov.co/index.php?option=com_content&view=article&id=89&Itemid=57. Accessed November 2011.

De Soto, H. 1986. *El Otro Sendero*. Lima: Instituto Libertad y Democracia.

De Wandeler, K., and A. Khanaiklang. 1992. Low-Income Rental and Rent-Free Housing. In Y. K. Sheng, ed., *Low-Income Housing in Bangkok: A Review of Some Housing Submarkets*. Bangkok: Asian Institute of Technology.

Deakin, E. 1989. Growth Controls and Growth Management: A Summary and Review of Empirical Research. In D. Brower, D. Godschalk, and D. Porter, eds., *Understanding Growth Management: Critical Issues and a Research Agenda*. Washington, DC: The Urban Land Institute.

Deininger, K., and G. Feder. 2009. Land Registration, Government and Development: Evidence and Implications for Policy. *World Bank Research Observer* 24(2): 233–66.

Di Tella, R., S. Galiani, and E. Schargrodsky. 2007. The Formation of Beliefs: Evidence from the Allocation of Land Titles to Squatters. *Quarterly Journal of Economics* 122(1): 209–41.

DiPasquale, D., and E. L. Glaeser. 1999. Incentives and Social Capital: Are Homeowners Better Citizens? *Journal of Urban Economics* 45(2) March: 354–84.

Doebele, W. A. 1977. The Private Market and Low-Income Urbanization: The "Pirate" Subdivisions of Bogotá. *American Journal of Comparative Law* 25(3) Summer: 531–64.

Dowall, D. E. 1992a. Benefits of Minimal Land-Use Regulations in Developing Countries. *Cato Journal* 12(2) Fall: 413–23.

———. 1992b. A Second Look at the Bangkok Land and Housing Market. *Urban Studies* 29(1): 25–38.

———. 2007. Brazil's Urban Land and Housing Markets: How Well Are They Working? In Gregory K. Ingram and Yu-Hung Hong, eds., *Land Policies and Their Outcomes*. Cambridge, MA: Lincoln Institute of Land Policy.

Dowall, D. E., and G. Clarke. 1996. A Framework for Reforming Urban Land Policies in Developing Countries. Urban Management Programme Discussion Paper no. 7. World Bank, Washington, DC.

Dowall, D. E., and P. A. Treffeisen. 1991. Spatial Transformation in Cities of the Developing World: Multinucleation and Land-Capital Substitution in Bogotá, Colombia. *Regional Science and Urban Economics* 21(2) July: 201–24.

Drayton, B., and Ashoka. 2008. Transforming Urban Markets for the Poor through Collective Entrepreneurship. *Global Urban Development* 4(2) November: 1–7.

Duffau, A. A. 2011. Construcción industrializada para la vivienda social en Chile: análisis de su impacto potencial. Independent Consultant. Unpublished.

Duranton, G. 2008. Viewpoint: From Cities to Productivity and Growth in Developing Countries. *Canadian Journal of Economics* 41(3): 689–736.

ECLAC (United Nations Economic Commission for Latin America and the Caribbean). 2009. La reacción de los gobiernos de las Américas frente a la crisis internacional: una presentación sintética de las medidas de política anunciadas hasta el 30 de septiembre de 2009. Santiago, Chile. October. Available at http://www.eclac.org/publicaciones/xml/8/37618/2009-733-Lareacciondelosgobiernos-30septiembre-WEB.pdf.

———. 2010. *Social Panorama of Latin America 2010*. Santiago: ECLAC. Available at http://www.eclac.org/cgi-bin/getProd.asp?xml=/publicaciones/xml/1/41801/P41801.xml&xsl=/dds/tpl/p9f.xsl&base=/tpl-i/top-bottom.xslt.

———. 2011. Social Statistics Unit. Available at http://www.eclac.org/estadisticas/default.asp?idioma=IN. Accessed on November 15, 2011.

The Economist. 2011. Some Like It Hot: Which Emerging Economies Are at Greatest Risk of Overheating? July 2, p. 65.

Ellen, I. G., S. Susin, A. E. Schwartz, and M. Schill. 2001. Do Homeownership Programs Increase Property Value in Low-Income Neighborhoods? Working Paper no. LIHO-01.13. Joint Center for Housing Studies, Harvard University, Cambridge, MA.

Esrey, S. A., J. B. Potash, L. Roberts, and C. Shiff. 1991. Effects of Improved Water Supply and Sanitation on Ascariasis, Diarrhoea, Dracunculiasis, Hookworm Infection, Schistosomiasis, and Trachoma. *Bulletin of the World Health Organization* 69(5): 609–21.

Eurostat. 2011. Statistics Explained. Available at http://epp.eurostat.ec.europa.eu/statistics_explained/index.php/Housing_statistics. Accessed August 2011.

Fack, G., and J. Grenet. 2010. When Do Better Schools Raise Housing Prices? Evidence from Paris Public and Private Schools. *Journal of Public Economics* 94(1–2) February: 59–77.

Fallis, G., and L. B. Smith. 1984. Uncontrolled Prices in a Controlled Market: The Case of Rent Controls. *American Economic Review* 74(1) March: 193–200.

———. 1985. Price Effects of Rent Control on Controlled and Uncontrolled Rental Housing in Toronto: A Hedonic Index Approach. *Canadian Journal of Economics* 18(3) August: 652–59.

Fay, M., ed. 2005. *The Urban Poor in Latin America*. Washington, DC: World Bank. Available at: http://www.siteresources.worldbank.org/…/Home/…/UrbanPoorinLA.pdf.

Feler, L., and J. V. Henderson. 2008. Exclusionary Policies in Urban Development: How Under-Servicing of Migrant Households Affects the Growth and Composition of Brazilian Cities. NBER Working Paper no. 14136. National Bureau of Economic Research, Cambridge, MA.

Ferguson, B. 1999. Micro-Finance of Housing: A Key to Housing the Low or Moderate-Income Majority? *Environment and Urbanization* 11(1): 185–99.

Ferguson, B., J. Rubinstein, and V. Domínguez Vial. 1996. The Design of Direct Demand Subsidy Programs for Housing in Latin America. *Review of Urban and Regional Development Studies* 8(2) July: 202–19.

Ferguson, B., and P. Smets. 2010. Finance for Incremental Housing: Current Status and Prospects for Expansion. *Habitat International* 34(3) July: 288–98.

Fernandes, E. 1997. *Access to Urban Land and Housing in Brazil: Three Degrees of Illegality*. Cambridge, MA: Lincoln Institute of Land Policy.

———. 2011. *Regularization of Informal Settlements in Latin America*. Cambridge, MA: Lincoln Institute of Land Policy.

Fernández-Maldonado, A. M., and J. Bredenoord. 2010. Progressive Housing Approaches in the Current Peruvian Policies. *Habitat International* 34(3) July: 342–50.

Ferre, C., F. Ferreira, and P. Lanjouw. 2010. Is There a Metropolitan Bias? The Inverse Relationship between Poverty and City Size in Selected Developing Countries. Policy Research Working Paper no. 5508. World Bank, Washington, DC.

Field, E. 2007. Entitled to Work: Urban Property Rights and Labor Supply in Peru. *Quarterly Journal of Economics* 122(4): 1561–602.

Figlio, D., and M. Lucas. 2004. What's in a Grade? School Report Cards and the Housing Market. *American Economic Review* 94(3): 591–604.

Fischel, W. A. 1985. *The Economics of Zoning Laws*. Baltimore, MD: Johns Hopkins University Press.

Flood, J. 2006. Secure Tenure Survey. Final Report. January. Available at http://zunia.org/post/global-secure-tenure-survey-final-report-1/. Accessed November 2011.

Fontenla, M., and F. González. 2009. Housing Demand in Mexico. *Journal of Housing Economics* 18(1): 1–12.

Fontenla, M., F. González, and J. C. Navarro. 2009. Determinants of Housing Expenditure in Mexico. *Applied Economics Letters* 16(17): 1731–34.

Frumkin, H. 2002. Urban Sprawl and Public Health. *Public Health Reports* 117(3): 201–17.

FTA (Federal Transit Administration). 2009. Characteristics of Bus Rapid Transit for Decision-Making. United States Department of Transportation, Washington, DC. Available at: http://www.fta.dot.gov/documents/CBRT_2009_Update.pdf. Accessed July 2011.

Galiani, S., P. Gertler, and E. Schargrodsky. 2005. Water for Life: The Impact of the Privatization of Water Services on Child Mortality. *Journal of Political Economy* 113(1) February: 83–120.

Galiani, S., and E. Schargrodsky. 2004. Effects of Land Titling on Child Health. *Economics and Human Biology* 2(3): 353–72.

———. 2010. Property Rights for the Poor: Effects of Land Titling. *Journal of Public Economics* 94(9–10) October: 700–29.

Gallup. 2007. Gallup World Poll. Available at http://gallup.com/consulting/worldpoll/24046.about.spx.

Garabato, N., and M. Ramada-Sarasola. 2011. Are Uruguayan Housing Policies Reaching the Poor? An Assessment of Housing Deficit, Housing Informality and Usage of Housing Programs in Uruguay. Technical Note no. IDB-TN-278.

Department of Research and Chief Economist, Inter-American Development Bank, Washington, DC.

Gattoni, G. 2009. Guyana: A Case for the Incremental Housing Process in Sites-and-Services Programs. Paper presented at the Inter-American Development Bank conference, Self-Help Housing and Incremental Housing: A Discussion on the Likely Directions for Future Housing Policy, July 28, Washington, DC.

Gattoni, G., R. Goethert, and R. Chávez. 2011. El Salvador: Self-help and Incremental Housing: The Likely Directions for Future Housing. Inter-American Development Bank, Washington, DC. Unpublished.

Gilbert, A. 1998. *The Latin American City.* Second edition. London: Latin America Bureau (LAB).

———. 1999. A Home Is Forever? Residential Mobility and Homeownership in Self-Help Settlements. *Environment and Planning A* 31(6): 1073–91.

Gillingham, K., R. G. Newell, and K. Palmer. 2009. Energy Efficiency Economics and Policy. NBER Working Paper no. 15031. National Bureau of Economic Research, Cambridge, MA.

Gischler, C., and N. Janson. 2011. Perspectives for Distributed Generation with Renewable Energy in Latin America and the Caribbean: Analysis of Case Studies for Barbados, Chile, Jamaica and Mexico. Paper presented at the Fifth Americas Competitiveness Forum, October 5–7, Santo Domingo.

Glaeser, E. L. 2011. *Triumph of the City: How Our Greatest Invention Makes Us Richer, Smarter, Greener, Healthier, and Happier.* New York: The Penguin Press.

Glaeser, E. L., J. Gyourko, and R. Saks. 2005. Why Is Manhattan So Expensive? Regulation and the Rise in Housing Prices. *Journal of Law and Economics* 48(2) October: 331–69.

Glaeser, E. L., and M. E. Kahn. 2010. The Greenness of Cities: Carbon Dioxide Emissions and Urban Development. *Journal of Urban Economics* 67(3): 404–18.

Glaeser, E. L., and E. F. P. Luttmer. 2003. The Misallocation of Housing under Rent Control. *American Economic Review* 93(4) September: 1027–46.

Gonzales Arrieta, G. M. 1998. Access to Housing and Direct Subsidies: Lessons from Latin American Experiences. *Housing Finance International* 13(1) September: 43–53.

Goodman, J. 1997. The Costs of Owning and Renting Housing: 1985–1995. National Multi Housing Council, Washington, DC. Unpublished.

Goux, D., and E. Maurin. 2005. The Effect of Overcrowded Housing on Children's Performance at School. *Journal of Public Economics* 89(5–6) June: 797–819.

Goytia, C., C. de Mendoza, and R. Pasquini. 2010. Land Regulation in the Urban Agglomerates of Argentina and Its Relationship with Households' Residential Tenure Condition. Working Paper no. WP10CC1. Lincoln Institute of Land Policy, Cambridge, MA.

Green, R. K., and P. H. Hendershott. 2001. Homeownership and Unemployment in the U.S. *Urban Studies* 38(9) August: 1509–20.

Green, R. K., S. Malpezzi, and S. K. Mayo. 2005. Metropolitan-Specific Estimates of the Price Elasticity of Supply of Housing, and Their Sources. *American Economic Review: Papers and Proceedings* 95(2): 334–39.

Greene, M. 2011. Self-Help Housing and Incremental Housing in Chile: The Likely Directions for Future Housing Policy. Inter-American Development Bank, Washington, DC. Unpublished.

Greene, M., and E. Rojas. 2008. Incremental Construction: A Strategy to Facilitate Access to Housing. *Environment and Urbanization* 20(1) April: 89–108.

Gyourko, J., and P. Linneman. 1989. Equity and Efficiency Aspects of Rent Control: An Empirical Study of New York City. *Journal of Urban Economics* 26(1) July: 54–74.

Gyourko, J., C. Mayer, and T. Sinai. 2006. Superstar Cities. NBER Working Paper no. 12355. National Bureau of Economic Research, Cambridge, MA.

Gyourko, J., A. Saiz, and A. Summers. 2008. A New Measure of the Local Regulatory Environment for Housing Markets: The Wharton Residential Land Use Regulatory Index. *Urban Studies* 45(3): 693–729.

Habitat for Humanity Argentina. 2011. Online portal. Available at http://www.hpha.org.ar/programs.html. Accessed August 2011.

Habitat for Humanity International. 2011. Online portal. Available at http://www.habitat.org/how/factsheet.aspx. Accessed August 2011.

Hamilton, B. 1978. Zoning and the Exercise of Monopoly Power. *Journal of Urban Economics* 5(1): 116–30.

Hammond, A. L., W. J. Kramer, R. S. Katz, J. T. Tran, and C. Walker. 2007. *The Next 4 Billion: Market Size and Business Strategy at the Base of the Pyramid*. Washington, DC: World Resources Institute and International Finance Corporation/World Bank Group.

Haurin, D. R., and H. L. Gill. 2002. The Impact of Transaction Costs and the Expected Length of Stay on Homeownership. *Journal of Urban Economics* 51(3) May: 563–84.

Haurin, D. R., T. L. Parcel, and R. Haurin. 2001. The Impact of Homeownership on Child Outcomes. Working Paper no. LIHO.01–14. Joint Center for Housing Studies, Harvard University, Cambridge, MA.

Henao Padilla, M. J. 2011. Análisis del proceso de producción privada de Vivienda de Interés Social (VIS) en Colombia en el período 2007–2010 a partir del Macroproyecto de Interés Social Nacional Ciudad Verde. Case study. Facultad de Ciencia Política y Gobierno, Universidad Colegio Mayor de Nuestra Señora del Rosario, Bogotá. Available at http://repository.urosario.edu.co/bitstream/10336/2633/13/1010182205-2011.pdf. Accessed November 2011.

Herbert, C. E., and E. S. Belsky. 2008. The Homeownership Experience of Low-Income and Minority Households: A Review and Synthesis of the Literature. *Cityscape* 10(2) July: 5–60.

Hofstetter, M., J. Tovar, and M. Urrutia. 2010. A History of Mortgage Loans in Colombia. Inter-American Development Bank, Washington, DC. Unpublished.

———. 2011. Effects of a Mortgage Interest Rate Subsidy: Evidence from Colombia. IDB Working Paper Series no. IDB-WP-257. Department of Research and Chief Economist, Inter-American Development Bank, Washington, DC.

HUD (U.S. Department of Housing and Urban Development). 2011. Low-Income Housing Tax Credits Data Sets. Available at http://huduser.org/portal/datasets/lihtc.html. Accessed November 2011.

IBGE (Instituto Brasileiro de Geografia e Estatística). 2011. Sistema Nacional de Pesquisa de Custos e Índices da Construção Civil (Historic Database). Available at http://www.ibge.gov.br/home/estatistica/indicadores/precos/sinapi/default.shtm. Accessed August 2011.

IDB (Inter-American Development Bank). 2004. *Unlocking Credit: The Quest for Deep and Stable Bank Lending.* Economic and Social Progress in Latin America: 2005 Report. Washington, DC: IDB.

———. 2008. Guyana: Second Low-Income Settlement Program. IDB Loan Proposal GY-L1019. Inter-American Development Bank, Washington, DC. Unpublished.

———. 2010a. *The Age of Productivity: Transforming Economies from the Bottom Up.* Development in the Americas series. New York: Palgrave Macmillan.

———. 2010b. BA-L1022: Support for Sustainable Energy Framework for Barbados (SEFB) I. Available at http://idbdocs.iadb.org/wsdocs/getDocument.aspx?DOCNUM=35232781; http://idbdocs.iadb.org/wsdocs/getdocument.aspx?docnum=35425963. Accessed November 2011.

———. 2011a. BA-L1021: Support for Sustainable Energy Framework for Barbados (SEFB) II. Available at http://www.iadb.org/en/projects/project,1303.html?id=BA-L1021. Accessed November 2011.

———. 2011b. Opportunities for the Majority Sector (OMJ). Online portal. Available at http://www.iadb.org/en/about-us/departments/about,1342.html?dept_id=OMJ. Accessed November 2011.

———. 2011c. RG-T2015: Caribbean Hotel Energy Efficiency and Renewable Energy Action - Advanced Program. Available at http://www.iadb.org/en/projects/project,1303.html?id=RG-T2015. Accessed November 2011.

INDEC (Instituto Nacional de Estadística y Censos de la República Argentina). 2011. Índice del Costo de la Construcción (ICC) (Historic Database). Available at http://www.indec.gov.ar/principal.asp?id_tema=733. Accessed August 2011.

INE (Instituto Nacional de Estadística de Bolivia). 2011. Índice del Costo de la Construcción (ICC) (Historic Database). Available at http://www.ine.gob.bo/indice/indice.aspx?d1=0201&d2=6. Accessed August 2011.

INEGI (Instituto Nacional de Estadística y Geografía). 2011. Índice del Costo de la Construcción (ICC) (Historic Database). Available at http://www.inegi.org.mx/est/contenidos/proyectos/inp/inpp.aspx. Accessed August 2011.

INEI (Instituto Nacional de Estadística e Informática). 2011. Índices Unificados de Precios de la Construcción (Historic Database). Available at http://www.inei.gob.pe/web/aplicaciones/siemweb/index.asp?id=003. Accessed August 2011.

Jacobsen, G. D., and M. J. Kotchen. 2010. Are Building Codes Effective at Saving Energy? Evidence from Residential Billing Data in Florida. NBER Working Paper no. 16194. National Bureau of Economic Research, Cambridge, MA.

Jalan, J., and M. Ravallion. 2003. Does Piped Water Reduce Diarrhea for Children in Rural India? *Journal of Econometrics* 112(1) January: 153–73.

Jaramillo, S., and M. Ibáñez. 2002. Elementos para orientar una política estatal sobre alquiler de vivienda urbana en Colombia. Documento CEDE no. 2002-14. Centro de Estudios sobre Desarrollo Económico (CEDE), Universidad de los Andes, Bogotá.

JCHS (Joint Center for Housing Studies). 2010. Long-Term Low-Income Housing Tax Credit Policy Questions. Harvard University, Cambridge, MA. Unpublished.

Katz, L., J. Kling, and J. Liebman. 2001. Moving to Opportunity in Boston: Early Results of a Randomized Mobility Experiment. *Quarterly Journal of Economics* 116(2): 607–54.

Kellogg School of Management. 2011. Patrimonio Hoy 2.0: Private Enterprise Innovation Lab. Kellogg School of Management, Northwestern University, Evanston, IL. Unpublished.

Kiviat, B. 2010. The Case against Homeownership. *Time* 176(10) September: 40–46.

Kling, J. R., J. B. Liebman, and L. F. Katz. 2007. Experimental Analysis of Neighborhood Effects. *Econometrica* 75(1) January: 83–119.

Kumaran, G. B., and S. Martínez González. 2008. Evolución reciente de la industria de cemento: un estudio comparativo entre México y la India. *Revista mexicana de estudios sobre la Cuenca del Pacífico* 2(3): 165–202.

Kutty, N. K. 2005. A New Measure of Housing Affordability: Estimates and Analytical Results. *Housing Policy Debate* 16(1): 113–42.

Laferrère, A., and D. Le Blanc. 2004. How Do Housing Allowances Affect Rents? An Empirical Analysis of the French Case. *Journal of Housing Economics* 13(1) March: 36–67.

Landis, J. D., and K. McClure. 2010. Rethinking Federal Housing Policy. *Journal of the American Planning Association* 76(3): 319–48.

Lanjouw, J., and P. Levy. 2002. Untitled: A Study of Formal and Informal Property Rights in Urban Ecuador. *Economic Journal* 112(482): 986–1019.

Lansley, S. 1979. *Housing and Public Policy.* London: Croom Helm.

Le Blanc, D. (with R. Green and C. Taffin). 2009. Residential Rental Housing Finance. In Loïc Chiquier and Michael Lea, eds., *Housing Finance Policy in Emerging Markets.* Washington, DC: World Bank.

Lee, L. F., M. R. Rosenzweig, and M. M. Pitt. 1997. The Effects of Improved Nutrition, Sanitation, and Water Quality on Child Health in High-Mortality Populations. *Journal of Econometrics* 77(1) March: 209–35.

Letelier, M. F., F. Flores, and C. Spinosa. 2003. Developing Productive Customers in Emerging Markets. *California Management Review* 45(4) Summer: 77–103.

Lizarralde, G., and D. Root. 2008. The Informal Construction Sector and the Inefficiency of Low Cost Housing Markets. *Construction Management and Economics* 26(2): 103–13.

López-Silva, M., R. Abreu-Lastra, A. Saracho-Martínez, and A. Paulín-Hutmacher. 2011. Housing Finance in Mexico: Current State and Future Sustainability. Technical Note no. IDB-TN-287. Department of Research and Chief Economist, Inter-American Development Bank, Washington, DC.

Lora, E., A. Powell, and P. Sanguinetti. 2008. Urban Quality of Life: More Than Bricks and Mortar. In Inter-American Development Bank, ed., *Beyond Facts: Understanding Quality of Life.* Development in the Americas series. Washington, DC: Inter-American Development Bank and Cambridge, MA: David Rockefeller Center for Latin American Studies, Harvard University.

Lora, E., A. Powell, B. M. S. van Praag, and P. Sanguinetti. 2010. *The Quality of Life in Latin American Cities: Markets and Perception.* Washington, DC: Inter-American Development Bank and World Bank.

MacDonald, J. 2004. Pobreza y precariedad del hábitat en ciudades de América Latina y el Caribe. Serie manuales no. 38. United Nations Economic Commission for Latin America and the Caribbean (ECLAC), Santiago, Chile.

MacDonald, J., and D. Simioni. 1999. Consensos urbanos: aportes del Plan de Acción Regional de América Latina y el Caribe sobre asentamientos humanos. Serie medio ambiente y desarrollo no. 21. United Nations Economic Commission for Latin America and the Caribbean (ECLAC), Santiago, Chile.

Magrin, G., C. Gay García, D. Cruz Choque, J. C. Giménez, A. R. Moreno, G. J. Nagy, C. Nobre, and A. Villamizar. 2007. Latin America. In M. L. Parry, O. F. Canziani, J. P. Palutikof, P. J. van der Linden, and C. E. Hanson, eds., *Climate Change 2007: Impacts, Adaptation and Vulnerability. Working Group II Contribution to the Fourth Assessment Report of the IPCC.* London: Cambridge University Press.

Malpezzi, S., and S. K. Mayo. 1987. The Demand for Housing in Developing Countries: Empirical Estimates from Household Data. *Economic Development and Cultural Change* 35(4) July: 687–721.

Marcano, L., and I. J. Ruprah. 2008. An Impact Evaluation of Chile's Progressive Housing Program. OVE Working Paper no. 06/08. Office of Evaluation and Oversight, Inter-American Development Bank, Washington, DC.

Marcello. 2010. Estudio sobre el mercado de viviendas de alquiler en Uruguay. Consultant report. Inter-American Development Bank, Washington, DC. Unpublished.

Markandya, A., R. Arigoni Ortiz, S. Mudgal, and B. Tinetti. 2009. Analysis of Tax Incentives for Energy-Efficient Durables in the EU. *Energy Policy* 37(12) December: 5662–74.

Marques, E., and H. Torres. 2005. *São Paulo: segregação, pobreza e desigualdades sociais*. São Paulo, Brazil: Editora Senac.

Martin, C. 2008. Going to Scale with Housing Microfinance: The Role of Commercial Banks. Micro Report no. 92. United States Agency for International Development (USAID), Washington, DC. March.

Martins, B., E. Lundberg, and T. Takeda. 2011. Housing Finance in Brazil: Institutional Improvements and Recent Developments. IDB Working Paper Series no. IDB-WP-269. Department of Research and Chief Economist, Inter-American Development Bank, Washington, DC.

Mayagoitia, F. 2009. Manual básico para diagnóstico y guías de implementación de la vivienda industrializada. Federación Interamericana del Cemento (FICEM-APCAC). Available at http://www.ich.cl/docs/vivienda/archivos/MANUAL%20BASICO%20SIST%20INDUS%20OCT%208%2008_ESP.pdf. Accessed on November 5, 2011.

Mayer, C. J., and T. C. Somerville. 2000. Land Use Regulation and New Construction. *Regional Science and Urban Economics* 30(6): 639–62.

Mboweni, T. T. 2004. The South African Banking Sector: An Overview of the Past Ten Years. Address by Mr. T. T. Mboweni, Governor of the South African Reserve Bank, December 14, Johannesburg. Available at http://www.bis.org/review/r041231f.pdf. Accessed November 2011.

McBride, B. 2009. Building Capital: The Role of Migrant Remittances in Housing Improvement and Construction in El Salvador. IDB-MIF Presentation.

Inter-American Development Bank, Washington, DC. Available at http://www.microfinancegateway.org/gm/document-1.9.43951/Building%20Capital.pdf. Accessed November 2011.

McNeil, M., R. Van Buskirk, and V. Letschert. 2006. The Value of Standards and Labelling: An International Cost-Benefit Analysis Tool for Standards and Labelling Programs with Results for Central American Countries. Unpublished.

Mehrotra, S., C. Rosenzweig, W. D. Solecki, C. E. Natenzon, A. Omojola, R. Folorunsho, and J. Gilbride. 2011. Cities, Disasters and Climate Risk. In C. Rosenzweig, W. D. Solecki, S. A. Hammer, and S. Mehrotra, eds., *Climate Change and Cities: First Assessment Report of the Urban Climate Change Research Network*. New York: Cambridge University Press.

Merrick, T. W. 1985. The Effect of Piped Water on Early Childhood Mortality in Urban Brazil, 1970 to 1976. *Demography* 22(1) February: 1–24.

MGI (McKinsey Global Institute). 2011a. Building Globally Competitive Cities: The Key to Latin American Growth. Report. Available at http://www.mckinsey.com/Insights/MGI/Research/Urbanization/Building_competitive_cities_key_to_Latin_American_growth. Accessed January 2012.

———. 2011b. Urban World: Mapping the Economic Power of Cities. Report. Available at: http://www.mckinsey.com/mgi/publications/urban_world/pdfs/MGI_urban_world_full_report.pdf. Accessed June 2011.

Micco, A., E. Parrado, B. Piedrabuena, and A. Rebucci. 2011. Understanding Housing Finance in Chile. Inter-American Development Bank, Washington, DC. Unpublished.

Ministerio de Ambiente, Vivienda y Desarrollo Territorial. 2011. Online portal. Available at http://www.minambiente.gov.co/contenido/contenido.aspx?conID=2910&catID=818. Accessed November 2011.

Miraftab, F. 1997. Revisiting Informal-Sector Home Ownership: The Relevance of Household Composition for Housing Options of the Poor. *International Journal of Urban and Regional Research* 21(2) June: 303–22.

Monkkonen, P. 2010. Measuring Residential Segregation in Urban Mexico: Levels and Patterns. Working Paper no. 2010–05. Institute of Urban and Regional Development (IURD), University of California, Berkeley, CA. Available at http://www.escholarship .org/uc/item/6hf1q7hg. Accessed November 2011.

Moya, R. 2011. The Rental Market in Argentina. Consultant report. Inter-American Development Bank, Washington, DC. Unpublished.

Naipaul, V. S. 1959. *Miguel Street*. First edition. London: André Deutsch Limited.

Newman, S. J., and A. B. Schnare. 1997. "... And a Suitable Living Environment": The Failure of Housing Programs to Deliver on Neighborhood Quality. *Housing Policy Debate* 8(4): 703–41.

O'Flaherty, B. 2005. *City Economics*. Cambridge, MA: Harvard University Press.

Olsen, E. O. 2001. Housing Programs for Low-Income Households. NBER Working Paper no. 8208. National Bureau of Economic Research, Cambridge, MA.

Ortalo-Magné, F., and S. Rady. 1998. Housing Market Fluctuations in a Life-Cycle Economy with Credit Constraints. FMG Discussion Paper no. 296. Financial Markets Group, London.

O'Sullivan, A. 2008. *Urban Economics*. Seventh edition. New York: McGraw-Hill/Irwin.

Oswald, A. J. 1996. A Conjecture on the Explanation for High Unemployment in the Industrialized Nations: Part I. The Warwick Economics Research Paper Series (TWERPS) no. 475. Department of Economics, University of Warwick, Coventry, England.

Pagano, M., ed. 2001. *Defusing Default: Incentives and Institutions*. Washington, DC: Inter-American Development Bank and Paris: Organisation for Economic Co-operation and Development.

Page-Adams, D., and N. Vosler. 1997. Homeownership and Well-Being among Blue-Collar Workers. CSD Working Paper no. 97–5. Center for Social Development, Washington University, St. Louis, MO.

Palomino, M., and R. Wong. 2011. Housing Finance in Peru: What Is Holding It Back? Technical Note no. IDB-TN-288. Department of Research and Chief Economist, Inter-American Development Bank, Washington, DC.

Parliamentary Office of Science and Technology. 2003. Modern Methods of House Building. Postnote no. 209. London. December. Available at http://www.parliament.uk/documents/post/postpn209.pdf. Last accessed on November 5, 2011.

Parry, I., and G. Timilsina. 2010. How Should Passenger Travel in Mexico City Be Priced? *Journal of Urban Economics* 68(2): 167–82.

Payne, G. 2001. The Mystery of Capital: Why Capitalism Triumphs in the West and Fails Everywhere Else. *Habitat Debate* 7(3) September: 23.

Payne, G., and E. Fernandes. 2001. Legality and Legitimacy in Urban Tenure Issues. Working Paper no. WP01GP1. Lincoln Institute of Land Policy, Cambridge, MA.

Peters, P. A., and E. H. Skop. 2007. Socio-Spatial Segregation in Metropolitan Lima, Peru. *Journal of Latin American Geography* 6(1): 149–71.

Peterson, G. E., and O. Kaganova. 2010. Integrating Land Financing into Subnational Fiscal Management. Policy Research Working Paper no. 5409. Economic Policy and Debt Department, World Bank, Washington, DC.

Piza, C., J. Litchfield, and F. Balderrama. 2011. Housing Demand in Brazil: Evidence from the Formal and Informal Sectors. IDB Working Paper Series no. IDB-WP-261. Department of Research and Chief Economist, Inter-American Development Bank, Washington, DC.

Pomeroy, S. 1998. *Residualization of Rental Tenure: Implications for Housing Policy in Canada*. Ottawa: Canada Mortgage and Housing Corporation (CMHC) and the BC Real Estate Foundation.

Pomeroy, S., and M. Godbout. 2011. Development of the Rental Housing Market in Latin America and the Caribbean. Discussion Paper no. IDB-DP-173. Institutional Capacity and Finance Sector, Inter-American Development Bank, Washington, DC.

Pomeroy, S., G. Lampert, and K. Mancer. 1999. *Private Rental Policies and Programs: Review of the International Experience*. Ottawa: Canada Mortgage and Housing Corporation (CMHC).

Potepan, M. J. 1996. Explaining Intermetropolitan Variation in Housing Prices, Rents and Land Prices. *Real Estate Economics* 24(2): 219–45.

Prahalad, C. K. 2005. *The Fortune at the Bottom of the Pyramid: Eradicating Poverty through Profits*. Upper Saddle River, NJ: Prentice Hall.

Presidencia de Colombia. 2011. Law 1469. Available at http://wsp.presidencia.gov.co/Normativa/Leyes/Documents/ley14693006201l.pdf. Accessed November 2011.

Quigley, J. M., and S. Raphael. 2005. Regulation and the High Cost of Housing in California. *American Economic Review* 95(2) May: 323–28.

Quigley, J. M., and L. A. Rosenthal. 2005. The Effects of Land Use Regulation on the Price of Housing: What Do We Know? What Can We Learn? *Cityscape* 8(1): 69–137.

Quigley, J. M., and A. Swoboda. 2007. The Urban Impacts of the Endangered Species Act: A General Equilibrium Analysis. *Journal of Urban Economics* 61(2) March: 299–318.

Reese, E. 2009. Planificación e instrumentos de gestión del territorio. Paper presented at Seminario Taller, October 21, Buenos Aires.

Retsinas, N. P., and E. S. Belsky, eds. 2002. *Low-Income Homeownership: Examining the Unexamined Goal*. Washington, DC: Brookings Institution Press and Cambridge, MA: Joint Center for Housing Studies, Harvard University.

Roberts, B. R., and R. H. Wilson, eds. 2009. *Urban Segregation and Governance in the Americas*. New York: Palgrave Macmillan.

Robinson, M. S. 2001. *The Microfinance Revolution: Sustainable Finance for the Poor*. Washington, DC: World Bank.

Rohe, W. M., R. G. Quercia, and S. Van Zandt. 2007. The Social-Psychological Effects of Affordable Homeownership. In W. M. Rohe and H. L. Watson, eds., *Chasing the American Dream: New Perspectives on Affordable Homeownership*. Ithaca, NY: Cornell University Press.

Rohe, W. M., S. Van Zandt, and G. McCarthy. 2002. Home Ownership and Access to Opportunity. *Housing Studies* 17(1): 51–61.

Rojas, E. 1995. A Review of the IDB Experience in Low-Cost Housing. DPP Working Paper no. 102. Strategic Planning and Operational Policy Department, Inter-American Development Bank, Washington, DC.

———. 2001. The Long Road to Housing Sector Reform: Lessons from the Chilean Housing Experience. *Housing Studies* 16(4) July: 461–83.

———, ed. 2010. *Building Cities: Neighbourhood Upgrading and Urban Quality of Life*. Washington, DC and Cambridge, MA: Inter-American Development Bank, Cities Alliance, and David Rockefeller Center for Latin American Studies/Harvard University.

Rojas, E., F. Cuenin, C. Piedrafita, and N. Medellín. 2010. Housing Policy Matters for the Poor: A Study of the Housing Sector and Housing Policies in Argentina, Chile and Colombia: Part One—Urban Housing Conditions and Public Policies in Latin America. Discussion Paper no. IDB-DP-152. Institutional Capacity and Finance Sector, Inter-American Development Bank, Washington, DC.

Rojas, E., and P. Masci. 2007. Promoting Private Sector Participation in Low-Income Housing Finance: Diagnosis and Policy Recommendations for Latin America and the Caribbean. Sustainable Development Department, Inter-American Development Bank, Washington, DC.

Rojas, E., and N. Medellín. 2010. Housing Policy Matters for the Poor: A Study of the Housing Sector and Housing Policies in Argentina, Chile and Colombia: Housing Conditions in LAC 1995–2006. Discussion Paper no. IDB-DP-151. Institutional Capacity and Finance Sector, Inter-American Development Bank, Washington, DC.

———. 2011. Housing Policy Matters for the Poor: Housing Conditions in Latin America and the Caribbean 1995–2006. IDB Working Paper Series no. IDB-WP-289. Institutional Capacity and Finance Sector, Inter-American Development Bank, Washington, DC.

Rosendahl, K. E., and J. Strand. 2009. Simple Model Frameworks for Explaining Inefficiency of the Clean Development Mechanism. Policy Research Working Paper no. 4931. World Bank, Washington, DC.

Rossi, P. H., and E. Weber. 1996. The Social Benefits of Homeownership: Empirical Evidence from National Surveys. *Housing Policy Debate* 7(1): 1–35.

Ruprah, I. J. 2009. The Housing Gap in Latin America: 1995–2015. Office of Evaluation and Oversight, Inter-American Development Bank, Washington, DC. Unpublished.

———. 2010a. Does Owning Your Home Make You Happier? Impact Evidence from Latin America? OVE Working Paper no. 02/10. Office of Evaluation and Oversight, Inter-American Development Bank, Washington, DC.

———. 2010b. Do Social Housing Programs Increase Poverty? An Empirical Analysis of Shelter Induced Poverty in Latin America. OVE Working Paper no. 05/10. Office of Evaluation and Oversight, Inter-American Development Bank, Washington, DC.

———. 2010c. Ex Post Thematic Report: ABC Housing Programs. Office of Evaluation and Oversight, Inter-American Development Bank, Washington, DC.

———. 2011. The Welfare Impacts of Social Housing Programs in Latin America: A Meta-Impact Analysis. OVE Working Paper no. 05/11. Office of Evaluation and Oversight, Inter-American Development Bank, Washington, DC.

Ruprah, I. J., and L. T. Marcano. 2007. A Meta-Impact Evaluation of Social Housing Programs: The Chilean Case. OVE Working Paper no. 02/07. Office of Evaluation and Oversight, Inter-American Development Bank, Washington, DC.

Ryser, J., and T. Franchini. 2008. *International Manual of Planning Practice*. Volume 5. The Hague, The Netherlands: ISOCARP.

Sabatini, F. 2003. The Social Spatial Segregation in the Cities of Latin America. Sustainable Development Department, Inter-American Development Bank, Washington, DC. Unpublished.

Sabatini, F., G. Wormald, C. Sierralta, and P. A. Peters. 2009. Residential Segregation in Santiago: Scale-Related Effects and Trends, 1992–2002. In B. R. Roberts and R. H. Wilson, eds., *Urban Segregation and Governance in the Americas*. New York: Palgrave Macmillan.

Sampson, R. J., and S. W. Raudenbush. 1999. Systematic Social Observation of Public Spaces: A New Look at Disorder in Urban Neighborhoods. *American Journal of Sociology* 105(3): 603–51.

Sanchez, M., R. Brown, and G. Homan. 2008. EPA Energy Star: Tackling Growth in Home Electronics and Small Appliances. ACEEE Summer Study on Energy Efficiency in Buildings. Environmental Energy Technologies Division, Lawrence Berkeley National Laboratory, Berkeley, CA. Available at http://eec.ucdavis.edu/ACEEE/2008/data/papers/9_129.pdf. Accessed on November 6, 2011.

Sancho, F., L. Rivera, and J. Rosales. 2010. Housing Finance in Central America: What Is Holding It Back? Inter-American Development Bank, Washington, DC. Unpublished.

Schmidt, S., and V. Budinich. 2006. Housing Solutions Serving Low-Income Populations: A Framework for Action. Ashoka, Arlington, VA. Unpublished.

SDP (Secretaría Distrital de Planeación). 2009. 1.187 Lotes no seguirán en "engorde" [1,187 Lots Will Not Continue "Fattening"]. Bogotá. Available at http://www.grupo-bahia.com/archivos/noticias/2577_lotes.pdf. Accessed November 2011.

Shalizi, Z., and F. Lecocq. 2009. Climate Change and the Economics of Targeted Mitigation in Sectors with Long-Lived Capital Stock. Policy Research Working Paper no. 5063. World Bank, Washington, DC.

Sinai, T., and J. Waldfogel. 2005. Do Low-Income Housing Subsidies Increase the Occupied Housing Stock? *Journal of Public Economics* 89(11–12) December: 2137–64.

Smolka, M. O. 2002. Regularización de la ocupación del suelo urbano: el problema que es parte de la solución, la solución que es parte del problema [Urban Land Regularization: Part of the Solution, Part of the Problem]. Document prepared for the professional development course, Informal Land Markets: Regularization of Land Tenure and Urban Upgrading Programs (on CD-ROM). November. Lincoln Institute of Land Policy, Cambridge, MA. Available at http://www.territorioy-suelo.org/documentos.shtml?x=11389529. Accessed November 2011.

Smolka, M. O., and L. Mullahy. 2000. La política del suelo en América Latina. *Land Lines* 12(5) September. Available at http://www.lincolninst.edu/pubs/284_La-pol%c3%adtica-del-suelo-en-Am%c3%a9rica-Latina. Accessed November 2011.

Somerville, C. T. 1999. Residential Construction Costs and the Supply of New Housing: Endogeneity and Bias in Construction Cost Indexes. *Journal of Real Estate Finance and Economics* 18(1) January: 43–62.

Stafford, D. C. 1978. *The Economics of Housing Policy.* London: Croom Helm.

Stein, A. 1990. Critical Issues in Community Participation in Self-Help Housing Programmes: The Experience of FUNDASAL. *Community Development Journal* 25(1): 21–30.

Suárez, E. 2011. The House Building Sector in Latin America and Caribbean Cities. Study commissioned by the Department of Research and Chief Economist, Inter-American Development Bank, Washington, DC. Unpublished.

Szalachman, R., and M. P. Collinao. 2010. Estimaciones de gasto social en vivienda y desarrollo urbano para algunos países de América Latina y el Caribe. Serie medio ambiente y desarrollo no. 142. United Nations Economic Commission for Latin America and the Caribbean (ECLAC), Santiago, Chile.

Telles, E. E. 1992. Residential Segregation by Skin Color in Brazil. *American Sociological Review* 57(2) April: 186–97.

Thorson, J. A. 1996. An Examination of the Monopoly Zoning Hypothesis. *Land Economics* 72(1): 43–55.

Torres, J. E. 2011. Estudio sobre el mercado de arrendamiento de vivienda en Colombia. Consultant report. Inter-American Development Bank, Washington, DC. Unpublished.

Torres, J. E., and A. Torres. 2009. El contexto económico, social y tecnológico de la producción de vivienda social en América Latina. Paper presented at the event, Encuentro Latinoamericano de Gestión y Economía de la Construcción (ELAGEC), September 9–11, Bogota.

Trivelli, P. 2010. *Urban Structure, Land Markets and Social Housing in Santiago, Chile.* Unpublished.

Turner, B., and C. M. E. Whitehead. 2002. Reducing Housing Subsidy: Swedish Housing Policy in an International Context. *Urban Studies* 39(2): 201–17.

Turner, J. F. C. 1976. *Housing by People: Towards Autonomy in Building Environments.* London: Marion Boyars Publishers.

Turner, J. F. C., and R. Fichter, eds. 1972. *Freedom to Build: Dweller Control of the Housing Process.* New York: The Macmillan Company.

UAECD (Unidad Administrativa Especial de Catastro Distrital). 2008. Base catastral [Cadastral Base]. Bogotá.

UN (United Nations). 1988. Global Strategy for Shelter to the Year 2000. 83rd Plenary Meeting A/RES/43/181. Available at http://www.un.org/documents/ga/res/43/a43r181.htm. Accessed November 2011.

———. 2007. Department of Economic and Social Affairs. World Urbanization Prospects.

UNEP (United Nations Environment Programme). 2010. *Global Environment Outlook: Latin America and the Caribbean: GEO LAC 3.* Panama City, Panama: UNEP. Available at: http://www.unep.org/pdf/GEOLAC_3_ENGLISH.pdf. Accessed July 2011.

UNFPA (United Nations Population Fund). 2007. *State of World Population 2007: Unleashing the Potential of Urban Growth.* New York: UNFPA. Available at http://www.unfpa.org/swp/2007/presskit/pdf/sowp2007_eng.pdf. Accessed July 2011.

———. 2010. *State of World Population 2010: From Conflict and Crisis to Renewal: Generations of Change.* New York: UNFPA. Available at: http://www.unfpa.org/webdav/site/global/shared/swp/2010/swop_2010_eng.pdf. Accessed July 2011.

UN-HABITAT (United Nations Human Settlements Programme). 2003a. *The Challenge of Slums: Global Report on Human Settlements 2003.* London, England and Sterling, VA: Earthscan Publications Ltd.

———. 2003b. Rental Housing: An Essential Option for the Urban Poor in Developing Countries. Nairobi: UN-HABITAT.

———. 2007. What *Are* Slums and Why Do They Exist? Paper presented at the Twenty-First Session of the Governing Council, April 16–20, Nairobi.

———. 2010. Global Urban Indicators Database. Available at http://www.unhabitat.org/downloads/docs/global_urban_indicators.pdf.

———. 2011a. *Cities and Climate Change: Global Report on Human Settlements, 2011.* Washington, DC and London: Earthscan.

———. 2011b. *A Policy Guide to Rental Housing in Developing Countries*. Quick Policy Guide Series—Volume 1. Nairobi: UN-HABITAT.

Uribe, M. C., and J. C. Bejarano. 2009. Annotated Bibliography on Property Tax in Latin America. Working Paper no. WP09MU1. Lincoln Institute of Land Policy, Cambridge, MA.

Vance, I. 2010. Gap Analysis: Opportunities for Expanding Patrimonio Hoy in Mexico and Regionally. Unpublished.

———. 2011. Housing Microcredit in Latin America: El Salvador Case Study. Inter-American Development Bank. Washington, DC. Unpublished.

Van der Heijen, H., and P. Boelhouwer. 1996. The Private Rented Sector in Western Europe: Developments since the Second World War and Prospects for the Future. *Housing Studies* 11(1) January: 13–34.

Vargas Garzón, B. 2007. Industrialización de la construcción para la vivienda social. *Revista nodo* 2(3) July–December: 25–44.

Velásquez, L. 2011. La importancia de los bienes públicos en la calidad de vida local: el caso de Manizales, Colombia. IDB Working Paper no. IDB-WP-255. Department of Research and Chief Economist, Inter-American Development Bank, Washington, DC.

Vetter, D. M., and M. Vetter. 2011. Land-Based Financing for Brazil's Municipalities. *Land Lines* 23(4) October: 14–19.

Wakely, P., and E. Riley. 2010. The Case for Incremental Housing. CIVIS Special Issue, World Urban Forum 5. March. Available at wwww.cities alliance.org.

Ward, P. 1986. *Welfare Politics in Mexico: Papering over the Cracks*. London: Allen and Unwin.

Warnock, V. C., and F. E. Warnock. 2008. Markets and Housing Finance. *Journal of Housing Economics* 17(3) September: 239–51.

———. 2011. *Housing Finance Systems and Financial Stability*. University of Virginia, Charlottesville, VA. Unpublished.

Whitehead, C. 1996. Private Renting in the 1990s. *Housing Studies* 11(1) January: 7–12.

Wilbanks, T. J., P. Romero Lankao, M. Bao, F. Berkhout, S. Cairncross, J.-P. Ceron, M. Kapshe, R. Muir-Wood, and R. Zapata-Marti. 2007. Industry, Settlement and Society. In M. L. Parry, O. F. Canziani, J. P. Palutikof, P. J. van der Linden, and C. E. Hanson, eds., *Climate Change 2007: Impacts, Adaptation and Vulnerability. Working Group II Contribution to the Fourth Assessment Report of the IPCC*. London: Cambridge University Press.

World Bank. 1993. *Housing: Enabling Markets to Work*. Washington, DC: World Bank.

———. 2010. *Doing Business 2011: Making a Difference for Entrepreneurs*. Washington, DC: World Bank and International Finance Corporation.

———. 2011a. Doing Business—Historic Data Sets and Trends Data. Available at http://www.doingbusiness.org/custom-query. Accessed July 2011.

———. 2011b. Doing Business—Registering Property Methodology. Available at http://www.doingbusiness.org/methodology/registering-property.

———. 2011c. World Development Indicators Database. Available at http://data.worldbank.org/data-catalog/world-development-indicators. Accessed July 2011.

World Resources Institute. 2005. Carbon Dioxide Emissions by Economic Sector 2005. EarthTrendsDataTables:ClimateandAtmosphere.Availableat:http://earthtrends.wri.org/pdf_library/data_tables/cli2_2005.pdf. Accessed July 2011.

———. 2011. National CO2 Emissions, 1990–2007. Available at: http://cait.wri.org/cait.php?page=graphcoun. Accessed July 2011.

Zabel, J. 2004. The Demand for Housing Services. *Journal of Housing Economics* 13(1): 16–35.

Index

ABC (Ahorro, Bono y Credito) programs, 31, 47, 246, 248, 252, 276, 278, 280
Abiko, A., 144, 168
Acioly Jr., C., 147
affordability, 55–73
  credit and, 59–62
  effect of house prices on, 67
  financial markets and, 59–62
  future of, 184–85
  gap in, 69–73
  housing supply in Bogota, 68
  income and, 56–58
  increase in home prices, 62–69
  interest rates, 61
  lack of affiliation to social security, 64
  mortgage interest rates and, 60
  overview, 55–56
  plot size effect on, 132
  price of cheapest private-sector housing, 65
  self-employment and, 63
Alcázar, L., 286
Altermatt, E.R., 11
Andrews, D., 104
Angel, S., 14–15, 18, 27, 39, 42–43, 145, 215, 246
Anzorena, J., 222
Apgar, W., 87, 170
Arbeláez, M.A., 75–76, 77, 88, 207, 208–9
Argentina
  affordability, 71
  construction and, 151–54, 158–59, 168, 170
  elasticity and, 83
  families and, 81
  Habitat for Humanity and, 105–6
  housing deficits, 28–29, 31–33
  housing policies, 65–66, 239, 246–49, 254–58, 261–79
  land markets, 117–20
  land titling programs, 10
  mortgage debt, 190
  neighborhood conditions, 39–40
  population growth, 52–53
  privatization and, 9
  regulation, 98–99, 136–41, 199
  rentals, 83, 88, 94–95
  slum population, 37–38
  tenure choices, 75–77
  urban migration and, 6, 28–29
Arnott, R., 282
Arriagada, C., 27
Artiga de Soundy, E., 112, 131, 133, 151–53, 159, 161
Auguste, S., 199, 285
AVC (Ahorro Voluntario Contractual), 253, 260, 278
Azariadis, C., 281

Bahl, R., 142–43
Bailey, M., 126
Banco Estado, 201
Banco Nacional de la Vivienda, 229
Banco Santander, 228
bankruptcy, 197, 285
Barata, M., 20
Basu, K., 282

Brazil
  construction, 150–55, 158, 174
  home ownership, 97
  housing choices, 75–76
  housing deficits, 28–29
  housing finance, 190, 199, 200–3
  housing informality, 36–38
  housing market, 80, 83
  interest rates, 59
  labor informality, 77
  land markets, 122–23
  land titling and, 10
  mass transport and, 19
  prices, 83, 117
  renting, 83, 88, 94
  residential segregation, 44–45
  self-help, 236
  slums, 23, 141–44, 227–28
  subsidies, 236, 246

Caja de Compensación Familiar, 62
CAVs (housing savings corporations), 206–7
CCF (Cajas de Compensación Familiar), 253, 266, 275
CEMEX, 223–24
Chile
  credit and, 201–2, 248, 250, 252
  finance housing market and, 201–2
  housing policy and, 250–52, 256–57
  mortgages and, 201–2, 248, 250
  private sector and, 250–52, 255
  subsidies and, 250–54
Citibank, 230
Colombia
  affordability and, 59–60, 71
  construction and, 154–63, 169
  credit and, 206–9, 253
  heads of household in, 75
  housing deficits, 28–29, 34
  housing finance market, 206–9
  housing policy, 66, 246–48, 252–58, 276–79
  housing prices, 80–81, 88
  labor informality and, 59–62, 76
  land regulation, 146
  macroproyectos, 146–47
  mortgages in, 60, 206–9
  Patrimonio Hoy and, 223–24
  perception of dwelling surroundings in, 40
  private sector and, 242, 253, 267, 270–74
  renting, in, 76, 77, 88–96, 98–99, 101
  securitization, 194–96
  slum population, 37–38
  subsidies, 206–9, 228, 270
  targeting and, 261, 264–66
  urban growth rate vs. general population, 53
CONAVI, 204, 229
construction
  concentration and dispersion of industry, 159
  costs, 150–55
  industrialization of, 163–76
  overview, 149–50
  permits, 161–63
  regulation, 160–63
  sector in Latin America, 155–60
  technology and, 164
consumer price index (CPI), 197, 283
core houses, 183, 214, 216–20, 234, 251
  basic starting options for, 217
  expansion possibilities for, 218
CRECE (Centro de Estudios Nacionales, Cafeteros y Empresariales), 271, 287
credit
  affordability and, 55–56
  Argentina and, 10
  borrower information and, 193, 195–201, 206
  Chile and, 201–2, 248, 250, 252
  Colombia and, 206–9, 253
  construction and, 101, 145, 152, 167, 219
  cost of, 84, 139
  El Salvador and, 234
  FUNDASAL and, 223
  government-sponsored, 189

housing policies and, 270, 275–76, 278–80
income and, 31
labor informality and, 59–62, 77
lack of access to, 2, 10, 51, 84–85, 197, 211, 239, 242
land-based revenue and, 142–43
LIHTC, 102–3
NGOs and, 237, 267
obstacles to obtaining, 22, 31, 59, 147, 174, 176
Patrimonio Hoy and, 224
rental housing and, 96
subsidies and, 206–9, 231–33
see also ABC programs; FONAVI; microcredit; microfinancing; mortgages

crime, 5–6, 13, 20
see also violence

De Soto, Hernando, 136
disease, 5, 7–9, 20, 281
Doing Business, 133, 197–99, 284, 285
see also World Bank

earmarks, 201–3, 209, 254
elasticity, 82–84, 136, 281
energy efficiency
Barbados and, 178–82
building codes and, 183
economic case for, 177–78
policies to promote, 182–84
taxes vs. subsidies, 184

finance market, housing
Brazil and, 202–3
Chile and, 201–2
Colombia and, 206–9
factors favoring provision of housing finance, 198
international benchmarks, 190–200
international comparison of house price levels, 188
market share of government-sponsored credit institutions, 189
Mexico and, 204–6
mortgage debt as percent of GDP, 191–93
overview, 187–90
securitization and mortgage financing, 194–97

FONAVIPO (Fondo Nacional de Vivienda Popular), 234–35
FONVIVIENDA (Fondo Nacional de Vivienda), 147, 254, 260, 262–64, 266, 275
FOVISSSTE, 62, 196, 204–5
FUNDASAL, 223, 225, 236

gated communities, 13, 140

Habitat for Humanity, 105–6, 230
heads of household, 75–76, 81, 264–65, 268
health, 1, 6–11, 13, 15, 20–25, 74, 85, 96–97, 111, 160, 271, 273
Hogar de Cristo, 225
Honduras, 28, 59, 93–95, 154, 228, 231
housing
city size and, 31–35
climate change and, 19–20
conditions by income quintile, 30–31
deficits, 28, 31–35, 48
education and, 11–12
environmental impact, 14–19
health and, 7–9
housing gaps, 24–28
housing markets, 14–19, 39–43
income and, 31–35
keys to finding better homes, 22
land titling, 10
location, 35–39
perception of dwelling surroundings, 40–41
price tag of closing housing gaps, 46–49
quality of life and, 20–21
report card for Latin America, 28–31, 32
segregation and, 12–14, 43–46
shape of cities, 39–43
shortages, 26, 33–34

housing choices
  buyers, renters, or builders, 73–74
  distribution of monthly household income per capita by tenure choice in Brazil, 78
  easing demand constraints on housing, 84–85
  families and, 81
  measuring, 74–78
  residential mobility, 82–84
  tender choices by gender of household head, 76
  valuing housing attributes, 79–81
housing policy
  Argentina and, 248–50, 256–57
  Chile and, 250–52, 256–57
  Colombia and, 252–54, 256–57
  constitutional provisions concerning, 240
  dos and don'ts of enabling market approach to housing, 243
  economic and political factors affecting, 254–55
  evolution of, 248
  housing programs in Latin America and Caribbean, 244–45
  management of, 274–75
  overview, 239–41
  results of, 255–61
  successful programs, 241–47
  suggestions for improving, 275–80
  see also public housing

ICT (Instituto de Crédito Territorial), 248, 252, 254
illegal development, 22, 35–36, 42, 74, 117, 127, 136, 137, 212–13, 215–16, 220, 228
incremental housing, 213–25
  autonomy and, 236–37
  building basic units, 216–20
  core houses, 216–20
  division of labor in, 233–37
  financing, 225–33
  government support for housing microfinance, 231–33
  improvements, 220–22
  land access, 214–16
  microfinancing and, 225–31
  new partnerships, 222–25
  remittances and, 231
industrialized construction
  advantages/disadvantages of, 166–67
  development of, 165–69
  energy efficiency and, 177–84
  environmental concerns and, 176–84
  laying building blocks for, 175–76
  overview, 163–65
  savings of, 171
  stumbling blocks to, 170–75
  technology and, 168
  value of, 169–70
INFONAVIT, 62, 196, 204–6
informality
  construction and, 158–59, 276
  housing market, 35–36, 39, 74, 75, 83, 114, 145, 147
  income, 253
  labor market, 57, 59–62, 76, 77, 123–24, 226
  regulation and, 124, 136, 140
infrastructure
  access to services and, 6, 247, 256
  Argentina and, 271, 277
  construction and, 150, 158, 173
  core houses and, 216
  government intervention and, 242, 253
  growth and, 18
  housing deficits and, 26–27, 29–32
  housing gap and, 2–3, 47
  housing informality and, 35, 38, 39
  housing policies and, 49, 84–85
  incremental housing, 214–16, 233–34
  land markets and, 110–13, 122, 127, 137–48
  lot-only option and, 219
  microfinance and, 226–27
  renting and, 87, 89, 94, 100, 106

risk mitigation and, 20
rural areas and, 1
segregation and, 13
Inter-American Development Bank (IDB), 47, 113, 178–82, 230, 242, 283, 287
interest rates, 55–56, 59–61, 63, 71–73, 101–3, 123, 152, 167, 193–95, 197, 202, 207–9, 227, 243, 256, 260, 269, 282, 286, 287
INURBE (Instituto Nacional de Desarrollo Urbano), 248, 252, 254

land markets
affordability and, 113–15
Argentina and, 117–20
effect of land prices on affordability, 115–16
housing costs and, 112–13
housing supply and population distribution, 118–19
income and, 114
overview, 109–11
prices, 111–23f
Rio de Janeiro and, 120–22
Santiago and, 122–23
land regulation, 123–34
need for policy overhaul, 146–48
price and, 136–41
land titling, 10
lot-only option, 219

Mexico
access to services, 80
affordability, 65–67, 70, 80
construction, 154–56, 158–62, 175
families in, 81
government programs, 9, 66, 228, 231, 242
incremental housing, 213–14
informal housing, 38
labor informality, 59–62
mass transportation, 19
mobility, 82–84
mortgages, 189–90, 192, 194–96, 199
poverty, 57
price elasticity, 82–84
promotion of finance, construction, and ownership, 204–6
rental market, 88, 90–95
residential segregation, 44–46
self-help, 222
SHF, 233
see also Patrimonio Hoy
microcredit, 69, 224–26, 228–29, 236
see also credit; microfinancing
microfinancing
credit and, 285
examples of, 227–28, 229
explained, 225-31
government support for, 231–33
housing gap and, 2
housing policies and, 279, 284
low-income housing and, 234–36
progressive housing and, 212–13
see also credit; microcredit; remittances
migration, 20, 75, 100, 127, 228
MINVU (Ministerio de Vivienda y Urbanismo), 248, 287
MISN (Macroproyectos de Interés Social Nacional), 146–47
mobility, 3, 74, 82–84, 87, 89, 97, 107, 220
Monkkonen, P., 44–45
mortgages
access to, 54, 73–74, 149
affordability and, 21–22, 55–56, 57, 62–65, 100–1
Argentina and, 248, 279
AVC and, 278
Brazil and, 202–3
Chile and, 201–2, 248, 250
Colombia and, 206–9, 253
construction and, 173
debt and, 190–91, 193, 197–200
doing it yourself and, 211–12
FONAVI and, 265
housing market and, 3, 87, 187, 200–1
housing policies and, 84–85, 97, 106, 232–33, 242–43

mortgages—*Continued*
improving market, 209–10
labor informality and, 59–62
market downturn and, 89
Mexico and, 204–6
microfinancing and, 226
Paraguay and, 229
price elasticity and, 83
private sector and, 2
securitization and, 194–97
see also credit; interest rates; microfinancing

Naipaul, V.S., 236
nongovernmental organizations (NGOs), 105–6, 212, 223, 229, 230, 234, 251

OECD (Organisation for Economic Co-operation and Development), 59–60, 92, 94, 97–98, 100–1, 103–5

Paraguay, 93–94, 97, 129, 229, 230
partnerships, housing value and, 222–25
Patrimonio Hoy, 223–25
Peru, 10, 23, 31, 39, 45, 83, 90, 93–94, 154, 160, 170, 172, 228, 242, 246
Piso Firme, 9
population
changes in density, 42
urbanized population density, 43
prefabricated homes, 154, 164, 168, 173–74, 220
private sector
autonomy and, 237
Chile and, 250–52, 255
Colombia and, 253
construction and, 22, 69, 79, 84, 149–50, 155, 170, 173, 184
El Salvador and, 235
environmental concerns and, 106
financing and, 189, 199, 201–2, 204, 210, 242–43
government programs and, 242–43, 246, 249
home prices and, 62–69, 134, 235
housing gaps and, 24, 28, 31
housing value chain and, 222
incentives for, 55, 147
interest rates, 59
investments by, 47–49
leveraging resources, 267–69
microfinancing and, 2–3, 229, 232
rental market and, 87
self home building and, 212
public housing
coverage, 267
impact of, 269–72
leveraging private sector resources, 267–69
satisfaction, 272–74
targeting, 261–67
see also housing programs
public transportation, 1, 5–6, 14–15, 19–20, 23, 39, 74, 145–48, 255, 261, 273
see also transportation costs

remittances, 231
see also microfinancing
rental market
constraints to development of, 96–101
demand for, 90–96
expanding, 104–7
Habitat for Humanity and, 105–6
housing shortage and, 88–90, 95
mobility and, 89
mortgage financing and, 100–1
overview, 87–88
policy bias toward home ownership, 96–98
preferential funding, 103
public housing, 102
public interventions in developed countries, 101–4
regulatory framework and, 98–99
rental tenure, 91–93
scarcity of land and, 99–100
shelter from financial exposure, 89–90

subsidies, 103–4
tax incentives, 102–3
rental tenure, 91–93
city size and, 92
evolution of, 93
Latin America vs. select EU countries, 91
in select cities worldwide, 92

sanitary core option, 219–20
segregation, residential, 2, 11–14, 20, 25, 35, 43–46, 88, 126, 146
self-help
home building, 212–14
importance of autonomy, 236–37
incremental building, 214–25
incremental housing, 213–14
overview, 211–12
progressive housing, 212
SFV (Subsidio Familiar de Vivienda), 252–54, 266–67, 269, 271, 273–74, 280, 287
SHF (Sociedad Hipotecaria Federal), 196, 233
SISBEN (Sistema de Identificación de Potenciales Beneficiarios de Programas Sociales), 263, 266, 278
slum population, 37–38
slums
attempts to combat, 141–45, 233
Brazil and, 23, 227–28
creation of, 134–36
financing and, 187
gated communities and, 13
government policies and, 147
growth of, 36–38, 44
housing informality and, 35–39, 123
housing market and, 25
labor and, 81
land prices and, 110
Latin American cities and, 6
self-help and, 220
upgrading, 227–28, 233, 243
small and medium enterprises (SMEs), 179
SMLMV (legal minimum salary), 266
Social Protection Certificate (FPS), 266, 278
SOFOLES, 196, 204–5
SOFOMES, 196
subsidies
affordability and, 63
Argentina and, 248, 250
Brazil and, 203, 227–28
Chile and, 250–54
Colombia and, 206–9
demand subsidies, 103–4
eligibility for, 77
El Salvador and, 235
government programs and, 79, 84, 176, 189, 201, 242–44, 246, 255–80
home ownership and, 96, 98, 144–45
housing policies and, 3–4, 28, 57, 74, 234, 248
Mexico and, 146–47, 204–6
microfinance and, 231–33
Paraguay and, 229–30
prefabricated homes and, 174
renting and, 96, 101–5
self-help and, 219–20
taxes vs., 184
Superintendencia de Bancos e Instituciones Financieras (SBIF), 194

tax credits, 102–3, 184
tenure
elasticity and, 83
home building and, 212–15
housing choices and, 73–78
housing gaps and, 25–26
housing policies and, 246–47
housing programs and, 234, 243–44
informal housing and, 36–37
neighborhood programs and, 233
private investment and, 138
renting and, 90–94, 96, 98
security and, 28–29, 31–32
slums and, 143–44
transportation costs, 109–11, 123–24, 165, 174–75

UN-HABITAT, 14–15, 36–38, 87, 89, 92, 94, 96–97, 214, 246, 281, 284
United Nations World Habitat Award, 225
UPAC accounts, 206–7, 286
urban planning, 42–43, 79, 128–30, 215, 227
urban regions, 52–56
 change in growth rate and total population, 53
 composition of GDP growth in, 54
 housing demand, 55
Uruguay, 31, 75, 80–84, 94, 98, 101, 130
US Low-Income Housing Tax Credit (LIHTC) program, 102–3

vector-borne diseases, 7, 20, 281
violence, 8, 12, 228, 262, 264, 277
 see also crime
Vision Banco, 230
vivienda digna, 239

World Bank, 36, 133, 197, 242, 283, 284
 see also Doing Business